SHAKESPEARE

THE MAN AND HIS ACHIEVEMENT

Not quite God.
Igor Stravinsky

Our English fortune is to share particularities with him.
Geoffrey Grigson

When we read we are looking in the words for someone for whom we can feel affection.
Frederick M. Keenes

It might be said that Shakespeare appeared, in a world grown more passionate and more secular, just at the right time to define the rules of poetic realism.
Manzoni

Shakespeare, tu dis toujours Shakespeare! Il'y a un en toi; trouves-le.
Jules Romains

Shakespeare

The man and his achievement

Robert Speaight

Cooper Square Press

First Cooper Square Press edition 2000

This Cooper Square Press paperback edition of *Shakespeare* is an unabridged republication of the edition first published in Briarcliff Manor, New York in 1977. It is reprinted by arrangement with the Estate of Robert Speaight.

Published by Cooper Square Press,
An Imprint of Rowman & Littlefield Publishers, Inc.
150 Fifth Avenue, Suite 911
New York, New York 10011

Distributed by National Book Network

The hardback edition of this book was previously catalogued by the Library of Congress as follows:

Speaight, Robert, 1904–1976
  Shakespeare, the man and his achievement.
  Bibliography : p.
  Includes index.
  1. Shakespeare, William, 1564–1616. 2. Dramatists, English—Early modern, 1500–1700—Biography. I. Title.
PR2894.S65
822.3'3   76-12979

ISBN 0-8154-1063-8 (pbk. : alk. paper)

♾™ The paper used in this publication meets the minimum requirements of American National Standard for Information Sciences—Permanence of Paper for Printed Library Materials, ANSI/NISO Z39.48-1992.
Manufactured in the United States of America.

Contents

Illustrations

For Harriet Laura (remembering a performance of *Macbeth*)

SHAKESPEARE

THE MAN AND HIS ACHIEVEMENT

Introduction

This book is addressed to the general reader, and I am tempted to describe it as a bird's-eye view of territory mapped out by professional cartographers, not always in agreement among themselves. Anyone setting out to write about Shakespeare leans on other men's shoulders, and I have leant on a good many of them. At the same time I have done my best not to lean too heavily. The last three-quarters of a century has seen the golden age of Shakespeare scholarship, though of little else. There is no aspect of the poet's life and work which has not been exhaustively discussed, and the discussion will go on. The assurance of this continuity must stand as my excuse for adding to it. For although there may be little now to discover about Shakespeare's life, he is not only 'for all time' but for all people, and no one person will see him in exactly the same way. We are ourselves reflected in the mirror of our admiration.

My debt to the scholars will be evident in particular references, and in a select bibliography. In a very brief treatment of Shakespeare's sources, I have been guided by Professor Geoffrey Bullough's *Narrative and Dramatic Sources of Shakespeare.* If Professor Bullough's introductions could be published separately from his cited texts, our gratitude for a monumental work would be even greater — for his scholarship would then be brought within the reach of those who cannot afford the eight volumes of the total series. For biographical details and historical background I have relied, with other material, upon the *Life* by Sir Sidney Lee, Dr Schoenbaum's *Shakespeare's Lives,* Dr A. L. Rowse's *William Shakespeare,* and Clara Longworth de Chambrun's unduly neglected *Shakespeare — a Portrait Restored.* These complement, and occasionally correct, each other. But when all is said, we are left, on many essential matters, with conjecture rather than certainty.

Shakespeare was an actor; yet we have no idea how well or ill he acted. He was a dramatist; yet we cannot be sure what proportion of his work was the fruit of collaboration. We do not know whether he was happily or unhappily married; and of his relations with his children we know nothing whatever. Nor can we speak with any certainty about his religious opinions; how far, at different periods of his life, his sympathies were Catholic, Anglican, or ambivalent. All we can say is that he was no friend to the Puritans. That the *Sonnets* were the record of a personal experience surely admits of no doubt, and I follow Dr Rowse, and others, in believing that the bulk of them were addressed to Southampton. Yet even here we lack the clinching evidence that would put the matter beyond question. And what of Shakespeare's emotional life after he had finished with the Dark Lady? Only the doubtful rumour of an affair with Mistress Davenant tickles, but does not satisfy, our curiosity.

The most assiduous research has left these gaps unfilled, and I certainly do not pretend to fill them. It occurred to me, however, that many of Shakespeare's biographers have concentrated on what could be known, or plausibly guessed, about his life to the neglect of his life's work; and, conversely, that most of his critics have discussed his work with scant reference to his life. This is the natural result of intensive, and valuable, specialization. But the time had come, I felt, to set a discussion of his art within a biographical framework; and it was borne in upon me, as I attempted to do this, that Shakespeare's life and work are inseparable — or, more exactly, that his plays *constitute* his biography. Not in the sense that they give us factual details of his doings, or even, I think, that they were designed as an exercise in 'self-expression'; but in the sense that the writing, acting, and production of them occupied by far the greater part of his time. Except for the story of the *Sonnets*, however we interpret them, what we know or can guess of Shakespeare's life is of very limited interest. Other men have invested in real estate, or sat and drank with their cronies, and acquired a coat-of-arms. These details are accidental, and deserve their mention; but we should not mention them at all unless the essential matter of the biography lay elsewhere. I think it just conceivable that a man who had never met Shakespeare on a good night at the Mermaid, and knew him only as a senior citizen of Stratford, might have said of him, as Rémy de Gourmont said of Flaubert, that 'apart from his writings he was not a very interesting person'.

This, then, must be my excuse for devoting the greater portion of this book to a discussion of Shakespeare's plays and of their original performance. Here, too, we are groping in the dark, and I have been forced to choose, though still without any certainty, between conflicting theories of what could, or could not, be done on the Elizabethan and Jacobean stage. I am writing for those, never more numerous than today, who flock to see Shakespeare in the theatre, and argue furiously about what they see when they get there. If there is a rendezvous on which the Christian, the Marxist, and the humanist can agree, it is wherever they can join hands in applause at a Shakespeare play. For myself, I disclaim any authority beyond that of a common reader; of a spectator with sixty years of playgoing behind him; and of one who has tried to grapple, intermittently, with the problems of Shakespearean acting and production. My particular thanks are due to Professor Nevill Coghill, Professor Geoffrey Bullough, Dr Stanley Wells, Dr A. L. Rowse, Professor Glynne Wickham, and the Librarian of London University. My wider indebtedness will, I hope, be apparent in these pages.

I am indebted to Collins, Publishers, for permission to incorporate brief passages from *Shakespeare on the Stage* and to Hollis & Carter and Gage Educational Publishing Ltd of Toronto for allowing me to include similar passages, respectively from *Nature in Shakespearean Tragedy* and *Shakespeare at Stratford.*

I am grateful, as always, for the patience and skill with which Mrs Pat Brayne has deciphered a complicated MS.

Benenden: February 1976

Part One

Elizabethan

Chapter 1

The Stratford Boy

1

William Shakespeare is generally thought to have been born on 23 April 1564, and the registers of Holy Trinity Church at Stratford-upon-Avon record his baptism on the 26th of that month. The rite was performed by the vicar, John Bretchgirdle, a stout Protestant from Christ Church, Oxford, and therefore according to the new Anglican liturgy which had been in force for only two years. William was the eldest son of John and Mary Shakespeare. Described as 'gentle' in his manhood, he was also gentle in his birth. The Shakespeares, under various spellings of their name, had left their traces in many parts of England, and in Ireland as well, from later medieval times. Of yeoman stock, they were by now firmly established in Warwickshire, and in the neighbourhood of Stratford. Richard Shakespeare, the poet's grandfather, had settled at Snitterfield, four miles north-east of the town, by 1529. He died in 1560 or 1561, leaving a fairly substantial estate in land, and two sons, John and Henry. The latter was an unstable character, although on his death in 1596 it was stated that he had 'money in his coffers, a mare in his stable, and plentiful corn and hay in his barn'.[1] A slightly disreputable uncle is a traditional feature of English family life, and in this respect Shakespeare was typical as in other ways he was unique.

John Shakespeare was given the administration of his father's estate, but whatever interest he still retained in land — and this was considerable — he had already moved into Stratford where he carried on a prosperous trade as a glover, occupying two houses — later joined together — in Henley Street, and owning another with a garden and croft, in Greenhill Street nearby. In 1557 he was appointed ale-taster of the borough — Stratford was already reputed for its brewing — and in the same year he married Mary Arden, the daughter of Richard Shakespeare's Snitterfield landlord. The Ardens were gentry, slightly above the Shakespeares in the social scale. The

[1] S. Schoenbaum, *Shakespeare's Lives* (1970), p. 17.

wedding would have taken place in the bride's parish church at Aston Cantlow, and since Queen Mary was still on the throne the union was blessed by a priest about whose ecclesiastical status and religious opinions there could be no dispute. In 1558 their first daughter, Joan, was born and died in infancy; a second, Margaret, was born in 1562. Meanwhile, John was steadily climbing the municipal ladder: burgess in 1558, one of the four constables in 1559, chamberlain of the borough from 1561 to 1565, and in the latter year an alderman in his furred gown. 'Robes and furr'd gowns hide all'[1] — in the case of John Shakespeare there was nothing to hide except honest industry, the passionate desire to acquire a coat-of-arms, and, it would seem, a fluctuating fidelity to the old religion. In the case of his wife this fidelity was probably stronger.

Two measures passed in the early months of 1559 gave warning of what might well be described as the Elizabethan Unsettlement. The Act of Supremacy decreed severe penalties against anyone who by word or writing refused to recognize the Queen's supreme authority in ecclesiastical as well as temporal affairs. The Act of Uniformity was directed against anyone professing a faith at variance with that promulgated in the Prayer Book of 1559. This was allowed a fairly wide latitude of interpretation. The Queen disliked the Puritans far more than she disliked the Catholics — or Papists as they now came to be called. She was a natural ritualist, and her definition of the Real Presence in the Eucharist adroitly avoided the issue

> Christ was the word that spake it,
> He took the bread and brake it;
> And what his words did make it
> That I believe and take it.

Nevertheless the celebration of Mass, publicly or privately, was forbidden, and attendance at church as by law established was compulsory. Elizabeth was very much her father's daughter; her attitude, though she was forced to compromise, was Henrician rather than Protestant. It was not surprising that when Pope Paul IV published his Bull, *Cum ex apostolatus,* in the year following her accession, advocating the deposition of all rulers encouraging heresy, she should have preferred the security of the throne to the sanctity of the altar.

Such pronouncements did nothing to endear the Papacy to Englishmen for whom it was already remote. The Marian persecutions were odious, and the Spanish alliance unpopular. The Shakespeares, and countless other families like them, were untroubled by theological disputes. They minded little about the

[1] *King Lear,* IV, vi, 169.

suppression of the monasteries, but they minded a great deal about the suppression of the Mass. Since they were obliged to go to church, and had no reluctance in doing so, it mattered immensely what they found when they got there. The 'deep consent of all great men' which Elizabeth set out to achieve could have been acquired by schism; it was from the first prejudiced by heresy. Warwickshire was deeply divided, the eastern districts centred upon Coventry being less opposed to the religious changes. Around Stratford, however, most of the gentry were Catholic — the Ardens of Parkhall, the Catesbys of Lapworth, the Cloptons who had built the bridge over the Avon that bears their name, the Throckmortons of Coughton, and several others. An important exception was Sir Thomas Lucy at Charlecote, who became assiduous in his pursuit of recusant priests as they came over from William Allen's seminary at Douai. Sir Roger Dyos, the Stratford vicar who baptized Shakespeare's elder sister, was the first priest to be deprived of his living and sent into exile. When orders were given, in the year of Shakespeare's birth, to whitewash the frescoes in the Gild Chapel of Holy Cross and dismantle the rood screen, and when, seven years later, the vestments were disposed of, the townsfolk must have realized that a whole way of popular worship was at stake.

A strict literary censorship was in force. No book or pamphlet could be published in any language which was not in conformity with the Book of Common Prayer; nothing could appear without a licence from the Queen, six members of her Privy Council, or certain dignitaries of the Church. These measures were, of course, freely evaded. Catholic publications from Douai, Rheims, and Antwerp could be bought under the counter at the London bookshops. Where the Shakespeares stood in these early years of transition and transformation it is hard to determine. Any conclusion about William's personal religious beliefs, as distinct from his religious background, is hazardous in the extreme. No doubt the family allowed themselves a contradiction between private opinion and public appearances. As a municipal official John Shakespeare would have been obliged to attend services in the parish church. John Bretchgirdle's successor, William Butcher, formerly President of Corpus Christi College, Oxford, had Catholic sympathies, but after the Northern rising in 1569 he was replaced by an unequivocally Protestant incumbent. Stratford was a microcosm of deep national divisions as the screw tightened; and Pope Pius V's excommunication of Elizabeth in 1570 did much to tighten it.

William was still in his cradle when the plague — a constant threat in any town of middling or larger size — claimed 250 victims in 1564. The world was lucky in his escape. Five more children were born to

John and Mary Shakespeare: Gilbert (1566), Joan (1569), Anne (1571), Richard (1574), and Edmund (1580). Anne died in 1579, but Joan survived her eldest brother, married a hatter of the town, William Hart, and inherited the house in Henley Street. Edmund became an actor, and died young. He is buried in the chancel of St Saviour's cathedral at Southwark. The brothers and sisters did not play much part in a story enacted on a larger stage.

John Shakespeare's rising fortunes and civic status enabled him to send William to the local grammar school. John may himself have been illiterate, since he always signed a document with his trade mark — a pair of compasses — but education, encouraged by a highly educated Queen, and by the impetus which the Reformation had given to the vernacular, was now a status symbol — and John cared about status. Elementary teaching was provided in the home, and it is fair to conclude that William, with his genius for assimilation, was a quick and even a precocious learner. The children were taught from an ABC, or horn-book, with its rows of letters and figures. This, we are told, was a primer framed in wood and covered with a thin plate of transparent horn. It included the alphabet in small letters and in capitals, with combinations of the five vowels with b, c, and d, and the Lord's Prayer in English. The first of these alphabets, which ended with the abbreviation for 'and', began with the mark of the cross. Hence the alphabet was known as the 'Christ cross row' — the cross-row of *Richard III*, I, i, 55. A short catechism was often included in the 'A—B—C book (the "absey book" of *King John*, I, i, 196).'[1] Dr Rowse[2] refers us to a line from *The Two Gentlemen of Verona*

> To sigh, like a schoolboy that has lost his ABC

and to Hero's 'What kind of catechising call you this?' in *Much Ado*. 'To make you truly answer to your name' replies Claudio — who, with Bertram in *All's Well That Ends Well*, takes pride of place among Shakespearean cads.

The grammar school had been founded in 1553, and both the sympathies and careers of its masters illustrate a confusion which no doubt extended to their pupils. Of the five who were in charge during the years of Shakespeare's schooling, three were obliged to leave on account of their adherence to the proscribed faith. John Acton left at Christmas 1571, and his successor, Walter Roche, remained only a short time before turning from a profession which obviously had its dangers. He was followed by Simon Hunt, an

[1] Sir John Edwin Sandys, *Shakespeare's England*, Vol. 2, p. 230.
[2] A. L. Rowse, *William Shakespeare* (1963), p. 35.

Oxford man, who weathered the storm, not without difficulty, until 1575. The weather was not improved by the Massacre of St Batholomew, which excited a gang of Puritans to break up his classroom. The activities of continental Catholics did not always make things easy for Englishmen disposed to sympathize with them, while beyond the Border Mary Stuart inflexibly pressed her claims to the succession. Hunt retired from Stratford to the seminary at Rheims, and later became Grand Penitentiary in Rome. At the age of eleven Shakespeare was not too young to have felt his influence; and whatever he imbibed of his beliefs, it may well have remained with him. Hunt's successor, Thomas Jenkins, was a ludicrous pedagogue who accepted six pounds to hand over his teaching to John Cottam; but when Cottam's brother, Thomas, was hanged at Tyburn with Edmund Campion in 1580, he too was obliged to disappear. With his 'small Latin and less Greek' Shakespeare had also learnt that Elizabeth's England was taking its time in arriving at the 'deep consent' for which she had striven.

We may presume, then, that he entered the lower school in 1571, where he was taught by an usher. Three years later — shortly before Simon Hunt's departure — he moved up and came under Jenkins. If he regarded schoolmasters as objects of ridicule — Sir Hugh Evans in *The Merry Wives of Windsor* is an example — Jenkins was probably responsible. It is, of course, the prerogative of schoolboys to make fun of schoolmasters; but it is the educators, and not the education, that get the brunt of Shakespeare's satire. We can derive from a contemporary publication, Seager's *The Schoole of virtue and the Book of good Nourture for chyldren and youth*, a picture of how he spent his day. After saying his prayers, combing his hair, and greeting his parents, he would set out 'with his satchel / And shining morning face, creeping like snail / Unwillingly to school'.[1] No need to assume that he was any more willing than his fellows. It was a short walk from Henley Street; others would have had to come from much further afield. On the last stroke of 5.45 a.m. in summer, and 6.45 a.m. in winter, he was expected to be in class. After an overture of singing in chorus, lessons continued with a short break until eleven o'clock. The boys went home for dinner, returned two hours later, and stayed at their desks until five, with only a quarter of an hour's recreation. Thursday and Saturday were half-holidays, when the afternoon was given up to games. Shakespeare would seem to have developed a particular fondness for bowls. Costard, in *Love's Labour's Lost*, can find no better excuse for Sir Nathaniel's incompetence on the stage than to explain to that discourteous

---

[1] *As You Like It*, II, vii, 145-7.

patrician audience that he was 'a very good bowler'. Before many
years had gone by — so runs the legend — the game was to be
canonized by Sir Francis Drake when he sighted the Armada.
Discipline at the school was enforced by methods to which the
English — and in particular what used to be their governing classes —
are pathologically addicted. The delinquent was held over a desk by
four of his fellows — boys, it was specified, of muscular strength and
exemplary character — while the teacher applied the birch.

The incredible richness of Elizabethan literature owed much to the
fact that, generally speaking, there were only good books to read,
and relatively few people to read them. The academic curriculum was
happily circumscribed. There are several references to Lyly's *Latin
Grammar* in Shakespeare's plays. Two editions had already been
published before he entered the school. It was the source of Act IV,
Scene I of *The Merry Wives of Windsor* where the Welsh
schoolmaster examines the boy William; of '*homo* is a common name
to all men' from *Henry IV, Part One* (II, i, 104); of Sir Toby's
'*diluculo surgere*' from the drinking scene in *Twelfth Night*; of
'*integer vitae*' from *Titus Andronicus,* to which Chiron replies,
speaking for the author, 'O 'tis a verse in Horace; I know it well: I
read it in the grammar long ago' (IV, ii, 20-3). In Lyly, and also in
Thomas Wilson's *Arte of Rhetorike,* the boy would find
commentaries on Seneca, Terence, Cicero, Horace and Plautus. The
Bucolica, or Ecloques of Baptista Spagnolo (1448-1510), commonly
known as Mantuanus, was much in use. Holofernes, the amiable
schoolmaster in *Love's Labour's Lost,* quotes the first line of this,
and then adds: 'Ah, good old Mantuan! . . . Who understandeth thee
not, loves thee not' (IV, ii, 101-2). But Shakespeare's favourite was
evidently Ovid. This predilection stamps him as a child of the
Renaissance, and earned him a Puritan rebuke for his attachment to
such 'lascivious' verses. We shall see what *Venus and Adonis* owed to
the *Metamorphoses,* and *The Rape of Lucrece* to the *Fasti.* Francis
Meres was to describe him, some years after he had made his name as
a playwright, as the 'English Ovid'; and at times when he felt divided
between the poetry of the play and the poetry of the printed page,
the example of Ovid may well have summoned him to emulate it.

History competed with mythology because, in those years of
England's great awakening, history had the generating power of
myth. Plutarch's *Lives of the noble Graecians and Romans,*
translated from the Greek by James Amyot, and out of the French
by Thomas North, was published in 1579. It showed how much that
was then happening, and had recently happened, in England had
happened before. Man was an incurably political animal, and the
Renaissance looking at antiquity discovered its own face in the

mirror. Raphael Holinshed, produced his *Chronicles of England, Scotland, and Ireland* in 1577. Here was the quarry, not only for the historical plays, but for *King Lear, Cymbeline,* and *Macbeth.* How far were the seeds of future achievement sown in those last years at the grammar school, when North and Holinshed were received with the excitement of best-sellers? We cannot tell; but Shakespeare would have read them at the age of discovery and, for him, every age was the age of assimilation.

His familiarity with the Bible and the Prayer Book was just as evident. Of the first there were four accessible translations by the time he was able to read: William Tyndale's, Miles Coverdale's, the Great Bible — known as Cranmer's — and the Bishops' Bible published in 1568 under the supervision of Archbishop Parker. A more popular version was the Geneva Bible used in the family circle. It is from this, and the Bishops' Bible, that Shakespeare usually quotes — although in the later plays Geneva is generally preferred, not necessarily because it was more Protestant but because it had a wider circulation and was more readily to hand. By 1589, however, the Catholics had produced their own translation of the New Testament from Rheims. There are echoes of this in the poet's use of 'cockle' for 'tares' in *Love's Labour's Lost* and *Coriolanus;* and in *All's Well That Ends Well* the Clown refers to the 'gate' as 'broad' and 'narrow' rather than 'wide' and 'strait'. In *The Tempest* Ariel assures Prospero that 'not a hair' of the shipwrecked mariners had 'perished' where the Protestant versions have 'fall'. But Shakespeare's indefectible ear may well have preferred 'perished' to 'fallen'; and in any case the translations smuggled over from the continent could only have been procured and read at risk. His memory retained whatever he heard, or whatever his eye had lighted upon; he would not have worried about its provenance.

For the Psalms, from which the references are frequent, he follows the Great Bible, because this was the translation used in the Book of Common Prayer. The evidence is conclusive that he regularly attended the services of the Church of England, whether or not he was encouraged to recite an 'Ave Maria' at home. Mistress Page in *The Merry Wives of Windsor* is commended as one 'that will not miss you morning nor evening prayer' (II, ii, 97). *The Merry Wives* is Shakespeare's only study of middle-class life, and his was a very typical middle-class family. It is worth remarking that the majority of England's greatest writers have come from the middle classes, although the greatest of them all shared the Elizabethan reverence for nobility — a reverence that did not die with Elizabeth. Echoes of the Litany come to us from *Henry VI, Part One,* where Salisbury and Gargrave prepare to meet their Maker

> *Sal.* O Lord! have mercy on us, wretched sinners.
> *Gar.* Lord! have mercy on me, woeful man.
>
> (I, iv, 61-2)

Shakespeare's ear has again preferred 'wretched' to 'miserable'. In *The Taming of the Shrew* 'From all such devils, good Lord, deliver us' seems to echo the petition 'From all evil and mischief, from sin, from the crafts and assaults of the devil . . . good Lord, deliver us'. Othello's warning to Desdemona

> If you bethink yourself of any crime
> Unreconcil'd as yet to heaven or grace . . .
> Solicit for it straight
>
> (V, ii, 27-9)

and Hamlet's pleading to Gertrude 'Confess yourself to heaven' recall the exhortation from the Communion Service to 'confess yourselves to Almighty God with full purpose of amendment of life'. The newly baptized child is enjoined 'to continue Christ's faithful soldier and servant': and Richmond, on the eve of Bosworth, prays as follows: 'O thou whose *captain* I account myself', while Mowbray in *Richard II* is described as rendering

> his pure soul unto his *captain* Christ,
> Under whose colours he had fought so long.[1]
>
> (IV, i, 99-100)

The point to be emphasized here is not that Shakespeare was a particularly pious boy — he was obliged to go to church whether he wanted to or not — and still less that he was theologically inclined. What mattered to him was language. Words that, for many people today, have become staled, if they have not become hallowed, by repetition, fell upon his ear like an adagio of Mozart to a man who has never heard Mozart before. It would be unjust to Chaucer and Malory to suggest that the English language had found itself; but it had, so to speak, shed its medieval skin. New potentialities were released, both in poetry and prose. People enjoyed listening to sermons of what to us would seem intolerable length, because great preachers could express themselves in words that moved the heart and satisfied the mind. Going to church, if the parson knew his business, could be an aesthetic pleasure. It was natural for the older generation to long for the Latin Mass — as an older generation of Catholics long for it today, without the compensation of Cranmer's collects. But Shakespeare had never known the Latin Mass, unless he had heard it in a rare and perilous clandestinity. The Middle Ages

---

[1] For a full treatment of Shakespeare's knowledge of the Bible and Prayer Book, see Peter Milward, *Shakespeare's Religious Background* (1973).

were not without an effect upon his thought, because they still influenced the thought of his time and, not least, the Reformation itself. The misericordes on the choir stalls of Holy Trinity Church would have given him a glimpse of their grosser fantasies, for his eye missed nothing. A lion with two bodies; a naked woman astride a stag; a man castigating a woman with a birch for no better reason than because a dog is biting her; a chained ape providing a specimen of its urine in a flask. But of medieval nostalgia Shakespeare shows no trace whatever; Friar Lawrence comes out of Wardour Street rather than a dissolved monastery.

If a parson were short of a text, or of the talent to preach from it, he would subject his congregation to one of the prescribed *Homilies.* No doubt these were often as tedious as the 'homily of love' with which Rosalind accuses Celia of 'wearying' her 'parishioners'. But those concerned with civil disobedience left an enduring imprint on the boy's mind. He had only to look back for little more than half a century into the history of his own country. The Wars of the Roses; the Tudor dynasty, questionable in its origin, and still questioned by many whose habits of belief and worship it had upset; the Henrician schism, and the Marian reaction — these gave colour to the doctrine that if the ruler were not admitted to rule by Divine Right, he or she was unlikely to rule for very long. Hierarchy was the only safeguard against anarchy, and authority the only preservative of peace. 'Almighty God hath created and appointed all things, in heaven, earth and waters, in a most excellent and perfect order.' This, remembered from a Sunday matins in Holy Trinity Church, gave Ulysses his cue in *Troilus and Cressida*

> How could communities
> Degrees in schools and brotherhoods in cities,
> Peaceful commerce from dividable shores,
> The primogenitive and due of birth,
> Prerogative of age, crowns, sceptres, laurels,
> But by degree, stand in authentic place?
> Take but degree away, untune that string,
> And hark! what discord follows.

(I, iii, 103-10)

England had heard it and, however divided she might be, was in no mood for an encore. Shakespeare, as life taught him its lesson, would have his second thoughts about 'man, proud man / Dressed in a little brief authority';[1] but the seeds of his political thinking were sown by some 'gentle' — or not so gentle — 'pulpiter' at Stratford-upon-Avon.

---

[1] *Measure for Measure*, II, ii, 117-18.

'All sins, I say, against God and all men heaped together nameth he that nameth rebellion' inspired Macduff's outcry

> Confusion now hath made his masterpiece.
> Most sacrilegious murder hath broke ope
> The Lord's anointed temple, and stolen thence
> The life o' th' building.

(Macbeth, II, iii, 68-71)

Unlike the preacher, however, Shakespeare not only condemned rebellion, but he understood it. Was there, indeed, anything that he did not understand?

Notwithstanding a quick imagination, and the feeling that he might one day do as well as Ovid, I do not see him as a bookworm. He was, and remained, a countryman. It has justly been observed that his early comedies are outdoor plays. He was a poet of the open air. In this attachment there was no trace of Wordsworthian pantheism. He did not look for God in the green fields, though he may have caught a glimpse of Pan when he got there. The world he knew was enough for his comment, his celebration, or his censure. Michael Drayton, his fellow poet, was also a Warwickshire man, and in the thirteenth Song of the *Polyalbion* he has left us a lively and affectionate picture of their native county and its 'rough woodlands', in particular of the Forest of Arden 'her one hand touching Trent, the other Severn's side'. It was of considerable extent, but Warwickshire was still equally divided

> with woodland as with plaine,
> Alike with hill and dale: and every day maintaine
> The sundry kind of beasts upon our copious wast's
> That men for profit breed as well as those of chase.

He described

> How Arden of her rills and riverets doth dispose;
> By Alcester how Alne to Arro easily flowes,
> And mildly being mixed, to Avon hold their way.

It was in Arden, far 'from the loathsome ayres of smoky cittied townes' — though he would be obliged to breathe them later on — that Shakespeare learnt the secrets of nature.

Drayton lovingly enumerates the birds: the merle, or thrush, the wood-lark, goldfinch, robin-redbreast and 'counterfetting jay'. He gives a vivid account of hunting 'both sorts of seasoned deere', the 'freckle fallowe' and the 'stately red'.

> The bucks and stags amongst the rascalls strew'd
> As sometime gallant spirits amongst the multitude

and the hart which was 'the hunter's noblest game', until at last

> He who the mourner is to his own dying corse,
> Upon the ruthless earth his precious tears lets fall.

Shakespeare must have had such a scene in mind when he introduced Jaques and the Lords bearing, presumably, the carcass of a dead deer in Act IV of *As You Like It*. The episode has nothing to do with the play, but it reminded him of the Forest of Arden which he transplanted without difficulty to the Ardennes — although the transplantation would have deceived nobody. One suspects that geography had a very modest place in the grammar school curriculum.

In *Venus and Adonis* he showed that he knew all about coursing the hare; and the death of the hare inspires the same compassion as Drayton's death of the hart

> Then shalt thou see the dew-bedabbled wretch
> Turn and return, indenting with the way;
> Each envious briar his weary legs do scratch,
> Each shadow makes him stop, each murmur stay.
> For misery is trodden on by many,
> And being low never relieved by any.
>
> (703-8)

The lines run smoother than Drayton's, and the last couplet suggests that by the time he wrote them Shakespeare knew as much about the back streets of Shoreditch as the backwoods of Arden. Sir Toby Belch extolled Maria as a 'beagle true-bred' — which indicates that the poet exempted hounds, even of lesser breed, from his general denigration of the species. Theseus in *A Midsummer Night's Dream* delights in the

> musical confusion
> Of hounds and echo in conjunction

and Hippolyta, in the single speech that makes her part worthwhile, remembers how

> they brayed the bear
> With hounds of Sparta. Never did I hear
> Such gallant chiding; for, besides the groves,
> The skies, the fountains, every region near
> Seemed all one mutual cry. I never heard
> So musical a discord, such sweet thunder.
>
> (IV, i, 113-21)

Shakespeare, then, was sensitive to the aesthetics of the chase; and he would have been out of tune with his time if the nobility of the horse had left him cold. Listen to the Dauphin on the eve of Agincourt

> The man hath no wit that cannot, from the rising of the lark to the lodging

of the lamb, vary deserved praise on my palfrey: it is a theme as fluent as
the sea; turn the sands into eloquent tongues, and my horse is argument
for them all: 'tis a subject for a sovereign to reason on, and for a
sovereign's subject to ride on . . .

(Henry V, III, vii, 32-8)

The subjects of Queen Elizabeth I rode horses as the subjects of
Queen Elizabeth II drive motor-cars. The horse was human, even in
its infidelity: the groom who visits Richard II in his cell at Pomfret
remembers Bolingbroke's coronation

O! how it yearn'd my heart when I beheld
In London streets, that coronation day
When Bolingbroke rode on roan Barbary
The horse that thou so often hast bestrid,
The horse that I so carefully have dress'd.

(V, v, 76-80)

The plays are garlanded with Shakespeare's precise knowledge of
flowers: Ophelia's 'rosemary . . . for remembrance', 'pansies . . . for
thoughts', fennel and columbines; Perdita's

Hot lavender, mints, savory, marjoram,
The marigold that goes to bed wi' the' sun
And with him rises weeping

(The Winter's Tale, IV, iv, 164-6)

and the flowers of spring no longer at hand for the plucking on that
hot summer afternoon of the sheep-shearing

Daffodils
That come before the swallow dares, and take
The winds of March with beauty; violets dim,
But sweeter than the lids of Juno's eyes,
And Cytherea's breath; pale primroses
That die unmarried ere they can behold
Bright Phoebus in his strength . . .

(IV, iv, 118-24)

The 'pale primrose' recurs in *Cymbeline* when Arviragus is standing
over the supposed corpse of Imogen

thou shalt not lack
The flower that's like thy face, pale primrose, nor
The azur'd harebell, like thy veins, no, nor
The leaf of eglantine, whom not to slander,
Out-sweeten'd not thy breath.

(Cymbeline, IV, ii, 220-4)

All this natural and sportive lore was the fruit of observation in the
gardens of Stratford, or in the glades of the Forest of Arden; and as
the dramatist got into his stride it was related to the *dramatis
personae*, and attuned to the dramatic situation. The horns of

Theseus and Hippolyta, musical enough in themselves, woke the quartet of lovers from their sleep; Perdita's catalogue acted as a counterpoint to the subsequent confrontation with Polixenes; and Ophelia's pathetic bunch of flowers heralded the willow that grew 'aslant the brook', and the

> crow-flowers, nettles, daisies, and long purples
> That liberal shepherds give a grosser name.
>
> (*Hamlet*, IV, vii, 169-70)

Shakespeare knew at an early age how the shepherds talked; an Elizabethan rural festival or fairground was some distance from Arcadia.

2

I do not see the adolescent Shakespeare as a brooding solitary. He was evidently sociable, more interested, I suspect, in other people than in himself. Was he not always more interested in other people than in himself? He had many friends in that small community. Hamnet and Judith Sadler gave their names to his twins. Thomas Russell, a recusant of noble birth, kept up with him in London, and returned to Stratford before he died. John Trussel was a first cousin on his mother's side, who collaborated with Samuel Daniel and Francis Bacon in a *History of England*, published in 1585. He twice evaded the censor in publishing the verses of the Jesuit, Robert Southwell. Richard Quiney was a fellow pupil of the grammar school, and his son Thomas married Judith Shakespeare. Another school-fellow, Robert Dibdale, became a recusant priest and was hanged at Tyburn on 8 October 1586. His family were friends of the Hathaways, who now enter the story.

Richard Hathaway was a fairly prosperous farmer, living at Shottery, only a mile out of Stratford. John Shakespeare had known him for some years, and in 1566 had stood surety for one of his debts. The two families were of similar status, and William was quick to form an attachment to Richard's eldest daughter, Anne, though she was eight years older than himself. If he was as precocious as his future achievement would indicate, it was natural for him to fix his affections on a woman of some maturity. He would quickly have tired of a milkmaid. Nor was it unlikely, with the hot blood stirring at eighteen and Ovid's *Amores* in his head, that he should have got Anne Hathaway with child towards the end of August 1582. Richard had died in the previous year, leaving several children adequately provided for. Anne moved out of the house at Shottery to her relatives at Temple Grafton, and by November, when there was no doubt of her pregnancy, William, with two friends of hers, rode off to Worcester to obtain a marriage licence. Advent, a close season for marriages, was upon them, and for this, and other obvious reasons, there was no time to lose.

There could be no question of William leaving Anne, literally, to hold the baby, and there is no evidence that he wished to do so. But he was still a minor, and his parents' consent had to be obtained. This was naturally given. The two were married, probably at Temple Grafton where the assembled relatives would have helped to preserve the conventions, on 30 November or 1 December 1573. The marriage would have been blessed by John Frith, an old Marian priest, who had been left undisturbed in his orthodoxy. The Puritan *Survey of the Ministry* for Warwickshire describes him as follows: 'Unsound in doctrine, he can neither preach nor read well, his chiefest trade is to cure hawks that are hurt or diseased, for which purpose many do usually repair to him.' Both in his readiness to help people in delicate situations, and in his preference for natural science to pastoral theology, he reminds one of Friar Lawrence. The Catholic ceremony may have preceded the official registration by several months, thus allowing the supposition that Susanna, Shakespeare's eldest daughter, had been conceived in wedlock. He is not likely to have minded one way or the other; his attitude was probably that of Claudio in *Measure for Measure* who 'upon a true contract', had 'got possession of Julietta's bed'. What mattered was the truth of the contract, not the time of the ceremony.

Shakespeare's views on marriage are not in doubt, to whatever degree in practice he may have contradicted them

> A contract of eternal bond of love,
> Confirm'd by mutual joinder of your hands
> Attested by the holy close of lips
> Strengthened by interchangement of your rings.
> (*Twelfth Night*, V, ii, 159-62)

Shakespeare did far more than any other dramatist to provide romantic love with its marriage lines. Gone is the medieval distrust of sexual relationship, the grudging Pauline concession that it is 'better to marry than to burn'. Gone, too, are the artifice and casuistry of the Courts of Love. Jaques, in *As You Like It*, may well have been speaking for his author when Sir Oliver Martext, the local incumbent, is sent quickly packing. 'Get you to church' Touchstone is told 'and have a good priest that can tell you what marriage is; this fellow will but join you together, as they join wainscot; and then one of you will prove a shrunk panel, and, like green timber, warp, warp' (III, iii, 82-6). Shakespeare would discover a good deal about the warping as the years went by, both in his own life and in other people's; but in the meantime old John Frith of Temple Marston was as safe a bet as he could find within an easy reach of Stratford.

We know nothing of Anne Shakespeare, except that she bore three children to her husband, survived him for seven years, and was bequeathed his 'second best bed'. The rest is silence, and had better remain so. Her role in his emotional life has been obscured, perhaps unfairly, by the lovely youth and the Dark Lady of the *Sonnets*. They were certainly separated for long periods of time, but when Shakespeare retired to Stratford his wife was there. That is all — and it is much — that one can say about many marriages. Difficulties faced them from the outset, for John Shakespeare had fallen upon hard times. In 1578 he had mortgaged a house and land in Wilmcote to his brother-in-law Edmund Lambert to raise £40 in ready money. Two years later he was unable to repay what he had borrowed. This led to unpleasant litigation. Also in 1578 the Shakespeares conveyed eighty-six acres of their property in Wilmcote to another relative, on the understanding that it was to revert to them or to their heirs after a specified period of time. In 1579 they sold a ninth share of their property in Snitterfield, and in the following year John Shakespeare incurred two fines, each of £20, from the Queen's Bench. His name heads a long list of gentlemen-landowners from Stratford, and with them were summoned 140 recusants from the adjoining counties accused of disturbing the peace of the realm. John was himself fined on two occasions for non-attendance at church. This does not in itself prove his recusancy, as he was said to be afraid of meeting his creditors under those hallowed vaults. He evidently went in some fear of them, for in 1582 he petitioned the Bench for sureties of the peace against four men, 'for fear of death and mutilation of his limbs'.[1]

It was not a moment for the young Shakespeares to set up house in the style John Shakespeare would have wished, or to which his daughter-in-law was accustomed. They presumably went to live in Henley Street. Susanna was born in May 1583, and was baptized on the 26th of the month in Holy Trinity Church. A pair of twins, Hamnet and Judith, followed in 1585 and were baptized on 2nd February. Anglican appearances were kept up. Meanwhile Shakespeare had no profession; to what were his thoughts now turning? It would have been natural for him to proceed to Oxford or Cambridge, where Sir Hugh Clopton had provided scholarships for the best pupils from the grammar school. This had a good academic reputation, and the 'magister' was paid a higher salary than an Eton master of the time. But genius cannot be equated with scholarship,

[1] See Rowse, p. 55.

and there is no proof that Shakespeare was a promising candidate for a First in Honour Moderations. Moreover the decline in his father's fortunes may well have prohibited a university career. There was a world elsewhere, and Shakespeare already had a glimpse of it.

With the accession of Elizabeth the secular drama was boisterously filling the void left by the disappearance of the Mystery Plays which, not long before Shakespeare's birth, had drawn big audiences to Coventry for the celebration of Corpus Christi. The Queen and the people alike could not have enough of pageantry. Those who were undernourished did not mind if others were overdressed. John Shakespeare, during the years of his mayoralty, had encouraged the performance of stage plays at Stratford, although the only stages available were the inn yards of the Bear, the Swan, and the Falcon. The companies played under the patronage of the noblemen who employed them: the Earl of Leicester in 1573 and 1577; the Earl of Warwick in 1576, 1577, 1581 and 1582; Lord Strange and the Countess of Essex in 1579; the Earl of Derby in 1580; Lord Berkeley and Lord Chandos in 1581 and 1583; the Earls of Oxford, Warwick, and Essex in 1584. The young Shakespeare could have seen all these performances. More spectacular were the celebrations for the Queen at Kenilworth in July 1575 recalled, it would appear, by Oberon in *A Midsummer Night's Dream*. The eleven-year-old boy, and certainly his father as alderman, would have

> heard a mermaid on a dolphin's back
> Uttering such dulcet and harmonious breath
> That the rude sea grew civil at her song

applauded the fireworks when 'certain stars shot madly from their spheres', and seen

> Flying between the cold moon and the earth
> Cupid all armed. A certain aim he took
> At a fair vestal thronéd by the west,
> And loosed his love shaft smartly from his bow,
> As it should pierce a hundred thousand hearts.
> But I might see young Cupid's fiery shaft
> Quenched in the chaste beams of the wat'ry moon,
> And the imperial votaress passed on
> In maiden meditation, fancy-free.
> (*A Midsummer Night's Dream*, II, i, 150 *et seq.*)

Leicester failed to win the hand of his 'imperial votaress', and in a play evidently written to celebrate a wedding, the reference is clear to a wedding which did not take place.

The companies were of uneven merit, some of no merit at all. The 'tragedians of the city' that Hamlet welcomed to Elsinore were of better quality, driven from their normal playhouse, maybe, by an outbreak of the plague. The strolling players were like the touring actors of the day before yesterday, not good enough to find employment in the capital. Nor was their precarious existence, regulated by law but socially discredited, likely to have appealed to a burgher of Stratford, itching for a coat-of-arms, as a profession for his son, or to a wife and mother with three children as a proper way of life for her husband.

But the clouds were gathering over Stratford. In 1583 John Somerville who had married Margaret Arden, a cousin of Mary Shakespeare, was arrested and condemned to death for allegedly plotting against the Queen. He appears to have been mentally unbalanced, but his wife was described by the prosecution as 'a very perverse and malitious Papist' whose faith had been strengthened by a visit to the Continent. The result of this celebrated case was a strenuous search for recusants in and around Stratford. Edward Arden, Margaret's father, his wife Mary, and the family chaplain, Father Hall, were also arrested. Edward and the priest were sentenced to be hanged, and Mary to be burnt alive. Francis Throckmorton, another respected landowner of the district, confessed under torture that he had carried letters to the Queen of Scots, and was executed shortly afterwards.

No one did more to encourage the round-up of suspects than Sir Thomas Lucy of Charlecote, and this brings us to the first of the legends which have embroidered Shakespeare's name. The story cannot be discounted altogether for lack of first-hand documentary evidence. William Fulman, who died not far from Stratford in 1688, had spent half a century in collecting a miscellany of local lore. His works were completed by Richard Davies and presented to Corpus Christi College, Oxford. Here, on the first page, Davies records that Shakespeare was 'much given to all unluckiness in stealing venison and rabbits particularly from Sir Lucy who had him whipped and sometimes imprisoned and at last made him fly his native country to his great advancement'. Thomas Betterton, the leading actor of the Restoration, heard the story at Stratford, and passed it on to Nicholas Rowe, Shakespeare's first biographer (1719). Twenty years later, William Oldys had it from the Duke of Buckingham, who had heard it from Sir William Davenant, Shakespeare's godson. Both Davies and Rowe state that Lucy was satirized in the person of Justice Shallow in *The Merry Wives of Windsor,* and Oldys quotes from the ballad which the poet was said to have indicted against his adversary.

> A parliamente member, a justice of peace,
> At home a poor scare-crow, at London an asse

and so on. The verses are pretty poor doggerel; they hardly suggest a poet soon to have his footsteps on the ladder of fame. Later editors, Capel (1767) and Jordan (1790), repeated the story. The latter claimed to have found additional stanzas to the poem, evidently not by Shakespeare, in a house at Shottery belonging to Dorothy Wheeler, the descendant of a councillor friend of the poet. They showed how unpopular Lucy had become in the neighbourhood.

Here, then, is no evidence to bring before a jury. But if it was based on fact, it is reasonable to see a portrait of Lucy in Justice Shallow of *The Merry Wives*. Shallow has the title of *'custos rotulorum'*, which would also have been Lucy's title when Shakespeare was said to have been brought before him. He accuses Falstaff as follows: 'You have beaten my men, killed my deer, and broken open my lodge; the Court shall hear of it; it is a riot' (I, i, 109). This echoes the ballad reported to have been hung on the gates at Charlecote

> He said 'twas a riot
> His men had been beat
> His venison had been stole
> And clandestinely ate.

There can be no certainty in the matter, but more than a faint probability.[1] Poaching has always been among the more respectable misdemeanours answerable to the law. If the Shakespeares were hard up, as appears likely, a haunch of venison would have been a welcome addition to the larder; and if Stratford had become too hot for Shakespeare, something in Shakespeare — call it genius or ambition — may have become too hot for Stratford. Sometime in 1586 or 1587 he packed his bags.

---

[1] For a detailed treatment, see Clara Longworth de Chambrun, *Shakespeare — a Portrait Restored* (1957), pp. 52-8.

Chapter 2

The Discord of Nobility

1

Had he packed them once or twice already? John Aubrey, writing from reliable hearsay — the family of Christopher Beeston, the actor — reports that Shakespeare 'had been in his younger days a schoolmaster in the country' since he 'understood Latin pretty well'. I modestly agree with Dr Rowse that this would not have been at all improbable. The Shakespeares, *père et fils*, were glad of any increment to the dwindling fortunes of the family; and a schoolmaster, especially if he were tutor to a squire or nobleman of substance, escaped the stigma of a 'rogue and vagabond' — as the strolling players were then commonly regarded. Nevertheless such employment, if Aubrey's story is to be believed, did nothing to satisfy any of the three vocations which for Shakespeare were now imperative — to write plays, to act in plays, and to write poetry. It was a case of London calling.

For a distance of 120 miles the road ran, as it still does, either through Oxford and High Wycombe, or through Banbury and Amersham. The two met at Uxbridge, and Shakespeare seems generally to have preferred the Oxford route. He would have ridden over the fourteen stone arches of Clopton Bridge — lucky not to be setting out two years later when both ends of it were broken by the Avon in flood. If he were riding his own horse he might have sold it when he got to London; if he took a post-horse he would have been charged 3*d.* a mile, and 6*d.* for a mounted post-boy to bring it back from one stage to another. On a good road, and at a good pace, ten miles could be covered in an hour. Shakespeare probably rode as quickly as he wrote; everything we know about him — and not least his marriage — points to a young man in a hurry. Inns were numerous, hospitable, and well appointed; one paid according to one's means. Fynes Moryson, who was well acquainted with inns on the Continent, writes that 'The world affords not such inns as England hath, either for good and cheap entertainments at the guest's own pleasure, or for humble attendance on passengers.' Harrison, in his *Description of England*, assures us that clean sheets were provided for everyone 'wherein no man hath been lodged since they came from the laundress, or out of the water wherein they were last washed'. It is possible, of course, if money were short, that Shakespeare made the journey on foot; thirty years later Ben Jonson walked from London to Edinburgh, as Will Kempe had danced, intermittently, from London to Norwich. In that case a four-days' march — perhaps a little longer — would have brought him past the gallows at Tyburn on his way to the City. Most of the strolling players toured on foot; but Shakespeare was not yet a strolling player, nor, when he became one, do we know how far, or how fast, he strolled.

Sir William Davenant told Betterton that when Shakespeare came to London 'he was without money and friends, and being a stranger knew not to whom to apply nor by what means to support himself'. This should warn us against treating hearsay evidence as historical fact. He may have been without money, but he was not without friends. Two of them, William Combe and Richard Field, were already established in the capital. Combe was a barrister at the Middle Temple; his brother left Shakespeare £5 in his will, and Shakespeare left his sword to Thomas Combe, the barrister's nephew. Richard Field was the son of Henry Field, a tanner of Stratford, whose goods and chattels had been valued by Shakespeare's father. Richard had served his apprenticeship as a printer with Thomas Vautrollier, a French Huguenot from Rouen; married his widow; and inherited his business in Blackfriars. Among the many books he published were Sir John Harrington's translation of *Orlando Furioso*, fifteen books of Ovid's *Metamorphoses*, the second edition of North's *Plutarch*, and Puttenham's *Arte of English Poesie*. This was an important work of literary criticism from which Shakespeare must have learnt much — not least a certain obedience to 'the mystery of things'; the 'negative capability' which Keats singled out as a mark of his genius; the middle road between fanaticism and indifference. If he frequented Field's shop, Puttenham may well have been among the *littérateurs* that he met there.

Shakespeare had come to London at a critical moment in the reign. On 8 February 1587, the Queen of Scots had been executed, and in 1588 Philip IV's Armada sailed up the Channel. The Catholic minority (which was still large) faced a choice between incompatible loyalties. An incandescent patriotism was in the air; we should call it the 'spirit of Dunkirk'. As George Wyndham put it: 'All the talk was of sea-fights and new editions: Drake and Lyly, Raleigh and Lodge, Greene and Marlowe and Grenville were names in every mouth.'[1]

[1] George Wyndham, *The Poems of Shakespeare* (1898), Introduction, xxviii.

How Shakespeare responded to this was made clear before long

> Come the four corners of the earth in arms
> And we shall shock them

but the condition of victory should be noted

> Nought shall make us rue
> If England to itself remain but true.
>
> (*King John*, V, vii, 112-18)

The scattering of the Armada secured the national independence, and confirmed a general, if not unanimous, loyalty to the throne; it did not procure the 'deep consent' which it was beyond even Elizabeth's statesmanship to achieve. The next fifteen years were to see an extraordinary florescence of literature, but they secreted a disillusionment which is the constant sequel to euphoria, and Shakespeare reflected it as the years went by.

'The man who is tired of London', said Dr Johnson, 'is tired of life.' The moment came when Shakespeare was tired of London — although the moment was not yet — but I do not think he was ever tired of life. London, in 1587 and 1588, was a book in which a man might 'read strange matters'. 'If he throws himself among the people,' wrote La Bruyère, 'he quickly makes strange discoveries, sees things he had never imagined, of which he could not have the least suspicion. Continuous experience takes him forward in the knowledge of humanity.' Shakespeare lodged, it appears, in Shoreditch, and what he gleaned from the city, as ever with his eyes as well as his wits about him, is suggested by Henry James in his Preface to *The Princess Casamassima*. Speaking of 'the assault directly made by the great city upon an imagination quick to react', he continues

> One walked of course with one's eyes greatly open, and I hasten to declare that such a practice, carried on for a long time and over a considerable space, positively provokes, all round, a mystic solicitation, the urgent appeal, on the part of everything, to be interpreted and, so far as may be, reproduced. Subjects and situations, character and history, the tragedy and comedy of life, are things of which the common air, in such conditions, seems pungently to taste; and to a mind curious, before the human scene, of meanings and revelations the great grey Babylon easily becomes, on its face, a garden bristling with an immense illustrative flora.

As James Baldwin has written, 'Shakespeare walked the streets and tried not to lie about what he saw there.' The Babylon that he saw was less grey than it afterwards became, but it lacked neither interest nor iniquity. Cheek by jowl, it exhibited the cruelty and charm, the spendour and squalor, the indigence and luxury of the time. The Bishop of Winchester's palace on the south bank of the Thames stood close by the 'stews' of which the profits filled his purse. In

Henry VI, Part One (I, iii, 36) a previous Bishop of Winchester is accused of giving 'whores indulgences to sin'. The narrow, pestiferous streets were already so congested with the coaches of the well-to-do, which multiplied as fast as motor-cars do today, that before the end of Elizabeth's reign a Bill was introduced to restrain their 'excessive and superfluous use' within the realm. Most people preferred to use the river, where the wherries were for hire at all the public stairs — 2,000 of them according to John Taylor — and there was much unemployment among the watermen as the coaches threatened their monopoly. The north bank was lined with the mansions of the nobility — Leicester House which passed to the Earl of Essex after Leicester's death in 1588; Durham House on the site of the Adelphi which was occupied by Sir Walter Raleigh. Superb above the crowded thoroughfares and the animated river stood old St Paul's. This was a place not only of worship, but of commerce and assignations. The central aisle was known as 'Paul's Walk' where Falstaff recruited Bardolph into his company. We learn that Inigo Jones added the portico to the west end as 'an ambulatory for such as usually walking in the body of the church, disturbed the solemn service in the choir'. Two impressive services were held in the cathedral shortly after Shakespeare's arrival in the city. On 16 February 1586-7,[1] 700 mourners followed the funeral procession of Sir Philip Sidney; and on 24 November 1588, the Queen drove from Somerset House to give thanks for the defeat of the Armada. The poet's eye could not have failed to register the power and the glory; and it registered much else besides.

Fleet Street was a fairground where puppets, naked Indians, and exotic fishes were displayed for the amusement of the people. Trinculo was reminded of them when he discovered Caliban

> A strange fish! Were I in England now, as once I was, and had but this fish painted, not a holiday fool there but would give a piece of silver: there would this monster make a man; any strange beast there makes a man.
>
> (*The Tempest*, II, ii, 28-32)

Bear-baiting would always draw the crowd, for the Elizabethans were not squeamish. Like young Richard in *Henry VI, Part Two* (V, i, 151-4), Shakespeare would

> Oft have . . . seen a hot o'erweening cur
> Run back and bite, because he was witheld;
> Who, being suffer'd with the bear's fell paw,
> Hath clapp'd his tail between his legs and cried.

'Fleet' was also the name of the prison to which Falstaff is consigned

---

[1] The year began in April in Shakespeare's time.

after his repudiation by the newly crowned Henry V, and Ben Jonson speaks of 'the cries of the damned' that could be heard there. Prisons for the people were as numerous as palaces for the patricians — five of them in Southwark alone. The Tower, guarding the city on its eastern side, was at once a treasury, an armoury, a mint, a place of royal assembly, and a 'Prison of Estate' for political offences. It is to the Tower that Gloucester in *Henry VI, Part One* (I, i, 168) sets off to view the artillery and munitions. If Shakespeare, to outward appearances, was more convivial than contemplative, we can picture him going the rounds of the taverns; the Dagger in Holborn, where the ale was strong and the company doubtful; the Mitre and the Mermaid in Cheapside; the Boar's Head in Eastcheap; the Devil at Temple Bar. The great days of the Mermaid did not come until 1603, but Jonson, it seems, had already been frequenting it; and who knows but that Shakespeare might have met him there before either of them had reached the meridian of their fame?

In contrast to the narrow streets were the open spaces and gardens. The Bishop of Ely in *Richard III* is asked to fetch strawberries from Ely Place; in the gardens of the Temple, leased to Sir Christopher Hatton in 1576, the roses bloomed, symbolically, red and white. Moreover the country, on either side of the river, was never far away. London and Westminster on one side, and Southwark on the other, were two narrow zones of ribbon development, divided by the bustling fairway of the Thames. With its brothels and bear-gardens, its riots and revelry, its Puritans and pandars, its pageantry and processions, its taverns and tournaments, it tapsters and gamesters, its rough justice, and its manners rude or refined, the city might well have been described as 'swinging'; but it 'swung' with a fantasy and extravagance which had never been seen before, and was not to be seen again. The men wore jewels on their doublets and roses in their ears; and the fashion in boots and shoes was so eccentric that legislation was brought in to restrain it.

2

It was, of course, upon the theatres that Shakespeare's ambition was principally fixed. In May 1574 James Burbage, by trade a carpenter, with four other of Leicester's men, was given the right to perform plays in the City of London and elsewhere, subject only to the censorship of the Master of the Revels. But the City fathers, with whom Puritan prejudice was strong, asserted their own rights of censorship, and Burbage was obliged to build his 'Theatre' in the fields beyond Shoreditch, outside the City limits. This was opened in 1576. It was essentially an amphitheatre where a movable stage could be put up for the performance of plays — a sketch for the Globe for

which its timbers eventually served. Other theatres quickly followed:
the Curtain in Shoreditch, the Rose on the south bank, with
Henslowe as its impresario and Edward Alleyn as its principal
tragedian, and a third at Newington Butts, also on the south bank,
were in use when Shakespeare came to London. There were two
'private' theatres: the first Blackfriars where the Children of the
Chapel Royal at Windsor played under Richard Farrant, and
Sebastian Westcott's playhouse near St Paul's. Westcott was master
of the cathedral choir-boys, who acted there.

There were good reasons why Shakespeare should have looked to
Burbage's 'Theatre'. Burbage had passed through Stratford on tour
with Leicester's men, and they may have met. He was to produce
several plays by Marlowe, Greene, Peele, Lodge, and Kyd; also, very
probably, the 'Ur-Hamlet' which was later to set Shakespeare's
imagination ablaze. Lodge and Kyd were London men; the others
had all been to the University. Shakespeare was only two months
younger than Marlowe, but very much his junior in the ways of the
literary world. That Shakespeare already regarded him as a rival
seems clear, if it was *Hero and Leander* that spurred him to *Venus
and Adonis*. But the two men were totally different; Marlowe was
homosexual and, as Dr Rowse has shrewdly pointed out, had
evidently no ear for music — except in iambic verse where
Shakespeare had still a little time to catch up with him. Marlowe was
contestataire, Shakespeare more naturally conformist.

The story that Shakespeare held the horses of Burbage's wealthier
patrons outside the door of the 'Theatre' came to Betterton from Sir
William Davenant. It should not be taken for gospel, but is not
inherently improbable. If a man wants to write plays or to act in
them, he can do worse than loiter around the stage door. An easy
way to get his foot inside would be to try his hand at collaboration.
This explains Shakespeare's part in *The Booke of Sir Thomas More*
(*c.* 1590), an unpublished and unacted play, where H. W. Pollard and
five other specialists have identified his handwriting beyond reasonable doubt. Thomas Dekker, Anthony Munday, and Henry Chettle
are thought to have written the greater part of it. What Jaques
Copeau wrote of Molière is equally applicable to Shakespeare. 'I
think it is an excellent thing for a dramatist, at the outset of his
career, if he is not obliged to bother too much about originality and
distinction, but if, on the contrary, he is content straightaway to
please his public.'[1] Shakespeare had dealt with the incident where
More saves the lives of some foreign workers threatened by a crowd
blaming them for the rise in the cost of living. These 127 lines follow

[1] *Registres II* (1976), p. 79.

the text in Holinshed, and they have the Shakespearean ring. Without laws, proclaims More, 'men like ravenous fishes would feed on one another'; Coriolanus proclaims that 'without the Senate to control them, the Roman plebs would feed on one another'. Or again 'You'll hold the majesty of law in liom to slip him like a hound', where Coriolanus is accused of 'holding Corioli in the name of Rome even like a fawning greyhound in the leash to let him slip at will'. In taking up arms against authority, the crowd were rebelling against God Himself

> For to the King God hath his office lent
> Of dread, of justice, power and command
> Hath bid him rule and will'd you to obey.

This was the lesson of the Homilies. Shakespeare's anti-democratic sentiments are already evident; London had given him glimpses of the majesty, and even closer glimpses of the mob. The Master of the Revels, Sir Edmund Tilney, had written on the first page of the manuscript: 'Leave out the insurrection wholly and the cause thereof', evidently afraid lest the spectacle of English citizens in violent protest against foreign workers might injure relations with the foreign power. Cecil was just as careful for the rights of workers from across the Channel, and Shakespeare follows him in an equal concern for order and compassion.

This precious fragment is undated. It is important, however, in showing that Shakespeare was prepared to collaborate with other people, as they would collaborate with him. The extent of their collaboration, particularly in the early plays, is beyond my purpose, and certainly beyond my competence, to decide. I can only refer the reader to responsible authorities — notably to the eight volumes of Professor Bullough's *Shakespeare's Sources* — and for a general discussion of the problem to Professor G. E. Bentley's *The Profession of Dramatist in Shakespeare's Time* (1971). He estimates that 'as many as half of the plays by professional dramatists in the period (1590-1642) incorporated the writing at some date of more than one man. In the case of the 282 plays mentioned in Henslowe's diary . . . nearly two-thirds are the work of more than one man' (p. 199). Shakespeare's assimilative genius cannot be emphasized too strongly; he laid his hands, so to speak, on anything lying about. If a certain passage appears to have been written by Marlowe or Peele, it may simply mean that he had been reading Marlowe or Peele. He had not yet found his distinctive poetic style; his sense of drama was stronger than his sense of poetry. It is tempting to ascribe to him the gold, and leave the dross to his collaborators. But, as Geoffrey Grigson has wisely written

The appalling uniqueness of each great writer includes the different proportions in him of fudge and gold. And what writer ... is not a warning against demands for a sustained perfection in literature, as if the great writer's graph ascended steeply, and at the worst flattened to a long high level.[1]

Moreover it was not only in reading other men's plays, and helping them to write them, that Shakespeare found his feet in the theatre. He had already trod its boards — modestly enough no doubt — with the Earl of Pembroke's men.

History appealed to him, not least because it was good Box Office. The test of a nation's greatness is its readiness to look back into its past, and to learn from it. Futurism, to be distinguished from inventive genius, is too often a sympton of decline. Shakespeare had many sources to draw upon: the *Chronicles of England* printed by Caxton in 1480; the *Polychromicon* of Ramalf Higden, translated in 1387, modernized by Caxton, and reissued by Peter Treveris in 1527; Matthew Paris's *Chronica Majora*; Thomas Walsingham's *Historia Anglicana*; Froissart's Chronicles mentioned in *Henry VI, Part One*; the verse-chronicle of John Hardyng, who had served as page to Hotspur and was attending on his master at the Battle of Shrewsbury; Polydore Vergil with his 'cyclical theory of history'[2], and giving the clue to both of Shakespeare's tetralogies when he wrote that 'the sovereignty extorted forcibly by Henry IV, grandfather to Henry VI, could not be long enjoyed of that family'. But Shakespeare's principal source was Edward Hall, who began the story with Richard II and ended it with Henry VIII. Hall's avowed purpose was to glorify the Tudors, under the second of whom he sat in the House of Commons. For him, as for Polydore Vergil, 'King Henry the Fourth was the beginning and root of the great discord and division'. Hall was followed by Holinshed whose *Chronicles* were first published in 1578. A second edition came out in 1587, and would therefore have been 'hot' reading when Shakespeare arrived in London. According to Professor Bullough, he 'took over not only the attitude but the pattern of Hall's history'[3], but drew increasingly on Holinshed when he tackled his second tetralogy. It seems to be generally agreed that Holinshed was the better writer.

For their general philosphy of history both Hall and Polydore Vergil owed much to *A Mirror for Magistrates*, first published in 1559, and brought up to date in 1587 — once again providentially for Shakespeare's perusal. This series of fictitious soliloquies by the

---

[1] *The Times Literary Supplement*, 5 October 1973.
[2] See Geoffrey Bullough, *Narrative and Dramatic Sources of Shakespeare* (1975), Vol. III, p. 9.
[3] ibid., p. 15.

ghosts of certain British statesmen who had come to a bad end, and interspersed with comments by the authors of the book, had become a breviary of political thought, inheriting as it did medieval notions of authority and applying them to past and present. The logic of cause and effect in history is seen to depend on Fortune (or the stars) the will of God, and the misbehaviour of mankind. The following quatrain put it in a nutshell

> Thus of our heavy hopes chief causes be but twain,
> Whereon the rest depend and underput remain.
> The chief the will divine, called destiny and fate;
> The other sin, through humours holp, which God
>   doth highly hate.

The period covered by the *Mirror* is the same as that covered by Hall's *Chronicle* and by Shakespeare's tetralogies. How Shakespeare, consciously or otherwise, turned didacticism into drama will soon be apparent.[1]

In approaching *Henry VI, Part One* three questions arise. Was Shakespeare the principal author of the play? If so, did he already have both tetralogies in mind? And in that case why did he treat the second period before the first? When was the play first performed? Critics have been condescending about *Henry VI*, wishing with the misplaced zeal of bardolatry to acquit Shakespeare of its crudities. It has been left to productions in the theatre — by Douglas Seale in Birmingham and at the Old Vic, and by Peter Hall and his associates at Stratford — to prove its stageworthiness. Even at Stratford, however, the three parts were telescoped into two, with abridgement and a good deal of pastiche to bridge the gaps. (M. Roger Planchon who had the plays in mind for performance at his theatre in Lyons gave me his opinion that it was sacrilege to cut a word.) The best reason for believing that Shakespeare was the main author of *Part One* is that Heminge and Condell included it in the First Folio. That the plays as a whole were popular is shown by the Epilogue to *Henry V*

> Henry the Sixth, in infant bands crown'd King
> Of France and England, did this King succeed;
> Whose state so many had the managing,
> That they lost France and made his England bleed:
> *Which oft our stage hath shown . . .*

The other ground for maintaining Shakespeare's essential authorship is the overall conception and design. The conventional prosody has nothing to compare with Marlowe's flights in *Tamburlaine*; but

---

[1] A detailed discussion of *A Mirror for Magistrates* may be found in E. M. W. Tillyard, *Shakespeare's History Plays* (1948).

Marlowe lacked altogether Shakespeare's grasp of dramatic architecture. In Marlowe one thing follows another; in Shakespeare one thing leads to the next. It is encouraging to note that both Tillyard and Bullough allow him to have been the author.

I find it hard to believe that he did not plan the entire sequence, however vaguely, from the start. But the public, in their post-Armada mood, would have been restless to see the Tudors on the throne as soon as possible; to be shown how the divisions were healed before being shown how they were brought about. There was also a further reason. France — where the action in *Part One* mainly takes place — was in the news, for in 1591 Elizabeth's troops were besieging Rouen, just as Talbot's troops besiege it in the play. Shakespeare would not have disdained the title of commercial dramatist; at this stage he could not have afforded to. As for the date of the play, Nashe refers, as early as 1592, to the popular enthusiasm for the Talbot scenes[1]

> How it would have joyed brave Talbot, the terror of the French, to think that after he had been dead two hundred years in his tomb he should triumph again on the stage, and have his bones embalmed with the tears of ten thousand spectators (at least at several times) who, in the tragedian that represents his person, behold him fresh bleeding.

Since Talbot is so obviously the hero of *Henry VI, Part One*, the reference is fairly conclusive. Already, according to Henslowe's Diary, 'Henry . . . the Sixth' was performed as a 'new' play in March 1591. The title page of QI tells us that it had been acted by Lord Pembroke's company to which Shakespeare had belonged. The theory that it was written after *Parts Two* and *Three* can be discounted by the fact that it so clearly leads up to them, and that the later parts have a greater variety and verve. Shakespeare was a quick learner, although there is no knowing how far he was working, at first, on the intractable material of an earlier play by another hand or hands, of which we have no trace.

The subject is how the English territories in France were lost, in spite of Talbot's feats of arms, through the witchcraft of Joan of Arc, and dissension at home. Henry V is hardly cold in his coffin before a Messenger warns Duke Humphrey of Gloucester, Protector of the Kingdom during the minority of the young King, that defeat has been due to

> want of men and money.
> Amongst the soldiers this is mutteréd,
> That here you maintain several factions,
> And whilst a field should be dispatch'd and fought,

[1] *Pierce Penniless* (1592).

> You are disputing of your generals:
> One would have lingering wars with little cost;
> Another would fly swift, but wanteth wings;
> A third thinks, without expense at all,
> By guileful fair words peace may be obtained.
>
> (I, i, 70-7)

Plus ça change . . . before the scene is over, Humphrey and Beaufort are snarling at each other, and presently they will bite. Talbot, defeated by Joan of Arc at Orleans, gets his revenge at Rouen, and only loses Bordeaux because Plantagenet and Somerset — respectively Yorkist and Lancastrian — quarrelling between themselves, fail to bring up reinforcements. Shakespeare must not be held primarily responsible for the caricature of Joan. As a good Protestant, Hall did not believe in divine locutions; witchcraft was a better explanation. And as a good patriot he could not be expected to agree that the French had the right to expel the English from territory that did not belong to them. Dramatically speaking, however, Joan justifies her place in the structure of the play. Talbot, from Shakespeare's point of view, is fighting on the right side, and fighting valiantly; but his efforts are brought to nothing by domestic rivalries. The young Henry is an ineffectual figure, and Exeter, acting as a Chorus, predicts

> More rancorous spite, more furious raging broils,
> Than yet can be imagined or supposed.
> But howsoe'er, no simple man that sees
> This jarring discord of nobility,
> This shouldering of each other in the court,
> This factious bandying of their favourites,
> But that it doth presage some ill event.
>
> (IV, i, 185-91)

The characterization, generally weak, gains in definition when Margaret of Anjou is introduced with Suffolk in Act V, and their future liaison clearly foreshadowed. In promoting her claims to Henry's hand over the wealthier Countess of Armagnac — for she brings no dowry, and England will lose Anjou and Maine as the price of her betrothal — Suffolk is no doubt speaking for Shakespeare when he argues that

> Marriage is a matter of more worth
> Than to be dealt with by attorneyship

and asks

> For what is wedlock forcéd but a hell,
> An age of discord and continual strife?
>
> (V, v, 55-6; 62-3)

If anyone likes to believe that this is why Shakespeare took the road
to London, they are free to do so. But when Talbot, helpless in front
of Bordeaux for want of reinforcements, remembers his hunting
days, the autobiographical note is unmistakably sounded

> How are we park'd and bounded in a pale,
> A little herd of England's timorous deer,
> Mazed with a yelping kennel of French curs!
> If we be English deer, be then in blood;
> Not rascal-like, to fall down with a pinch,
> But rather, moody-mad and desperate stags,
> Turn on the bloody hounds with heads of steel
> And make the cowards stand aloof at bay.
>
> (IV, ii, 45-52)

Shakespeare is finding his voice at the same time as he is finding his
feet.

3

The 'discord of nobility' reaches a crescendo in the second part of
Henry VI. York is now the dominating figure, although Margaret
increasingly asserts herself. His claim to the throne is based on
descent from Lionel, Duke of Clarence, the third son of Edward III,
through the female line, and he retails it at great length to Warwick
and Salisbury who know it by heart already, and to an audience of
amateur genealogists who apparently cannot hear it too often. His
way is barred, however, not only by a king

> Whose church — like humours fits not for a crown
>
> (I, i, 244)

and by a queen who does her best to stiffen him, but by the good
Duke Humphrey of Gloucester who is still the Lord Protector and
popular with the crowd. York, therefore, makes common cause with
his Lancastrian opponents, Somerset, Warwick and Suffolk, who
cherish their own ambitions, to displace Humphrey and Cardinal
Beaufort, his rival and probable successor. Only Salisbury, Warwick's
father, holds himself above their intrigues, appealing both to York
and to his own son

> While these do labour for their own preferment
> Behoves it us to labour for the realm.
> I never saw but Humphrey, Duke of Gloucester,
> Did bear him like a noble gentleman
>
> (I, i, 181-4)

and as for Beaufort

> Oft have I seen the haughty cardinal
> More like a soldier than a man o' the church . . .

> Sweat like a ruffian, and demean himself
> Unlike the ruler of a commonweal.
>
> (I, i, 185-8)

Humphrey's wife, Dame Eleanor, is ambitious for the crown, but the Duke is not to be persuaded. She therefore hires Sir John Hume to find her a witch and conjuror who will give her the answer to certain leading questions. But Hume is also in the pay of York, and through the exposure of the Duchess' indiscretion Humphrey is persuaded to resign the Lord Protectorship. He is afterwards brought to trial, and then murdered by Suffolk, while Eleanor is exiled to the Isle of Man — a fate she regards as only slightly worse than death. Suffolk's crime is denounced to the King by Warwick, and he too is exiled. He leaves after an emotional parting from Queen Margaret, and is killed by pirates during the channel crossing.

With Suffolk, Humphrey, and Beaufort all removed — for the Cardinal, impenitent to the last, has died from natural causes — the way looks clear for York. For the moment, however, it is blocked by an uprising in Ireland which he is sent to quell. This gives him the cue to stir up Jack Cade's rebellion, and Shakespeare a chance to broaden his social panorama. The 'people of England' — or at any rate a section of them — who 'had not spoken yet' discover their voice in Cade. We remember the opening of *Henry VI, Part One*

> Comets — importing change of times and states,
> Brandish your crystal tresses in the sky

resounding, feudal rhetoric as an overture to a battle of iron-clads; but here, in Act IV, Scene 2 of *Part Two*, are home truths in homespun prose after all those cantering iambics

> Well, I say it was never merry world in England
>   since gentlemen came up —
> The nobility think scorn to go in leather aprons —
> There is no better sign of a brave mind than a hard
>   hand

and so we have 'Best's son, the tanner of Wingham', and Dick the butcher, and Smith the weaver, all flocking to join Jack Cade the clothier who 'means to dress' the commonwealth, and turn it, and set a new nap upon it. Cade is, of course, shown as a preposterous demagogue, claiming, on instructions from York, that his father was a Mortimer — whereas, as a fellow-insurgent reminds us, he was merely a 'good bricklayer', and his mother a Plantagenet, whereas she was merely a midwife. He promises that 'all the realm shall be in common' — the familiar demand that because some people have too little, no one shall have anything at all; that seven half-penny loaves shall be sold for a penny; and he promises that, for the first year of his reign, the city's 'pissing-conduit shall run nothing but claret wine', and that the Savoy, the Inns of Court, and the Record Office shall all be pulled down. He accuses Lord Say of having 'most traitorously corrupted the youth of the realm in erecting a grammar school', of 'causing printing to be used', of building a paper mill, and of tolerating in his entourage conversation about 'nouns and verbs'. There is no question of Shakespeare's sympathy with Cade, but he is not a caricature. His language is that of the Paris students who sacked the Odéon in 1968, and his philosophy is the nihilism of the 'giddy multitude'.

Shakespeare had evidently drawn upon Holinshed's or Grafton's account of the Peasants' Revolt in 1381, also led by a Kentishman. Wat Tyler and Jack Straw professed a similar contempt for literacy.[1] The scenes in which Cade and his rabble appear have a vernacular vigour, hinting at the greater things to come. They show how well, by now, Shakespeare knew his London — 'Up Fish Street! Down St Magnus Corner!' — and the scene where Cade meets his end gave him the opportunity for a different social contrast. It is no longer the mob versus the nobility, but the mob versus the middle classes. Alexander Iden, with his five servants, comes from the same stratum as Shakespeare's mother — a little higher, that is to say, than John Shakespeare himself. He describes himself, and his situation, not without complacency

> Lord! who would live turmoiléd in the court,
> And may enjoy such quiet walks as these?
> This small inheritance my father left me
> Contenteth me, and worth a monarchy.
> I seek not to wax great by other's waning,
> Or gather wealth I care not with what envy;
> Sufficeth that I have maintains my state,
> And sends the poor well pleaséd from my gate.
>
> (IV, x, 16-23)

The picture is one of moderate fortune; such fortune as Shakespeare himself was later to enjoy. The inheritance is small, and Iden has no wish to augment it. (We shall not be able to say the same of Shakespeare.) If the poor come to the gate, they will not be sent empty away; but they will always be there to come. And, needless to say, trespassers will be prosecuted. Iden little guesses that Cade, in his flight from justice, has climbed over the garden wall, 'having eat no meat these five days', and prepared to take on, single-handed, Iden and his five servants. Iden has no wish to invoke these considerable odds against a 'poor famish'd man' but, forced to it, slays him in single combat.

[1] See Bullough, Vol. III, pp. 96 *et seq.*

No tears are solicited for Cade, and we do not grudge Iden his accolade. Men have been knighted for less. But if you compare the speeches of the two antagonists before they fall to blows, the palm for self-expression does not go to the man of property.

> *Iden*: Is't not enough to break into my garden
> And like a thief to come to rob my grounds,
> Climbing my walls in spite of me, the owner . . .
>
> *Cade*: Steel, if thou turn the edge, or cut not out the burly-boned clown
> in chines of beef 'ere thou sleep in thy sheath, I beseech Jove on
> my knees, thou may'st be turned to hobnails.
>
> (IV, x, 32-5; 56-9)

The Cade sequence, for all its novelty, is integral to the play. York has fostered the rebellion to create anarchy in the commonwealth; and when he returns from Ireland to challenge the rival power of Somerset, the King can only complain

> Thus stands my state, 'twixt Cade and York distress'd;
> Like to a ship that, having 'scaped a tempest,
> Is straightway calm'd and boarded with a pirate.
>
> (IV, ix, 31-3)

The King gives way, and Somerset is consigned to the Tower. He is presently released, however, and both Warwick and his father, Salisbury, endorse York's claim to the throne. Now, for the first time, York's son — the 'foul indigested lump / As crookéd in thy manners as thy shape' — whom we shall know, and enjoy, as Richard III — makes his appearance at his father's side. The opposing forces meet at St Albans, with Margaret railing at her husband's vacillation

> What are you made of? You'll nor fight, nor fly.
>
> (V, iii, 74)

The Yorkists are victorious, and the Wars of the Roses have begun.

The play is rich in classical allusions, as if Shakespeare were not averse to showing off his shreds and patches of scholarship. York, smarting under the loss of Anjou and Maine, compares himself to 'Ajax Telamonius', and speaks of his 'brows'

> Whose smile and frown, like to Achilles' spear
> Is able with the change to kill and cure.
>
> (V, i, 100)

Young Clifford takes up his father's body on the battlefield

> As did Aeneas old Anchises bear
>
> (V, ii, 62)

thus anticipating Cassius in Julius Caesar

I, as Aeneas our great ancestor
Did from the flames of Troy upon his shoulder
The old Anchises bear, so from the waves of Tiber
Did I the tiréd Caesar.

                                        (I, ii, 12-15)

The verse, rarely less than vigorous, escapes at times from the conventions of rhetoric. 'The silvery livery of adviséd age' is inimitably Shakespearean; and young Clifford, as he contemplates his dead father at St Albans, can exclaim in the same speech

            O let the vile world end
And the premiséd flames of the last day
Knit earth and heaven together.
Now let the general trumpet blow his blast,
Particularities and petty sounds
To cease.

                                        (V, ii, 40-4)

This, in feeling and prosody, is closer to *Othello* than to *Tamburlaine*

Methinks it should be now a huge eclipse
Of sun and moon, and that th' affrighted globe
Should yawn at alteration.

                              (*Othello*, V, ii, 98-100)

Shakespeare, like Icarus, has no fear of stretching his wings; and if he should fall to the ground, he will soon be in the air again. His passion for the chase is so strong that he will bring (not to say drag) in a hunting scene whenever he can. It is two game-keepers who discover the King wandering in a northern forest.

First Keep: Under this thick-grown brake we'll
                 shroud ourselves,
                 For through this land anon the deer
                 will come.
Second Keep: I'll stay above the hill, so both may shoot.
First Keep: That cannot be: the noise of thy cross-
                 bow will scare the herd, and so my shoot is
                 lost.

                                        (III, i, 1-2; 5-8)

The images drawn from country life in *Henry VI, Part Two*, are so persistent that one is tempted to guess that the poet had refreshed his memory by several visits to Stratford. York, on learning that he cannot further his fortunes in France, compares his hopes to

        blossoms blasted in the bud
And caterpillars eat my leaves away.

                                        (III, i, 89-90)

Humphrey, on his arrest, warns the King

> Thus is the shepherd beaten from thy side,
> And wolves are gnarling who shall gnaw thee first.
>
> (III, i, 191-2)

Warwick, after Humphrey's murder, compares the 'commons' to

> an angry hive of bees
> That want their leader, scatter up and down
> And care not who they sting in his revenge.
>
> (III, ii, 125-7)

Margaret observes that

> Now 'tis the spring, and weeds are shallow-rooted;
> Suffer them now, and they'll o'ergrow the garden,
> And choke the herbs for want of husbandry
>
> (III, i, 31-3)

and Suffolk that 'The fox barks not when he would steal the lamb' (III, i, 55). Certain lines echo or initiate popular sayings. Suffolk's 'Smooth runs the water where the brook is deep' (III, i, 53), Cade's 'If I do not leave you all as dead as a door-nail' (IV, x, 43), and his contempt for the mob that deserts him: 'Was ever feather so lightly blown to and fro as this multitude?' (IV, viii, 55). The images of bear-baiting are so frequent that they show a close familiarity with this popular sport. York summons Warwick and Salisbury

> Call hither to the stake my two brave bears,
> That with the very shaking of their chains
> They may astonish these fell-lurking curs.
>
> (V, i, 143-5)

Most of these examples — and there are many more — suggest that, however loudly London might be calling, the call of the countryside went deeper, and it was never to be silenced.

Nevertheless, in the second part of *Henry VI*, it is the unity both of style and construction that strikes one. Gone, now, are the antiphonal exchanges of dialogue which looked back to the old Moralities. The uses of soliloquy, generally by York, are being explored — though not, as yet, for introspection. They are addressed to the audience, not to the character himself. Of characterization in the fuller sense there is still very little, though Humphrey is all the more alive for having lost his temper.

> Now, lords, my choler being overblown
> With walking once about the quadrangle . . .
>
> (I, iii, 155-6)

How usefully the mention of a quadrangle particularizes the scene on a stage that gave a minimal indication of locality! And note, once again, how the emergence of young Richard Crookback, and the Yorkist victory at St Albans, would have excited an audience impatient to know how the story was 'to be continued in our next'.

4

It is continued, virtually, in the next paragraph, for *Henry VI, Part Three* begins with Warwick's question to York

> I wonder how the King escaped our hands.

The play has not the even texture of its forerunner, and the writing in the fourth act is so inferior to the rest that one is tempted to think that other hands may have been at work on it, and that Shakespeare got tired of revising intractable material. The style, too, has subtly changed with a good deal of stichomythia, and a reversion to the formalism of the Moralities. It seems as if the dramatist felt that the Chronicle Play as such, of which *Part Two* is so good an example, was inadequate to express the philosophy of history that he had in mind. Providence, or nemesis, or a mixture of both, must be allowed their say. Two passages are overtly prophetic. The first is where Henry, facing Gloucester in the Tower, predicts that

> many an old man's sigh and many a widow's,
> And many an orphan's water-standing eye
> Men for their sons, wives for their husbands,
> And orphans for their parents' timeless death
> Shall rue the hour that even thou wast born.
>
> (V, vi, 39-43)

The second is where Henry lays his hand on the head of young Harry Richmond, and prophesies that

> This pretty lad will prove our country's bliss
>
> (IV, vi, 70)

— a compliment to the reigning dynasty which doubtless earned its applause.

No single character predominates. As one protagonist is removed, another takes his place; Warwick succeeds York, and Richard Warwick. These transitions are carefully prepared for, so that by the end of the play Richard is already the man we are to meet at the opening of *Richard III*. His ambition, cold-bloodedness, sexual frustration, and sardonic humour are illustrated, not at first by extended rhetoric, but by short stabbing comments on whatever matters he is engaged upon. In the very first scene, as each of York's sons relates what he has done in the battle, Richard throws down Somerset's head with the terse observation

> Speak thou for me and tell them what I did.
>
> (I, i, 16)

When Henry reminds the Yorkists that it was not he, but the Lord Protector who had lost the French possessions, and adds

> When I was crown'd I was but nine months old
>
> (I, i, 112)

Richard interpellates

> You are old enough now, and yet, methinks, you lose.
> Father, tear the crown from the usurper's head.
>
> (I, i, 113-14)

But York has taken an oath to leave it there for as long as Henry is alive. Richard meets this objection with casuistry

> An oath is of no moment, being not took
> Before a true and lawful magistrate . . .
>
> (I, ii, 22-3)

If some critics have thought *Richard III*, or much of it, was written by Marlowe, it is perhaps because Richard is a Marlovian character, and here he captures the Marlovian melody

> And, father, do but think
> How sweet a thing it is to wear a crown
> Within whose circuit lies Elysium
> And all that poets feign of bliss and joy.
>
> (I, ii, 28-31)

These, and for Shakespeare exceptionally, are the accents of Tamburlaine. Or again, before the brothers hear the news of their father's death

> See how the morning opes her golden gates,
> And takes her farewell of the glorious sun.
>
> (II, i, 21-2)

After their strange vision of the three suns, Edward declares

> henceforward will I bear
> Upon my target three fair-shining suns
>
> (II, i, 39-40)

and Richard, knowing his elder brother's lascivious disposition, caps his resolution with a realistic play upon it

> Nay, bear three daughters; by your leave I speak it,
> You love the breeder better than the male.
>
> (II, i, 41-2)

When Edward is reluctant to hear the atrocious details of his father's execution, it is in character for Richard to interrupt

> Say how he died, for I will hear it all
>
> (II, i, 49)

and in character, too, for him to confess when he has heard it

> I cannot weep.
>
> (II, i, 79)

To Margaret — and it will not be the end of her invective — who compares him to a 'foul, misshapen, stigmatic', he can give as good as he has got from her

> Iron of Naples,[1] hid with English gilt . . .
>
> (II, ii, 139)

Misshapen in mind as well as body, he is also superstitious, wishing to decline the dukedom of Gloucester because 'Gloucester's dukedom is too ominous'. His asides on his brother's wooing of Elizabeth Woodville — 'much rain wears the marble' — look forward to his later soliciting of Elizabeth for her daughter's hand. And when Edward has won his suit, Richard wishes

> he were wasted, marrow, bones and all
> That from his loins no hopeful branch may spring
> To cross me from the golden time I look for.
>
> (III, ii, 125-7)

This introduces the first of two long soliloquies in which Richard reveals himself to the audience. They can be described as explanatory introspection, and their gist is both repeated and condensed in the opening soliloquy of *Richard III*. The crown is still a long way off — for Clarence stands between himself and Edward — and if power is out of his immediate reach, so too is love. With his arm shrivelled 'like a withered shrub', his legs 'of an unequal size', it was all too obvious that 'love forswore me in my mother's womb'. Nevertheless if he cannot charm in one way, he will do so in another

> Why, I can smile, and murder whiles I smile . . .
> I can add colours to the chameleon,
> Change shapes with Proteus for advantages
> And set the murderous Machiavel to school.
>
> (III, ii, 182; 191-3)

Here the medieval panorama begins to fade, and we are in the full glare of Renaissance amorality — once again, closer to Marlowe than to Shakespeare. The rhythm and classical allusions both reinforce the comparison

> I'll play the orator as well as Nestor,
> Deceive more slily than Ulysses could,
> And, like a Sinon, take another Troy.
>
> (III, ii, 188-90)

---

[1] Margaret was the daughter of Reignier, King of Naples, as well as of his French possessions.

In the second soliloquy, after he has murdered King Henry, Richard strikes a deeper note

> I have no brother; I am like no brother;
> And this word 'love' which greybeards call divine,
> Be resident in men like one another,
> And not in me: I am myself alone.

(V, vi, 80-3)

Richard is the first of Shakespeare's 'outsiders'. He has something in common with a character out of Graham Greene. The triumphant villain of *Richard III* is only to be fully understood if we have been introduced to the psychotic youth of the preceding play.[1]

Opposed to him, in stark relief, stands the 'pious founder' of Eton and King's, although there is no mention of his foundations. Henry comes into his own as a character, though not as a king, in *Henry VI, Part Three*. The scene in which he meditates on the happiness of the shepherd's life, and contemplates from the modest eminence of a molehill the father who has mistakenly killed his son, and the son who has mistakenly killed his father, revives the convention of the Moralities to preach a gospel of peace. There was need of it to relieve the monotony of discord, and the meanders of diplomacy. For the play is built around three battles — Wakefield where the Yorkists are defeated; Towton where they take their revenge; and Barnet where they consolidate their victory — and Warwick's embassy to France in the hope of winning King Lewis's sister for the man whom he has made king. When he learns that Edward has married Elizabeth Woodville, he changes sides, joins forces with Queen Margaret, and pays with his life for it. The 'Kingmaker' had found it easier to make a king than to unmake him; and the fortunes of the house of Lancaster are lost for ever when Richard stabs Prince Edward at Tewkesbury. Clarence, deserting his brothers, has also changed sides, but doubles back in time; too late, however, to escape the opprobrium that falls upon him in the following play — 'false, fleeting, perjured Clarence' — and the death that he meets there in a butt of malmsey.

Margaret has grown from her girlish beginnings in *Part One* into a figure of ferocious strength. The scene in which she mocks the captured York with a paper crown, and a napkin stained with the blood of his son, Rutland, excels in dramatic intensity anything else in the first three plays of the tetralogy. She will always be a virtuoso of invective, which here goes far beyond the clichés of rhetorical

---

[1] For the psychological division in Richard, and the eventual disintegration of a split personality I refer the reader to William B. Toole's illuminating essay in *Shakespeare Survey*, 27 (1974).

tragedy. It has an almost colloquial immediacy

> Where are your mess of sons to mock you now?
> The wanton Edward and the lusty George?
> And where's that valiant crook-back prodigy,
> Dicky your boy, that with his grumbling voice
> Was wont to cheer his dad in mutinies?
> Or, with the rest, where is your darling Rutland?
>
>   (I, iv, 72-7)

Shakespeare had no personal experience of queens, but he was probably familiar with fishwives, and guessed that on occasion they could talk alike. York vituperates with equal force, and greater dignity

> O tiger's heart wrapp'd in a woman's hide . . .
>
>   (I, iv, 137)

provided Robert Greene with his text to accuse Shakespeare of plagiarism

> There is an upstart crow, beautified with our feathers, that with his *Tiger's heart wrapt in a player's hide,* supposes he is as well able to bombast out a blank verse as the best of you, and being an absolute *Johannes Factotum,* is in his own conceit the only Shake-scene in the country.

This proves that the play was already well known before June 1592, when the theatres were closed; that Shakespeare was reputed as an actor as well as a playwright; and that his popularity was already a cause for envy in his fellow-dramatists. We know that others beside Shakespeare himself resented Greene's attack upon him. Henry Chettle, writing in December of the same year (1592), speaks of his 'demeanour no less civil than he excellent in the quality he professes. Besides, divers of worship have reported his uprightness of dealing, which argues his honesty, and his facetious grace of writing that approves his art.'[1] Other testimony confirms this. Aubrey had learnt from Beeston that the young poet was 'the more to be admired *quia* he was not a company-keeper . . . wouldn't be debauched, and, if invited writ — he was in pain' — the classic excuse of the reluctant guest.

According to Dover Wilson, *Henry VI, Parts Two* and *Three* were both played at Burbage's 'Theatre' in 1591-2 by a company calling itself Lord Pembroke's men.[2] Shakespeare's transpositions of historical sequence, as distinct from his obedience to historical fact, were due, no doubt, to the complicated material he had to work upon, and the sheer necessities of playwriting. He invented, however, a number of incidents involving Richard better to prepare the audience

---

[1] Preface to *Kind-Heart's Dream.*
[2] J. Dover Wilson (ed.), *The Second Part of King Henry VI* (1952), p. xiii.

for the dominating figure of his next play. It is worth noting that *A Mirror for Magistrates* makes Richard the murderer of the King; by then he had a very 'bad press' — *vide* the history of his reign by Sir Thomas More, of which Shakespeare was to make full use. Generally speaking, as Professor Bullough reminds us, 'Shakespeare darkens the landscape as he makes the chief characters behave even worse than they did in the Chronicles'.[1] If the groundlings were calling out for blood and thunder, her certainly gave it to them. They were not squeamish; neither, at this point of his development, was he.

The three parts of *Henry VI* should be judged as a whole, and the whole is more impressive than the parts. Here, you would say, is a great dramatist in embryo; not, as yet, the greatest poet in the language. Jan Kott's *Shakespeare Our Contemporary* must not be taken *au pied de la lettre* and much of it is arrant nonsense; but his view of Shakespeare's history plays as an illustration of the *'grand méchanisme du pouvoir'* — an ineluctable process of rise and fall — is justified in *Henry VI*, as it will be in *Richard III* and in the second tetralogy. And these characters, exulting in the free will of their ambition, are yet moved by historical necessity and an apparently sleeping Providence which they do not recognize. No doubt, as Tillyard has pointed out, the chief *persona*, if not the chief protagonist, is the *respublica* of late medieval England. And there is a tragic irony in its personification by a King who is at once too good and too incompetent to rule. Shakespeare's Henry authenticates to the letter the verses which have been attributed to him

> Kingdoms are but cares;
> State is devoid of stay:
> Riches are ready snares,
> And hasten to decay

> Who meaneth to remove the rock
> Out of his slimy mud,
> Shall mire himself, and barely scape
> The swelling of the flood.

5

Richard III has provided the historians and textual critics with several bones of controversy. Many have wished, in restoring his character to Richard, to deprive Shakespeare of his protagonist. Josephine Tey's *A Daughter of Time* presents the case for rehabilitation with an attractive plausibility. But here we are concerned with the history that Shakespeare found in his sources, or deduced from them — not with a history that no contemporary would have dared to write, even had he wished to. Depending on Hall and Holinshed,

[1] See Bullough, Vol. III, p. 167.

and through them on Sir Thomas More who had got his facts from Cardinal Morton — the Bishop of Ely of the play — he was the spokesman — or, as some would say, the prisoner — of the Tudor myth. More complicated are the claims of the Folio and the Quarto texts. Of the latter no less than six were published before the Folio. These versions vary slightly in length and verbal detail, but the essential matter is preserved in all of them. For an exhaustive discussion of the problem I refer the reader to A. Hamilton Thompson's introduction to the play in the Arden Shakespeare. The question hinges on whether QI (1597) was taken from Shakespeare's own text, or from that of a 'nameless transcriber'. Mr Hamilton Thompson 'while giving full weight to the editor or editors' responsibility for errors, in F, is unable to distinguish its debt to "a nameless transcriber" from that which it may owe to the author's original version of the play'.

The unusual number of Quartos at least prove its popularity. Richard has always tempted the virtuoso tragedian, and it was among Burbage's great parts. Manningham's Diary for 13 March 1601 records a trick played on Burbage by Shakespeare 'upon a time when Burbage played Richard III'. Burbage had made an assignation with a lady in the audience, but when he reached her lodging he found Shakespeare on the threshold. 'William the Conqueror', Shakespeare reminded him, 'came before Richard III.' And there is Bishop Corbet's account[1] of a visit to Bosworth where his host had reconstructed the battle for him

> Besides what of his knowledge he could say,
> He had authenticke notice from the Play;
> Which I might guesse, by's mustring up the ghosts,
> And policyes, not incident to hosts,
> But chiefly by that one perspicuous thing,
> Where he mistook a player for a king,
> For when he would have said, King Richard dyed,
> And called — A horse! a horse! he Burbidge cryed.

As in the previous plays, but even more drastically, Shakespeare telescopes time as it suits him. The events of seven years are crammed into eleven days. Where the Chronicles merely insinuate, he positively affirms. Shakespeare follows *A Mirror for Magistrates* in making Richard directly responsible for the murder of Clarence; and in Clarence's dream the verse throbs with an electricity and incandescence which go far beyond the rhetoric of which he was by now a master. But there is no historical or literary warrant for the scene in which Richard woos Lady Anne Nevill (though she became his wife),

[1] Written before 1635.

or for his soliciting Queen Elizabeth for her daughter's hand —
afterwards given to Richmond. *Richard III* completes the tetralogy in
accordance with the grand design, but it is a different kind of play.
The principal character holds the stage throughout, and I use the
phrase advisedly. Shakespeare is forced to provide a complement to
Richard's triumphant theatricality if his deeper message is to get
across. Richmond cannot supply it because he arrives on the scene
too late. It is Queen Margaret — returned, unhistorically, from
France — Queen Elizabeth, and the Duchess of York who compose a
chorus of condemnation on Richard's misdeeds, and to this, on the
eve of Bosworth, the ghosts of his victims add their voices. Nor is
Margaret the termagant who set a paper crown on the head of York,
and wiped his face with a napkin dipped in the blood of Rutland.
Age and adversity have given her invective a deeper, more impersonal, note; it is the voice of Nemesis that gives its warning to
Buckingham and the wrangling nobility

> O, but remember this another day,
> When he shall split thy very heart with sorrow,
> And say poor Margaret was a prophetess.
> Live each of you the subjects to his hate,
> And he to yours, and all of you to God's.
>
> (I, iii, 299-303)

A similar *gravitas* colours the later imprecations of the Duchess of
York

> Either thou wilt die, by God's just ordinance,
> Ere from this war thou turn a conqueror,
> Or I with grief and extreme age shall perish
> And never look upon thy face again.
> Therefore take with thee my most heavy curse;
> Which in the day of battle, tire thee more
> Than all the complete armour that thou wear'st!
> My prayers on the adverse party fight;
> And there the little souls of Edward's children
> Whisper the spirits of thine enemies,
> And promise them success and victory.
>
> (IV, iv, 183-93)

Richard III is balanced, not at all insecurely, between a Morality and
a melodrama. In *Henry VI* God is rarely mentioned, except by the
'pious Founder'; in *Richard III* He is invoked no less than seventy-
three times — more often than in any other Shakespearean play.

Richard has become, traditionally, a part 'to tear a cat in'. Rob
him of his humour, the exultation in his own wickedness, and you
are left either with a monster, like Marlowe's Barabbas in *The Jew of
Malta,* or the subject from a psychoanalyst's case-book. He must be
at once human and Satanic; the Vice from an old Morality, whose

company the audience enjoys at the same time as they reprobate his behaviour. At a later stage in his development Shakespeare would have made him, as he made Iago, simultaneously both of these things. This, however, was at present beyond him; Richard is, instead, alternately man and monster. Flesh and blood, with an engaging sense of humour, to begin with, his personality diminishes once he has seized the crown, and then asserts itself on the eve of Bosworth when it attains a tragic grandeur. A casuist to the end, he at last comes to grips with conscience — a more formidable foe than Richmond

> O coward conscience how thou does afflict me:
> The light burn blue. It is now dead midnight.
> Cold fearful drops stand on my trembling flesh . . .
> Alack, I love myself. Wherefore? for any good
> That I myself have done unto myself?
> O no, alas, I rather hate myself
> For hateful deeds committed by myself . . .
> All several sins, all used in each degree,
> Throng to the bar, crying all 'Guilty! guilty!'
> I shall despair. There is no creature loves me;
> And if I die, no soul will pity me:
> Nay, wherefore should they, since that I myself
> Find in myself no pity for myself?
> (V, iii, 179-81; 187-90; 198-201)

The significance of this introspection has been overlooked by certain critics. There is nothing like it elsewhere in the tetralogy, unless it be Richard's 'I am myself alone', prefiguring his ultimate sensation of loneliness. In perceiving self-hatred as the principal ground of despair, Shakespeare strikes the note of real as distinct from rhetorical tragedy. It is not, after all, so far a cry from

> There is no creature loves me;
> And if I die, no soul will pity me

to Macbeth's

> And that which should accompany old age
> As honour, love, obedience, troops of friends,
> I must not look to have; but in their stead,
> Curses not loud, but deep . . .
>
> (V, iii, 24-7)

The curses which had accompanied Richard's waking and sleeping hours were both loud and deep, and now his own conscience reiterates them. It may be that the nudity — even the crudity — of the versification has concealed the new dimension which the soliloquy opens up, so that here — and afterwards in the fight with Richmond — Richard proves himself to be a man both in his weakness and his strength, facing the fact of his moral as well as his physical deformity, neither glorying in the one nor brooding on the other.

Of the four plays that compose the tetralogy, only *Richard III* has consistently held the stage. Not until the later scenes when his self-control, and even his voracious appetite, desert him does the central character develop, and this makes for a certain monotony which judicious abridgement may counteract. But the theatrical vitality never flags, and the scene of Clarence's murder contains not only the magnificent 'set piece' of the dream which foreshadows it, but a passage in prose, Falstaffian in its casuistry, that forms, as it were, a counterpoint to Richard's last soliloquy. The second murderer is speaking of his conscience

> I'll not meddle with it: it is a dangerous thing: it makes a man a coward: a man cannot steal but it accuseth him; he cannot swear, but it checks him; he cannot lie with his neighbour's wife, but it detects him; it is a blushing shame-faced spirit that mutinies in a man's bosom; it fills one full of obstacles; it made me once restore a purse of gold that I found; it beggars any man that keeps it; it is turned out of all towns and cities for a dangerous thing; and every man that means to live well endeavours to trust to himself and to live without it.
>
> (I, iv, 137-48)

In both cases conscience is aroused and subsequently stifled.

Critics have been disconcerted by the abrupt passage from prose to verse when the murderers, after talking to each other, engage in conversation with Clarence. But it was an accepted convention that characters assumed the verbal idiom of their superiors in rank — even when they were proposing to murder them! Thus the 'bleeding Sergeant' in *Macbeth* describes the battle to Duncan in language far removed from that of the Sergeants' mess. Shakespeare's use of language in *Richard III* is a clue to an understanding of Richard's character or, more precisely, of his function. The repetition of his favourite oath, which Shakespeare had taken from More

> By the apostle Paul, shadows tonight
> Have struck more terror to the soul of Richard
> Than can the substance of ten thousand soldiers
> Arméd in proof, and led by shallow Richmond
>
> (V, iii, 216-19)

his parting shot to Clarence — who of course does not hear it

> Simple, plain Clarence, I do love thee so,
> That I will shortly send thy soul to heaven
>
> (I, i, 117-18)

and his pious wish that God will 'take King Edward to his mercy', illustrate the ambiguity of a character who cannot escape from his inherited beliefs however flagrantly his behaviour contradicts them. Deprive Satan of his Deity, and he loses his *raison d'être*; the unbeliever does not bother to blaspheme. There is here a double irony, for it is Richard's diabolism that promises the salvation of his victims. 'False, fleeting, perjured Clarence', the voluptuous Edward, and the licentious Hastings all have time to make an act of contrition which is anything but habitual. Conversely, if Shakespeare had wished to suggest that Richard was the first Puritan, he could not have done better than make him swear 'by St Paul'. Even his wooing of Lady Anne is an exercise of power, not of profligacy.

Here again the language should warn us against invoking the sanctions of realism. As a French critic has written, it is the *'force de frappe d'une stratégie amoureuse'*[1], and Shakespeare had taken the hint from Petrarch — the model of Wyatt and Surrey, and now, more recently, of Sidney whose *Astrophel and Stella* was published in 1591. Richard's salutation of Anne as his 'sun'; his declaration that she is at once 'his life and his death', and that her beauty has made him weep, are all Petrarchan echoes, and would have been understood as such by the cultivated members of an audience for whom Petrarch was all the rage. Those who were content to enjoy the scheming of Machiavelli would have had all, and more than, their money's worth. For others who remembered the Mystery Plays the scene of Richard's wooing of Anne would have been recognized as an analogue of Satan's temptation of Eve, and there would have been nothing surprising in his conquest. Unless the play is seen as a 'serious attempt at Christian dramaturgy'[2] — closer to *Doctor Faustus* than anything Shakespeare had written as yet, or was to write again — we overlook the most important part of his debt to Marlowe; and the power, more subtly demonstrated in the second tetralogy, to show the workings of Nemesis in the logic of events, and through the development of human character beyond its historical context. *Richard III* leads up to Bosworth, but to something bigger than a battlefield.

Richmond, when he appears, is St George in Tudor armour, uniting heraldically the white rose and the red. In his final speeches he invokes the Deity five times, and assures us that he will 'take the sacrament'. The assurance was necessary, for one or two people in the audience might have read *A Mirror for Magistrates*, and remembered that 'whosoever rebelleth against any ruler either good or bad, rebelleth against God, and shall be sure of a wretched end; for God cannot but maintain his deputie'. Richard, after all, had been duly

[1] Francois Fleure, *Etudes Anglaises*, T.XXIII, No. I (1970).
[2] ibid.

crowned; but the *Mirror* also specified that the crown shall 'not have been injuriously procured by rigour of sword and open force, but quietly by title or inheritance, succession, lawful bequest, common consent, or election'. Shakespeare would bear these conditions in mind when he came to tackle the source of all those troubles which, in *Richard III,* he had now brought to an end. It is likely, however, that he was already looking a century beyond Bosworth; and would have been glad to underwrite the verses of Fulke Greville[1]

> Under a throne I saw a virgin sit,
> The red and white rose quartered in her face
> Star of the north, and for true guards to it
> Princes, church, states, all pointing out her grace.

Chapter 3

Comical... Tragical

1

Greene's denigration of Shakespeare as a 'Johannes Factotum' was at least a tribute to his versatility, and it is not too soon to bring other witnesses into the box. In the Address by two of his fellow-actors, Heminge and Condell, which introduces the First Folio, they affirm that 'what (he) thought he uttered with that easiness that we have scarce received from him a blot in his papers'; and Ben Jonson was often told by members of the company that 'whatsoever he penned he never blotted a line'. Jonson, though prolific, was also a perfectionist, and his admiration for Shakespeare did not prevent him wishing that he had 'blotted a thousand'. But Shakespeare was not that kind of writer. He wrote with a precocious facility, and obviously in haste. He had his own living to earn; and a wife and three children to maintain, with now, perhaps, two establishments. John Shakespeare's affairs had gone from bad to worse. Already, when his son was leaving Stratford, his name was removed from the roll of aldermen because he 'doth not come to the halls when they are warned, nor hath not done for a long time'.

Nevertheless it was a considerable achievement to have written the first tetralogy, and seen it produced, within five years of coming to London. This argued a prodigious industry as well as an easy pen; small wonder that he did not always accept an invitation to dinner. Nor was this all. Shakespeare was a natural romantic, and the Wars of the Roses were not a romantic theme. He had an ebullient sense of humour, and for this, too, they offered little scope. Audiences demanded fun as well as fury, a neat plot as well as a coherent chronicle. They did not mind where it came from, and neither did he. Moreover if they did not want to spend their afternoons watching the same kind of play, he was equally relieved, no doubt, not to spend his mornings or his midnights, his late or his early hours, in composing it.

The theme of mistaken identities was an old one, and it had always been popular. Shakespeare was to use it again to different, and deeper, effect. For *The Comedy of Errors* he turned to the *Menaechmi* of Plautus and, in one scene (I, i) to his *Amphitruo*. Of the former no translation in English was printed till 1595, but it seems possible that Shakespeare may have read it in William Warner's MS, since a copy of this was handed round to the translator's friends. He was also quite capable of reading it in Latin. *The Comedy of Errors* is the shortest of his plays (1,777 lines), but even so it is longer by over 600 lines than the original. It has both the economy and the symmetry of farce. Yet Shakespeare was never content with comedy, pure and simple; and the slightly greater elbow room that he gave himself here allowed the occasional, discreet introduction of a more serious note. Aegeon's exposition of how he, his wife, their sons, and two servants became separated after the shipwreck might have served as a prelude to a wholly different play. The characters of Adriana's sister, Luciana, and the two Dromios, are Shakespeare's invention; as Coleridge wrote, 'farce dares add the two Dromios, and is justified in doing so by the laws of its end and constitution. In a word, farce commences in a postulate, which must be granted.'[1] Luciana's homily on the prerogatives of a husband anticipates Katharina's sermon in the fifth act of *The Taming of the Shrew*. It is another example of Shakespeare's doctrine of 'degree'

> There's nothing situate under heaven's eye
> But hath his bound, in earth, in sea, in sky:
> The beasts, the fishes, and the wingèd fowls,
> Are their males' subjects and at their controls:
> Men more divine, the masters of all these,
> Lords of the wide world and wild watery seas,
> Indued with intellectual sense and souls,
> Of more pre-eminence than fish and fowls,
> Are masters to their females, and their lords;
> Then let your will attend on their accords.

(II, i, 16-25)

Adriana herself is a first study in jealousy; not altogether without cause, since Antipholus of Ephesus, mistakenly refused entrance to his own house, seeks consolation with a courtesan in spite of his civic respectability

> His company must do his minions grace,
> Whilst I at home starve from a merry look.
> Hath homely age the alluring beauty took
> From my poor cheek? then he hath wasted it;
> Are my discourses dull? barren my wit?

(II, i, 87-91)

[1] *Shakespeare and the Elizabethan Dramatists.*

Here is the not uncommon complaint of the too long married woman. The play gave Shakespeare the chance to exchange one kind of discord for another, and it gave him a total relief from nobility. The scene is set in Ephesus, but it might just as well have been set in Southampton. There is talk of the capon burning, and the pig falling from the spit; of the meat getting cold, or dry for lack of basting. We are told that 'every churl' can afford 'good meat'. Dromio of Syracuse, in describing the physical geography of the kitchen-maid on whom he has fixed his affections, declares in a characteristic Shakespearean pun that France is 'in her forehead; armed and reverted, making war against her heir'. This reference to the wars of religion, and another to 'armadoes of caracks', dates the play between 1589 and 1591. In one respect, however, Shakespeare's Ephesus recalls the city which St Paul describes as full of 'curious arts'. Antipholus of Syracuse is warned that

> this town is full of cozenage;
> As, nimble jugglers that deceive the eye,
> Dark-working sorcerers that change the mind,
> Soul-killing witches that deform the body . . .
>
> (I, ii, 97-100)

Professor Bullough[1] suggests that these Pauline associations led Shakespeare to make Emilia the Abbess of a Priory, and not the priestess of a temple. On the other hand, the exorcism is performed by a doctor with the unimpeachably English name of Pinch.

The first recorded performance of what appears to have been Shakespeare's *The Comedy of Errors* was at Gray's Inn on 28 December 1594, when it only got a hearing after a good deal of licentious revelry. But it was almost certainly acted before then by one of the regular companies. Francis Meres mentions it in his *Palladis Tamia* (1598) as one of the poet's six 'excellent' comedies. In one respect Shakespeare's masterpieces have done him a disservice in that they have chased his lesser works from public view. Yet *The Comedy of Errors* proved its armour-plated professional competence in a recent production at Stratford, and was given for a command performance before the Queen at Windsor. At the supper which followed, the Queen and her guests mingled with the actors, meeting them as Southampton or Pembroke might have met Shakespeare and Burbage. It was a typically Elizabethan evening. The verse may be described as utility iambic, which ripples along easily enough, interspersed with racy dialogue in prose from the Dromios. Here, as elsewhere in Shakespeare, conversation was notably enlivened by the acceptance of class distinctions. Derived as it is from classical

[1] See Bullough, Vol. I, p. 10.

sources, *The Comedy of Errors* alone among Shakespeare's plays, if we except *The Tempest,* preserves the classical unities of time, place, and action. Like the best of its kind, it has the mathematical beauty of a fine clock, or the sheen of the chassis on a good motor-car.

The Taming of the Shrew presents a nice problem for the exegete. The only published text was that included in the First Folio (1623). Was this an adaptation of another play, *The Taming of A Shrew,* already popular in 1594 when it was described by the printer, Peter Short, as having been 'at sundry times acted by the Right Honourable the Earle of Pembroke his servants'? Was it, as Dover Wilson thought, the revision of yet another version of the same story? Was *A Shrew,* as Professor Bullough thinks possible, Shakespeare's 'first shot at the theme'?[1] The date of its first performance cannot be determined, but subject, treatment, and style alike suggest that it was written shortly after *The Comedy of Errors.* Shakespeare was quite capable of working on more than one play at a time for different companies, and both these plays would have given him a respite from the sterner challenge of the tetralogies.

Assuming, then, that *A Shrew* was his springboard, it is instructive to note the differences. Shakespeare expands the Induction into two scenes, but where *A Shrew* has Christopher Sly watching most of the play, interrupting four times, and conversing with the Tapster at the end of it, Shakespeare forgets all about him after the end of Act I. Perhaps he found him a nuisance, and others have felt the same; at Stratford, Bridges-Adams had him away altogether. The dramatist's instinct may have told him that by the end of the play the audience would have become too involved in the plot to take any further interest in a spectator who was already sound asleep. Perhaps the actor — Will Kempe or Dick Tarleton — objected to an interminable session on the upper stage. But for so long as he is there, Sly is given as much head as small ale has left him. The Boy who plays his wife improvises with a lively invention, and the tapster of *A Shrew* is turned into a shrewish Hostess. The Lord is not provided with a name, but he might well have been Lord Willoughby de Broke returning, like his die-hard descendant, from a meet of the Warwickshire[2]

> Lord :   Huntsman, I charge thee, tender well my hounds:
> Brach Merriman, the poor cur is emboss'd;
> And couple Clowder with the deep-mouth'd brach.
> Saw'st thou not, boy, how Silver made it good
> At the hedge-corner, in the coldest fault?

[1] See Bullough, Vol. I, p. 58.

[2] See *The Passing Years* by Lord Willoughby de Broke. He was an M.F.H. and prominent opponent of the Parliament Act in 1911.

	I would not lose the dog for twenty pound.
First Huntsman:	Why, Belman is as good as he, my lord;
	He cried upon it at the merest loss,
	And twice today picked out the dullest scent:
	Trust me, I take him for the better dog.
Lord:	Thou art a fool: if Echo were as fleet,
	I would esteem him worth a dozen such.
	But sup them well and look unto them all.

(Induction: I, 16-28)

Shakespeare paints the scene with a number of Warwickshire place-names — Wincot and Burton-heath — but he sets the play proper in Italy rather than in Athens. He always seemed to share the view of Dr Johnson that 'the chief object of travel is to see the shores of the Mediterranean' — though, as far as we know, he never saw them. He elaborated the sub-plot of Bianca and her suitors, but where *A Shrew* had given two sisters to Katharina, Shakespeare leaves her with only one. For the sub-plot he drew directly on Gascoigne's *Supposes* (1566); and the theme of the pauper translated into a magical enjoyment of riches goes back to the *Arabian Nights*. The story ran that the example of Haroun Al Raschid was followed by Philip the Good of Burgundy and the Emperor Charles V. There was ample precedent both for the entertainment of the tinker, and the taming of the shrew.

Although the play is set in Italy, the *ambiente* is only initially Italianate — just enough to mark the difference between the actors and the audience. Here and there the dialogue is sprinkled with Italian phrases: Grumio's *'Basta'*, Tranio's *'Mi Perdonato'*, Petruchio's greeting to Hortensio *'Con tutto il core ben trovato'*. But *The Taming of the Shrew* is not even distantly related to the Commedia del Arte, although some directors who wince at boot and saddle have tried to force a match between them. Here are social and moral values that we have long since discarded, whether for better or worse; humours that have hardly survived the disappearance of the music hall; assumptions that in Shakespeare's time were still common to all Europe, and whose later echoes we catch in Molière rather than in Congreve.

But Shakespeare is generally happier on his home ground. As Jonson had written in *Every Man in his Humour*

> Our scene is London, 'cause we would make known
> No country's mirth is better than our own.

Grumio's repartee has the edge of Cockney wit; and once the action has removed to Petruchio's country house, the smell comes unmistakably from a Cotswold kitchen — 'neat's foot', 'beef and mustard', 'a fat tripe finely broiled'. This is an English winter with

Grumio 'sent before to make a fire'. He is evidently a small man; the part written, no doubt, for a small actor

> Now were not I a little pot, and soon hot, my very lips might freeze to my teeth, my tongue to the roof of my mouth, my heart in my belly, ere I should come by a fire to thaw me; but I, with blowing the fire, shall warm myself; for considering the weather, a taller man than I will take cold.
>
> (IV, i, 5-12)

No street in Padua was ever called Long Lane End, and this quintessential Englishry was wonderfully brought out in John Barton's production at Stratford in 1961. The revolving stage showed the inside and outside of a Cotswold inn, according as the action took place within doors or in the open air and, as it revolved, one caught a glimpse of the players making ready for their next entrance. When the play was over they had changed, and were off to their next one-night stand; and Sly wandered off in their wake, ruminating about his wife at Burton-heath. This was magnificent, although it was not Shakespeare.

Moreover Peggy Ashcroft, in a flash of fine insight, wrote large what is legible between the lines of the play — that Katharina has fallen in love with Petruchio at first sight. For the moment she must keep up the contrary appearances; nevertheless Petruchio is not only the one man who can tame her, but the one man who can attract her — as she is the woman of his chance, if not exactly of his choice. Their battle of wills is a duel, not a discord, and its end is

> love, and quiet life,
> An awful rule, and right supremacy
> And to be short, what not, that's sweet and happy?
>
> (V, ii, 108-10)

Katharina could have refused the marriage; nothing would have brought her to church if she had not secretly wanted to go. Petruchio's tyranny is teasing pushed to an extreme; his manners to Katharina have a conquering charm; it is only to others that he is rough, albeit at her expense. He is masterful, not sadistic; and so far from being thoughtless, there is no move in the game that he has not thought out beforehand. With another woman, no doubt, he would have played it differently. Here is the first, flamboyant, example of what Middleton Murry has called the 'Shakespearean man' — virile, extrovert, and not a little fantastic. We shall follow him through various incarnations, each different, but all members of the same family or, at least, members of the same club. When Petruchio explains to Hortensio what has 'blown' him to Padua

> Such wind as scatters young men through the world

To seek their fortune farther than at home
Where small experience grows.

                                                              (I, ii, 50-2)

one is easily reminded of Shakespeare himself setting out over
Clopton Bridge.

In short, the dramatist has considerably refined the character he
found in his sources, and he allows Katharina to preach the homily.
No doubt he believed marriage to be a sacrament, but this is the
nearest he came to giving it a written constitution. The two plots are
neatly dovetailed; the irony should not escape us that it is Bianca,
not Katharina, who makes the clandestine marriage, and she, not her
sister, who proves finally recalcitrant. The play has ridden the seas of
changing fashion like a battleship; it can stand up even to a society
dedicated to the proposition that all men are created equal, and the
women equal to the men.

With *The Two Gentlemen of Verona* we are faced at once with the
objection that one of them is not a gentleman at all. Its theme is the
conflicting claims of love and friendship and, as we shall presently
see, Shakespeare already knew how they could clash. His principal
source was a Portuguese play, *Diana Enamorada* (1542), where
treachery to a friend was compounded by treachery to a mistress. He
may have read a French translation of this, published in 1578, or
even a MS of Bartholomew Yonge's English version which had been
completed by 1582. The style of *The Two Gentlemen*, with two
references to Hero and Leander suggesting that Shakespeare may
have had a preview of Marlowe's poem, although it had not yet been
published, and clear reminiscences of Lyly's *Eupheus and Endimion*,
probably date the play just after *The Taming of the Shrew*. It
certainly represents a new departure. Shakespeare is exploring, a
little tentatively as yet, the possibilities of romantic comedy, and of
romantic tragedy as well. Silvia's window and balcony; the rope
ladder by which she gets down from them; her intention to make her
confession at 'Friar Patrick's cell'; and the mention of a 'Friar
Lawrence' wandering about in the forest — all suggest that
Shakespeare had already been reading George Brooke's poem of
Romeus and Juliet (1562). Valentine's despair when he is banished
from Milan prefigures Romeo's when he is banished from Verona —
and the mediocre verse (if Shakespeare wrote it) is proof of early
composition

And why not death, rather than living torment?
To die is to be banished from myself,
And Silvia is myself: banished from her
Is self from self . . . Ah! deadly banishment:

> What light is light, if Silvia be not seen?
> What joy is joy, if Silvia be not by?
>
> (III, i, 170-6)

This is sorry stuff compared with

> 'Tis torture, and not mercy: heaven is here,
> Where Juliet lives; and every cat and dog
> And little mouse, every unworthy thing,
> Live her in heaven and may look on her,
> But Romeo may not.
>
> (III, iii, 29-33)

Indeed the play is an anthology of anticipations. Julia, catechized by Lucetta about her suitors, looks forward to Nerissa's catechism of Portia in *The Merchant of Venice* — although it is a faint and lame foreshadowing. Had the dramatic possibilities of male disguise been suggested by the St George's play at Stratford in 1583? Julia, now dressed as a page, recalls to Silvia how

> At Pentecost,
> When all our pageants of delight were played,
> Our youth got me to play the woman's part,
> And I was trimmed in Madame Julia's gown,
> Which servéd me as fit, by all men's judgments,
> As if the garment had been made for me
> And at that time I made her weep agood,
> For I did play a lamentable part:
> Madam, 'twas Ariadne passioning
> For Theseus' perjury and unjust flight:
> Which I so lively acted with my tears
> That my poor mistress, movéd therewithal,
> Wept bitterly . . .
>
> (IV, iv, 156-69)

Speculation runs further: was this Shakespeare's own theatrical début?[1] Julia is the first of his heroines to put on male attire in an emergency; and in other respects, too, she attests what Quiller-Couch well described as 'that catholic kinship which communicates to us, as we wander in Shakespeare's great portrait gallery, a delightful sense of intimacy, of recognition'.[2] When she hears Proteus' hired musician singing under Silvia's window, her reply to the elderly innkeeper who has brought her there has the mute agony of heartbreak

> *Host*:   You would have them always play but one thing
> *Julia*:   I would always have *one* play but one thing.
>
> (IV, ii, 70-1)

The perfunctory ending to the play presents a problem with which

---

[1] See Rowse, p. 53.

[2] Introduction to *The Two Gentlemen of Verona*, Cambridge University Press (1921), XII.

editors have heroically wrestled. Proteus' treachery is unmasked, and Valentine demands

> Who should be trusted, when one's own right hand
> Is perjured to the bosom?

Proteus replies

> My shame and guilt confound me . . .
> Forgive me, Valentine . . . if hearty sorrow
> Be a sufficient ransom for offence,
> I tender't here; I do as truly suffer
> As e'er I did commit.

Before accepting this facile contrition, Valentine proceeds

> And that my love may appear plain and free,
> All that was mine in Silvia I give thee.

It is not surprising that Julia should faint at this monstrously misplaced magnanimity; it is only surprising that Silvia, who detests the sight of Proteus, does not faint as well. Perhaps she does; we are not told; she utters not another word before Valentine concludes the play with the comforting assurance

> Come Proteus, 'tis your penance but to hear
> The story of your loves discovered . . .
> That done, our day of marriage shall be yours —
> One feast, one house, one mutual happiness.
>
> (V, iv, 67 *et seq.*)

But the wedding bells still jangle discordantly in the ears of the spectator.

An Elizabethan audience could accept — and so can we — the convention by which Proteus does not recognize Julia disguised as a boy. It could hardly accept — what was not a convention at all — the proposed handing over by the hero of the play, for whom all its sympathy had been won, of the girl he loved to the friend who had betrayed him. Two explanations have been offered, the second by far more plausible than the first. A comparison has been suggested with Sonnet 40: 'Take all my loves, my love, yea, take them all.' Was Shakespeare so besotted with his passionate friendship for Southampton — assuming that it was he to whom the *Sonnets* were addressed — that he did not see the gross inconsistency of Valentine's proposal? I think it most unlikely. More probable is Quiller-Couch's conjecture, endorsed by Dover Wilson, that 'the botcher's hand — or maybe the hands of several botchers — may be detected in our text and throughout it'; and 'that Shakespeare invented a solution which at the first performance was found to be ineffective; that the final scene was partly rewritten — not by Shakespeare — . . . that in this mutilated form it remained the play-copy; and that so it reached the printer.'¹ For the play shows other signs of carelessness. One did not travel from Verona to Milan by sea, although one might have done so by canal; nor would Speed have welcomed Launce to Padua when they had both met in Milan. Other considerations apart, Padua was in the opposite direction.

Proteus' servant, Launce, appears a first thought for Launcelot Gobbo in *The Merchant of Venice*; if so, one can only say that here first thoughts were best. Launcelot Gobbo is the most tedious of Shakespeare's 'clowns', and an unpleasant character into the bargain. I cannot recall a performance of *The Merchant* when I did not long for him to quit the stage. Launce, on the contrary, with his dog makes admirable fooling. In Shakespeare's time, as in ours, there was obviously no limit to the Englishman's patience with domestic animals

> I have sat in the stocks for puddings he hath stol'n, otherwise he had been executed: I have stood in the pillory for geese he hath killed, otherwise he had suffered for't . . . Nay, I remember the trick you served me, when I took my leave of Madam Silvia: did not I bid thee still mark me, and do as I do? When dids't thou see me heave up my leg, and make water against a gentlewoman's farthingale?
>
> (IV, iv, 28-36)

This is the only place where Shakespeare introduces a live animal; did Crab, one wonders, misbehave at a performance? Launce does, it is true, echo a few tags of popular anti-semitism. If Speed will not go with him to the ale-house, it is because he is a 'Hebrew, a Jew, and not worth the name of a Christian'. If Launce was indeed the father of Launcelot Gobbo, one can only say that in this respect the child had bettered his father's instruction. Nor should the scenes between Launce and Crab be read simply as comic relief. They underpin, so to speak, the principal motif of the play, which is man's ingratitude for the love that is lavished on him. Just as Crab gets forgiveness from his master, so Proteus gets foregiveness from his mistress; and both are undeserved.

The *Two Gentlemen of Verona* is a short play, but in its verbal fencing it is too long by half.

> *Speed*:   How now, Signior Launce! What news
> with your mastership?
> *Launce*: With my master's ship? Why, it is at
> sea.
> *Speed*:   Well, your old vice still: mistake the word.
>
> (III, i, 276-8)

¹ Introduction to *The Two Gentlemen of Verona*, Cambridge University Press (1921), XVI.

Shakespeare had caught the 'vice' from Lyly; presumably it raised its laughs, and it was to be a little time before he grew out of it. When he did so, *Love's Labour's Lost* showed how it could be turned to satiric purpose. *The Two Gentlemen* is naturally classed with the early comedies, but it is also something of a problem play born out of due season. Proteus, like Bertram in *All's Well That Ends Well*, is rewarded with an undeserved forgiveness, although Helena goes to even more ingenious lengths to get her man.

It is, at any rate, some way from the 'light and jocund Italianate comedy' of Quiller-Couch's description. The hot sunshine of Lombardy is already throwing the long shadows that were quite absent from *The Taming of the Shrew*. The deeper theme is the theme of the problem plays — the need to reconcile what reason alone would declare to be irreconcilable. Would Mariana have wanted to marry Angelo, or Helena Bertram? In a most illuminating essay[1] John Vyvyan has shown that in *The Two Gentlemen* Shakespeare is feeling his way towards allegory, clearly influenced by Chaucer's *The Romance of the Rose*, and by the Neo-Platonic doctrine that the soul is itself divine. Love is perfect in Julia and Silvia; it is imperfect in Proteus and even, at first, in Valentine

> If haply won, perhaps a hapless gain;
> If lost, why then a grievous labour won . . .
> . . . by love the young and tender wit
> Is turn'd to folly.

(I, i, 32-3; 47-8)

Valentine is educated by adversity — the Duke's opposition to his marriage with Silvia; Proteus by Julia's constancy, Silvia's scorn, and the magnanimity of his friend. Seen in this light, the last scene becomes understandable in its aim, though unacceptable in its execution. Shakespeare was trying to do a most difficult thing — although most of his critics have failed to see what it was; found that it did not come off with an audience; and left someone else to make a worse job of it than he had made himself. But it is still possible to hear through these entanglements, so crudely untied, 'the inly voice of love'; and to watch, in its earliest functioning, the operation of Shakespearean justice.

2

Almost certainly before he had completed *The Two Gentlemen*, the young poet was fumbling after pure tragedy. A Quarto edition of *Titus Andronicus* was published in 1600, stating that the play had been performed 'at sundry times by the Right Honourable the Earl

---

[1] 'Shakespeare and the Rose of Love' (1960).

of Pembroke, the Earl of Derby, the Earl of Sussex, and the Lords Chamberlain their servants'. This was printed by James Roberts of the Barbican, who was also the printer of the theatrical play-bills, and well placed to judge what plays would please the town. The Earl of Derby was one of those who gave their names to the company for which Shakespeare wrote, before it came under the patronage of the Lord Chamberlain. Langbaine's *Account of the English Dramatic Poets* states that a previous Quarto had been published in 1594, and a single copy of this was found in 1905 among the books in a Swedish library. Francis Meres, in 1598, mentions the play as already well known. And Edward Ravenscroft, who revived and altered it in 1678, repeats what he had been told in theatrical circles, that another, unnamed, author had brought it to Shakespeare who merely added a few master-touches to one or two of the principal characters. Sir Israel Gollancz, introducing the play for the Temple edition, allows Shakespeare only sixty lines of the entire text. Such critical cocksureness is breath-taking.

Why then, we may ask, did the editors of the First Folio include *Titus Andronicus* and exclude *Pericles*, where many more than sixty lines are certainly authentic? Was the play still so popular in 1623 that Shakespeare's reputation would be damaged by its exclusion? The play's kinship with the 'revenge' tragedies of Kyd is clear; and although the Stationers Registers and Henslowe's Diary refer to three other plays on the same subject, Jonson may well have had Shakespeare's in mind when he writes in *Bartholomew Fair* (1614), 'He that will swear, Jeronimo or Andronicus are the best plays yet, shall pass unexcepted at here, as a man whose judgment shows it is constant, and hath stood still these five and twenty or thirty years.' If there had been a better play on the subject, surely we should have heard of it? Henslowe mentions a *Titus Andronicus* as a 'new' play on 22 January 1593-4; and a *Titus and Vespasia*, also as 'new', acted by Lord Strange's men on 11 April 1591. Vespasia was a character in the German tragedy of *Titus Andronicus*, and it may be that Shakespeare was working on this, since no alternative source has been discovered. Sir Sidney Lee's conclusion seems reasonable enough. 'The play was in all probability written originally in 1591 by Thomas Kyd, with some aid, it may be, from Greene or Peele, and it was on its revival in 1594 that Shakespeare improved it here and there.'[1] There is much matter, as Touchstone would have said, in that 'here and there', and the 'where' has continued to keep the critics guessing. Jan Kott was acute in summarizing the play as follows: '*C'est déjà le théâtre Shakespearien, ce n'est pas encore le*

---

[1] *A Life of William Shakespeare* (1898), p. 129.

texte Shakespearien.[1] True enough; but this is not to deny Shakespeare a responsible share of the authorship.

We should not discredit *Titus Andronicus* as a repellent exercise in Grand Guignol without trying to understand Shakespeare's motives for writing it (or substantial parts of it). This was what the public wanted, and Shakespeare was not the kind of *précieux* to turn up his nose at popularity. The genre was perfectly respectable, for Kyd had touched it with genius, reaching in *The Spanish Tragedy* depths as yet beyond Shakespeare's grasp. One does not ask of a young poet on the threshold of fame, and intoxicated with beauty in all its forms, to be possessed by the tragic sense of life. Shakespeare would find his own way to it, but it would not be the way of Kyd. Already in *Richard III*, and even in *The Two Gentlemen*, there are hints of it. But his natural vein, at present, was for robust or romantic comedy; when he was at grips with a tragic theme, he treated it, as it were, from the outside — in the first historical tetralogy as an historical dramatist, in *Titus Andronicus* as a 'French falconer' flying at anything he saw.

The proof of the play is in the playing. With Topcliffe busy at the rack, and the corpses dangling at Tyburn, and recent memories of Cranmer at the stake, the Elizabethans had 'supped full with horrors'. Small wonder, then, that they found in *Titus Andronicus* a catalyst, only slightly amplified, of their own experience. Dr Rowse is remarkably perceptive about this play. To a generation that has learnt, from irrefutable witnesses, of the horrors of Auschwitz and Buchenwald, and seen the return of torture as a recognized instrument of policy among nations that like to think of themselves as civilized, there is nothing to defy the imagination in the horrors of *Titus Andronicus*. When the play was performed at Stratford in 1955, under the masterly direction of Peter Brook, the worst of them did not raise a titter. Who that heard it will ever forget Olivier's agonized outcry: 'I *am* the sea!'; or the stabbing Shakespearean simplicity of the single line: 'When will this fearful slumber have an end?' — where the author of *Hamlet* and *Macbeth* peeps out from behind the curtain that conceals the future panorama of his genius?

One is on the alert for such moments as these. Aaron, the Moor, appears at first a two-dimensional figure of Marlovian monstrosity, but he suddenly springs into life when Tamora's sons threaten to deprive him of the child she has borne him. He is the same man, but redeemed by a quickened humanity. The scene of Titus' madness when he shoots arrows at the gods is vividly theatrical. In 1593 the theatres were closed on account of the plague, and Dr Rowse

[1] *Shakespeare notre contemporain.*

plausibly suggests that Shakespeare spent the year at Stratford, working on this and other plays shortly to follow it. Rome has not yet taken hold of this imagination. There are the familiar allusions to the chase: the hounds in full cry, and the chorus of bird-song, accompany Tamora's advances to Aaron

> The birds chant melody on every bush;
> The snake lies rollèd in the cheerful sun;
> The green leaves quiver with the cooling wind,
> And make a chequered shadow on the ground . . .
> We may, each wreathèd in the other's arms,
> Our pastimes done, possess a golden slumber;
> While hounds and horns and sweet melodious birds
> Be unto us as is a nurse's song
> Of lullaby to bring her babe asleep.
>
> (II, iii, 11 *et seq.*)

It does seem as if Shakespeare is glad to forget the ghastly mechanism of revenge; and that he imagines Tamora engaged in doing what he would willingly be doing himself. Aaron, too, can clothe his passion for Tamora, and his limitless ambition, in imagery of which Marlowe might not have been ashamed

> As when the golden sun salutes the morn,
> And having gilt the ocean with his beams,
> Gallops the zodiac in his glistering coach,
> And overlooks the highest peering hills;
> So Tamora . . .
> I will be bright, and shine in pearl and gold,
> To wait upon this new-made empress.
> To wait, said I? to wanton with this queen,
> This goddess, this Semiramis, this nymph,
> This siren, that will charm Rome's Saturnine,
> And see his shipwreck and his commonweal's.
>
> (II, i, 1-10; 19-24)

The magniloquence and the monotony are both Marlovian.

The play is rich in classical allusions. Lavinia lets fall a copy of Ovid's *Metamorphoses,* and Titus offers to read 'the tragic tale of Philomel' which 'treats of Tereus' treason and his rape'. This obviously haunted Shakespeare, for many years later, in *Cymbeline,* the same story is Imogen's bedside reading, and provides an useful addition to Iachimo's inventory

> She hath been reading late
> The tale of Tereus; here the leaf's turned down
> Where Philomel gave up.
>
> (II, iii, 44-6)

Nor would the poet have forgotten that Lucius, who pronounces justice on Aaron and Tamora at the conclusion of the play, was reputedly the first Christian king of Britain.

The themes of rape and treason were now very much in the poet's mind, for *The Rape of Lucrece* was published in the following year — if we are right in thinking that he took the material for *Titus Andronicus* down to Stratford in 1593, and that this was the new play mentioned by Henslowe as performed twelve months later at the Rose. To celebrate the quatercentenary of Shakespeare's birth in 1964 an exhibition was organized at Stratford purporting to illustrate the life of his times. One spectator observed that it told one everything one could want to know about them, except that he ever for a single moment thought life worth living. It certainly explained why his audiences enjoyed *Titus Andronicus.*

We have now examined seven of Shakespeare's plays, and of these only two, *Richard III* and *The Taming of the Shrew*, have enjoyed a perennial popularity. If this had been the sum of his achievement, rather more in quantity than that of Marlowe, one might have quoted Marlowe to the purpose

> Cut is the branch that should have grown full straight
> And wither'd is Apollo's laurel bough
>
> (Dr Faustus)

but one would not have said that a greater poet than Marlowe had met an untimely end. One would have saluted a dramatist of exceptional promise and versatility, witty and occasionally wise, a master of theatrical effect, capable of sound construction and unusual breadth of design, lyrical in a conventional mode. But what had happened to turn the author of *The Two Gentlemen of Verona* into the author of *Romeo and Juliet?* Was it enough for Shakespeare to have fallen upon material that set his imagination alight, unless his imagination had been ready to receive the spark?

I shall suggest an answer to these questions in the next chapter; let us consider the event before we trace the cause of it. The story in its main outlines goes back to an Italian novel, *Il Novellino*, by Masuccio Salerintano, who was himself indebted to Boccaccio. Indeed one detail, the heroine's use of a potion to avoid a compulsory marriage, is found in the late Greek novelist, Xenophon of Ephesus. But Shakespeare's principal source was *The Tragicall Historye of Romeus and Juliet, written first in Italian by Bandello, and nowe in English by Ar(thur) Br(ooke).* This had been published in November 1562. Arthur Brooke was a young poet drowned while crossing the channel in 1570. Shakespeare follows his laborious poem of 3,000 lines very faithfully, but altering and adding as he sees fit. Brooke insists that the tragic end of the 'star-cross'd lovers' is the work of Fortune who 'nothing constant is, save in unconstancie'. It is due in no way to a flaw in the lovers themselves. This, too, is Shakespeare's guiding idea; he is writing a tragedy of circumstance, not of character. But he condenses the action of the play into a space of four or five days, where Brooke spreads it over several weeks. The lovers meet on Sunday evening; they are married early on Monday morning; by noon Romeo has killed Tybalt and been sentenced to banishment; the marriage is consummated the same night; early on Tuesday morning Romeo leaves for Mantua, and by the evening Juliet has obtained her opiate from the Friar; on the night of Thursday both are found dead in the Capulets' funeral vault. The rapidity of action matches the rapidity of passion that precipitates it. Shakespeare had the nose of a foxhound for dramatic irony; so he invents the scene where Mercutio invokes Rosaline's private parts, while Romeo is languishing under Juliet's balcony, and has Mercutio killed because Romeo has tried to stop the fight. While the newly wedded pair are consummating their marriage, Capulet was discussing with Paris the date of his wedding to Juliet; and Juliet, in quest of advice that will get her out of her dilemma, meets Paris in the Friar's cell. As Professor Bullough has pointed out, 'the irony and pathos here are doubled, since Paris is so likeable'.[1] The pathos is redoubled when the Romeo of the play, but not of the poem, is obliged to kill Paris at the entrance to the tomb. The character of the Nurse was taken over pretty well intact from Brooke, but Mercutio — a lay figure in the poem — was wholly Shakespeare's creation. He was the kind of person that Shakespeare, now and for some years to come, found irresistible. Indeed audiences have found him so difficult to resist that the going is hard for the other characters once he has been killed — as many an aspiring Romeo and Juliet have discovered to their cost. In killing Mercutio, Shakespeare ran the risk of killing his play, and another dramatist, less possessed by his central theme, would have done so.

Romeo and Juliet, if well produced and acted, is so compelling on the stage that it is easy to forget that two themes are at work — the tumultuous and yet consecrated passion of the lovers, and the hatred of their two families which only their sacrifice can heal. This is formally set out in the prologue, leading us to expect that Montague and Capulet, with their respective spouses, will engage our attention far more closely than in fact they do. Capulet is a lively portrait of a Warwickshire squire, though not of an Italian nobleman — Shakespeare may be forgiven for not having first-hand experience of Italian noblemen — but Lady Capulet is good for nothing better

---

[1] See Bullough, Vol. I, p. 283.

than to open the local flower show, and both the Montagues are ciphers. There was simply no time to explore the labyrinth of a family feud, when the dramatist was racing hell for leather down the fairway of love at first sight. So little time indeed that all too often, in the theatre, the ending is drastically abridged, or even cut altogether. It is certainly a dramatic fault, or at least a theatrical misfortune, that Friar Lawrence has to explain to the bereaved parents what the audience know already. But the parents must know it too if they are to be reconciled; and if they are not reconciled one of the two themes is left hanging in the air. By this time, however, the average audience does not greatly care whether they are reconciled or not.

More insidious, because Shakespeare makes it seem endemic, is the incomprehension of the world at large in face of a love so exclusive as that of Romeo and Juliet. Mercutio is *un homme moyen sensuel*: his banter does not invalidate his good nature; and the defiant pathos of his death is unforgettable. But he is not a sensitive character. Coleridge could write of 'that exquisite ebullience and overflow of youthful life, wafted on over the laughing waves of pleasure and prosperity'[1]; nevertheless the aerial fantasy of the 'Queen Mab' was wafted from lips that were elsewhere cheerfully earth-bound. His baiting of the Nurse, good-tempered as it is, does not betray an excess of chivalry. Just as earth-bound is the Nurse herself; she is the prisoner of a society and its conventions, which the young lovers have set at defiance, and to preserve them she is prepared to connive at bigamy. Paris is pleasant and well-bred — the very type that parents would choose for their daughter, and that a strong-minded daughter would reject. With all these characters we are in the world we know, and it is part of the lovers' tragedy that only through death can they escape from a world which is 'too much with them'. Like astronauts who have tasted the freedom of outer space, there is nowhere else that they can go. To argue that if the plague had not prevented Friar John from delivering the explanatory letter, they might have lived happily ever after is to reduce a tragedy to an accident. I have described the play as a tragedy of circumstance; but the tragedy of Oedipus was no less circumstantial.

Shakespeare did, however, have rather too much on his plate, or at any rate on his mind. The meeting of boy and girl — and they *were* only boy and girl, with Juliet four years younger than in Brooke's poem — moved him to a lyrical exaltation which has no parallel in dramatic literature. Here was that perfect identity of artist and subject which alone can produce a masterpiece. For all that,

[1] *Shakespeare and the Elizabethan Dramatists.*

however, *Romeo and Juliet* is a flawed masterpiece. Is it, as George Moore suggested, 'an exquisite love-song', but no more than 'a love-song in dialogue'?[1] Not at all; the first half of the play has an impetus and vitality, a total integration of verse and prose, of one kind of verse and another, of character and situation, which even Shakespeare never surpassed. The rhymed couplets of Romeo's mooning after Rosaline perfectly express a Romeo who is in love with love, while the *aubade* of the balcony scene expresses just as perfectly a Romeo who is in love with Juliet. We need not suppose, as critics once thought, that the two were written at different times; the difference is between an accomplished versifier and a dramatic poet who is possessed.

But after the death of Mercutio, and Romeo's sentence of banishment, the case is somewhat altered. In the scene of despair in Friar Lawrence's cell Romeo betrays a surprising weakness of character. Is this the boy who had defied the family feud with a clandestine marriage, and showed an initial self-control when Mercutio became embroiled with Tybalt? Juliet reacts with less hysteria, but, again, would she have allowed Romeo to leave Verona without her? She could easily have gone with him as his page. If she had the courage to swallow a drug which would give her the semblance of death, would her native resourcefulness not have spared her the necessity of doing so? Shakespeare was here the prisoner of his material, and the character he had built up was inconsistent with the circumstances imposed upon it.

Of course he keeps things going with the magnificent potion soliloquy, but we can observe already a certain tendency to tire when he is two-thirds of his way through a story. The conventional lamentations over Juliet's supposed corpse, and the musicians' chit-chat, are so prolonged that they defeat their ironic purpose. Nor do we need them as a breathing space. After this momentary halting, however, the play recovers in the last act, but no longer, be it emphasized, under the opposing signs of love and hate. The dramatist has discovered a new dimension to replace the theme of hatred, in which he was only formally interested, and it is this that makes *Romeo and Juliet*, after all, something more than a tragedy of circumstance. Already, like Keats, Shakespeare is 'half in love with easeful death'.

The acceptance and facing of death transform Romeo from a boy into a man; they are, for anyone, a certificate of maturity. Banishment from Verona to Mantua — no great distance off — was a small matter compared with the death of one's newly married wife, even

---

[1] *Confessions of a Young Man* (1888), p. 233.

before one had been given the chance of a honeymoon. Yet to the first Romeo had reacted with hysteria, and to the second with resolution. A single, pregnant line

> Is it e'en so? Then I defy you, stars
>
> (V, i, 24)

against reams of emotional self-indulgence. No doubt it was Shakespeare's intuition of death as the reconciler of all human antinomies that made him bring Paris to the tomb and be killed there, and Romeo to extend forgiveness to Tybalt in his 'bloody sheet'. There is no romanticizing of the 'palace of dim night'. It is quite as grim as Juliet had foreseen in her soliloquy; Romeo's flaring torch falls on 'grubs and eyeless skulls' — just such a charnel-house as lay outside the church of Holy Trinity at Stratford. But Juliet and her beauty could transform it into a 'feasting presence full of light'; and it is by defiance, not by despair, that the 'yoke of inauspicious stars' could be lifted from shoulders which had done nothing to deserve its burden.

The readiness of two young people, whose observance of Christian morality is otherwise punctilious, to commit suicide incurs no rebuke from the Friar, nor, by implication, from the dramatist. Shakespeare always takes suicide in his stride; it had the imprimatur of theatrical convention. Here, too, it carries the significance that if perfect love has expelled hatred from a society torn apart by it, love itself can be so perfect that there is no place for it in society. Death, in *Romeo and Juliet*, is both a frustration and a fulfilment; and by the end of the play more is reconciled than two families who have for so long disturbed the peace.

Much evidence points to an early composition of the play. In Weever's *Epigrams,* written before 1595, Romeo is referred to as one of Shakespeare's popular characters. The Nurse's allusions to an earthquake 'eleven years' ago may refer to an earthquake which had shaken London in 1580. Passages from Samuel Daniel's *Complainte of Rosamunde* (1592) are strongly reminiscent of Romeo's speeches over Juliet in the tomb; and Daniel was reputed for his literary pilfering

> Only let him more sparingly make use
> Of others' wit and use his own the more.[1]

Once again, there are echoes of Marlowe: Juliet's 'Gallop apace, you fiery-footed steeds' recalls 'Gallop apace bright Pheobus thro' the sky' from *Edward II*. The play on words, descending on occasion to bathos

[1] *The Return from Parnassus.*

> Flies may do this, but I from this must fly

Juliet's violent antitheses

> Beautiful tyrant, fiend angelical,
> Dove-feather'd raven, wolvish-ravening lamb

the frequency of rhyme

> Vile earth to earth resign, end motion here,
> And thou and Romeo press one heavy bier

all suggest that Shakespeare was still emerging from one convention of prosody to another as his imaginative barometer went up or down. As Professor Duthie has written, the play reveals 'an excited Shakespeare and a developing Shakespeare'.[1] In the course of development he had learnt to develop his characters; and what had excited him is the subject of our next inquiry.

---

[1] Introduction to *Romeo and Juliet*, Cambridge University Press (1955), XV.

Chapter 4

Pastoral... Tragical...
Poem Unlimited

1

Obliged, and ready, to write plays for his living, it would not be
surprising if Shakespeare had written poetry for his pleasure. This
appears to have been the case during the difficult years of 1592 and
1593 when, for much of the time, the plague had put a stop to
playgoing. Poetry was more respectable than playwriting and, let us
admit, Shakespeare was not averse to respectability. His father was
even less averse to it; that coveted coat-of-arms was still an exasper-
ating prospect. Poetry gave one easier access to noble patronage, and
by 1592, or earlier, Shakespeare had found a patron who quickly
became a friend. Henry Wriothesley, the young Earl of Southampton, was between nine and ten years Shakespeare's junior.
Baptized and brought up a Catholic, he became the ward of Lord
Burghley who sent him to St John's College, Cambridge. In 1590
Burghley was pressing him to marry Lady Elizabeth Vere, but the
young man showed no disposition to do so. His temperament was
unstable, and his sexual inclinations ambivalent.

How, or when, Shakespeare met Southampton we do not know.
The young Earl may have seen him act, sitting with other sprigs of
the nobility at the side of the stage. Southampton House, where he
lived with his mother, stood on the site of Southampton Buildings
where Chancery Lane runs into Holborn — a huddle of late medieval
buildings round an open courtyard. Here Shakespeare could have met
John Florio, the translator of Montaigne, and Southampton's Italian
tutor, for the Southamptons gave hospitality to Renaissance scholars
as well as to recusant priests. The Earl was described by Nashe, who
unsuccessfully sought his patronage, as 'a dear lover and cherisher as
well of the lovers of poets as of the poets themselves'. One has only to
look at Nicholas Hilliard's miniature painted about this time to
understand Shakespeare's passionate, and yet dutiful, affection for
him. The sweeping forehead, delicate mouth, finely arching eyebrows, and the hair falling in long curls over his shoulder, were
irresistible to a young poet who worshipped at the shrine of physical
beauty, wherever else he may have bent the knee. Yet, as Dr Rowse

has pointed out, there is strength in the face as well — a certain wilfulness not unnatural in one so favoured of the gods; a man of action, you would say, and not only a man of taste.

If, as I believe, it was Southampton who inspired the *Sonnets*, this was probably the deepest emotional experience in Shakespeare's life. He may well have projected it in various and ideal forms on to several of those heroines who challenge Fortune in masculine attire through the early comedies, and throw their chequered sunshine on the gathering shadows of the nineties. For the moment, however, we must trace its effect on the poems which preceded, or perhaps coincided with, the writing of the *Sonnets*. There is no date for the composition of *A Lover's Complaint*. It was published with the first Quarto of the *Sonnets* in 1609, but it seems to have been written much earlier. The style is modelled on the seven line Spenserian stanza — a, b, a, b, b, c, c — and the vocabulary contains certain archaisms and Latinisms that you do not find elsewhere in Shakespeare's work: 'invis'd' for 'unseen', 'acture' for 'action', 'unexperient' for 'inexperienced', 'fluxive eyes'. Shakespeare was always capable of inventing a word if he wanted to, but these have an old-fashioned and affected ring.

The subject is the conventional lamentation of a maid who has been seduced, yet has found the experience so agreeable that she would willingly be seduced again if only the seducer would come her way. Shakespeare displays no moral prejudice against consenting adults. The maid is like any girl he might have met on the road to Shottery. She wore

> Upon her head a platted hive of straw
> Which fortified her visage from the sun
>
> (8-9)

and the young man bears a remarkable resemblance to Hilliard's miniature of Southampton, although Shakespeare would hardly have attributed such falsity to his patron. It merely seems that, in depicting an irresistible youth, he cannot get Southampton out of his mind's eye

> His browny locks did hang in crooked curls,
> And every light occasion of the wind
> Upon his lips their silken parcels hurls . . .
> Small show of man was yet upon his chin;
> His phoenix down began but to appear
> Like unshorn velvet on that termless skin . . .
>
> (85-7; 92-4)

Southampton's ambivalence and uncertain temper are both hinted at

> His qualities were beauteous as his form,

> For maiden-tongu'd he was, and thereof free;
> Yet, if men mov'd him, was he such a storm
> As oft 'twixt May and April is to see

(99-102)

his horsemanship

> Well could he ride, and often men would say
> 'That horse his mettle from his rider takes:
> Proud of subjection, noble by the sway,
> What rounds, what bounds, what course, what stop
>   he makes!'

(105-9)

his popularity, and success with men and women

> That he did in the general bosom reign
> Of young, of old, and sexes both enchanted,
> To dwell with him in thoughts, or to remain
> In personal duty, following where he haunted;
> Consents bewitch'd, ere he desire, have granted,
> And dialogu'd for him what he would say,
> Ask'd their own wills and made their wills obey.

(127-33)

'Will' was, of course, an Elizabethan euphemism for both the male and female reproductive organs. What emerges from the poem is Shakespeare's greater interest in the young man 'with his art in youth and youth in art' than in the girl he has seduced. It is a celebration, rather than a censure, of 'most potential love'.

With the publication of *Venus and Adonis* in 1593, and its dedication to Southampton, Shakespeare's devotion to his patron comes out into the open, though as yet not fully. This was the first of his works to be printed, and its popularity was immediate. Cambridge undergraduates slept with it under their pillows, and it ran through sixteen editions before 1640. Like Molière, Shakespeare appears to have been indifferent to the publication of his plays, but he saw his poems carefully through the press. *Venus and Adonis*, printed by his old friend, Richard Field, and sold 'at the sign of the White Greyhound in Paul's Churchyard' presents none of the problems with which the Quarto and Folio texts have teased the critics. In so far as Shakespeare was eager for fame, he seems to have relied on his poems to earn it for him. Neither his contemporaries, nor his close posterity, disappointed him.

The poem itself merits close attention, but let us first examine the Dedication

> Right Honourable, I know not how I shall offend in dedicating my unpolished lines to your Lordship, nor how the world will censure me for choosing so strong a prop to support so weak a burden. Only, if your

> Honour seemed but pleased, I account myself highly praised; and vow to take advantage of all idle hours, till I have honoured you with some graver labour. But if the first heir of my invention prove deformed, I shall be sorry it had so noble a godfather, and never after ear [till] so barren a land, for fear it yield me still so bad a harvest. I leave it to your honourable survey, and your Honour to your heart's content, which I wish may always answer your own wish, and the world's hopeful expectation. Your Honour's in all duty, William Shakespeare.

The prose is at once easy and scholarly, the tone respectful. Whatever deeper feelings the poet may have entertained for his patron could hardly have been expressed in the dedication of a poem designed for public circulation. Other things apart, the difference in rank would have forbidden it.

The subject was a popular theme in classical mythology, and Shakespeare's principal debt was to Ovid's *Metamorphoses* (Book X), which he would have known from Arthur Golding's translation, and could also have read in Latin. But whereas Ovid's Adonis is merely indifferent to Venus' advances, Shakespeare's is positively hostile. For this stronger reaction he went to the Hermaphroditus of Ovid's fourth book. The similar tale of Glaucus and Scylla had been worked over by Lodge in 1589, with the roles reversed. Here Glaucus repels the amorous invitations of Scylla, and this may have given Shakespeare a cue that he was not unwilling to take up. The vivid description of the boar-hunt was taken from Meleager's encounter with the boar in the eighth book of the *Metamorphoses*. The metre chosen is the 'staffe of six verses' (ab, ab, cc) which Puttenham had described as 'not only most *usual*, but also very pleasant to th' eare'. The narrative poem, like the sonnet, was a popular genre; *The Lover's Complaint* was already a first essay in a poetry of situation which had dramatic as well as lyrical appeal.

It is a pity that the sensitivity of certain Shakespeare critics is not equal to their scholarship. When Edward Dowden declares, with only minor qualifications, that *Venus and Adonis* 'is not a good poem', one's hair stands up on end. It is not a perfect poem like Marlowe's *Hero and Leander,* written about the same time and probably known to Shakespeare in manuscript form. For one thing, it is a good deal too long. But its beauties put its imperfections in the shade. Among those of an earlier generation who have written on it at length, only George Wyndham did justice to its quality — and Wyndham was a Member of Parliament! Its 'wealth of realistic detail' reminded him of 'the West Porch of Amiens', and its whole colouring and *ambiente* of Botticelli's Venus rising from the sea; of that 'debatable dawntime which we call the Renaissance'.[1] He had good precedent for his

[1] Introduction to *The Poems of Shakespeare* (1898), lxxxv.

admiration. Coleridge wrote of 'an endless activity of thought with thought, thought with feeling, or with words, of feelings with feelings, and of words with words ... Shakespeare writes in this poem as if he were of another planet, charming you to gaze on the movements of Venus and Adonis, as you would on the twinkling dances of two vernal butterflies.'[1]

The theme is playful sensuality — not a theme which an earlier generation of dons were accustomed to take seriously. But like any other game it is a very serious matter for those engaged in it. Shakespeare shows considerable expertise

> And yet not cloy thy lips with loath'd satiety,
> But rather famish them amid their plenty,
> Making them red and pale with fresh variety;
> Ten kisses short as one, one long as twenty ...
>
> (19-22)

> Art thou asham'd to kiss? then wink again,
> And I will wink; so shall the day seem night;
> Love keeps his revels where there are but twain;
> Be bold to play, our sport is not in sight:
> These blue-vein'd violets whereon we lean
> Can never blab, nor know not what we mean
>
> (121-6)

and then Adonis

> He wrings her nose, he strikes her on the cheeks,
> He bends her fingers, holds her pulses hard,
> He chafes her lips; a thousand ways he seeks
> To mend the hurt that his unkindness marr'd:
> He kisses her; and she, by her good will,
> Will never rise, so he will kiss her still.
>
> (475-80)

Here is the high comedy of love, and it is acted in the open air. Shakespeare cannot help digressing to describe the pursuit of the 'timorous flying hare', or the points of Adonis' horse when he breaks loose from the tree to which Adonis has tethered him

> Round-hoof'd, short-jointed, fetlocks shag and long,
> Broad breast, full eye, small head, and nostril wide,
> High crest, short ears, straight legs and passing strong,
> Thin mane, thick tail, broad buttock, tender hide.
>
> (295-8)

This is quite different from the liquid grace and enamelled surface of *Hero and Leander*. The excessive length of the poem is a defect of its quality — a tireless, superabounding, energy.

Landscape is used as a metaphor of love

---

[1] *Shakespeare and the Elizabethan Dramatists.*

'Fondling' she saith 'since I have hemmed thee here
Within the circuit of this ivory pale,
I'll be a park and thou shalt be my deer:
Feed where thou wilt, on mountain or in dale;
Graze on my lips, and if those hills be dry,
Stray lower where the pleasant fountains lie.'

(229-34)

The wooing of Adonis is paralleled, with the roles reversed, by the horse's wooing of the jennet

He looks upon his love, and neighs unto her;
She answers him as if she knew his mind;
Being proud, as females are, to see him woo her,
She puts on outward strangeness, seems unkind,
Spurns at his love and scorns the heat he feels,
Beating his kind embracements with her heels.

(307-12)

Two stanzas anticipate the opening sequence of the *Sonnets*, refer-ring — as they well may do — to Southampton's reluctance to marry the young woman Lord Burghley had chosen for him

Torches are made to light, jewels to wear,
Dainties to taste, fresh beauty for the use,
Herbs for their smell, and sappy plants to bear;
Things growing to themselves are growth's abuse:
Seeds spring from seeds, and beauty breedeth beauty;
Thou wast begot; to get it is thy duty.

(163-8)

Upon the earth's increase why should'st thou feed,
Unless the earth with thy increase be fed?
By law of nature thou are bound to breed,
That thine may live when thou thyself art dead;
And so in spite of death thou dost survive,
In that thy likeness still is left alive.

(169-74)

Venus can say to Adonis what Shakespeare could not have said to an aristocratic patron in a published work. In the *Sonnets*, of course, he said much more, but there is no reason to think that he authorized their publication.

2

Venus and Adonis is a pagan poem, untroubled in its inspiration though much troubled in its subject; a hymn to ideal Beauty, and when Beauty is slain by the boar, the poet can exlaim

And beauty dead, black Chaos comes again

(1020)

in almost the same words as Othello foresees the loss of his love for

Desdemona 'and when I love thee not/Chaos is come again.' (III, iii, 91). *The Rape of Lucrece* is that 'graver labour' which Shakespeare had promised Southampton. The two face each other like the Comic and the Tragic Muse; the one an *aubade*, the other a nocturne. *Lucrece* was published by Richard Field in 1594, and by 1640 had run into ten editions. The tone of the Dedication, again to Southampton, is notably warmer

> The love I dedicate to your Lordship is without end: whereof this Pamphlet without beginning is but a superfluous Moiety. The warrant I have of your Honourable disposition, not the worth of my untutored Lines makes it assured of acceptance. What I have done is yours, what I have to do is yours, being part in all I have, devoted yours. Were my worth greater, my duty would show greater, meantime, as it is, it is bound to your Lordship; to whom I wish long life still lengthened with all happiness.
>
> Your Lordship's in all duty,
>
> William Shakespeare.

The poet still speaks of duty to his patron, but he also speaks of love. The relationship had obviously ripened.

The poem is written in the seven-line stanza — a, b, a, b, b, c, c — which Chaucer had borrowed from Guillaume de Machaut. Puttenham had commended this 'Heroicall' metre as 'very grave and stately' and 'most usual with our auncient makers'.[1] *Lucrece* owed not a little to Chaucer, as well as to Ovid's *Fasti* from which Chaucer had taken the Fifth Story in his *Legend of Good Women*. The *ambiente* of the poem, though it is set in Rome, is medieval rather than Roman or Renaissance. Lucretia was 'the grand example of conjugal fidelity throughout the Gothic Ages'[2]; and Shakespeare must have come across the story in North's *Plutarch*. Chaucer and Ovid both tell it with economy, where Shakespeare expands it over 1,855 lines. His narrative is deeply introspective and moralizing, as well as passionately emotional. *Venus and Adonis* and *Lucrece* both look forward, obliquely, to the *Sonnets*, though in different ways; the first to the lovely boy and the second to the Dark Lady. In *Lucrece* the 'two loves' of which the poet was afterwards to speak stand tragically opposed, but not in the same character. As Professor Bullough has neatly put it, 'having described desire unaccomplished against reluctance, Shakespeare now gives desire accomplished by force'.[3] And in the second case desire is equally disappointed.

Slow and repetitive as the narrative becomes, it sets off at the gallop

---

[1] *Art of English Poesie.*
[2] Warton, *History of English Poetry* (1824).
[3] See Bullough, Vol. I, p. 179.

> From the besieged Ardea all in post
> Borne by the trustless wings of false desire
> Lust-breathéd Tarquin leaves the Roman host . . .
>
> (1-3)

He introduces himself to Lucrece with a cautious courtesy

> nothing in him seem'd inordinate
> Save sometime too much wonder of his eye . . .
>
> (94-5)

When they have separated, it is not fanciful to think that Shakespeare is speaking for himself in analysing such stirrings of conscience as may deter Tarquin from his criminal intent

> So that in venturing ill we leave to be
> The things we are for that which we expect;
> And this ambitious, foul infirmity,
> In having much, torments us with defect
> Of that we have: so then we do neglect
> The thing we have, and, all for want of wit
> Make something nothing by augmenting it.
>
> (148-54)

He was to say it all again, and even better, in Sonnet 129

> Past reason hunted; and no sooner had
> Past reason hated, as a swallowed bait
> On purpose laid to make the taker mad.

As Tarquin stalks — the word was Chaucer's — to Lucrece's chamber

> No noise but owls' and wolves' death-boding cries
>
> (165)

disturb the heavy silence of the house — as, later, in *Macbeth*, they sound an accompaniment to crime

> It was the owl that shriek'd
> The fatal bellman that gives the stern'st good night.
>
> (II, ii, 3)

Conscience stabs him again, yet more sharply

> What win I, if I gain the thing I seek?
> A dream, a breath, a froth of fleeting joy.
> Who buys a minute's mirth to wail a week?
> Or sells eternity to get a toy?
>
> (211-14)

As he passes from one room to another, the dramatist in Shakespeare takes command

> The threshold grates the door to have him heard
> Night-wand'ring weasels shriek to see him there;
> They fright him, yet he still pursues his fear . . .
>
> (306-8)

As each unwilling portal yields him sway
Through little vents and crannies of the place
The wind wars with his torch to make him stay
And blows the smoke of it into his face.

(309-12)

He picks up Lucretia's glove from the rushes, and pricks his finger
with the needle sticking out of it; but all these omens are defied as he
enters, at last, her chamber, and discovers her very much as Iachimo
was to discover Imogen in *Cymbeline*

Her lily hand her rosy cheeks lies under,
Coz'ning the pillow of a lawful kiss

(386-7)

while her hand

Show'd like an April daisy on the grass.

(395)

It is, for Shakespeare as for Lucrece, a mark of Tarquin's villainy that
being a King he does not behave like one

Thou seem'st not what thou art, a God, a King;
For Kings like Gods should govern everything

(601-2)

— not least themselves. Or again — and how Elizabeth would have
relished the lines

For Princes are the glass, the school, the book
Where subjects' eyes do learn, do read, do look.

(615-16)

After the rape, described without any gloating on its lubricious
details, Tarquin's victory turns to ashes in his mouth. A very sure
psychology is here at work

Pure Chastity is rifled of her store,
And Lust, the thief far poorer than before

(692-3)

and a Christian conscience also

Feeble Desire, all recreant, poor and meek,
Like to a bankrupt beggar wails his case:
The flesh being proud. Desire does fight with Grace,
For there it revels; and when that decays,
The guilty rebel for remission pays.

(710-14)

Lucrece's impassioned outburst against the agents of her fall —
Tarquin, Time and Opportunity — continues for 450 lines: 'Misshapen Time' is the 'ceaseless lackey to Eternity'; and Opportunity is

its servant. Only one thing remains for her

> To clear this spot by death, at least I give
> A badge of fame to Slander's livery;
> A dying life to living infamy . . .
>
> (1053-5)

The poet's favourite simile recurs as she compares herself to

> the poor frighted deer that stands at gaze
> Wildly determining which way to fly
>
> (1149-50)

and with her, as with Tarquin, a Christian dimension is given to a story which Chaucer had already baptized

> My body or my soul, which was the dearer,
> When the one pure, the other made divine?
> Whose love of either to myself was nearer,
> When both were kept for Heaven and Collatine?
>
> (1163-6)

Lucrece is a sombre, claustrophobic poem, letting in no chink of daylight. Like *Venus and Adonis* it is too long. Freed from the necessity of holding an audience in thrall through the two (or more) hours' traffic of his stage, Shakespeare gives unbridled rein to his verbal and intellectual invention. Nothing can stop him from going on and on; and on and on he goes, now in this direction and now in that. A painting of the siege of Troy distracts him — where had he seen it? — and distracts Lucrece in the depth of her shame and grief. This is good for a digression of twenty-four stanzas. The picture is meticulously observed, for Shakespeare was eminently a *visuel*

> Here one man's hand lean't on another's head,
> His nose being shadow'd by his neighbour's ear;
> Here one being throng'd bears back, all boll'n and red;
> Another smother'd seems to pelt and swear . . .
>
> (1415-18)

Achilles is represented by his spear

> Gripp'd in an arméd hand; himself behind
> Was left unseen, save to the eye of mind
>
> (1425-6)

and all leads up to the splendid line

> Show me the strumpet that began this stir
>
> (1471)

the embittered question

> Why should the private pleasure of some one
> Become the public plague of many more?
>
> (1477-8)

d an image that was to serve the poet in another context, as
ucrece recalls the words of Priam that

> like wildfire burnt the shining glory
> Of rich-built Ilion, that the skies were sorry
> And little stars shot from their fixéd places,
> When their glass fell wherein they view'd their faces
>
> (1523-6)

and so to the inevitable confession when Collatine and his Knights
arrive on the scene, and

> this pale swan in her watery nest
> Begins the sad Dirge of her certain ending.
>
> (1611-12)

What happens in *Lucrece* occurs with a brutal, though deliberate,
rapidity. Shakespeare gives one the impression of events recorded in
slow motion; the impetus of narrative is continually checked. We can
believe that his heart was not wholly in the theatre, and that it never
would be until he had made poetry perfectly at home there. He had
gone some way to doing this in *Romeo and Juliet*, although the
'Queen Mab' and 'Gallop apace' are arias, pure and simple; and the
'Queen Mab' has little to do with Mercutio. In *Venus and Adonis* and
Lucrece he was packing in, at the risk of no matter what digression,
everything that life had taught him; and hinting, here and there, at
the bitter-sweet instruction which, at the same time, he was receiving
from the experience recorded in the *Sonnets*. He had always been in
love with ideal as well as carnal Beauty; now the ideal had become
incarnate.

Chapter 5

'Two Loves I Have'

1

The problems raised by the *Sonnets* may be summarized as follows. When were they written, and to whom? Can the rival poet and the Dark Lady be identified? What is the meaning of the Dedication? Were the poems no more than a literary exercise and only indirectly inspired by personal experience? Even so fine a scholar as Sir Sidney Lee thought this explanation possible — to which one is tempted to reply, with the Duke of Wellington, that if he believed that, he would believe anything. No responsible commentator believes it today. For one thing, the first and second pronouns are used more frequently than in any other Elizabethan sonnet sequence. The formal artefact is infused with urgent feeling.

On the other points, however, opinion has been sharply divided. Those who wish to study both sides of the question should refer to J. Dover Wilson's *Shakespeare's Sonnets* (1964) and A. L. Rowse's *Shakespeare's Sonnets — the Problems Solved* (1973). My own conclusion, in the main, is Dr Rowse's, but Dover Wilson's insight and scholarship carry a weight that cannot be ignored, although his exegesis rarely errs on the side of caution. What follows here is a summary of the conflicting arguments with such additional comment as I am bold enough to make.

The *Sonnets* were published as a Quarto in 1609 by Thomas Thorpe and sold by John Wright 'dwelling at Christ Church gate'. They are described as 'never before imprinted'; but in fact two of them, 138 and 144, with three other poems also by Shakespeare, had appeared ten years earlier in a miscellaneous collection of verse entitled *The Passionate Pilgrim* to which his name was dishonestly attached, obviously to promote its sales. Both of these sonnets reflect his torment of conscience and emotion over the affair with the Dark Lady. There are no signs that he had seen Thorpe's complete edition through the press, or even that he approved of his story being given to the world. Francis Meres had referred, in 1598, to the poet's 'sugared sonnets' as circulating 'among his private friends'. But this was a very different matter from the wider publicity now given to them. On the other hand, he counted on them, if on nothing else, eventually to secure his fame.

> You still shall live — such virtue hath my pen —
> Where breath most breathes, even in the mouths of men . . .
>
>   (81)

If Shakespeare did not authorize, or facilitate, this publication, how did Thorpe — a reputable publisher — get hold of them? This brings us to the mysterious Dedication — by Thorpe, be it noted, not by Shakespeare himself. Here was a case where an author's Dedication, over which the poet had been scrupulous in *Venus and Adonis* and *Lucrece*, would have been either superfluous or indiscreet.

> To the only begetter of these ensuing sonnets Mr W.H. all happiness and that eternity promised by our ever-living poet wisheth the well-wishing adventurer in setting forth. T.T.

Our first instinct is to assume that 'Mr W.H.' had inspired the sonnets, if only because it was to him that Shakespeare had promised 'eternity'. On second thoughts, however, we realize that whoever had inspired them, 'Mr W.H.' was by no means their 'only begetter'. The Dark Lady had had a considerable hand in the business; nor had 'Mr W.H.' come out of it particularly well. Would a publisher wishing to pay a fulsome compliment to a nobleman — never mind his identity for the moment — have so advertised his infidelity and his indiscretions?

This point has been overlooked by most of those who have scratched their heads over the problem. Nevertheless Sir Edmund Chambers and Dover Wilson were not alone in arriving — I will not say jumping — at the conclusion that 'Mr W.H.' must have been William Herbert, who succeeded his father as Earl of Pembroke in 1601. He had much to recommend him for the part: his initials to begin with; Shakespeare's association with his father's company; his reluctance, in 1597, to marry Burghley's grand-daughter, Bridget Vere; his notorious affair with Mary Fitton, who thus became a favourite candidate for the role of the Dark Lady; his high rank, romantic looks, and keen intelligence. Aubrey writes that he and his brother Philip were 'the most popular Peers in the West of England', and that William was 'a most noble Person and the Glory of the Court . . . He was a good scholar and delighted in Poetry . . . Wilton will appear to have been an Academy, as well as Palace, and was (as it were) the Apiary, to which men that were excellent in Arms, and Arts, did resort, and were caressed; and many of them received honourable Pensions.' This sounds too good to be true; but Clarendon, after praising Herbert's liberality and readiness to welcome 'all who were displeased and unsatisfied in the Court or with

the Court', qualifies his appreciation. 'He indulged to himself the
pleasures of all kinds, almost in all excesses . . . he was immoderately
given up to women . . . And some who were nearest his trust and
friendship were not without apprehension that his natural vivacity
and vigour of mind began to lessen and decline by those excessive
indulgences.'[1]

All this adds up to a persuasive likeness of the young man who had
captured Shakespeare's affections; but look a little further, and the
solution bristles with difficulties. In the first place, Mary Fitton
disappeared from the picture when it was discovered that she was a
smashing blonde! Then, is it remotely probable that a publisher
would have addressed the 'most popular Peer . . . one might boldly
say, in the whole Kingdom'[2] as '*Mr* W.H.', unless he had wished to
conceal his identity; and if he had wished to conceal his identity,
would he have given him his correct initials? Coronets in Elizabethan
times, and for long afterwards, were not so lightly disregarded.
Moreover, to plant Shakespeare's patron on Herbert dates the
composition of the *Sonnets* not earlier than the turn of the century.
If the alternative theory holds good — that they were written
between 1591 and 1594 — the person who snatched Shakespeare's
mistress away from him and gave his favours to a rival poet would
have been only twelve years old. Here it is no answer to reply that
Juliet was only two years older.

So the identification of Herbert is crucially dependent on the date
of composition. Much play has been made of Sonnet 107, which is
taken to refer to the death of Elizabeth in 1603

> The mortal moon hath her eclipse endured
> And the sad augurs mock their own presage;
> Incertainties now crown themselves assured,
> And peace proclaims olives of endless age.

This interpretation seems to me perverse in the extreme. The point
of the first line is that the mortal moon has *survived* her eclipse; nor
are these the accents in which the greatest poet of the day would
lament the death of a revered sovereign. Another explanation has
been suggested, which I shall discuss in due course. Again, parallels
have been found between the language of the *Sonnets* and the
language of the plays written in 1597 or thereabouts.

> Anon permit the basest clouds to ride
> With ugly rack on his celestial face

(33)

---

[1] *History of the Rebellion*, Vol. I.
[2] Aubrey.

and

> the sun
> Who doth permit the base contagious clouds
> To smother up his beauty from the world.
>
> (*I Henry IV*, I, ii, 221)

> Therefore are feasts so solemn and so rare,
> Since, seldom coming, in the long year set . . .
> So is the time that keeps you as my chest,
> Or as the wardrobe which the robe doth hide,
> To make some special instant special blest
>
> (52)

and

> My presence, like a robe pontiféd,
> Ne'er seen but wonder'd at; and so my state,
> Seldom but sumptuous, showéd like a feast
> And won by rareness such solemnity . . .
>
> (*I Henry IV*, III, ii, 56)

Other parallels between the *Sonnets* and *Henry IV*, and also *Hamlet*, have been noticed by Dover Wilson: the contrast between the wild rose and the garden rose, and the comparison between the eye in its socket and a star moving in its sphere. The Professor modestly disclaims any wish to press the argument further than it will go; I confess that I do not find it even a starter. We have already seen how frequently an image employed by Shakespeare in the poems and the earlier plays lives on to illuminate a later theme.

It might be argued, on the other hand, that the turn of the century coincided with the sexual revulsion explicit in *Hamlet* and *Troilus and Cressida*, and that this is equally explicit in many of the *Sonnets* inspired by the Dark Lady. That experience, however, was so painful that Shakespeare may well have suffered from it for some time to come. More apposite are his references to Rosaline in *Love's Labour's Lost* — a play, revised, it is true, in 1597, but certainly written much earlier. And even if we accept the later date for the *Sonnets,* and consequently Herbert as their 'only begetter' — dubious as I have shown this to be — we are still left with the problem of the rival poet.

> Was it the proud full sail of his great verse?

There was only one person to whom these words could have been applied without absurdity — and that was Marlowe. Shakespeare would not have scattered such praise on a rival unless he had felt it was deserved. But Marlowe had been killed in 1593; so, if we accept the subsequent dating, an alternative candidate must be found. Chapman has been suggested; but no one comparing Marlowe's beginning to *Hero and Leander* — published in 1598 — with

Chapman's completion of it, could have spoken of the 'proud full sail' of Chapman's verse without putting himself out of court as a judge of poetry. Marlowe had other points in his favour, and these will emerge as we pursue the argument. There remains, of course, the mystery of 'Mr W.H.'; but this must await our examination of a different theory, both of the young man and of the date when the poems were written to him.

Of Shakespeare's devotion to Southampton, and dependence on him, the Dedications to *Venus and Adonis* and *Lucrece* have already given us ample proof. Of his personal acquaintance with Herbert there existed only one piece of documentary evidence: a letter, now lost, referring to a visit of 'the man Shakespeare' to Wilton Park with a performance of *As You Like It*. The terms of the reference do not point of any great degree of intimacy with the Pembroke circle. Malone, the most reliable among earlier editors of Shakespeare's works, did not question that the poet's friend was Southampton; and Hyder Rollins, who edited the *Sonnets* for the *New Variorum*, realized that in order to identify the persons one had first to establish the date of the events in which they were involved.

I think it is wholly arbitrary to assume, because the *Sonnets* are greater poems than *Venus and Adonis* and *Lucrece*, that they were therefore the fruit of Shakespeare's maturity. A great poem is born, not of years but of experience, and we have already noted the leap forward registered by *Romeo and Juliet*, compared with any play written by Shakespeare before that time. I am more impressed by the similarity of expression in the *Sonnets* to certain expressions in the previous poems, where the themes of the *Sonnets* are adumbrated, than to echoes of these in the subsequent plays. In the Dedication of *Venus and Adonis* Shakespeare had written: 'But if the first heir of my invention prove deformed, I shall be sorry it had so noble a godfather and never after *ear* so barren a land, for fear it yield me still so bad a harvest.' In Sonnet 3 he asks his friend

> For where is she so fair whose *unear'd* womb
> Disdains the tillage of thy husbandry.

Venus begs Adonis to enjoy her favours in exactly the same terms as Shakespeare begs his friend to get married

> By law of nature thou art bound to breed
> That thine may live when thou thyself art dead;
> And so in spite of death thou dost survive,
> In that thy likeness still is left alive.

> (171-4)

This surely indicates that the two were closely connected in time as well as inspiration.

Absence is a recurring motif of the *Sonnets*. We have seen that during 1592 and 1593 the London theatres were closed on account of the plague, and we should therefore expect to find Shakespeare on tour. Here the evidence is coercive. He speaks of himself as 'weary with toil', and of

> The dear repose for limbs with travel tired
>
> (27)

of the day and night which conspire to torture him

> The one by toil, the other to complain
> How far I toil, still farther off from thee . . .
>
> (28)

He expostulates against 'Injurious distance', but assures his friend that

> Thyself away art present still with me . . .
>
> (47)

He describes himself on horseback ambling or trotting the weary miles from one provincial town to another — perhaps along the south coast, collecting those images of the sea which were to serve him until he brought Lear and Gloucester face to face on the cliffs of Dover, and, in his last plays, raised *The Tempest* and restored Marina to Pericles

> The beast that bears me, tired with my woe,
> Plods dully on, to bear that weight in me
> As if by some instinct the wretch did know
> His rider loved not speed, being made from thee
>
> (50)

and the opening of a later sonnet, as he looks back on these prolonged absences when his profession had called him away from the happy proximity of Southampton House

> From you I have been absent in the spring . . .
>
> (98)

The plague, and other causes, had taken a heavy toll of his friends, and of one who was not a friend. Kyd, Nashe, Greene and Peele had all died in those two years, and Marlowe had been killed in a squalid brawl

> Then can I drown an eye, unused to flow,
> For precious friends hid in death's dateless night
>
> (30)

and in the succeeding sonnet

> Thy bosom is endearéd with all hearts,
> Which I by lacking have supposéd dead;

And there reigns love, and all love's loving parts
And all those friends which I thought buried.

(31)

If, as I hope to demonstrate, Marlowe was the rival poet, there is
much significance in the opening line of the last poem that treats of
his association with Shakespeare's friend

Was it the proud full sail of his great verse?

Here, and here alone, the poet speaks of him in the past tense, and
Marlowe was killed in May 1593. At the same time Shakespeare was
at work on *Love's Labour's Lost,* and the mockery of his own
infatuation with the Dark Lady is clear in the lines of Berowne

A wightly wanton with a velvet brow,
With two pitch balls stuck in her face for eyes;
Ay, and by heaven, one that will do the deed
Though Argus were her eunuch and her guard

(III, i, 198-201)

where present pain is mixed with present laughter.

Lastly, it is now widely recognized that the 'mortal moon', which
has led to a later dating of the *Sonnets,* refers to Queen Elizabeth's
escape from poisoning by her personal physician, Dr Lopez, who was
found to be in touch with Spanish agents. The evidence against him
was not conclusive, but he was duly tried, and executed in June
1594. In March of the same year Henry of Navarre thought Paris
worth a Mass, and the wars of religion in France were brought to an
end. This plausibly explains the two lines from the same sonnet
(107)

Incertainties now crown themselves assured,
And peace proclaims olives of endless age

lines which strike a strangely impersonal note in a sequence otherwise inspired by intense personal feeling. The only other allusion to
external events is the puzzling couplet which ends Sonnet 124.
Shakespeare describes his love as

Hugely politic,
That it ne'er grows with heat nor drowns with showers.
To this I witness call the fools of time,
Which die for goodness, who have lived for crime . . .

According to Dr Rowse, this refers to the persecution of the Jesuit
missionary priests after the exposure of the Lopez conspiracy in
1594. The dilemma was very real for men forced to choose between
a régime which had robbed the English people of their religion, and a
foreign power that promised to restore it. For some of them, no
doubt, patriotism was 'not enough'. Shakespeare evidently took the

official view of their activities, but admitted that a man might be
guilty in the eyes of the law, and yet good in the sight of God. Thus,
with the clue given in Sonnet 104

> Three winters cold
> Have from the forests shook three summers pride,
> Three beauteous springs to yellow autumn turn'd
> In the process of the seasons have I seen,
> Three April perfumes in three hot Junes burn'd,
> Since first I saw you fresh, which yet are green

we may fairly safely date the writing of the *Sonnets* over three years
— between 1591 and 1594.

We are now in a position to see how the character and features of
Southampton fit the portrait that Shakespeare has left us of his
friend. Here then is the popular young patrician, not yet come of age

> The lovely gaze where every eye doth dwell.
>
> (5)

> beloved of many,
> But that thou none lovest is most evident
>
> (10)

whom Burghley, no less than Shakespeare, is imploring to beget an
heir, and whose 'living flowers' many a débutante would prefer to his
'painted counterfeit' — a reference, maybe, to Hilliard's miniature.
The sheer physical beauty

> Such heavenly touches ne'er touched earthly faces . . .
>
> (17)

The poet speaks of the 'buds of marjoram' which had 'stolen' his hair,
and Dover Wilson observed that these more resemble Herbert's
close curls than Southampton's dangling tresses. But the difference
between a close curl and a flowing ringlet is a doubtful peg on which
to support a theory. Here is the youth with everything before him

> Now stand you on the top of happy hours
>
> (16)

and the feminine streak in his character legible in his features

> A woman's face with Nature's own hand painted . . .
> Which steals men's eyes and women's souls amazeth . . .
>
> (20)

The boy of noble birth whose qualities

> Entitled in thy parts do crownèd sit
>
> (37)

and make him an easy target for temptation

> For still temptation follows where thou art
>
> (41)

the

> Lascivious grace in whom all ill well shows
>
> (40)

but not saving him from the *mauvaises langues* of those equally lascivious, though less privileged and gifted

> That thou art blamed shall not be thy defect,
> For slander's mark was ever yet the fair
>
> (70)

in fine, what the world would describe as an attractive and rather spoilt young man

> You to your beauteous blessings add a curse,
> Being fond on praise, which makes your praises worse . . .
>
> (84)

Of his 'inconsistency' and 'sensual fault' there will be more to say, but enough has been said to confirm his resemblance to everything we know of Southampton.

Once Mary Fitton had been disqualified, all hope was abandoned of identifying the Dark Lady until Dr Rowse claimed to have run her to earth, quite by accident, in the Bodleian Library. On 13 May 1597, a woman called Emilia Lanier came to consult the well-known astrologer, Simon Forman. She was twenty-seven years old, the daughter of Baptist Bassano, one of the Queen's Italian musicians, and his English wife. For some years she had been the mistress of Lord Hunsdon, later the Lord Chamberlain, by whom she had a son; and in 1593 she had married Will Lanier, also a musician, on whose behalf she wished to consult the astrologer. He noted her very dark complexion, and as time went on formed a pretty low opinion of her. Hunsdon had maintained his own company of players from 1564, to which it appears James Burbage had once belonged, and when the new company was founded in 1594, it was named after the office which he then held. Thus the evidence collected by Dr Rowse from Forman's diary, and other sources, tells us that Emilia Lanier, at the time when Shakespeare might be supposed to have met her, was married, of a musical family and modest birth, promiscuous, on the fringe both of theatrical and noble society, dark-complexioned, and twenty-three years old.

Critics have not been slow to point out the gaps in Dr Rowse's confident conjecture; and indeed, taken by itself, it fails to indicate any connexion with either Shakespeare or his friend. For this we must turn to the *Sonnets* themselves. But it is interesting to note that Dover Wilson, who was no longer alive to enter the controversy — if he had been, the correspondence columns of *The Times* would have made lively reading — himself imagined a Dark Lady very similar to Dr Rowse's candidate[1]

> The probability is that she was a woman of his (Shakespeare's) own class and, one fancies, of much about his age. She was a married woman, and there is more than a hint that she had not only broken her 'bed-vows' for Shakespeare's sake (152-3) but was at times open to the charge of promiscuity (135-5; 137-6; 142-8). Yet she was certainly no common courtesan. If sonnet 128 be not mere flattery, she could play and . . . probably sing charmingly.

Dover Wilson acquits her of being a courtesan; he would perhaps have agreed with Dr Rowse that she was a 'cocotte'.

So what do the *Sonnets* tell us? Unambiguously, that she was dark

> In the old age black was not counted fair,
> Or if it were, it bore not beauty's name;
> But now is black beauty's successive heir,
> And beauty slander'd with a bastard shame . . .
>
>   (127)

Worth noting, too, that Emilia Lanier was the only woman to be so described among Forman's dubious clientèle. Then that she was musical

> How oft, when, though, my music, music play'st,
> Upon that blessèd wood whose motion sounds
> With thy swift fingers, when thou gently sway'st
> The wiry concord that mine ear confounds
>
>   (128)

reminding us once again of how much music meant to Shakespeare. The following lines tell us that she was promiscuous

> Do I envy those jacks that nimble leap
> To kiss the tender inward of thy hand
> Whilst my poor lips, which should that harvest reap
> At the wood's boldness by thee blushing stand?

With its further reference to the 'dancing chips', and her fingers that 'walk' over them 'with gentle gait', the picture is extraordinarily vivid; the poet dumb with infatuation, and the gallants competing for her favours, all clustered round the harpsichord. Later she is described as 'the wide world's commonplace' and 'the bay where all men ride' (137). But the most substantial — if not coercive — evidence for Dr Rowse's theory is to be found in the two sonnets where Shakespeare plays with a wry, lubricious sarcasm on the meaning of 'Will' to Elizabethan ears. Bearing in mind that Emilia was married to a man called 'Will', and that the poet accuses her of

[1] A. L. Rowse, *Shakespeare's Sonnets* (1973), p. 49.

breaking her 'bed-vow', we can allow that here the scent becomes hotter

> Whoever hath her wish, thou has thy will,
> And will to boot, and Will in overplus . . .

(135)

In plain English, the lady has her own sex, her husband's, and Will Shakespeare's — not to mention a good many other people's as well. Emilia Lanier at least qualifies to sit for an examination in which she is the sole competitor.

We are left with the problem of 'Mr W.H.'. Much hangs on the meaning of 'begetter', Dover Wilson affirming that this cannot be understood in the sense of 'getting hold of', since no other example of such use exists in Elizabethan literature. To this Dr Rowse replied by quoting Hamlet's advice to the players: 'You must acquire and beget a temperance that may give it smoothness' (III, i, 8), where the association of the word with 'acquire' would appear to give it a similar sense. He supports this explanation by reminding us that 'W.H.' were the initials of Sir William Harvey whom the Countess of Southampton had married *en troisième noce.* To the objection that Thorpe would not have addressed a Knight as 'Mr', he tells us that this was common practice, and that Lady Southampton regularly referred to her second husband, Sir Thomas Heneage, as 'Master Heneage', whereas this would have been unthinkable in the case of a Peer. Lady Southampton had died in 1607, leaving all her household possessions to Sir William Harvey, and by 1609 when the *Sonnets* were published Harvey had married a young wife. This might well explain Thorpe's hope that he would enjoy 'all happiness and that eternity promised by our ever-living poet' — in other words, the posterity which Shakespeare had promised to his friend, if only he would get himself a wife. Nothing more likely than that Harvey had discovered the *Sonnets* among everything else that was left to him; and since fifteen years had passed since the events described in them, that he thought no harm would come of giving them to the world. In any case he would earn a fulsome Dedication.

2

C. S. Lewis wrote that 'In certain senses of the word "love" Shakespeare is not so much our best as our only love poet.' This is true in so far as he raised the love of one man to another on to a level where service is perfect freedom, and where, as Lewis put it, the 'transference of the whole self into another self without the demand for a return' had 'hardly a precedent in profane literature'. Shakespeare's friend is the god of his idolatry, and in the poems he inspires the categories of sacred and profane are transcended. Yet that is less than the whole story, for here too is the Dark Night of the senses and a premonition of the day when

> Love converted from the thing it was
> Shall reasons find of settled gravity . . .

                                                             (49)

Many of the poems are sublime; some are frankly sensual; one or two are bitterly or playfully obscene. 'The expense of spirit in a waste of shame' is set in tragic opposition to 'the marriage of true minds'. Idolatry and degradation, frustration and fulfilment, lust and satiety, inspiration and obsession, humility that is never servile and pride that is never presumptuous, answer each other in harmony or in discord according as one or other of the poet's 'two loves' possesses him. In this sense also there is nothing to compare with the *Sonnets* in profane literature. The light they shed upon the poet himself is so blinding that it puts the other *dramatis personae* of the story in the shade, and makes their identity a matter of secondary importance.

One or two general considerations are first of all in place. It should be superfluous by now to insist that Shakespeare was in no sense what is generally understood by a homosexual. Everything we know about his life, or can deduce from his writings — and not least from the *Sonnets* — attests the contrary. A man who is inclined to pederasty — whether he practises it or not — does not beseech the object of his affections to get married, or allow his conscience to torment him because he has committed adultery. Shakespeare was sexed — perhaps over-sexed — in the normal way. That he had a feminine strain in his make-up is nothing to the point; so have most men of imagination. That his feelings were more deeply engaged in friendship than most other people's feelings in physical desire merely proves that he was not like other people — a fact that we knew already. Physical encounter, to be distinguished from physical congress, was natural to men of that time. When Erasmus came to England in the reign of Henry VIII he remarked that Englishmen were for ever kissing each other.

A constant theme in the *Sonnets* is the tyranny of Time, which is generally given a capital letter, and Sonnet 123 is addressed to it. Time is 'injurious', 'wasteful', and 'never resting'; we read of his 'fell hand', 'scythe', 'fickle glass', and 'thievish progress to eternity'. The poet asks

> O how shall summer's honey breath hold out
> Against the wreckful siege of battering days,
> When rocks impregnable are not so stout,
> Nor gates of steel so strong but Time decays?
> O fearful meditation! where, alack,

Shall Time's best jewel from Time's chest lie hid?
Or what strong hand can hold his swift foot back?
Or who his spoil of beauty can forbid?

The poet answers the question in the concluding lines of the same sonnet

O, none, unless this miracle have might,
That in black ink my love may still shine bright

(65)

and again

Yet do thy worst, old Time: despite thy wrong,
My love shall in my verse ever live young.

(19)

Shakespeare's confidence in the immortality of his verse is not to be separated from its immediate object

Who will believe my verse in time to come
If it were filled with your most high deserts? . . .
But were some child of yours alive that time,
You should live twice, in it and in my rhyme.

(17)

He thus predicts a dual immortality

Nor shall Death brag thou wander'st in his shade
When in eternal lines to time thou grow'st:
So long as men can breathe, or eyes can see
So long lives this and this gives life to thee

and yet again

O let my books be then the eloquence
And dumb presagers of my speaking breast . . .

(23)

With an extraordinary abnegation the poet gives to his friend the credit for a fame which otherwise seems hardly to have preoccupied him at all. Later on he will plead guilty to

All frailties that besiege all kinds of blood

but vanity, the besetting sin of writers, was not one of them.

In the first group of sonnets — 1 to 26 — the poet plays exquisite variations on a single theme; the boy must marry that he may beget a son. In spite of his general popularity — 'beloved of many' — Shakespeare's affection is reciprocated

Presume not on thy heart when mine is slain;
Thou gavest me thine, not to give back again.

(22)

Then happy I, that love and am beloved
Where I may not remove or be removed.

(25)

The tone is ardent, and goes far beyond literary convention. It seems as if Shakespeare, in the presence of his friend, suffers something like 'first night' nerves

As an unperfect actor on the stage,
Who with his fear is put beside his part,
Or some fierce thing replete with too much rage,
Whose strength's abundance weakens his own heart;
So I, for fear of trust, forget to say
The perfect ceremony of love's rite,
And in mine own love's strength seem to decay
O'ercharged with burthen of mine own love's right.

(23)

He cannot help feeling the social gulf which patronage, and even reciprocated love, are unable to bridge

Let those who are in favour with their stars
Of public honour and proud titles boast,
Whilst I, whom fortune of such triumph bars,
Unlook'd for joy in that I honour most.

(25)

He is still 'a poor player that struts and frets his hour upon the stage'; and when the stage — such as it is — takes him away from London, he feels his 'outcast state' even more acutely

Wishhing me like to one more rich in hope,
Featured like him, like him with friends possessed,
Desiring this man's art and that man's scope,
With what I most enjoy contented least

(29)

as if, heaven knows, he did not have enough! The poet, like his patron, had been standing 'on the top of happy hours', but absence strains their relationship. The Dark Lady was hovering around Southampton House, and seized her opportunity. Some have thought Sonnets 33 to 36 misplaced, since they seem more naturally to belong to the group she dominates. There is here no conflict of conscience, no failure of fidelity

Yet him for this my love no whit disdaineth
Suns of the world may stain where heaven's sun staineth . . .

(33)

The poet has done no more than compare what has happened to the 'region cloud' which has masked the sun of his adoration. The next sonnet indicates some repentance on the patron's part, but Shakespeare is deeply hurt

> Though thou repent, yet I have still the loss;
> The offender's sorrow lends but weak relief
> To him that bears the strong offence's cross . . .

Nevertheless there is no limit to his forgiveness

> Ah, but those tears are pearls which thy love sheds
> And they are rich and ransom all ill deeds
>
> (34)

and in the following stanza he admits

> Such civil war is in my love and hate
> That I an accessory needs must be
> To that sweet thief which sourly robs from me
>
> (35)

and in Sonnet 36 he suggests that his own reputation has been hurt by his association with the woman they have both enjoyed

> I may not evermore acknowledge thee,
> Lest my bewailéd guilt should do thee shame,
> Nor thou with public kindness honour me,
> Unless thou take that honour from thy name.

The cloud passes, and even absence gives him leave

> To entertain the time with thoughts of love . . .
>
> (39)

The theft of his mistress no longer rankles

> Take all my loves, my love, yea, take them all

even though

> Lascivious grace, in whom all ill well shows,
> Kill me with spites; yet we must not be foes

and he cannot quite forget

> Those pretty wrongs that liberty commits
> When I am sometime absent from thy heart

and if his friend had felt in the mood for a love affair

> Ay me! but yet thou might'st my seat forbear

for he had broken a 'twofold truth'

> Hers, by thy beauty tempting her to thee,
> Thine, by thy beauty being false to me.
>
> (41)

In Sonnet 42, Shakespeare exercises all his casuistry to console himself

> That thou hast her, it is not all my grief,

And yet it may be said I loved her dearly;
That she hath thee, is of my wailing chief,
A loss in love that touches me more nearly . . .
But here's the joy: my friend and I are one;
Sweet flattery! then she loves but me alone.

Nevertheless he had learned that the very qualities he admired in his friend will always make him 'the prey of every vulgar thief' (48). During this 'sad interim' of absence, Shakespeare knows that he will fill his 'hungry eyes even till they wink with fullness', and the difference of status puts the poet at a disadvantage. There are times, at Southampton House maybe, when he is kept waiting — in the ante-room if not in the corridor

Being your slave, what should I do but tend
Upon the hours and times of your desire?
I have no precious time at all to spend,
Nor services to do till you require . . .

(57)

In the companion sonnet to this (58) he speaks of 'being at your beck'

Be where you list, your charter is so strong
That you yourself may privilege your time
To what you will

and Shakespeare must wait, 'though waiting so be hell'. His friend may have shed a few crocodile tears, but the reciprocal rapture has faded beyond recall.

After what seems to have been a short, and emotionally unsatisfying, stay in London, the poet is again on tour, and wonders as he lies awake in some provincial lodging

Is it thy spirit that thou send'st from thee
So far from home into my deeds to pry,
To find out shames and idle hours in me,
The scope and tenour of thy jealousy?
O, no! thy love, though much, is not so great . . .

(61)

Travelling round the country he might have seen the wreck of the monasteries

When sometime lofty towers I see down-razed
And brass eternal slave to mortal rage

and noting this

interchange of state
Or state itself confounded to decay;
Ruin hath taught me thus to ruminate
That Time will come and take my love away . . .

(64)

He is increasingly worried by the way tongues are wagging about him

> Then, churls, their thoughts, although their eyes were kind,
> To thy fair flower add the rank smell of weeds:
> But why thy odour matcheth not thy show,
> The soil is this, that thou dost common grow . . .
>
>   (69)

A note of sadness and apprehension creeps in; when he is dead

> Nay, if you read this line, remember not
> The hand that writ it; for I love you so
> That I in your sweet thoughts would be forgot,
> If thinking on me then should make you woe.
>
>   (71)

How often, one asks oneself, did Southampton read these lines
before they were published? Or were they left to moulder in that
labyrinth of a house until Sir William Harvey, maybe, brought them
along to Thomas Thorpe? Gratitude does not seem to have been a
mark of Southampton's character. Strange that we should have no
record of what he — or Herbert either for the matter of that —
thought of Shakespeare. 'The man Shakespeare', on a visit to Wilton
with *As You Like It*, is all that has come down to us. Shakespeare
already feels himself old at twenty-nine; and the thought of death —
faced, as we saw, in *Romeo and Juliet*, and reinforced by the loss of
so many friends — continuously haunts him

> In me thou see'st the glowing of such fire,
> That on the ashes of his youth doth lie,
> As the death-bed whereon it must expire,
> Consumed with that which it was nourish'd by . . .
>
>   (73)

One is almost ashamed that so great a man as Shakespeare should be
helplessly dependent on a youth who was at times too busy or too
indifferent to notice him

> Now counting best to be with you alone,
> Then better'd that the world may see my pleasure;
> Sometime all full with feasting on your sight,
> And by and by clean starvéd for a look
> Possessing or pursuing no delight
> Save what is had or must from you be took . . .
>
>   (75)

He might be writing something else but sonnets, but he has no will to

>   glance aside
> To new-found methods and to compounds strange

though he was to find them soon enough when this crisis was over

> O, know, sweet love, I always write of you,
> And you and love are still my argument.
>
> (76)

The reason for his friend's blowing hot and cool now becomes
apparent. Another 'alien pen' is soliciting, and winning, his patronage

> But now my gracious numbers are decay'd,
> And my sick Muse doth give another place.
>
> (79)

We have seen that the 'alien pen' was pretty certainly Marlowe's.
There were good reasons for this. Marlowe was at the height of his
fame, and better known than Shakespeare. Also he was homosexual,
and Southampton was ambivalent. There may well have been more
to the relationship than flattery on one side and patronage on the
other. Shakespeare reacts to the rivalry with a resurgence of belief in
the immortality of his own contribution to it

> Your monument shall be my gentle verse,
> Which eyes not yet created shall o'er-read;
> And tongues to be your being shall rehearse
> When all the breathers of this world are dead . . .
>
> (81)

He understands the temptation

>   to seek anew
> Some fresher stamp of the time-bettering days . . .
>
> (82)

Nevertheless

> There lives more life in one of your fair eyes
> Than both your poets can in praise devise.
>
> (83)

He does not question the rival poet's ability, and even speaks of his
own Muse as 'tongue-tied'

> While comments of your praise, richly compiled,
> Reserve their character with golden quill,
> And precious phrase by all the Muses filed
> I think good thoughts, whilst others write good words.
> And, like unletter'd clerk, still cry 'Amen'
> To every hymn that able spirit affords,
> In polish'd form of well refinéd pen.
>
> (85)

Marlowe was then at work on *Hero and Leander,* and if he had taken
Southampton as his model one can understand that the model was
well satisfied with the likeness

> His body was as straight as Circe's wand,

> Jove might have sipped out nectar from his hand.
> Even as delicious meat is to the taste,
> So was his neck in touching, and surpass'd
> The whites of Pelop's shoulder. I could tell ye,
> How smooth his breast was, and how white his belly.
>
> (61-6)

These were not the terms in which Shakespeare wrote to his friend, and of course it is only supposition that his friend inspired them. But then we stumble abruptly on the past tense and the full stop

> *Was* it the proud full sail of his great verse?

and the following allusion to Marlowe's dabbling in the occult — so often the atheist's substitute for faith — confirms an identity hardly beyond dispute

> Was it his spirit, by spirits taught to write
> Above a mortal pitch that struck me dead?
> No, neither he, nor his compeers by night
> Giving him aid, my verse astonishéd . . .
> But when your countenance fill'd up his line,
> Then lack'd I matter; that enfeebled mine.
>
> (86)

Sudden death had put an end to the rivalry, and Shakespeare's Muse — her tongue now loosened — was free to sing again, though not quite as she had before.

In the next group of sonnets the reproachful note, both to himself and to his friend, is recurrently sounded. The poet speaks of

> The injuries that to myself I do

and declares that he

> can set down a story
> Of faults conceal'd wherein I am attainted
>
> (88)

> and in my tongue
> Thy sweet beloved name no more shall dwell,
> Lest I, too much profane, should do it wrong,
> And haply of our old acquaintance tell.
>
> (89)

Things are going badly with him

> Now, while the world is bent my deeds to cross . . .
>
> (90)

His friend is once more evasive

> But do thy worst to steal thyself away

but even so

> Thou may'st be false, and yet I know it not
>
> (92)

and the *mauvaises langues* are still at work

> Making lascivious comments on thy sport . . .
>
> (95)

Yet admiration is always there to counteract them

> Rise, resty Muse, my love's sweet face survey,
> If Time have any wrinkle graven there
>
> (101)

though the words no longer come so easily

> O, blame me not, if I no more can write
>
> (103)

for all that his love remains

> Still constant in a wondrous excellence.
>
> (105)

> Even as when first I hallowed thy fair name . . .
>
> (108)

Once again he is touring the provinces, and morally at the end of his tether

> Alas! 'tis true I have gone here and there,
> And made myself a motley to the view,
> Gored mine own thoughts, sold cheap what is most dear,
> Made old offences of affections new . . .

But this must stop

> Mine appetite I never more will grind
> On newer proof to try an older friend . . .
>
> (110)

Fortune is to blame

> That did not better for my life provide
> Than public means which public manners breeds
>
> (111)

if only, that is to say, she had cast him for any other role but that of a strolling player. He is quite aware of the obloquy

> Which vulgar scandal stamp'd upon my brow
> For what care I who calls me well or ill
> So you *o'er-green* my bad, my good allow . . .
>
> (112)

Robert Greene is lately dead, but his slanderous tongue still bites from beyond the grave. At this point the Dark Lady returns, though not as yet explicitly, to cast her shadow over 'the marriage of true minds'. Shakespeare confesses that

> To bitter sauces did I frame my feeling
>
> (118)

and exclaims

> What potions have I drunk of Siren tears
> Distill'd from limbecks foul as hell within . . .
> How have mine eyes out of their spheres been fitted
> In the distraction of this madding fever!
>
> (119)

He looks back to the time when his friend has stolen his mistress; now his own infidelities make him the debtor

> That you were once unkind befriends me now,
> And for that sorrow which I then did feel
> Needs must I under my transgression bow,
> Unless my nerves were brass or hammer'd steel.
> For if you were by my unkindness shaken,
> As I, by yours, you've pass'd a hell of time;
> And I, a tyrant, have no leisure taken
> To weigh how once I suffer'd in your crime.
>
> (120)

He makes no excuses, but still can ask

> For why should others' false adulterate eyes
> Give salutation to my sportive blood . . .
> No, I am that I am, and they that level
> At my abuses reckon up my own
>
> (121)

and then in Sonnet 127 she is brought before us, just as we have known her for the past four hundred years, 'familiar' and yet still for many people, *pace* Dr Rowse, 'unidentifiable'.[1] Shakespeare's itinerary in the *Sonnets* is the reverse of Dante's in *La Divina Commedia*. Setting out from Paradise, he has passed through Purgatory, and now stands on the brink of an Inferno from which no Beatrice is in sight to liberate him

> For since each hand hath put on nature's power
> Fairing the foul with art's false borrow'd face,
> Sweet beauty hath no name, no holy bower,
> But is profaned, if not lives in disgrace.
> Therefore my mistress' eyes are raven black . . .

[1] T. S. Eliot, *Little Gidding*.

He is caught with his eyes open

> The expense of spirit in a waste of shame
> Is lust in action . . .
> All this the world well knows; yet none knows well
> To shun the heaven that leads men to this hell
>
>   (129)

nor will he contradict, except to himself, those who say

> Thy face hath not the power to make love groan
>
>   (131)

although 'a thousand groans' are the price of his infatuation; and the deepest of them is heaved

> For that deep wound it gives my friend and me!
> Is't not enough to torture me alone,
> But slave to slavery my sweet'st friend must be?
>
>   (133)

Moreover we learn from the next sonnet that it was through his friend that Shakespeare had come to know her

> He learn't but surety-like to write for me

and that she — not unnaturally, given the adventuress that she was — had preferred a coronet to a kind heart. It is not that he admires her looks or her voice — and Shakespeare was susceptible to the voice; 'gentle and low, an excellent thing in woman';[1] nothing in her person invites him

> To any sensual feast with thee alone . . .
>
>   (141)

Her promiscuity is notorious; he knows very well that she has

> Robb'd other beds' revenues of their rents

his cry is that of the semi-repentant sinner since men first discovered they had consciences

> Hate of my sin, grounded on sinful loving
>
>   (142)

and as for conscience

> Love is too young to know what conscience is;
> Yet who knows not conscience is born of love?
>
>   (151)

It is lines such as these that give a universal resonance to a personal dilemma. What holds him is, quite simply, her art in love

[1] *King Lear*, V, ii, 275.

That in the very refuse of thy deeds
There is such strength and warrantise of skill
That, in my mind, thy worst all best exceeds

(150)

and the whole story of Shakespeare, his friend, and their mistress is comprised in the sonnet from which I have taken the title of this chapter

Two loves I have of comfort and despair,
Which like two spirits do suggest me still:
The better angel is a man right fair,
The worser spirit a woman colour'd ill.
To win me soon to hell, my female evil
Tempteth my better angel from my side
And would corrupt my saint to be a devil
Wooing his purity with her foul pride.

(144)

We do not know how it ended, except that in the 'civil war' that tore the poet apart a 'better angel' than Southampton was at last victorious. Shakespeare had touched the heights and depths of passion, and come out on the other side, certainly not unscathed, but with a knowledge of good and evil from which future masterpieces were to be born. It is the alliance of intellect, imagination, and technique, working on the very raw material of personal experience, but never swamped by it, that has secured for the *Sonnets* their unique place in literature. And it speaks much for the poet's resilience that the misery of a divided mind should have been followed by, if it did not coincide with, the composition of a play where, as Puck was presently to proclaim

Jack shall have Jill
Nought shall go ill
The man shall have his mare again, and all shall be well.

(*A.Midsummer Night's Dream*, III, ii, 461-3)

Chapter 6

'Compounds Strange'

1

Shakespeare had told his friend that he had no will to

> glance aside
> To new-found methods and to compounds strange . . .

Nevertheless they were fermenting in his mind, and when they saw the daylight of the stage, or the candlelight of the 'great chamber', they were seen to be 'compounded' of disparate elements which he brought together into a flawless unity. *Love's Labour's Lost* is a gentle satire; *A Midsummer Night's Dream* is an epithalamium. Their points of similarity, both in structure and style, are as evident as their points of difference. Each instructs us that 'the course of true love never did run smooth'. Light-heartedly as Shakespeare carried his knowledge, he knew very well what he was talking about.

It is uncertain which of the two plays was written first, and the question is of little importance. The *Dream* was obviously composed for a wedding, and the occasion of its première has given rise to much speculation. Titania's long speech about the bad weather seems to refer to the severe winter of 1594, and the publication of Spenser's *Epithalamium* in 1595 would have given the poets their cue to ring the wedding bells. The Queen attended the marriage of William Stanley, Earl of Derby, and Lady Elizabeth Vere, the grand-daughter of Lord Burghley and the Queen's god-daughter and maid of honour, on 26 January 1595. Theseus' advice to Hermia not

> To live a barren sister all your life
> Chanting faint hymns to the cold fruitless moon.
> Thrice-blessèd they that master so their blood,
> To undergo such maiden pilgrimage;
> But earthlier happy is the rose distill'd
> Than that which, withering on the virgin thorn,
> Grows, lives, and dies in single blessedness
>
> (I, ii, 72-8)

has been taken, even by so great an authority as Sir Edmund Chambers, as a word in season to Elizabeth. But in spite of the Duke's half-hearted compliments to the single state, it is highly improbable that the Queen would have thanked him for comparing her to a rose 'withering on the virgin thorn'. Moreover, a winter wedding would have been an inappropriate occasion for a 'midsummer night's dream'. We should rather look for a ceremony at which the Queen was *not* known to have been present, and where such indiscreet allusions would not have incurred the reproach, and perhaps the punishment, of *lèse-majesté.* Dr Rowse's suggestion that the play was written for the wedding of the Countess of Southampton to Sir Thomas Heneage, on 2 May 1595, seems much more plausible. Shakespeare was a friend of the house, and the Countess would have been grateful for his pressure on her son to marry. Theseus' reference to 'the rite of May' brings us a good deal nearer to midsummer than the end of January; and his advice to Hermia can more properly be interpreted as a veiled hint to Southampton than a scarcely veiled hint to Elizabeth, who was in any case too old to have taken it.

A Midsummer Night's Dream is the first of Shakespeare's plays that can be described, without qualification, as a masterpiece. If he had written nothing else but this, his place would have been secure on the summit of Parnassus. The 'methods' are as 'new-found' as the 'compounds' are 'strange'. Where another poet might have composed a masque, or devised a pageant, appealing only to the eye and ear, Shakespeare produced a celebration which was also an entertainment. Indeed he produced a play within the play. Pageantry and poetry, dancing and music, fantasy and fun, were all integrated in a dramatic pattern which, as Coleridge wrote, is 'Very Anacreon in perfectness, proportion, grace, and spontaneity', and at the same time 'what wealth, what wild ranging, and yet what compression and condensation of, English fantasy!'[1] We have only to wander a few yards in this wood to realize how far it is from Athens.

Shakespeare began by placing his bridal pair — call them Lady Southampton and Sir Thomas Heneage — actually on the stage in the persons of Theseus and Hippolyta, borrowed for the evening from North's *Plutarch*, and Chaucer's *The Knighte's Tale*. They frame the play, which thus becomes part of the wedding it is designed to celebrate. The poet knew his way, if not about the Court, at least about the circles that frequented it. Philostrate might well have been the Lord Chamberlain of the hour whose business it was (and long remained) to sanction public or private entertainment. The lovers he got from his own imagination — lightly characterized, since they are more like figures in a dance than people in a play, puppets that react according as the puppet-master — blind Cupid — pulls the strings.

[1] *Shakespeare and the Elizabethan Dramatists.*

The Fairies he took from wherever he found them. Oberon, an Oriental figure, from Lord Berners' translation of *Huon of Bordeaux*; Titania from Ovid's *Metamorphoses*

> *dumque ibi perluitur solita Titania lympha*
>
> (III, 173)

and Puck, the earth demon or 'pixy' of Cornish folk-lore, is assimilated to the Robin Goodfellow of whose pranks any boy would have learnt in the nursery. But all this material is transformed — although we may yet see a production of the play in which Oberon is reduced to his original stature of a dwarf. With the exception of the artisans whom Shakespeare knows like his next door neighbour in Henley Street, the characters are seen in a kind of middle distance, or even, as Demetrius sees them

> small and undistinguishable,
> Like far-off mountains turnéd into clouds.
>
> (IV, i, 192-3)

Bottom and his companions do indeed bring us down to earth, but never with a bump; for when Titania embraces that ass's head heaven and earth have kissed each other, the immortal putting on mortality, and the mortal winning through mere innocence the privilege of 'a most rare vision'. Shakespeare had doubtless read in Reginald Scot's *Discovery of Witchcraft* how people smeared with a certain ointment were supposed to acquire the head of a horse or an ass. The story of 'Pyramus and Thisbe' he could have found in Chaucer's *The Legend of Good Women*, and in Golding's translation of Ovid's version from the *Metamorphoses* (IV). The miracle of the play is the fusion of these 'compounds strange', through the alchemy of poetry, and the counterpoint of poetry and prose, into an immaculate work of art; and also into a picture of society where each man has his place, and where the 'lords of misrule', after their interim of mischief, preside over a cosmic harmony.

The drama, however, proceeds from the cosmic discord, and here the new moon will have its large share of responsibility. Othello was to exclaim over the body of his murdered wife

> It is the very error of the moon;
> She comes more near the earth than she was wont
> And makes men mad . . .
>
> (V, ii, 109-11)

Juliet had spoken of

> the inconstant moon
> That monthly changes in her circled orb . . .
>
> (II, ii, 109-10)

The full moon was traditionally the season when men and women were not quite in their right minds, and when pretty well anything might happen. It was an agent of transformation. In the first eighteen lines of the *Dream* it is mentioned three times, and Egeus accuses Lysander of singing at Hermia's window by moonlight

> With feigning voice, verses of feigning love.
>
> (I, i, 31)

Theseus threatens Hermia with claustration in a nunnery if she will not agree to marry Demetrius 'by the next new moon'; and Lysander informs Helena of his intention to escape with Hermia the following night

> when Phoebe doth behold
> Her silver visage in the watery glass
> Decking with liquid pearl the bladed grass . . .
>
> (I, i, 209-11)

Titania is 'ill met by moonlight', and holds the moon responsible for the general arthritis which had followed the winter of 1594

> Therefore the moon, the governess of floods,
> Pale in her anger, washes all the air
> That rheumatic diseases do abound.
>
> (II, i, 124-6)

Oberon — like Shakespeare himself, maybe, at Kenilworth — had seen

> young Cupid's shaft
> Quench'd in the chaste beams of the watery moon
>
> (II, i, 162)

and Titania invites him to watch her 'moonlight revels'. Bottom solves the problem of producing moonlight for the meeting of Pyramus and Thisbe, giving us a clear picture of how and where the play was first produced

> Why, then may you leave a casement of the great chamber window, where we play, open, and the moon may shine in at the casement.
>
> (III, i, 57-9)

Incidentally, this solution might have excited some protest from the audience if, as some critics have supposed, the performance had taken place in January. The moon 'looks with a watery eye' as Titania leads Bottom to her bower, but it fades in the daylight of discovery, and only returns through the open window of the casement, and the mimesis of Starveling's lantern, just a few minutes before the 'iron tongue of midnight hath told twelve'. There would, of course, have been no casement when the play was acted at the

Globe; but Ronald Watkins — long before Peter Brook bettered his instruction — showed how easily the imagery of the *Dream*, alternately concrete and translucent, dispenses it from these accessories.[1] The moon which has presided over the mistakes and the misunderstandings gives place to the

> glimmering light
> By the dead and drowsy fire
>
> (V, i, 398-9)

as Oberon and Titania lead their fairies through the 'hallow'd house'. We have come indoors, and there is now no need for Lysander to 'lie further off'. But the moon in its fullness still shines outside, with only the wolf to 'behowl' it.

This succession of daylight, moonshine, and candlelight illuminates the poet's variations on the themes of appearance and reality. Depth upon depth of meaning underlie the shimmering surface of the play. Hazlitt quoted a 'celebrated person' of his own time — was it Coleridge? — who regarded Shakespeare 'rather as a metaphysician than a poet'. This was putting it too strongly; nevertheless there are metaphysics in the *Dream* if you choose to look for them. In *Romeo and Juliet* Shakespeare had said the last word about one aspect of love; in *A Midsummer Night's Dream* he shows that it is many-faceted and far from simple. It is simple for Theseus, although he had conquered Hippolyta in battle before winning her affections. But Theseus lacks imagination, bracketing 'the lunatic, the lover, and the poet' as seeing what they wish to see whether it is there or not. The relation between truth and imagination is beyond his military mind to fathom. He stands, when the play opens, upon the letter of the law; Hermia must marry Demetrius because her father says she must; to which she replies

> I would my father look'd but with my eyes

and this meets the objection

> Rather your eyes must with his judgment look.
>
> (I, i, 56-7)

We learn presently that Demetrius has already been betrothed to Helena — so love is subject to inconstancy. We learn, too, that Hermia and Helena are such 'sweet play-fellows' that Lysander lets Helena into the secret of his planned elopement. Helena, in her subsequent soliloquy, anticipates Theseus on imagination

> Love looks not with the eyes but with the mind:
> And therefore is wing'd Cupid painted blind . . .
>
> (I, i, 234-5)

[1] *Moonlight at the Globe* (1946).

But why does she encourage Demetrius to follow Hermia into the
wood? Might she not have hoped that 'out of sight' would also be
'out of mind'?

> for this intelligence
> If I have thanks, it is a dear expense;
> But herein mean I to enrich my pain
> To have his sight thither and back again.
>
> (I, i, 248-51)

The love affairs of the immortals are just as complicated; perhaps
more so, since they have become involved with mortality. It is often
overlooked that Hippolyta has been Oberon's 'buskin'd mistress' and
his 'warrior love'; and that Titania has led Theseus

> through the glimmering night
> From Perigenia whom he ravishéd
>
> (II, i, 77-8)

and persuaded him to break at least three other 'bed-vows' into the
bargain. Nevertheless her infidelities are now forgotten, and Oberon
is prepared to give his blessing to a marriage which — like the
marriage of Lady Southampton to Sir Thomas Heneage — can hardly
be called an initiation. The immediate bone of contention is the little
Indian boy whom Titania has brought up, and Oberon demands as
his page. She refuses, and Oberon plots his revenge. But while Puck is
away looking for the 'little western flower', Helena appears on the
heels of Demetrius, her love unrequited in proportion as it is abject.
Oberon, invisible to mortal eyes, takes note of her plight and
instructs Puck on his return to drop the juice of 'love-in-idleness' into
the eyes of Demetrius whom he will recognize

> By the Athenian garments he has on . . .
>
> (II, ii, 264)

Oberon is solicitous for other people's love affairs, but he does not
know that Lysander is also wandering in the wood, similarly dressed,
and he cannot prevent Puck from mistaking his man. Lysander,
awaking, sees Helena exhausted from her pursuit of Demetrius, and
declares his love for her. The irony of the passage should be noted;
Lysander appeals to reason just when his passion is most un-
reasonable

> The will of man is by his reason sway'd
> And reason says you are the worthier maid.
> Things growing are not ripe until their season:
> So I, being young, till now ripe not to reason . . .
>
> (II, ii, 115-18)

So the figure of the dance takes shape. Helena in love with

Demetrius; Demetrius in love with Hermia; Lysander in love with Helena; and Hermia in love with Lysander.

The appropriate comment comes from Bottom in the following scene: 'and yet, to say the truth, reason and love keep little company together now-a-days.' The point of Bottom's translation is missed unless we realize that in being transformed into an ass, he has also been transformed into a gentleman. He talks to the fairies very much as Theseus might have talked to him — with a patrician charm and condescension

> Good Master Mustardseed, I know your patience well: that same cowardly, giant-like, Ox-beef hath devoured many a gentleman of your house: I promise you your kindred hath made my eyes water ere now. I desire your more acquaintance, good Master Mustardseed.
>
> (III, i, 196-201)

The point is not that Bottom is immediately in love with Titania, but that he is instinctively at home in her entourage. The more intimate 'rarity' of that 'vision' is beyond Shakespeare s discretion, and Bottom's eloquence, to narrate. The joke is against Titania. If it is he who is made to look an ass, it is she who is made to look a fool.

When Demetrius appears in pursuit of Helena, Oberon realizes that Puck has laid the love-juice on the wrong pair of eyes, and Puck's excuse confirms Bottom's observation

> Then fate o'er-rules that, one man holding troth
> A million fail, confounding oath on oath.
>
> (III, ii, 92-3)

It is all very well for him to conclude that

> Lord, what fools these mortals be!
>
> (III, ii, 115)

but immortals too can make mistakes, and there is a power above them that neither can overrule. Oberon, however, does his best, pouring the juice on to the eyes of Demetrius, who wakes to find himself passionately in love with Helena. But this only makes confusion worse confounded, Helena disbelieving so sudden a conversion, and angry with Lysander for breaking his faith with her best friend. With the appearance of Hermia the maze of misunderstanding becomes more intricate, and the lovers cannot escape from it until Lysander has been anointed with 'love-in-idleness'. But this will only be possible when Puck has

> overcast the night . . .
> With drooping fog, as black as Acheron
>
> (III, ii, 356, 358)

and Lysander has fallen asleep, worn out from his desperate blind man's buff with Demetrius. It is a nice point, often escaping notice, that Titania's infatuation with Bottom makes her perfectly willing to give up the Indian boy to Oberon — so easily does one attachment exorcize another.

But there is no time to lose

> For night's swift dragons cut the clouds full fast,
> And yonder shines Aurora's harbinger . . .
>
> (III, ii, 379-80)

The fairies are familiar with the dawn

> I with the morning's love have oft made sport;
> And, like a forester, the groves may tread,
> Even till the eastern gate, all fiery-red,
> Opening on Neptune with fair blessèd beams,
> Turns into yellow gold his salt green streams
>
> (III, ii, 389-93)

but once it has opened, they must vanish into their native empyrean until moonlight and candlelight in conjunction summon them to the 'great chamber'. So Titania must be woken, and fall in love afresh with Oberon, and the last strains of the music he has commanded will hardly have died away before Theseus' hunting horns have warned us that we are now in 'the vaward of the day', and the sleeping lovers will awaken to their right minds. Theseus no longer stands upon the letter of the law, taking his cue from the 'gentle concord' that now reigns between the rival claimants to Egeus' daughter. Bottom, who has slept the soundest, and whose dream has had no taint of nightmare, only wakes up when the others have gone. Alone among them all, he is momentarily disappointed with the daylight; but he is also resolutely realist. 'The play's the thing'; and if Peter Quince will turn his dream into a ballad, he will sing it when the show is over. One way or another, he will 'steal the curtain'. The others were still only half awake; it is the weaver with the ass's head, who has slept with the Queen of the Fairies, that has his wits about him

> The eye of man hath not heard, the ear of man hath not seen, man's hand is not able to taste, his tongue to conceive, nor his heart to report, what my dream was.
>
> (IV, i, 217-20)

Is the analogy accidental between this and the way a mystic, more accurately suiting the verb to the substantive, might communicate his foretaste of the Beatific Vision? Like all genuine mystics, Nick Bottom was a highly practical person; he had his feet firmly on the ground, and just as firmly on the boards.

If Theseus could enjoy the feasts of royalty, he had also suffered its fatigues. In the following lines it is easy to recognize an

Elizabethan 'progress', past or present

> Where I have come, great clerks have purposéd
> To greet me with premeditated welcome;
> Where I have seen them shiver and look pale,
> Make periods in the midst of sentences,
> Throttle their practised accents in their fears,
> And, in conclusion, dumbly have broke off,
> Not paying me a welcome. Trust me, sweet,
> Out of this silence yet I picked a welcome.
>
> (V, i, 93-9)

How many Public Orators might have renewed their blushes if these words had fallen upon their ears! Moreover Philostrate had attended a rehearsal of 'Pyramus and Thisbe', and assures his master that it is 'nothing, nothing in the world'. But there is more than a touch of Malvolio in Philostrate, and Theseus insists on seeing a performance conceived in strict accordance with the principles of Berthold Brecht. For 'Pyramus and Thisbe' is a masterly exercise in alienation, set in a play where poetry and drama have combined to create illusion. Not only does the Prologue 'tell all', like the Dumb Show in *Hamlet*, but the actors 'present' their parts before they start to act them. There is a whole breviary of theatrical aesthetic in the exchange between Theseus and Hippolyta

> *Hip.* This is the silliest stuff that ever I heard.
> *The.* The best in this kind are but shadows; and the
> worst are no worse, if imagination amend them.
> *Hip.* It must be your imagination then, and not theirs.
> *The.* If we imagine no worse of them than they of
> themselves, they may pass for excellent men.
>
> (V, i, 212-19)

Shakespeare put a very modest price on his profession. Although these happy amateurs have freely addressed their audience, only Puck, in his last speech, addresses the audience in the 'great chamber'

> Give me your hands, if we be friends . . .
>
> (V, i, 426)

It is pleasant to think of Theseus and Hippolyta coming out through the double doors below the minstrels' gallery and shaking hands with the bride and bridegroom of the hour. Assuming that the story of the *Sonnets* is much as I have outlined it here, the extraordinary fact remains that the Shakespeare who wrote *A Midsummer Night's Dream* was a self-evidently happy man. Like all creative genius, working at this pitch of incandescence, the fact defies explanation. As Bernard Levin recently asked about Mozart: 'Where did it come from?' We do not know.

2

Puck's 'Lord, what fools these mortals be!' might have been applied
to Hazlitt when he declared *Love's Labour's Lost* to be Shakespeare's
worst play — and here Coleridge says nothing to give him the lie.
Fortunately, in the theatre, *Love's Labour's* has at last been won. It
appeared in Quarto in 1598 'as presented before her Highness this
last Christmas. Newly corrected and augmented by W. Shakespeare'
— which showed that it was not a new play. In the same year a
certain Robert Tofte described how he had been taken to see it by
his wife, much against his will. But having come to yawn, he
remained to applaud — with reservations

> Each actor played in cunning wise his part,
> But chiefly those entrapped in Cupid's snare;
> Yet all was feigned, 'twas not from the heart,
> They seemed to grieve, but yet they felt no care:
> 'Twas I that grief (indeed) did bear in breast,
> The others did but make a show in jest.[1]

This was sounder criticism than Hazlitt's; *Love's Labour's* does not
tug at the heart strings, nor was it intended to. A play of wit rather
than humour, it was the closest Shakespeare ever came to an
intellectual comedy. Both foreign and domestic affairs gave it topical
point. Henry of Navarre had just brought the wars of religion to an
end, but he had been a popular protagonist on the Protestant side,
and the Church took its time in lifting the ban of excommunication.
Moreover he had won victories in alliance with England against
Spain, and that would have increased his popularity. Since he had
broken his Protestant oath to achieve power as well as peace, and
since his love affairs were the talk of the town on both sides of the
Channel, there was fun to be had from a King of Navarre breaking his
oath to forswear the sight of women — if only for three years. We
catch an echo of his sensible and cynical statecraft from the presence
of Dumaine among his entourage; for Dumaine (Mayenne) had been
Governor of Paris under the League. Henry had been married to
Marguerite de Valois, daughter of Catherine de Medici, but they had
long been separated when, in 1578, she met him at Nérac in
Aquitaine, with a retinue of ladies-in-waiting. This may well have
given Shakespeare a hint for the visit of the Princess of France on her
diplomatic mission.

So much for the light context of foreign affairs. But the play's
satire bites deeper in its ridicule of Lyly and the University Wits,
whose sterile cerebration went against Shakespeare's grain. Ford
Madox Ford put it neatly when he wrote that

[1] *Alba; or the Month's Mind of a Melancholy Lover* (1598).

With *Amadis de Gaul* or *Euphues* ... you are for ever thinking of the author ... The prose and even the blank verse of that age sparkled with trope, metaphor, image, simile, play upon words, conceits and every type of verbal felicity, so that the last thing that comes to the mind in the case of almost any work of that age is the subject treated of.[1]

There is plenty of all this in *Love's Labour's Lost* — too much indeed for twentieth century taste — but Shakespeare is laughing up his sleeve; and scarcely have the reading party taken their oath than they get the red light from Costard's single immortal line: 'Such is the simplicity of man to hearken after the flesh.' Berowne, taking his name from the Marshal de Biron, Henry's liaison officer with Essex at the siege of Rouen in 1591, is not only the 'Shakespearean man' *par excellence*; he is as near as we shall find to a portrait of Shakespeare himself. A reluctant convert to provisional celibacy in the 'heyday of the blood', he goes along with the others out of good fellowship rather than good faith. Shakespeare may not have known much about Cambridge, but passing through Oxford on his way to Stratford he would have caught the whiff of the Common Rooms. No doubt he would have liked to be a lord, as he later became a man of property, but there is no evidence that he had longed to be an undergraduate. 'What is the end of study?' Berowne asks the King. And to the reply

Why, that to know, which else we should not know

he answers

Things hid and barr'd, you mean, from common sense?
(I, i, 56-7)

Very well, then; he will study

To know the thing I am forbid to know
As thus — to study where I well may dine,
When I to feast expressly am forbid;
Or study where to meet some mistress fine,
When mistresses from common sense are hid ...
Small have continual plodders ever won
Save base authority from others' books ...
(I, i, 60-64; 86-7)

But Berowne argues with such eloquence that he earns the King's rejoinder, as the dramatist himself might have earned it

How well he's read, to reason against reading!
(I, i, 94)

Shakespeare was a remarkably well-read man, and none the worse for not having read for a degree.

[1] *The English Novel* (1930), pp. 61-2.

In fact, of course, the gentlemen of Navarre have no time to open any of the books they have borrowed or purloined from the Bibliothèque Nationale, for the play is a sequence of interruptions. With the entrance of Dull, the constable — a first sketch for Dogberry — bearing a letter from Don Armado, and Costard in custody, we get the delicate suggestion of a great park and a reference to the 'curious-knotted' garden which adjoins the royal mansion. We might be at Knole or Compton Wynyates. But Don Armado has strayed over from the other side of the Pyrenees; a skit on contemporary and high-falutin *hispanidad*. Here was an exotic brand of pedantry, and Don Armado is first cousin to Don Quixote. The King describes him as

> A man in all the world's new fashion planted,
> That hath a mint of phrases in his brain . . .
> A man of compliments, whom right and wrong
> Have chose as umpire of their mutiny . . .
>
> (I, i, 165-8; 169-70)

In the event Armado umpires with such impartiality that, having accused Costard of consorting with Jaquenetta, he subsequently falls in love with her himself. His page, Moth, stands in relation to him very much as Feste in *Twelfth Night* stands to Olivia, or the Fool in *Lear* to his master — for the deflation of folly is the prerogative of Shakespearean Fools. Don Armado has been allowed to join the reading party, and the King hands Costard over to him while Jaquenetta stays at the lodge where she is employed as a dairy-maid. Don Armado is the first to break his oath — and the more blatantly because he falls in love below the station on which he sets such store

> I do affect the very ground, which is base, where her shoe which is baser, guided by her foot, which is basest, doth tread
>
> (I, ii, 172-4)

but when he gets down to brass tacks with Jaquenetta in a brief aside, magniloquence gives place to monosyllables

> *Arm.* Maid
> *Jaq.* Man
> *Arm.* I will visit thee at the lodge
> *Jaq.* That's hereby.
> *Arm.* I know where it is situate.
> *Jaq.* Lord! how wise you are!
> *Arm.* I will tell thee wonders.
> *Jaq.* With that face?
> *Arm.* I love thee
> *Jaq.* So I heard you say.
>
> (I, ii, 138-47)

This, at least, is real; and rather less ridiculous than the sonnet it will presently inspire if the 'extemporal god of rhyme' comes to the Don's assistance.

The arrival of the Princess and her ladies, and Boyet, her liaison-officer and elder statesman, brings an immediate change of style. Gone are the elaborate rhymes and euphuisms with which Shakespeare satirizes Lyly in his own idiom. She speaks in the fluent and finished blank verse of the poet's earlier prosody. Berowne now meets his Dark Lady, though in character, if not in looks, she is less dark than she had been in real life. In fact, they had met before, having 'danced in Brabant once', and she remembers his good humour

> a merrier man
> Within the limit of becoming mirth
> I never spent an hour's talk withal . . .

> > > > (II, i, 66-8)

They engage at once in a battle of wits that anticipates Benedick and Beatrice; the Princess's diplomatic business is speedily and successfully dispatched; and the King will lodge them in a pavilion until it can be formally settled on the morrow. While Berowne and Rosaline have exchanged wits, Dumain and Longaville are ready to exchange eyes with Katharine and Maria. But the ladies are giving nothing away.

Armado now employs Costard as his courier with a letter to Jaquenetta, giving him a 'remuneration' for his pains, and Costard — his affections now transferred to a lady called Frances — cheerfully goes on his errand. By chance, which proves unlucky, he meets Berowne who gives him a letter to Rosaline — for the ladies will presently be hunting in the park — and with it a shilling, which is better than Armado's 'remuneration' of a penny. Berowne is left to descant with a wry, robust humour on his susceptibility to

> This wimpled, whining, purblind, wayward boy;
> This senior-junior, giant-dwarf, Dan Cupid

> > > > (III, i, 169-70)

until Shakespeare himself takes over the character, as both the character and the verse get into their stride, remembering another

> whitely wanton with a velvet brow,
> With two pitch-balls stuck in her face for eyes.

> > > > (III, i, 186-7)

This is some way from Benedick and Beatrice, and also from Rosaline and Berowne when they had danced together in Brabant. Moreover, there is an odd discrepancy between the Berowne who was unwilling to take the oath because it might keep him from a mistress, and the Berowne who can now exclaim incredulously

> What! I love! I sue? I seek a wife.

But this is Cupid's revenge for neglecting

> his almighty dreadful little might.
> Well, I will love, write, sigh, pray, sue and groan
> Some men must love my lady, and some Joan
> > (III, i, 181 *et seq.*)

or — he might have added — Jaquenetta.

Shakespeare cannot resist yet another glimpse of the chase, as the Princess and her train enter with bows and arrows to shoot the deer that browse among the thickets of the park. The analogy with Dan Cupid would not have been lost upon the audience. It is only a glimpse, but enough to remind us where we are supposed to be — among the lower foothills of the Pyrenees

> Was that the King, that spurr'd his horse so hard
> Against the steep uprising of the hill?
> > (IV, i, 1-2)

but the sport of Kings is interrupted by the entrance of Costard bearing his two letters. Not being able to read — and no great wonder in that — he hands over to the Princess the one addressed to Jaquenetta. This gives rise to some delicately bawdy banter between Rosaline and Boyet — more accessible to Elizabethan than to modern ears. We begin to suspect that Berowne was accurate in guessing that his 'whitely wanton' would 'do the deed'.

The dramatist had now reached a point in his play where he must get a second wind. (In the *Dream* there was no need for this; the first one saw him through.) So he introduces two new characters — Holofernes the schoolmaster and Sir Nathaniel the curate — and another stratum of society. We are manifestly back at Stratford with the parson in the pulpit and the pedagogue in the front pew. Dull is with them, and they are talking about the hunt which they have just been watching. Holofernes' pedantry gives Shakespeare a fresh target for his satire. He declares that the Princess has killed a deer; Sir Nathaniel replies that it was 'a buck of the first head'; Holofernes answers in Latin: '*haud credo*'; and Dull rejoins tersely "Twas not a *haud credo*; 'twas a pricket'. Holofernes is shocked at Dull's illiteracy, but Sir Nathaniel excuses him

> Sir, he hath never fed of the dainties that are bred in a book; he hath not eat paper, as it were; he hath not drunk ink; his intellect is not replenished; he is only an animal, only sensible in the duller parts.
> > (IV, ii, 24-7)

We are left to infer that, beside Holofernes, he is none the worse for

his abstinence; and after much further talk he sticks to his point that
"twas a pricket'. If Holofernes sits under Sir Nathaniel in the pulpit,
the roles are evidently reversed elsewhere

> Sir (says Sir Nathaniel) I praise the Lord for you: and so may my
> parishioners: for their sons are well tutored by you, and their daughters
> profit very greatly under you; you are a good member of the common-
> wealth.
>
> (IV, ii, 75-9)

Perhaps Shakespeare had second thoughts about Thomas Jenkins?

Costard then returns with Jaquenetta to whom he has given
Berowne's letter to Rosaline. She is looking for someone capable of
reading it. Holofernes obliges and tells her to take it to the King.
Berowne enters by himself, with an unfinished sonnet in his hand.
The way he describes in prose the nature of his obsession is a comic
counterpart to the way Shakespeare had described his own obsession
in verse — and also in the shape of sonnets

> I am toiling in a pitch, — pitch that defiles . . . By the Lord, this love is as
> mad as Ajax; it kills sheep; it kills me . . . O, but her eye, — by this light,
> but for her eye, I would not love her; yes for her two eyes.
>
> (IV, iii, 3 *et seq.*)

Add the author of the *Sonnets* to the author of Berowne, and you
have the total Shakespeare at this stage of his development. This
leads up to the masterpiece of high comedy where all four gentlemen
of Navarre are discovered in *flagrant délit* of perjury — for
Jaquenetta has delivered Berowne's sonnet to Rosaline into the
hands of the King; and to Berowne's irresistible speech for the
defence. Shakespeare has seen through the Dark Lady, but he has
also seen beyond her to the creative power of which she is the
defacing image

> Love's feeling is more soft and sensible
> Than are the tender horns of cockled snails:
> Love's tongue proves dainty Bacchus gross in taste:
> For valour, is not Love a Hercules,
> Still climbing trees in the Hesperides?
> Subtle as Spinx; as sweet and musical
> As bright Apollo's lute, strung with his hair;
> And when Love speaks, the voice of all the gods
> Make heaven drowsy with the harmony . . .
>
> (IV, iii, 337-45)

The others rally to this manifesto of romanticism, and it only
remains for them to woo the women they had sworn to renounce.
But first, the women must be entertained.

Holofernes and Sir Nathaniel, with Dull in attendance, have dined
— perhaps a trifle too well. The schoolmaster's strictures on Don

Armado suggest that upper class Englishmen in Shakespeare's time made a point of their mispronunciations, as they do in ours. The Don says 'cauf' for 'calf', 'hauf' for 'half', and 'nebour' for 'neighbour'. No doubt he also said 'wescot' for 'waistcoat', and 'orffer' for 'offer'. The purpose of his visit is to communicate the King's wish that the ladies shall be entertained in the 'posteriors of the day', and Holofernes suggests the Masque of the Nine Worthies. There is a great deal of talk, and when Holofernes observes to Dull that 'thou hast spoken no word all this while', we are not surprised by the constable's reply, 'Nor understood none neither, sir'. There was not much to choose between the pedantry of the dominie and the circumlocution of the Don.

The ladies receive their gifts and love letters, and Rosaline speaks to the Princess very much as the Dark Lady might have spoken to herself. It is not an attractive self-portrait

> That same Biron I'll torture ere I go:
> O that I knew he were but in by the week!
> How I would make him fawn, and beg, and seek,
> And wait the season, and observe the times,
> And spend his prodigal wits in bootless rhymes,
> And shape his service wholly to my heart,
> And make him proud to make me proud that jests!
> So porttaunt[1] -like would I o'ersway his state,
> That he should be my fool, and I his fate.
>
> (V, ii, 60-8)

Boyet brings news that the men are about to return disguised as 'Muscovites or Russians' — subjects always calculated to appeal to an Elizabethan audience — to pursue their several suits. The ladies decide to wear masks and to exchange their distinguishing 'favours', so that Berowne will be making love to the Princess, and the King to Rosaline. The portrait of Boyet should be noted, and it is Berowne who draws it. Note, too, how the verse springs into spontaneity whenever the dramatist is speaking in his own person. Shakespeare was drawn to the aristocracy — and this play shows how easily he moved among them — but he did not romanticize the courtier. We shall meet Boyet again in Osric and Le Beau

> This fellow pecks up wit as pigeons pease,
> And utters it again when God doth please . . .
> This gallant pins the wenches on his sleeve;
> Had he been Adam, he had tempted Eve;
> A' can carve too, and lisp; why this is he
> That kiss'd his hand away in courtesy;
> This is the ape of form, monsieur the nice,
> That, when he plays at tables, chides the dice

[1] The word probably means 'tit-for-tat'.

In honourable terms . . .
            . . . the ladies call him sweet;
The stairs, as he treads on them, kiss his feet:
This is the flower that smiles on every one,
To show his teeth as white as whale's bone. . .
                                    (V, ii, 315 *et seq.*)

The trick works, and when the men return in their own persons, the
ladies expose them. They are now doubly forsworn, having declared
their love to the wrong partners. Berowne has had enough of the
game, even of his own ebullience. No longer will he woo in

Taffeta phrases, silken terms precise,
Three-piled hyperboles, spruce affectation,
Figures pedantical; these summer-flies
Have blown me full of maggot ostentation:
I do forswear them; and, I here protest,
By this white glove — how white the hand. God knows! —
Henceforth my wooing mind shall be express'd
In russet yeas, and honest kersey noes:
And to begin, wench — so God help me, la! —
My love to thee is sound, sans crack or flaw . . .

With that single 'wench' sincerity shatters the artifice; but Rosaline
does not take it as Beatrice would have taken it from Benedick

Sans sans, I pray you . . .
                                    (V, ii, 406-16)

It will be a long time before Berowne has worked his passage home,
and one cannot help wondering what kind of a home he will find
when he gets there.

The scene is now set for the masque of the Five Worthies — nine is
more than the village can muster. This echoes — if it does not
anticipate — the Athenians' 'Pyramus and Thisbe'. The behaviour of
the audience alternates between condescension and incivility; had
Shakespeare some bitter experience of country house theatricals?
When Costard announces himself as 'Pompey surnamed the Big',
Dumain corrects him: 'The Great'; and when he has finished and the
Princess has thanked him, he teaches them all a lesson in natural
manners. ''Tis not so much worth, but I hope I was perfect; I made a
little fault in "Great".' Sir Nathaniel as Alexander the Great is
mercilessly ragged and retires hurt; and again Costard makes exquisite amends

There, an't shall please you; a foolish mild man; an honest man, look you,
and soon dashed. He is a marvellous good neighbour, faith, and a very
good bowler: but, for Alisander, — alas! you see how 'tis, — a little
o'erparted.
                                    (V, ii, 584-8)

In a few lines, and through the mouth of the village simpleton, Shakespeare evokes the life of a whole community. But it is Holofernes as Judas Maccabeus, hardly allowed to speak, who delivers to these insolent patricians his annihilating rebuke

> This is not generous, not gentle, not humble
>
> (V, ii, 632)

three epithets that sum up everything that Shakespeare felt men ought to be; everything, one likes to believe, that he was himself. Don Armado as Hector fares no better, and then — in the general mêlée of audience participation as he prepares to fight with Pompey — the dramatist contrives one of his most stunning theatrical effects

> Enter Mercade
> *Mer.* God save you, madam!
> *Prin.* Welcome, Mercade;
>   But that thou interrupts our merriment.
> *Mer.* I am sorry, madam; for the news I bring
>   Is heavy in my tongue. The King your father —
> *Prin.* Dead, for my life!
> *Mer.* Even so; my tale is told.
> *Biron.* Worthies away! The scene begins to cloud . . .
>
> (V, ii, 723-30)

It was often to cloud in the comedies yet to be written, but never so suddenly and dramatically as here. In this play of many words reality had broken through with as few words as possible. The men had forsworn the favours of women for three years, and they must still forswear them for a twelve month, either in prayer and fasting, or in what the moral theologians call the corporal works of mercy. If Berowne wishes to exercise his wit he must do so in a hospital. The moonlit misunderstandings of the *Dream* come to mind as he pleads excuse for

> what in us hath seem'd ridiculous, —
> As love is full of unbefitting strains;
> All wanton as a child, skipping, and vain;
> Form'd by the eye, and therefore, like the eye,
> Full of strange shapes, of habits and of forms,
> Varying in subjects as the eye doth roll
> To every varied object in his glance.
>
> (V, ii, 769-75)

Variety could not stretch further than an ass's head. But love must abide its testing and, as Berowne wryly observes

> Our wooing doth not end like an old play;
> Jack hath not Jill: these ladies' courtesy
> Might well have made our sport a comedy.
>
> (V, iii, 862-4)

It is still a comedy, but its laughter is muted in the end, as twilight falls on the elms and beeches of Béarn. Even Don Armado must 'hold the plough' for Jaquenetta till three years are past, and the flowering and fading of the seasons answer each other, like the hopes and disappointments of lovers, in the two lyrics with which the Worthies bring the play to a close. Armado's last words — 'You that way, — we this way' — are evidently spoken to the spectators, as the stage slowly empties.

Love's Labour's Lost did not presuppose a popular appeal; much of it is an 'in' joke for the initiate, and in modern productions is sensibly abridged. More than any other play of Shakespeare's, except, perhaps, for *As You Like It*, it asks for the open air. I remember a performance, many years ago, in the gardens of Wadham College, Oxford, and the jet-black figure of Mercade striding from what seemed an immense distance down the greensward. This was the right place, and the right public also. The play was written for the discomfiture of dons, and it was not difficult to detect Holofernes among the audience.

Chapter 7

The Professional

1

Shakespeare's early experience, both as actor and dramatist, had been gained with Lord Strange's Men at James Burbage's 'Theatre' in Shoreditch, at the smaller theatre in the garden of the Earl of Warwick at Newington Butts, or, now and then, in the courtyard of the Cross-Keys, the Bull, and the Bell Savage. Afterwards they worked for Henslowe at the Rose on Bankside, and for a time joined forces with the Lord Admiral's Men under Edward Alleyn. This coalition did not last for long. Alleyn was the most famous actor of his day — the creator of Barabbas, Faustus, and Tamburlaine, whose method was well adapted to Marlowe's 'mighty line'. If Henslowe did not exactly have Alleyn in his pocket, Alleyn had done much to line it. Born in 1566, he was only a year older than Richard Burbage, the rising star of the Lord Chamberlain's Men; and although the parts they played were very different, contemporaries spoke of Alleyn's acting very much as they spoke of Burbage. He was no barnstormer, out-Heroding Herod; and in so far as such methods persisted at the Rose, and later at the Fortune, he should be taken as having 'reformed them altogether'. But where Alleyn had lost a dramatist, Burbage had found one. That affinity — personal as well as professional — may well have influenced Shakespeare in his choice of themes, and it now helped him to a more secure status in the company.

Clearly there was not room for Burbage and Alleyn in the same troupe, and in 1594 the alliance with the Lord Admiral's Men came to an end. Lord Strange's Men became the Lord Chamberlain's Men, a title they held until they became The King's Men on the accession of James I. Shakespeare, who was never to work for anyone else, now acquired an actor's share in the company. As a hired man, playing odd parts and doing odd jobs for eight to ten shillings a week, he could hardly have afforded to buy this out of his savings; everything he earned he would have needed for his board and lodging, and no financial help could have been expected from Stratford. There is reason to believe that Southampton put up a handsome sum to help his protégé, although it was more likely to have been £100 than the £1,000 which tradition has reported. But more significant is the fact that Shakespeare was considered worth his place, as actor as well as dramatist, in that illustrious 'fellowship of players'. In eight years he had come far.

The Lord Chamberlain's Men provide the outstanding example in theatrical history of a company of actors running their own affairs. The nearest parallel today is the Comédie Française, where the hands of the Administrator are pretty severely tied. It is the actors who have to approve the production of a new, or the revival of an old, play; or the admission of a new *sociétaire.* But the Comédie Française works on a substantial subsidy. The Lord Chamberlain's Men had no subsidy whatever; they enjoyed the patronage, but not the financial support, of the Lord Chamberlain. He gave them respectability, and even prestige; secured for them invitations to perform at Court; but he did not pay their bills. At the same time, they were obliged to watch their step. The fair copy of any new play — or of an old one if it were revived after some lapse of time — had to be approved by the Master of the Revels, Edmund Tilney, who came under the Lord Chamberlain's jurisdiction. Thus, in *A Midsummer Night's Dream*, Philostrate has read the script of 'Pyramus and Thisbe', and seen it rehearsed. He also has the scripts of several other plays in his wallet. Tilney held his rehearsals in the Great Chamber of St John's Priory at Clerkenwell by the light of candles and torches, and the warmth of a huge fire.

Censorship was strict. The policy and conduct of the government must not be criticized. Foreign powers and personalities 'with whom our relations continue to be friendly' must not be presented in an unfavourable light. No comment must be made on current religious controversy. Persons of influence must not be satirized. The authorities had no objection to a dirty joke or a four-letter word, but they would come down heavily on a disparaging allusion. The general orthodoxy of Shakespeare's views both on politics and religion must be read in the light of these restrictions, and of the way they would operate at any particular time. He is not to be accused of hypocrisy because he was not always free to speak his mind. Moreover the censorship of those who protected and patronized the theatre was an easy yoke compared to the persecution of the Puritans who wanted to do away with it altogether.

Once a play had been accepted for production, it remained the property of the Lord Chamberlain's Men. The 'book keeper' would make a fair copy from the dramatist's 'foul papers'; and if the few surviving specimens of Shakespeare's script are anything to go by, these were liable to be very foul indeed. The scriveners would then copy out the actors' parts, with their cues, to be memorized. The Quarto texts, especially when they are designated as 'bad', carried the authority neither of the author, nor of the company. They had been surreptitiously, and in many cases inaccurately, passed to a printer — for piracy in publishing was then as common as piracy on the high seas. There is no evidence that Shakespeare was concerned with the publication of his plays, or worried if — as in the case of nearly half of them — they were not published at all in his lifetime. It was to Heminge and Condell's *pietas* and foresight that he owed a large share of his immortality.

What therefore do the editors of the Folio mean when they tell us that in all the papers they received from Shakespeare there was 'scarce a blot'? What papers are they referring to; his first drafts or his finished fair copies, carefully preserved in the archives? That he wrote with phenomenal speed and facility is obvious; two, and sometimes three, plays a year in the last decade of Elizabeth's reign, and in only one of them — *The Merry Wives* — an audible boiling of the pot. But are we to imagine that in the heat of composition, or the cool of revision, he never admitted a second thought? The MS pages of *Sir Thomas More*, if we allow them to be in Shakespeare's handwriting — not to mention the application of common sense to uncommon genius — forbid one to suppose so. Even if he were not thinking of posterity, he was thinking of performance. How would this line speak? Would this scene prove too long — or perhaps too short? What he had written — probably on both sides of a folio sheet with fifty lines to a page — must have undergone certain changes before it had passed through the hands of the scriveners and reached the archives in what the editors of the Folio regarded as its definitive form. Here, indeed, it might be described as 'with scarce a blot'; and the editors allowed their exaggeration.

Piety now prescribes that Shakespeare should be played virtually uncut. The prescription was obeyed as faithfully by Granville-Barker, as it was disregarded — at least in his later years — by William Poel. It is very doubtful if Shakespeare — were he alive today — would have enforced it. We must presume that the Prologue to *Romeo and Juliet* means, roughly speaking, what it says. When Shakespeare referred to the 'two hours traffic of our stage', he may have had *The Comedy of Errors* or *The Two Gentlemen of Verona* in mind, either of which could have been acted within that time. But not *Richard III*, nor even *Romeo and Juliet* for the matter of that. There is no mention in any play of the period of an acting time of more than three hours. It has been suggested that the Elizabethan actor possessed a secret of rapid delivery subsequently lost, but there is no evidence for this. 'Suiting the action to the word and the word to the action', and

'overstepping not the modesty of nature' would very effectively put
the brakes on the kind of marathon to which certain theorists would
like to reduce an Elizabethan performance, in theatres where neither
size nor sight-lines were an aid to audibility.

It would be comforting to think that the plays were acted without
intervals. *Macbeth,* in recent productions by the Royal Shakespeare
Theatre in London and Stratford, was all the more effective for the
lack of them. In *A Midsummer Night's Dream,* produced in America,
I refused to allow the audience to leave their seats until the lovers had
left the wood. *The Tempest* should similarly never be permitted to
relax its spell. So presented, none of these plays would exceed two
hours in performance. But from what we read of the clatter of
bottles in the theatres of Shakespeare's time, it would seem that the
'bars' exercised their tyranny then very much as they do today. And
what of *Hamlet*? If a performance at the 'Theatre' or the Globe
began at 2 p.m. it would have to be over by 4.30 to catch the
daylight on a winter afternoon; and even by then the twilight would
already be obscuring Burbage's facial play. If the rest was silence, the
rest was darkness also. An 'entirety' performance of *Hamlet* lasts well
over four hours, and not a moment too long for an audience that
knows and loves its Shakespeare. But this does not prove that stage
conditions and audience receptivity in Shakespeare's time allowed
for a performance of such length. Since he cared so little about the
publication of his plays, he is unlikely to have minded their
abridgement — although he would doubtless have had his say as to
how they were abridged.

I am forced to the conclusion, therefore, that he wrote with two
audiences in mind. One was his professional audience of actors and
public — groundlings below, more prosperous citizens in the tiers
above, and perhaps Southampton himself on a stool at the side of the
stage. They all had to be pleased. With the actors he would rehearse
in the morning, perform in the afternoon, and confabulate when the
play was over. A new production had to be cast, prepared for, and
approved. It can only have been in the evening, and late into the
night, as the tallow candle burnt low and the embers died in the
hearth, that Shakespeare wrote for that other, secret, audience which
was himself. Then he could let his imagination run riot and his pen
keep pace with it, knowing very well that this or that might have to
come out in performance, but seeing in his mind's eye an ideal stage
for which he need not apologize, and an ideal audience for whom an
'entirety' *Hamlet* would not seem too long. His fair copy might never
see the daylight of the Globe or the candlelight of the Blackfriars,
but they could have it for the archives just to show them the play as
he would have liked to see it performed. It may be that much that we

find irrelevant, like the references to the 'little eyases' — or Children's Companies — which were then rivalling the Lord Chamberlain's Men in popularity, was retained for its topical appeal; and — who knows? — that 'To be or not to be' was allowed to drop because it was holding up the action of the play. Any production is the slave of the last bus or the last train, and of the hour at which people choose to dine. Shakespeare did not, it seems, jib at these exigencies. But we owe it to Heminge and Condell that the secret audience to which he addressed himself in the small hours has now spread to the remotest auditorium, and that his secret thoughts are inscribed in the common-place book of human wisdom.

2

In 1594 a new theatre, the Swan, was opened on Bankside not far from the Rose, and it seems likely that at the same time Shakespeare moved his living quarters across the water. The Swan was owned and managed by Francis Langley, and the Lord Chamberlain's Men almost certainly played there, from time to time, while they were without a permanent home. In 1886 a drawing was discovered in the University library at Utrecht, purporting to reproduce the Swan as a visitor, Johannes de Witt, remembered it in 1596, only two years after it was built. We do not know whether de Witt's report was oral or committed to writing, nor how accurate was his memory, nor how faithful were the reproduction and the description which accompanied it. This or that detail, perhaps important, may have been omitted or misunderstood. We are told that there were in London at that time 'four theatres of noteworthy beauty', and that of these the 'largest and most distinguished' was the Swan; that it accommodated 3,000 spectators — an estimate which I find very hard to accept; and that it was 'built of concrete of flint stones . . . and supported by wooden columns, painted in such excellent imitation of marble that it might deceive even the most cunning'. Other visitors remarked upon the elegance of the London theatres. The Swan drawing, though it raises as many questions as it answers, is the only pictorial evidence we possess as to what the interior of an Elizabethan playhouse looked like, and how the actors performed in it. Eighteen years separated the opening of James Burbage's 'Theatre' and Francis Langley's Swan; many lessons, no doubt, had been learnt in the meantime. Only five years separated the opening of the Swan and the opening of the Globe. Anything we can deduce from de Witt's drawing, presuming upon its accuracy, can reasonably be predicated of the Globe, while allowing for variety of detail. No two theatres at any one period are exactly alike, but they are rarely diametrically different. The Swan sketch, I repeat, and however we interpret it, is the only pictorial clue that exists to an understanding of Shakespeare's stagecraft. It cannot lightly be disregarded because it does not, in every respect, meet our preconceptions.

Here then is a performance in full swing, with the flag of the theatre announcing it from the gabled roof of the tiring house, out of which a man has stepped with a signboard. The theatre is an oval-shaped building of three tiers, with a rectangular stage thrust out into the middle of it, built flush with the surrounding walls and projecting well beyond the two entrances right and left. The stage looks as if it is supported on two broad trestles not more than 2 ft 6 in. high. Two solid and elaborate columns sustain the steeply graded 'heavens', or penthouse roof. Two pairs of doors give entrance to the tiring house below, and above them a gallery with a balustrade and divided by thin columns runs the entire width of the tiring house. Assuming that the doorways are not less than 6 ft 6 in. in height, the distance between the floor of the stage and the rim of the balustrade must be at least 13 or 14 ft. The action of the play is going on well to the front of the forestage. If the drawing was made three years after de Witt's visit, this might be a reminiscence of Olivia and Maria in *Twelfth Night*, and Malvolio obeying his mistress's instruction to 'run after that same peevish messenger'.

With this evidence before our eyes, and such knowledge of the Elizabethan theatre as we may possess or deduce from other sources, what are we to think of the Swan drawing? It certainly has surprises in store for us. To begin with, why is the artist apparently the sole spectator? Why all these empty seats, when there is still room for a man with a signboard? And who are all these people in the gallery? Examine them closely, and you will find that they are paying precious little attention to the play. Natural enough, since the actors have their backs to them, and are anyway so far forward as to be virtually inaudible. This disposes of the idea that the onlookers are privileged spectators, and also, in my opinion, of the idea that the artist is recording a public performance. What he is showing us is surely a rehearsal, and the indifferent onlookers are actors waiting for their cue. Easy enough for them to come down by an inside staircase and out on to the stage by one of the back doors. Or did the man who made the sketch — and who had never, remember, actually seen the Swan — just put them in for fun? As I look at de Witt's drawing I find myself back in Kyoto, watching the rehearsal of a Noh play — the sole spectator in a theatre more than a little reminiscent of the 'wooden O' where Shakespeare learnt and matured his stagecraft.

I now draw your attention to the pair of double doors, the only means by which the actors could make their entrances. You can see exactly the same thing in many college dining halls at Oxford or Cambridge, and in the dining halls of the Inns of Court. Sometimes there is a single pair in the middle; sometimes two at the sides. For purposes of play-acting the advantage of the latter was obvious, since two entrances are better than one. The parallel is also clear between the tiring house gallery and the minstrels' gallery which was a common feature in great houses of the period. Since plays were acted in such places before any theatres existed at all, the architect evidently had them in mind. A play could be acted at the Swan and then in the hall of Grays Inn with only minimal adjustments.

Here I can speak from some experience. The hall of Grays Inn was bombed to rubble during the Second World War and subsequently rebuilt. The occasion of its reopening was festive in the Elizabethan manner. The Queen and other members of the Royal Family attended the performance of *Gesta Grayorum,* a masque written by the Benchers of the Inn for the entertainment of Queen Elizabeth I, and I was called upon to lay the tribute of their abominable blank verse at the feet of Queen Elizabeth II. We entered the hall through two pairs of double doors, while the musicians and the 'lord of misrule' performed from the gallery. One cherished notion, however, de Witt's drawing lays by the heels, and that is the hypothesis of an 'inner stage'. Volumes have been written on how this feature was supposedly used in the production of Shakespeare's plays. It has served for Juliet's bedchamber, and Juliet's tomb, and Friar Lawrence's cell; for Gertrude's closet and Brutus' tent; for any domestic interior where two or more persons are gathered together. Neat alternations have been suggested between the inner and the outer stage, but no one has asked themselves how a scene could be played in a recess where the actors could be neither seen nor heard by large sections of the audience, and which in itself would be too shallow to accommodate dramatic movement. Moreover the space it was supposed to occupy would be needed for the stacking of properties required for the play in performance. If there had been an 'inner stage' at the Swan it is incredible that de Witt should not have recorded it; the sketch indicates that the actors played, wherever possible, well down on the forestage.

Nevertheless some such curtained-off space, both above and below, is called for in many of Shakespeare's plays. To leave the entrances free to right and left, it must have been placed in the centre — a space for discovery if not for action. Thus we can picture Nerissa drawing aside the curtain to reveal the caskets, and Portia's suitors taking them downstage to deliberate upon their choice; Ferdinand and Miranda shown at their game of chess; Falstaff discovered asleep in *Henry IV, Part One*; and Juliet closing the curtains round her bed when she has swallowed the potion, although I do not imagine her speaking the great soliloquy from so far back. A similar contrivance must have served for her tomb. Here at least it must have been set some feet forward from the back wall, though still connected with it, for the boy playing the part must have had time to exchange a nightgown for a shroud and to be laid out on the bier without being seen by the audience. This could only be done if he had access to the tiring house, and this in turn presupposes a possible opening — if not a formal entrance — in the back wall. In Middleton's *A Chaste Maid in Cheapside* we read of a bed being 'thrust out upon the stage', and in Heywood's *The Golden Age* of its being 'drawn in'. Desdemona's bed, and Imogen's, would certainly have been 'thrust out' from somewhere, and Imogen's would have been 'drawn in', or the curtains closed around it, once Iachimo had retired into his trunk. But how was the trunk, with a full-sized man inside it, got into position and removed without exciting a titter? It was revealed, I imagine, in one of the side openings, and then the double doors would have closed upon it. Desdemona's bed, with its 'tragic loading', would of course have remained in position until the end of the play.

The problem has been fully discussed by Mr C. Walter Hodges in his most valuable *The Globe Restored* (1973), and I rally to his conclusions. The essential question to answer, in default of firmer evidence, is simply: how would it have worked? The Induction to *The Taming of the Shrew* is a case in point. Sly with his supposed 'wife' must sit 'aloft' throughout the play and make their occasional comments; and in the previous scene where he wakes up from his drunken stupor, room must be found on the upper level for a bed, some chairs, six actors with speaking parts and one or two attendants. How could such a scene have effectively played, or been generally visible, in a narrow passage and behind a balustrade? The same difficulty is presented by Cleopatra's Monument where she and her maids — two of them at least -- must be 'aloft' to receive the dying Antony. Firstly, she must not be raised so high that Antony cannot be raised up and gathered in her arms with becoming dignity; secondly, the supremely important scene with its sublime poetry cannot be played too far back; thirdly, Cleopatra and her attendants must be able to enter and leave the Monument on the upper level, drawing curtains behind them in front and at the sides to conceal the body of Antony which cannot be left exposed there for the rest of the afternoon; and fourthly, they must have reasonable space to act in. This presupposes that the upper floor of the Monument should not stand more than seven feet above the level of the stage — significantly lower, that is to say, than the presumed level of the balcony. When, in Act V, we are supposed to be *inside* the Monument, the lower curtains need only be drawn aside to reveal Cleopatra's throne, and Proculeius — the upper curtains being now drawn back, and Antony's body removed — could surprise her from *above*, descending by a flight of steps attached to the structure of the Monument. This I imagine as remaining in place throughout the action of the play; and at the end the curtains would close upon Cleopatra and the two attendants dead beside her, while Caesar — 'ass unpolicied' — and the other Romans would leave the stage frustrated of their Roman triumph. But if it were thought desirable to bring the death of Cleopatra further forward, a throne could have been let down from the 'heavens'. One thinks also of the 'arbour' from which Benedick in *Much Ado About Nothing* overhears the conversation that tells him that Beatrice is in love with him. We know that a portable 'arbour' was required in Kyd's *Spanish Tragedy*; and if there is no 'inner stage' suggested in the Swan drawing, may not this have been because a serviceable inner, and also upper, stage were provided by such a structure as Mr Hodges has outlined in greater detail than I have space to elaborate here?

The uses of the permanent gallery are obvious. Here was Antony's rostrum in *Julius Caesar*, from which he would descend (by an inner staircase) for the second part of his speech over Caesar's body — set, one imagines, pretty well to the fore. Here were the battlements of Angiers in *King John*, and of Flint Castle in *Richard II*. From here Jessica would have thrown down her casket of stolen jewels to Lorenzo, and Silvia have listened to Proteus' *aubade*. Here, probably, was Juliet's balcony, although I do not exclude the possibility that this may have formed the upper part of an alcove serving alternately for her bed, her tomb, and the Friar's cell. It was certainly along the gallery that Salisbury and Talbot appeared 'on the turrets' before Orleans, and here that Joan of Arc entered with the Dauphin 'on the walls'.

I now turn to the forward pillars. These support the canopy, but they could also prove theatrically useful. Did one of them, wreathed perhaps with greenery, do service for the tree on which Orlando fixed his verses, or from which Berowne listened to the other members of the reading party give themselves away? Notches or nails would have discreetly facilitated his ascent. But a tree to support a man is one thing; a tree to support a poem is quite another. This could have been provided by the flimsiest imitation; something far more solid must have been improvised for Berowne, and there were no convenient pillars at the Blackfriars or in whatever other courtly setting the play may have been given. The development of scenic furnishing in the Elizabethan and Jacobean theatre was a progress from emblem to illusion; from a symbolic box hedge in *Twelfth Night* to something much more like the real thing. Whatever constructions were accommodated on the stage of the Swan or the Globe — even the 'transpicuous mansions' which Professor Hotson believes it inherited, in their pre-transpicuous form, from the medieval theatre — *stood* for something; once Inigo Jones had set the fashion, and the roofed-in theatres had ousted the open theatres in favour with the aristocracy, they *simulated* something. It is a shaky argument that the Elizabethans were better able than we are to 'piece out' a dramatist's 'imperfections' with their thoughts. Believing, as so many of them did, that magnificence was the whole duty of man, or a large part of it, they were only too glad when the necessity of doing so was spared them. Whether Shakespeare would have written his plays differently if his stage had been more elaborately equipped is a rather futile question. I do not believe that the amenity of a lighting panel would have exempted him from writing 'How sweet the moonlight sleeps upon this bank'; or that a realistic Forest of Arden would have prevented the banished Duke from expatiating on its compensations.

Any theory of Elizabethan staging must abide the test of practicability, and it is here that Professor Hotson's theory of an arena stage and 'transpicuous' mansions breaks down.[1] He accepts the Swan drawing because it does not show an inner stage, and then brings in his 'transpicuous' mansions to supply one. We know, of course, that plays can be produced in an arena with the audience on all four sides, although this forces the actors into a St Vitus' dance which I, personally, find extremely irritating. It is hard enough to accommodate de Witt's Swan in an arena, and harder still then to encumber the stage with mansions — 'transpicuous' because you must be able to see through them. Moreover, the 'mansions' would have prescribed just that immobility which the arena forbids. Let them be as transpicuous as you like, and the imagination of an Elizabethan audience as vivid as we may suppose it to have been, their vision did not possess the penetration of an X-ray. And what happened to a mansion when it was no longer wanted? Was Antony's rostrum left to encumber the field of Actium, and the 'Boars Head' the field of Shrewsbury? Did Capulet's house obscure his funeral vault, and Orsino's palace get in the way of Olivia's garden? There would have been many moments when you could not have seen the scene for the scene-shifters.

Returning to the (relatively) *terra firma* of the Swan drawing, we look for the trap-door. This was evidently concealed by the bench on

[1] See *The Wooden O* (1959).

which Olivia — if indeed it is she — is seated; it will be used later in the play for Malvolio's prison. And thus we are drawn to an evident inaccuracy. The trestles which support the platform are too short to allow the necessary space underneath. Here there must be room for the Ghost in *Hamlet* to move about from one point to another in the 'cellarage', and perhaps for the Apparitions in *Macbeth* to rise from the cauldron. Moreover the space between them, both in front and at the sides, must have been covered in by the 'concrete of flint stone' of which we are told in the description. The use of the trap-door can be vividly illustrated by the Porter scene in *Macbeth*; how does the Porter get on to the stage? Let us consider what has preceded his entrance. Macbeth has gone out through one of the double-doors on his way to Duncan's bedchamber, and Lady Macbeth has come in through the other. When Macduff's knocking is heard, they both go out by the same door through which she has come in. The stage is empty, and the knocking goes on. We then have the stage direction: 'Enter a Porter'. If he comes in through one of the double-doors, he will be coming from Duncan's bedchamber; if he comes in through the other, he will presumably collide with his master and mistress. I suggest — and here the effect, at once comic and macabre, of his entrance makes its impact — that he comes up, still befuddled from his hang-over in the servants' quarters, *through the trap-door*. To an Elizabethan audience the space underneath the stage represented the infernal regions, and when the Ghost of Hamlet's father speaks from there Hamlet begins to wonder whether 'the devil hath power to assume a pleasing shape'. The Porter's references to Beelzebub and the 'porter of hell's gate', and the 'equivocator' that cannot 'equivocate to heaven' — in other words Macbeth, although the Porter does not know it — all combine to emphasize the dramatic irony of the scene; and this is powerfully reinforced if the Porter has come up through the trap. Since the Elizabethan stage was *essentially* unlocalized, Macduff and Lennox would be able to come in through the door by which Macbeth and his Lady have gone out, and no one would have supposed them to have met on the way. Moreover a scene of forty-four lines has intervened between the exit of the first pair and the entrance of the second.

Nevertheless, in a modern production of the play on a stage built to the Elizabethan pattern, I suspect that Macduff and Lennox would be brought in from the front, after hammering on one of the doors labelled 'ingressus' in the Swan drawing. This conjecture — and it is no more — raises the question as to whether similar entrances and exits were made in Shakespeare's time; whether the yard — or space between the stage and the groundlings — formed part of the normal playing area. The question has been examined, in three specific instances, by Professor Nevill Coghill.[1] He quotes the conclusion of a theatrical historian, Professor Allardyce Nicoll, whose authority cannot be questioned, that 'there was provision in the Elizabethan theatre for some way of stepping up on to the acting area from the yard, although there is no positive evidence to support it'. Professor Coghill supplies the evidence from theatrical common sense. His first example is taken from Act V of *The Merchant of Venice*. Lorenzo's opening lines tell us that he and Jessica are at Belmont, clearly established by the tiring house from which they enter; that the moon is shining; and, a few lines later, that they are reclining on a bank in the garden — which presupposes an adequate scenic accessory. The scene could hardly be set more clearly; we know where we are, and that it is probably long past midnight. When Stephano enters with the news that Portia will be there 'before the break of day', Lorenzo cannot at first make out who it is that 'comes so fast in silence of the night'. Stephano must therefore have room to *run* upon the stage, and he must *not* come from the direction of the house. It is from here that Lancelot Gobbo appears to inform Lorenzo and Jessica that a post has come announcing that Bassanio, too, will presently arrive. He thus creates the expectation that Bassanio and Portia will meet from opposite directions; he returning home by the front door and she by way of the garden. With his 'sola, sola' shouted into the darkness, he helps to reinforce it. Stephano has meanwhile placed a candle on the balustrade of the gallery, and Portia's lines

> That light we see is burning in my hall:
> How far that little candle throws its beams

(V, i, 89-90)

demonstrate that she *must* have seen it from a certain distance, and that she and Nerissa *must* have come up on to the forestage from the yard by a flight of steps, easily removable when they were not wanted. Any other entrance would have been theatrically absurd.

Professor Coghill then takes the opening of Act II in *Henry V* — the Siege of Harfleur. The Chorus sets the scene; the 'chambers go off'; and on the cue 'down goes all before them' whatever fragile constructions do duty for the gates of the city obediently collapse. The Chorus makes his exit, and the King with Exeter, Bedford, and Gloucester, take the stage. Scaling ladders are prescribed, but there is no mention of soldiers on the stage itself. Might they not have swarmed into the yard from below while the King, from above, exhorted them 'to the breach', and then used their ladders to scale the apron? This would leave Pistol safely in the rear to parody the

---

[1] *The Triple Bond* (1975), pp. 234-9.

rhetoric, but not to imitate the courage, of his commander-in-chief. Similarly in *Macbeth* (V, iv) Professor Coghill imagines traverse curtains between the two pillars pulled back to reveal the greenery of Birnam Wood, and Malcolm's army marching towards it ('What wood is this before us?'). Obviously it could not be before them if they were approaching it from behind. When each soldier has armed himself with the leafy camouflage, Dunsinane stands clear in the background, with Macbeth ordering the banners to be hung out upon the walls. Other examples tempt one to speculate. How, in the last act of *Pericles*, did the barge in which Marina and her attendants are brought out to Pericles' ship with its black sails arrive on the scene? No difficulty about the black sails; these could have been let down from the 'heavens'. But might not the barge have been a practicable boat brought in through one of the entrances to the yard, and moored alongside the platform? Might not the characters at the end of *The Tempest* have departed in the same way, except for Ariel winging his way to freedom on wires, and Caliban, may be, relapsing from sight through the trap-door? Prospero could then appear alone on the empty stage to speak the Epilogue. In the early plays there are several references to actors on horseback. We know that they sometimes rode on hobby-horses — as they did, very effectively, in the Royal Shakespeare Theatre's recent production of *Richard II* — but I see no reason why they should not sometimes have ridden on real horses stationed round the yard, provided the horses were not left there too long to interfere with the sight-lines. One likes to imagine the effect of Mountjoy entering like this in *Henry V.*

An early drawing of a performance of *Titus Andronicus* — the only such drawing we possess — indicates that in Roman plays the actors wore Elizabethan dress with classical trimmings. Saturninus has a short toga looped over one shoulder and carries the staff of his imperial office; Tamora, wearing a high crown and voluminous robe, kneels before him, with Demetrius and Chiron in quasi-Elizabethan costume kneeling behind; Aaron's white tunic and buskins contrast with his coal-black legs, hands and face; and Saturninus' two attendant halberdiers are distinguished by their different head-gear, and the different cut of their breeches, much fuller in one case than in the other. Cleopatra's 'Cut my lace, Charmian' indicates the 'serpent of old Nile' as Tiepolo imagined her entertaining Antony to supper;[1] and Lucius' description of the conspirators in *Julius Caesar* when they appear at the gate of Brutus' orchard

> their hats are pluck'd about their ears,
> And half their faces buried in their cloaks

(II, i, 73-4)

[1] The picture is in the National Gallery at Melbourne.

suggests that Shakespeare's audiences had no need to look further than the Thames to feel themselves on the banks of the Tiber. Unless the Elizabethans changed their skins when they got inside a theatre, I am convinced that they delighted in as much spectacle as the theatre could give them, and that the theatre gratified them with a good deal more beauty and ingenuity than we commonly give it credit for. History was actual; it did not matter that its appearances should be accurate.

3

When all is said, however, this was an actor's and a dramatist's theatre – and an audience's also. The effect of the audience on Shakespeare's art will become apparent as we follow its development. No doubt Ulysses was speaking for his author when he argued that

> No man is the lord of anything,
> Though in and of him there be much consisting,
> Till he communicate his parts to others;
> Nor doth he of himself know them for aught
> Till he behold them form'd in the' applause
> Where they're extended; who, like an arch reverberate
> The voice again; or like a gate of steel
> Fronting the sun, receives and renders back
> His figure and his heat.
> (*Troilus and Cressida*, III, iii, 115-23)

Shakespeare never lost this essential contact, now flattering his public and now leading them on, generally a step or two ahead. For so long as Lyly was in fashion, he was worth the mockery – much of it, to us, incomprehensible – of *Love's Labour's Lost*; for so long as Marlowe's rhetoric resounded at the Rose, similar tunes would be popular elsewhere; for so long as audiences were in thrall to the epic of their own history, Shakespeare would honour his side of the contract with the plays we have already been looking at and the others that we have yet to consider. It would not be history without tears, but it would be history with a difference – differences that looked forward to plays that were not history at all; or, more exactly, plays that, like the good acting whose principles Hamlet was to enunciate at Elsinore, held the mirror up to the nature of the audience itself, so that history became the here and now, instead of being merely the once upon a time.

The close reasoning of Ulysses applied equally to the player and the playwright. Adam in *As You Like It* and the Ghost in *Hamlet* are among the parts that Shakespeare himself is reported to have played. This denotes him as a 'character' man; and such subsidiary rôles would have enabled him to lend an ear to Burbage and keep an eye on Kempe. He may well have discharged the function of 'guider' — which was Dekker's word for a stage director. But in whatever way he was employed, Hamlet is speaking from Shakespeare's experience when he gives his views on acting. The famous speech is not quite the irrelevance it appears, since Hamlet is desperately anxious that the players — a respectable company, we must suppose, good enough to be welcomed at Court — shall do justice to *The Murder of Gonzago*. It tells us all we want to know about what good judges considered good acting to be at the turn of the century, when the Globe had earned the right to Ben Jonson's encomium of 'the glory of the Bank'.

Just as Shakespeare was moulding his verse, with no loss of imagery and incandescence, to the rhythms of colloquial speech, and turning his back on rhetoric — the difference between a relaxed and a coiled spring — so the style of acting appropriate to Alleyn as Tamberlaine or Burbage as Richard III was no longer suited to Hamlet, and still less to Leontes or Prospero. The Globe invited a broader style than a performance at Court or the Blackfriars, where there were no groundlings with ears to be tickled. Shakespeare's own preferences are not in doubt. He enjoined the actors to speak 'trippingly', and not to encumber their speech with useless and inflated gestures; not to confuse restraint with insipidity; to preserve a certain 'smoothness' even in the height of passion; always to have something in reserve. The comedians were still a problem. Evidently Will Kempe had taken the bit between his teeth, and his gags had set the auditorium on a roar. But Shakespeare would have none of this, and Kempe took his talents elsewhere. The actor-sharers of that immortal company were educated men. Burbage was an artist in painting as well as interpretation — the portrait in the Dulwich Gallery is said to be by his own hand — and Kempe wrote a readable account of his dancing marathon to Norwich. Of Burbage's versatility there can be no doubt. To have shone equally as Hamlet and Richard III — two parts requiring very different styles — is exceptional in the annals of the stage. It could be said of Irving, but of no one else.

We simply do not know what an Elizabethan performance sounded like. It has been defined as a 'sustained tone' reaching without apparent effort to the furthest seats in the theatre, combining melody and meaning, and producing the effect of nature with the maximum of art. As Bernard Shaw put it, 'The score, not the libretto, keeps the word alive and fresh.' If we are tempted to wonder what Shakespeare would have done with his love scenes with actresses to play them, we shall reply that he could hardly have done better. The picture of an athletic boy Cleopatra 'hopping forty paces through the public street' is both seductive and plausible. Nevertheless I cannot help noting that there is no record of a performance of *Antony and Cleopatra* in Shakespeare's lifetime. Was Cleopatra too stiff a challenge for even the best of his boy actors? Did the convention, of which the dramatist never complains elsewhere, prove too severe a strain? Even when the convention had been swept away, performances of this astonishing work suggest that here, for once, Shakespeare was asking too much of theatrical flesh and blood. In general, however, it was just because there were certain things that he could not expect his boy actors to do that they were able to suggest them so convincingly. 'The iron tongue of midnight hath told twelve; lovers to bed.' Who wants a bedroom scene after a line like that? 'Where souls do couch on flowers we'll hand to hand.' Who regrets that we have not been shown Antony and Cleopatra couching on something else? It is true that Shakespeare likes to put his heroines into buskin and hose — Julia and Rosalind, Viola and Imogen — but genius can always turn convention to commodity. He left the sophisticates of a later time to puzzle out the Freudian complications of a Duke who fancies himself in love with a great lady, but is really in love with a girl dressed up as a boy (actually a boy pretending to be a girl dressed up as a boy), and the great lady falling in love with the same girl, but happily contenting herself with her twin brother, and the girl falling in love with the Duke, whose suit she is presenting to the great lady. The brain turns Pirandellian cartwheels when it troubles to explore the shimmering depths of *Twelfth Night*.

The absence of dramatic criticism at the time — and the theatre got along very well without it — leaves us in the dark about much that we should like to know. What, for example, were the uses of soliloquy? Did the actor begin by talking to the audience — easy enough when they surrounded him on three sides, not to mention a few gallants sitting on the stage itself; and then, as Shakespeare's art matured, and his experience of life deepened, did he increasingly talk to himself? May we not detect a difference of perspective between Richard III telling us frankly that he is going to 'play the villain', Viola wondering why Olivia has sent Malvolio after her with the ring, Edmund arguing the natural rights of bastardy, or Iago trying to rationalize his machinations — and Hamlet in the contemplation of suicide, or Macbeth in the meditation of murder? The perspective could shift easily for the same character in the same play; Hamlet, in his first soliloquy, informing the audience that he is burnt up inside because of his mother's marriage, and, in his last, asking no one but himself 'what is a man if the chief good and market of his time be but to sleep and feed?' Richard III's soliloquy on the eve of Bosworth, when the villain of melodrama becomes for a few moments a protagonist of tragedy, and Richard II's in the cell at

Pomfret, both invite introspection. So does Claudius' 'O my offence is rank, it smells to Heaven.' But it was easy to share even one's most secret thoughts with the spectator under that open sky and in that polygonal arena, and easier still in the candlelit interior of the Blackfriars. Whether they were spoken *to* the audience or *with* them was a matter of theatrical discretion.

We can speak with more certainty about the use of music. The golden age of lyric and dramatic verse in England was also a time of high musical accomplishment; and here, as in so many other respects, Shakespeare took advantage of his moment. The Englishman of that time was spoken of as *musicus vir*. The Court was musically minded; Elizabeth herself played the virginals, just as the Dark Lady of the Sonnets played the harpsichord. Music, for Shakespeare, was an analogue of the harmony which should reign on earth, and certainly reigned in Heaven

> The man that hath no music in his soul
> Nor is not moved by concord of sweet sounds
> Is fit for treasons, stratagems, and spoils . . .
> Let no such man be trusted . . .
> *(Merchant of Venice,* V, i, 83-6)

Music recalls Lear to sanity, and the statue of Hermione to life. Warwick, in *Henry IV, Part Two*, asks for 'music in the other room' to accompany the last moments of his sovereign. Cerimon in *Pericles* revives Thaisa to the 'still and woeful music of the viol'; and for Orsino in *Twelfth Night* music is 'the food of love'. These melodies would have been played on strings by musicians seated in a gallery above the upper stage, visible or hidden as required. The mysterious hautboys heard by the soldiers in *Antony and Cleopatra* would have come from underneath the stage — further confirmation that here there was a good deal more head room than the Swan drawing allows for. However music was employed, it reinforced dramatic meaning and very often illustrated human character — generally by a song. Here Shakespeare could draw upon the boys' voices, and there were certainly adult players in the company who could sing. One of them would be cast for Amiens in *As You Like It* and Balthazar in *Much Ado.* Robert Arnim would have been heard as Feste, Autolycus, and the Fool in *Lear.* From the boys who played Desdemona, Glendower's daughter in *Henry IV*, Ariel in *The Tempest*, and the fairies in *A Midsummer Night's Dream*, a reasonable competence was called for, but Ophelia could get through her snatches with less than professional skill. The songs were accompanied, or otherwise, as character or scene required. Feste might not have brought an instrument to Toby's drinking bout, or even to Orsino's court, while Iago could break spontaneously into 'Let me the canakin clink' at another drinking bout which had more serious consequences than Toby's defiance of the licensing laws in Olivia's household. On the other hand Ophelia is described as entering with a lute for her mad scene — a stage direction now more generally observed in the breach than the observance. Queen Katharine in *Henry VIII* commands her maid of honour to 'take thy lute, wench'; and Pandarus in *Troilus and Cressida* asks for an instrument before he embarks upon the song which distils the heated eroticism of the play.

The musicians disposed of whatever instruments were best adapted to their dramatic use — strings for magic and mystery and reconciliation, trumpets and drum for a battle, a military parley, or a royal entrance. Edgar, when he challenges Edmund in the last act of *Lear* enters 'armed, with a trumpet before him'. In *Hamlet* there is talk of the recorders which presumably accompanied the Dumb Show; and in *A Midsummer Night's Dream* Theseus commands his huntsmen to wake the sleeping lovers with their horns. The demand for music is more explicit in the later plays; *Coriolanus* and *Henry VIII* both call for woodwind, brass, and drums, and *Henry VIII* for 'four Quiristers singing'. The private theatres gave larger scope for musicians, and here we know that they played during the intervals. To a certain extent Shakespeare's use of music was following the theatre in the direction of masque — which was also, implicitly, the direction of opera. He wrested it, as he wrested everything else, to his own purposes; and these were the development of tragedy into what has been called romance, where the Muse of Tragedy and the Muse of Comedy meet and kiss each other. To the achievement of this harmony music made its natural contribution. For the general effect of a Shakespeare play performed on Shakespeare's stage I cannot do better than quote the definition of Professor Dover Wilson, because the same effect can, and should, be produced on other stages and in other times. 'The Shakespearean play is composed of a succession of waves through which the spectator moves like a swimmer.' What matters is that the succession should not be interrupted.

A word is here in place about the audience if only because no dramatist can afford to neglect it. An audience at the Globe would not be the same as an audience at Whitehall, the Blackfriars, the Middle Temple, or the courtyard of an inn. It would not be the same in London as on tour. Where Shakespeare had a special audience in mind, as in *Love's Labour's Lost*, he generally makes it clear. But in his greater plays the appeal is either so diversified, as in *Hamlet* or *Henry IV*, or so direct, as in *Julius Caesar*, that he seems to be counting on a public of whom some considerable part, at least, would be capable of responding to anything he chose to say. Even if it could not read, it could listen; but if it was bored, it evidently had no hesitation in letting one know it. Smoking — the new fashion — was apparently permitted, nuts were cracked, cards were shuffled, and the 'bona robas' of the town were visible for the picking. An Elizabethan audience had much in common both with the Old Vic and the Alhambra, as older playgoers now remember them. The Globe, at any rate, was the reverse of a coterie theatre; with a bear pit on the other side of the street, and the stews round the corner, it was competing with entertainment considerably less refined.

It has been suggested that the middle classes were as absent from Shakespeare's audience as they were from his plays. It seems, however, that this conclusion can be pushed too far. Thomas Platter of Basel, visiting England in 1599, observed that 'the English pass their time learning at the play what is happening abroad; indeed men and womenfolk visit such places without scruple.' This suggests the kind of people for whom *The Times* or the *Daily Telegraph* would today be their morning diet; and Ben Jonson's reference to 'the modest matron' in his audience implies that Puritan hostility did not always have its own way with the classes most subject to its influence. A minority of the audience at the Globe might have had a grammar school education, and could have caught the meaning of a Latin 'tag'; but a lesser dramatist than Shakespeare might have asked with Middleton

> How is't possible to please
> Opinion tossed in such wild seas?[1]

Variety of character, vivacity of action, and luxuriant imagery of speech were Shakespeare's answer to this question. Moreover he achieves his greatest effects — Beatrice's 'Kill Claudo', Cleopatra's 'Dost thou not see the baby at my breast?', Macduff's 'He has no children', Lear's five-fold 'Never' — with the simplest of means. H. S. Bennett has compared him to 'a broadcasting station transmitting a programme which is received well by some instruments, imperfectly by others, and scarcely at all by a few'.[2] But the essential parts of the programme would have been perfectly received by everyone.

---

[1] *No wit, no help like a Woman's.*
[2] 'Shakespeare's Audience' in *Studies of Shakespeare* (1964), p. 70.

Chapter 8

Tragical...Historical

1

The previous chapter marked a breathing space at a point in the story where Shakespeare's professional status had become secure, and where the nature of his profession asked for examination. On leaving the parish of St Helen's in Bishopsgate for a new residence in the Liberty of the Clink at Southwark he found several of the Lord Chamberlain's Men as his neighbours, with the Swan and the Rose, and also the Bear Garden, close at hand. Francis Beaumont and John Fletcher lived near by. He still owed £2 13s. 4d. to the Collectors of Taxes in the City, and these — to us not very considerable — arrears were eventually reclaimed by the steward of the Bishop of Winchester on whose estate the Liberty of the Clink then lay. John Shakespeare's affairs had gone from bad to worse, and by 1595 he seems to have retired from trade altogether. In January 1596 he conveyed a piece of land attached to the house in Henley Street to a local draper.

The great matter on William's mind, as the last decade of the reign began to throw its shadows, was the good estate of the realm. Mary Stuart was out of the way, and Philip's Armada was under the waves or on the rocks; the Church of England was the official religion of a substantial majority of Englishmen — Heminge and Condell were both churchwardens; but Shakespeare was too wise a man to believe in the stability of human affairs. The theatres were constantly menaced by the Puritans, or the plague. The Queen was ageing, and there was as yet no nominated heir. The moment was still propitious to read the lessons of history. Responsible authorities disagree as to whether *King John* was written before *Richard II*, or followed it. There can be no certainty in the matter. The fact that it was placed first among the Histories in the Folio tells us nothing, for here they follow the historical sequence. There is no record of its performance, or of any publication before the Folio. If Shakespeare had the second tetralogy on his mind, is it probable that he would have allowed himself to be distracted by another historical subject? On the other hand, if he had completed *Richard II*, would he have left

Bolingbroke looking forward to sleepless nights, Prince Hal diverting himself in the stews, and Hotspur already showing a trace of his mettle, while he involved himself in the story of another 'uneasy crown' and another 'discord of nobility'? Assuming this view, one can only conclude that the Bastard had so taken hold of his imagination, and so enlarged his vision of what was meant by 'England', that the character could not be resisted. You can argue, further, that the style of *Henry IV* is so different from that of *Richard II* that another play on a not dissimilar theme might have come between them with the Bastard opening up the prosody as well as the social horizons. Dover Wilson thought that *King John* was the earlier play; Professor Bullough, linking the style of *Richard II*, with its unusual number of rhymed couplets, to that of *Love's Labour's Lost*, inclines to the view that *King John* followed it; and that *Richard II* 'may be regarded as the tragedy most nearly correspond-ing to what *Love's Labour's Lost* is in comedy. For the latter is the comedy in which the mind of a Shakespearean character is first consciously alive to all that goes on in it, to the relation of thought to senses and passion, to the delight of words. It too is a heavily stylized play, and Biron is in comedy what Richard is in tragedy.'[1] I find this extremely suggestive, and prefer to consider *King John* as an interruption, rather than a prelude, to work in progress.

On 7 December 1595, Sir Edward Hoby invited Sir Robert Cecil to what appears to have been a private performance of *Richard II* on the 9th of that month, for supper was included in the invitation. This suggests that the play had already been performed elsewhere — presumably earlier in the same year. If Shakespeare was influenced by Samuel Daniel's epic poem, *The First Four Books of the Civil Wars*, registered in October 1594 and dated 1595 on the title page of the first edition, this indicates very quick composition, although he may have seen something of Daniel's work in manuscript. A play by Shakespeare was not obliged to go the rounds of theatrical manage-ments, and *Richard II* probably had its first performance in the summer of 1595 when the theatres had reopened after closure by the plague. The play was published in four Quartos before the Folio of 1623. This argued popularity — and, as we shall see, notoriety as well.

The second tetralogy is so different from the first, and so superior to it, that although Shakespeare may well have had the total sequence in mind from the moment he set his hand to *Henry VI, Part One*, the form it would take was probably still vague, and changed — perhaps radically — as his dramaturgy developed and his imagination

---

[1] See Bullough, Vol. III, pp. 381-2.

took wing. Always more interested in human beings than in the *idées fixes* that they weave out of their prejudices and beliefs, he was still constrained to illustrate a political idea. The Tudors had to be made respectable, and no doubt Shakespeare considered them respectable enough. But it was essential to show, not only the fault of Henry Bolingbroke in 'compassing the crown', but adequate reasons for his doing so — reasons answerable to human experience. He could not be justified, but he must be explained — and permitted, therefore, to excite a measure of sympathy.

With this necessity in mind, Shakespeare made his way with extraordinary skill through the various sources open to him, although the degree of his dependence on them must remain in doubt. He would certainly have read Marlowe's *Edward II*, another portrait of a weak King following a strong one, and brought to ruin by his own vices. But where Edward's homosexuality is central to his character, Richard's is only hinted at. Bushy, Bagot and Green are very far from playing the part in Shakespeare's play that Gaveston does in Marlowe's; and Richard has a tender affection, if not a compulsive passion, for his Queen. Shakespeare may well have read the anonymous play of *Woodstock* — Earl of Gloucester and Richard's uncle — which very considerably gilds the character of its hero, and makes Richard responsible for his death. This accusation is echoed by the Duchess of Gloucester in *Richard II* (I, ii, 9-36), and rebutted by Bolingbroke (I, i, 98-100). Shakespeare, with an equal disregard for historical accuracy, transfers to John of Gaunt some of the sterling qualities which the author of *Woodstock* had attributed to Gloucester; and Gaunt, in answering the Duchess's plea for revenge upon the man she believes to have been responsible for her husband's death — a crime in which he rather casually admits his share — already anticipates the answer of the whole tetralogy to those who might think that Bolingbroke was justified in his usurpation and, only a little less directly, for the murder of his lawful sovereign

> God's is the quarrel — for God's substitute,
> His deputy anointed in his sight,
> Hath caus'd his death; the which if wrongfully
> Let heav'n revenge, for I may never lift
> An angry arm against his minister.
>
> (I, ii, 37-41)

A. P. Rossiter has shown that out 'of some twenty-five resemblances in matter, phrase, or both' between *Woodstock* and *Richard II* twelve are to be found in this scene between Gaunt and the Duchess. Shakespeare leaves the question of Richard's responsibility for the death of Gloucester pretty open; by a fine stroke of irony he allows Bolingbroke to exempt him from the charge; and he does not refer to the matter again. He is concerned with Richard in the last phase of his reign, when he is no longer the same man that quelled Wat Tyler's revolt in 1381. He has other delinquencies to answer for, and Gaunt is prompt in bringing him to book for them.

Shakespeare takes his starting point from Hall's 'Introduction into the History of King Henry the Fourth', and relies on Holinshed for Bolingbroke's loyalty in the opening scene. In the main he follows Holinshed thereafter, though he may have borrowed from Sir Thomas Elyot's 'The Book named the Governor' (1531) the tradition of Prince Hal's 'misruly mates of dissolute order and life', which was to be a principal theme of the succeeding plays. More evident is his debt to Berners' translation of Froissart, who had visited England in 1395 and presented his poems to the King. Froissart, like Chaucer, took a Shakespearean view of John of Gaunt, and referred to Bolingbroke's popular way with the crowd. Most importantly, he gave Shakespeare the feeling not only of a medieval court, but of a medieval political and social order. *Richard II* is the most ceremonious of the poet's plays. The action proceeds to the rhythm of a slow motion; the characters appear to us like figures out of a tapestry; the verse is at once more formal and more lyrical than it is in either *King John* or *Richard III*. Richard's right to rule was absolutely unquestioned. Later monarchs — and the Tudors most certainly among them — were Kings *de jure* because they, or their predecessors, had first of all been Kings *de facto*. Richard, as he presides over the lists at Coventry, is not only King *de jure*, but King *de jure divino*; and indeed we can understand nothing whatever about the play unless we can enter into the doctrine of the Divine Right of Kings.

This is not to say, however, that Shakespeare understood the doctrine in the way of its more extreme apologists. As Professor Arthur Humphreys has written: 'The great debate which culminated in the seventeenth century between Kingship by Divine Right and Kingship by Contract (or consent of the governed) is the vast sounding-board which makes the contentions of the tetralogy the more resonant.'[1] Shakespeare would not have ventured to define the Contract; seeing all round the problem himself, he took care that his audience, and particularly his censors, should not see round it quite so clearly. But he demonstrates in *Richard II* that a King who acts unjustly must expect to be repaid in his own coin. The chief end of politics for Shakespeare, as for Hooker of whose teaching he may have picked up a hint or two, is the liberty of men to live within just laws. Hooker was exceptional among political philosophers of his time in postulating the consent of the governed and opposing this to

---

[1] *Stratford Papers on Shakespeare* (1964), p. 33.

the blind obedience preached in season and out by the Homilies. He was following Aquinas where others were following Machiavelli, and was indeed accused of following 'the schoolmen too strictly'[1]

> Howbeit over a grand multitude having no such dependence upon any one, and consisting of so many families as every politic society in the world doth, impossible it is that any should have complete lawful power, but by consent of men, or immediate appointment of God; because not having the natural superiority of fathers, their power must needs be either usurped, and then unlawful; or if lawful, then either granted or consented unto by them over whom they exercise the same, or else given extraordinarily by God unto whom all the world is subject.

Hooker safeguards his flank, as Shakespeare does, but in his *Conference on the Next Succession* he claimed the rights of a popular voice in the election of a King. Certainly Bolingbroke had that voice; and Shakespeare's stand is ambivalent between loyalty to a King, of whose 'immediate' and 'extraordinary' appointment by God neither John of Gaunt nor the Bishop of Carlisle has the slightest doubt, and the duty of that King to govern for the good estate of the realm. Just as Holinshed could turn from his record of Richard's misdemeanours to the prudent assertion that he was a 'bountiful and loving sovereign' and a 'prince the most unthankfully used of his subjects', so Shakespeare gives equal weight to the reasons why he should, and should not, have been deposed. When Richard banishes Bolingbroke he acts capriciously, but within his rights; the Council have approved the sentence, not even John of Gaunt dissenting from it. When he confiscates his lands, he breaks the laws which he has sworn to uphold, and puts a question to his own authority. 'For how art thou a King' asks York 'but by fair sequence and succession?' If we presuppose a moral contract between governor and governed, it is here the governor who has broken it; and if so, can it be maintained that God has cancelled his appointment? Shakespeare does not answer in the affirmative — far from it — but he allows the question to be asked; and it is asked more insistently by a modern than an Elizabethan audience.

The dialectic of the play is articulate in the characters. Richard takes his stand upon the Divine Right in proportion as the other grounds of his authority are weak

> Not all the water in the rough rude sea
> Can wash the balm off from an anointed King
>
> (III, ii, 54-5)

or again, as he faces Northumberland at Flint

> For well we know, no hand of blood and bone

Abednego Seller, *History of Passive Obedience since the Reformation* (1689).

> Can gripe the sacred handle of our sceptre
> Unless he do profane, steal or usurp . . .
>
> (III, iii, 79-81)

Yet almost in the same breath that he asserts his power

> Is not the King's name twenty thousand names?
>
> (III, ii, 85)

he admits his weakness

> Our lands, our lives, and all are Bolingbroke's . . .
>
> (III, ii, 151)

Richard has a half-conscious will to deposition, just as Bolingbroke has a half-conscious will to usurpation. Each allows himself to be guided by events; enemies in appearance, they are allies in reality. Richard, as acute in observation as he is inept in act, has observed his rival's 'courtship of the common people'

> As were our England in reversion his
> And he our subjects' next degree in hope . . .
>
> (I, iv, 35-6)

On the one hand is the man who has the right to rule and exercises it badly, and on the other hand is the man who has no right to rule, but looks already as if he might rule well; on the one hand the King appealing to prestige, on the other hand the usurper appealing to popularity. The *vox populi vox Dei* is beginning — though as yet only in whispers — to challenge the Divine Right of Kings.

It has been said that Bolingbroke gets what he wants because he never knows where he is going. He certainly has the politician's flair for taking advantage of events when they look like playing into his hands. No doubt he shares his father's disapproval of the parasites who have made the Court a byword for ostentation, frivolity, and perhaps unnatural vice; one sees him as a man of the marches, more at home with the rugged northern Percies than with the *jeunesse dorée* of Westminster. With the 'commons pilled with grievous taxes' — high taxation has never been the primrose path to popularity — and the nobles 'fined for ancient quarrels' — to provide money for Richard's Irish expedition — the King is in no position to meet the challenge of a man who has come, ostensibly at least, to claim a coronet to which he had an undisputed right rather than a crown to which he had no right at all. Bolingbroke, however, has first to reckon with York, whom Richard has appointed Regent during his absence. York is a good example of the politician whose bark is considerably worse than his bite, and who proves, when he is pushed to it, to have no bite at all. Realizing the strength of Bolingbroke's support, he would like

> to attach you all and make you stoop
> Unto the sovereign mercy of the King.
> But since I cannot, be it known unto you
> I do remain as neuter . . .
>
> (II, iii, 146-9)

Instead he offers him a bed for the night. Never, surely, in the history of politics was there a more lame and impotent conclusion.

By the opening of Act III Bolingbroke has acquired a notable accession of authority. Bushy and Bagot and Green must pay for the King's misdoings

> You have in manner with your sinful hours
> Made a divorce betwixt his queen and him.
>
> (III, i, 11-12)

This is all very well, but of course it is all quite illegal. The men are being sent to their deaths without the shadow of a trial; Bolingbroke is usurping the prerogative, though not as yet the title, of kingship. Moreover his motives are not disinterested. While he has been 'eating the bitter bread of banishment', Bushy, Bagot and Green have

> Dispark'd my parks, and felled my forest woods
> From mine own windows torn my household coat . . .
>
> (III, i, 23-4)

Unpopular as such hangers on to Establishment so often are, he will reap a certain popularity by dispatching them.

In politics, as in warfare, the secret of success is to look as if you have already won the battle. Bolingbroke is already Montgomery facing his Alamein. Richard, when he reappears at Berkeley Castle, is a defeated man. This is eloquent in his wonderful cadenzas — an expense of words in a waste of self-pity — to be matched by Bolingbroke's economy when the two men meet at Flint. Rather than confront the King directly, he sends Northumberland, thus underlining the rally of the feudal nobility to the rebel arms. The message is a masterpiece of diplomacy with teeth in it. He will lay down his arms provided his banishment is restored and his lands repealed. Otherwise he will 'lay the summer's dust with showers of blood'. This, however, is the last thing he wants; honey, you might say, would not melt in the mouth of this calculating man. The contrast is vivid between the appearance of Richard's royalty, and the reality of Bolingbroke's power; and ironically it is Bolingbroke's ally, Henry Percy, the Hotspur of the later play, who adds a last flickering lustre to Richard's crown

> See, see, King Richard doth himself appear,
> As doth the blushing, discontented sun
> From out the fiery portals of the east . . .
>
> (III, iii, 62-4)

How easily one pictures him on the gallery of the Swan, Bolingbroke well down on the forestage, and Northumberland going to and fro between them! Abruptly descending from his high horse — and he has never ridden higher — Richard agrees to Bolingbroke's demands, and then, just as abruptly, wonders if he had not better go back on his agreement. But Aumerle, who understands the facts of military life, prevents him

> No, good my lord, let's fight with gentle words,
> Till time lends friends, and friends their helpful swords.
>   (III, iii, 131-2)

Northumberland has a long word with Bolingbroke, while Shakespeare is building up our sympathy for Richard as a man and our admiration for him as an artist — for in losing his job he is discovering his vocation, which is the lyrical expression of his own tragedy. And what is the result of Bolingbroke's confabulation with Northumberland? It could hardly be more ominous. Richard is invited to come down, and as he does so one is reminded of General MacArthur receiving the Emperor of Japan in his short-sleeves. To Bolingbroke's softly spoken

> My gracious lord, I come but for my own

Richard's defeatism replies with a cutting edge

> Your own is yours, and I am yours, and all . . .
> What you will have I'll give, and willing too.
> For do we must what force will have us do.
> Set on toward London. Cousin, is it so?
> *Bol.* Yea, my good lord
> *Rich.* Then must I not say no.
>   (III, iii, 196-209)

How well these two men, cousins in blood and much of an age, understand each other! Without striking a blow, or so much as raising his voice, Bolingbroke has Richard in his grip. The sheer psychological pressure of superior force, and the mailed magnetism of his own presence, have given him the victory. Courteous and implacable, he stands there at the head of an insurgent army, the irresistible symbol of success. The idea and the reality, the shadow and the substance, could not be more nakedly opposed or more paradoxically reconciled. What has failed in Richard is the will or the ability to sustain his title; all he is left with, for our enrichment and the actor's opportunity, is the masochistic delight in his own misfortune.

The ceremonious convention of the play is maintained in the scene where the gardener, in conversation with his fellow, points the moral plainly. Why, he is asked

> should we in the compass of a pale

> Keep law and form and due proportion,
> Showing, as in a model, our firm estate,
> When our sea-walled garden, the whole land
> Is full of weeds, her fairest flowers chok'd up,
> Her fruit-trees all unprun'd, her hedges ruin'd,
> Her knots disorder'd, and her wholesome herbs
> Swarming with caterpillars?

and the other gardener replies

> He that hath suffer'd this disorder'd spring
> Hath now himself met with the fall of leaf.

(III, iv, 40-9)

Here is the commentary of the common man, very uncommonly phrased, on the ill estate of the commonwealth. Here, if anywhere, Shakespeare is speaking for himself — and for the *respublica* where legitimacy is no excuse for injustice. We have travelled a long way from Bolingbroke's initial grievances; he has become the catalyst of a general discontent. And now at last, as he takes the road to London, he knows exactly where he is going.

The scene in Westminster Hall gives us the measure of his authority. Abdication must be wrapped in the forms of legal fiction; Bolingbroke, like so many upstart rulers, is careful about these things. It is only when York brings word that Richard is prepared to abdicate that he takes the decisive step

> In God's name, I'll ascend the regal throne . . .

(IV, i, 12)

Here, then, is the Lancastrian title, and the Bishop of Carlisle foresees that it will not go uncontested

> And if you crown him, let me prophesy
> The blood of English shall manure the ground,
> And future ages groan for this foul act.

(IV, i, 136-8)

Shakespeare, when he wrote these lines, was remembering the earlier tetralogy, and his audience would have remembered it too. But Richard must be seen to abdicate and, also, to make public confession of his 'weaved up follies'. Lost in his private agony he calls for a mirror that he may still further play the artist with his grief. Northumberland, as usual left to do the dirty work, insists on the public confession while the mirror is being brought. Bolingbroke, anxious to preserve the appearances, intervenes

> Urge it no more, my lord Northumberland . . .

(IV, i, 271)

Northumberland persists in the name of those who have helped

Bolingbroke to the throne, but when the mirror is brought Richard is spared this ultimate humiliation. All through his soliloquy Bolingbroke watches him, and the power of his presence is conveyed by Richard's concluding lines as he dashes the mirror to the ground

> Mark, silent King, the moral of this sport
> How soon my sorrow hath destroyed my face . . .
>
> (IV, i, 290-1)

Shakespeare had given us through the Bishop of Carlisle the full enormity of Bolingbroke's usurpation, and through the gardener the measure of Richard's responsibility for his downfall. Yet there is one voice in the body politic which has not been heard — and that is the mob; the anonymous and fickle crowd for which Shakespeare never had anything but contempt. Bolingbroke had exerted his charm on them as he went into exile; how do they behave when the man who is ruler by right of law and the man who is ruler by right of will ride together into London as if, for all the world, they were the fastest friends? York gives us the picture in retrospect — letting us see, at last, the ace which Bolingbroke has up his sleeve

> You would have thought the very windows spake;
> So many greedy looks of young and old
> Through casements darted their desiring eyes
> Upon his visage; and that all the walls
> With painted imagery had said at once
> 'Jesu preserve thee! Welcome, Bolingbroke.'
>
> (V, ii, 12-17)

So much for the man and woman in the street; and Richard in his cell at Pomfret learns that even his favourite horse had sensed which way the wind was blowing — 'so proud that Bolingbroke was on his back'.

It had been no light matter to play fast and loose with the Divine Right of Kings, and Bolingbroke knows it. The Divine Right has been removed to Pomfret — for the Tower was uncomfortably close to Westminster Abbey — but though discrowned it was still incarnate. And so it is that Bolingbroke who rarely speaks an unnecessary word lets drop the word which is not only unnecessary but fatal. Sir Pierce Exton takes the hint, and Richard is murdered in his cell. Exton may not have been surprised at Bolingbroke's sombre reception of the news, and Bolingbroke does not deny the hint; but for the first time this man of single purpose betrays the fissure of a divided mind

> They love not poison that do poison need,
> Nor do I thee; though I did wish him dead,
> I hate the murderer, love him murderéd
>
> (V, vi 38-40)

and then turning to all that retinue of triumphant *arrivistes* he concludes

> Come mourn with me for what I do lament
> And put on sullen black, incontinent,
> I'll make a voyage to the Holy Land,
> To wash the blood off from my guilty hand.
>
> (V, vi, 47-9)

The later scenes of *Richard II* look forward in different directions; with Bolingbroke to the public and private troubles of the succeeding play, already foreshadowed by Aumerle's conspiracy; with Richard to the area of introspection, beyond politics altogether, where a man is alone with his own thoughts, and where Brutus and Hamlet already cast their silhouettes on the horizon. It does not escape the reader, or still less the spectator, that in *Richard II* private thoughts are publicly expressed; other people are generally standing around. Richard's descant on the common humanity of Kings is still an aria that does not lack its audience. But in his long soliloquy at Pomfret both the perspective and the prosody have changed

> I have been studying how I may compare
> The prison where I live unto the world:
> And for because the world is populous,
> And here is not a creature but myself,
> I cannot do it; yet I'll hammer it out.
> My brain I'll prove the female to my soul;
> My soul the father: and these two beget
> A generation of still-breeding thoughts.
> And these same thoughts people this little world
> In humours like the people of this world,
> *For no thought is contented.*
>
> (V, v, 1-11)

This is a new Shakespearean voice, and we shall hear more of it as the catharsis in the life of the individual comes to matter more than the chronicle of historical event. Bolingbroke will never escape from politics, but he too is from henceforth the prisoner of conscience, and the Jerusalem Chamber is the nearest he will ever get to the Holy Land. Thus these two *frères ennemis* are still locked in the rivalry which they have brought upon themselves, and locked the more closely when the one has been murdered by the other. In the meanwhile John of Gaunt has spoken for England, but he too is dead. Yet England is what the second tetralogy is about, and somebody must be found to speak for it in action as well as in iambics.

2

If, as I have presupposed, *King John* followed closely upon *Richard*

II, we are drawn to speculate as to what deflected Shakespeare from matter so ripe for development. Was it that he could not as yet see the wider social panorama that *Henry IV* was to open up; that although the sign of the 'Boar's Head' and the outline of Prince Hal's dissipations may already have been in his mind's eye, the gigantic figure of Falstaff had not yet come to occupy the hearth? Was it perhaps that he lighted by chance upon the anonymous *Troublesome Raigne of John King of England* published in 1591, and that this gave him a cue that he was eager to take up? Professor Bullough concludes — 'after some vacillation' — that Shakespeare rewrote the *Raigne* in 1596 'using the original plot but changing the emphasis, and above all the style, adding features to give it new topicality, reducing its length from 3,081 lines to 2,715, but expanding the first part . . . at the expense of the second'.[1] In the *Raigne* he would have discovered two characters that may well have met his mood at this particular moment. The first was the Bastard in whom he created a voice that could speak for England without benefit of royalty; for even if he was looking forward to Henry V as his patriot King, that coronation was two long plays ahead. The second was young Arthur who might have filled the role if he had lived. Shakespeare's only son, Hamnet, died when he was only eleven years old, and was buried at Stratford on 11 August 1596. If the play was written in that year, the lines of Constance when she is forcibly separated from Arthur have a poignant resonance

> Grief fills the room up of my absent child
> Lies in his bed, walks up and down with me,
> Puts on his pretty looks, repeats his words
> Remembers me of all his gracious parts,
> Stuffs out his vacant garments with his form . . .
>
> (III, iv, 93-7)

Shakespeare had no need to have lost a son to imagine a mother's grief, but the coincidence is too striking to pass unnoticed.

Nevertheless *King John* is not a satisfactory play; the material is intractable for the purposes Shakespeare had in mind. John is not the hero, nor even the character we most remember. For John Bale in his *King Johan*, for the author of the *Troublesome Raigne*, for Foxe in his *Booke of Martyrs,* and Holinshed in his *Chronicles,* King John stood for the rights of Englishmen against the pretentions of the Papacy. Shakespeare's view is far less *simpliste.* Chatillon, the envoy of King Philip of France, refers to John's 'borrowed majesty', and even his mother, the formidable Elinor of Aquitaine, insists on

---

[1] See Bullough, Vol. IV, p. 5.

Your strong possession much more than your right,
Or else it must go wrong with you and me

(I, i, 40-1)

for Arthur as the son of John's elder brother, Geoffrey, had a better title to the throne. Like Bolingbroke in the previous play, John is a King *de facto*; not even a double coronation can invest him with a Divine Right. Like Richard he is weak — and also violent, which Richard was not. So Shakespeare is compelled to find his hero elsewhere, and Falconbridge — the bastard son of Richard Coeur de Lion — steps into the breach. Country bred and a stranger to courtly manners, he is Shakespeare's first portrait of a self-made man, and in Shakespeare's view obviously the better for it. His humour, humanity, spontaneity, and self-deprecating cynicism link him with others of his kind — a Berowne born on the wrong side of the blanket, and plunged into the contemplation, and then the management, of great affairs. If he is not quite the patriot King he is at least the patriot Commoner; and as he keeps his head above the turmoil and trivialities of international diplomacy, he acts as a Chorus as well as a character. In so far as the play preserves a unity, it is he who gives it one.

The first two acts revolve around the English claim to the city of Angiers, and the French claim to it on Arthur's behalf. The First Citizen of the place refuses to open the gates and bids the rival armies fight it out. This they do, but inconclusively. Then the Citizen suggests that Lewis, the Dauphin, shall marry Blanche, King John's niece, and Queen Elinor urges the match for political reasons

For by this knot thou shalt so surely tie
Thy now unsured assurance to the crown,
That yon green boy shall have no sun to ripe
The bloom that promiseth a mighty fruit.

(II, i, 470-3)

Lewis and Blanche are acquiescent, and the several parties leave for 'this unlook'd for, unpreparéd pomp' — not without some apprehension of what Constance, Arthur's mother, will say to it; and she says a great deal. The novelty of the scene lies in this: that for the first time Shakespeare treats diplomacy with derision, and employs the Bastard as his mouth-piece

Mad world! mad Kings! mad composition!
John, to stop Arthur's title in the whole
Hath willingly departed with a part
And France, w͟ ͟se armour conscience buckled on,
Whom zeal and charity brought to the field
As God's own soldier, rounded in the ear

With that same purpose-changer, that sly devil . . .
That smooth-faced gentleman, tickling Commodity.

(II, i, 561-72)

The Kings of France and England have met at Angiers; they might as well have met at Helsinki.

In the third act a second theme, more strongly emphasized in *The Troublesome Raigne* than in the play which Shakespeare derived from it, is introduced. Pandulph, the Papal legate, demands from John redress of his wrongs against the Church, and when John refuses with a popular taunt against the sale of Indulgences, Pandulph excommunicates him and enjoins upon Philip to cancel the alliance. Philip reluctantly agrees; the newly wedded pair are parted; and John, with Arthur now in custody, prepares to return home, charging Falconbridge to 'shake the bags of hoarding abbots'. It should be noted throughout that John, not Falconbridge, is the fire-eating anti-clerical. Falconbridge is the servant of his master because he is the servant of his country; and the true character of his master, hitherto imperfectly defined, is shown in the following scene where John persuades Hubert to remove Arthur from a succession which he might claim, or that others might claim on his behalf.

The focus of the play now shifts to Arthur, and to Hubert's sparing of his life; to the nobles' resentment at the King's double coronation, and their request that Arthur shall be set at liberty; to Hubert's false report that the boy is dead; to John's conclusion that

There is no sure foundation set on blood
No certain life achieved by others' death.

(IV, i, 104-5)

and to the news that the Dauphin has landed at the head of a French army. Hubert gives a vivid picture of how the rumour has spread; an example of how Shakespeare's art illustrates the worldly wisdom of his hero

For he is but a bastard to the time
That doth not smack of observation.

(I, i, 207-8)

Hubert tells the King

I saw a smith stand with his hammer, thus,
The whilst his iron did on the anvil cool,
With open mouth swallowing a tailor's news,
Who with his shears and measure in his hand,
Standing on slippers, which his nimble haste
Hath falsely thrust upon contrary feet,
Told of a many thousand warlike French
That were embattaléd rank'd in Kent.

(IV, ii, 192-200)

Faced with a foreign invasion and the defection of his own nobility — a theme for which Shakespeare, in contrast to *The Troublesome Raigne*, has not left himself the necessary room — John's nerve begins to crack. He only recovers, momentarily, when Hubert reassures him that Arthur is, after all, alive. The revelation is ironical because, in the next scene, the boy jumps down from the walls of his prison and is killed. The nobles — Pembroke, Salisbury, and Bigot — have been summoned to meet the King at St Edmundsbury, and are discussing their refusal with the Bastard who quietly advises them to go

> Bas. Whate'er you think, good words, I think, were
>   best.
> Sal. Our griefs, and not our manners, reason now.
> Bas. But there is little reason in your grief;
>   Therefore 'twere reason you had manners now . . .
>
> (IV, iii, 28-31)

They all have reason for their grief, however, when they discover Arthur's body on the ground. Shakespeare gives the others more than twenty lines of fairly conventional rhetoric before the Bastard, who is not normally sparing of words, is allowed his brief and pregnant comment

> It is a damnéd and a bloody work;
> The graceless action of a heavy hand,
> If that it be the work of any hand.
>
> (IV, iii, 57-9)

For a sudden light on human character this reminds one of Benedick's 'Lady Beatrice, have you wept all this while?' from *Much Ado*. The Bastard is jumping to no conclusions; when Hubert enters, and Salisbury, suspecting him of murder, draws his sword, Falconbridge intervenes with the accents of Othello

> Your sword is bright, sir; put it up again.
>
> (IV, iii, 79)

The voice is just as firm — the voice of reason, not of passion — when he is left alone with Hubert. Satisfied at last of Hubert's innocence, he can speak for England, because he now realizes that England has no other voice; and in doing so he faces his own dilemma

> Go, bear him in thine arms.
> I am amazed, methinks, and lose my way
> Among the thorns and dangers of this world.
> How easy dost thou take all England up!
> From forth this morsel of dead royalty,
> The life, the right and truth of all this realm
> Is fled to heaven; and England now is left

To tug and scamble and to part by the teeth
The unowed interest of proud-swelling state.
Now for the bare-pick'd bone of majesty
Doth dogged war bristle his angry crest
And snarleth in the gentle eyes of peace:
New powers from home and discontents at home
Meet in one line; and vast confusion waits,
As doth a raven on a sick-fallen beast,
The imminent decay of wrested pomp.

(IV, iii, 139-54)

The Bastard has no doubts; if there is a Divine Right it is dead with Arthur. But there is another right, though it does not call itself divine — and that is the safety of the realm. So long as England is threatened, the King must be supported. That John has made his peace with Pandulph does not matter one way or the other, except that it reinforces his flagging authority. *The Troublesome Raigne* had made much play with the Bastard's indecorous adventures among the monks and nuns at St Edmundsbury, but Shakespeare omits all this as inconsistent with the character he has built up. *King John* is essentially a patriotic, and only incidentally an anti-Papal, play. Pandulph, who has been driven by John's defiance of the Pope to encourage the Dauphin, now agrees to mediate between them. The Bastard is doubtful whether he will succeed; and if he does

let it at least be said
They saw we had a purpose of defence.

(V, i, 75-6)

In the event, Lewis defies the Legate just as resolutely as John had defied him at Angiers

I, by the honour of my marriage-bed,
After young Arthur, claim this land for mine;
And, now it is half-conquer'd, must I back
Because that John hath made his peace with Rome?
Am I Rome's slave?

(V, ii, 93-7)

The Bastard brings John's defiance, and his manly rhetoric justifies the claim that 'thus his royalty doth speak in me'. But the keenest edge of his invective falls on the nobles who have deserted their sovereign

You bloody Neroes, ripping up the womb
Of your dear mother England, blush for shame.

(V, ii, 152-3)

As the armies engage word is brought to the King that Lewis' supply fleet has been wrecked on the Goodwin sands. If, as seems likely, this was suggested by the dispersal of Philip II's armada in the Bay of

Biscay during the autumn of 1596, it dates the play with a fair degree of certainty. John, however, suffering from poison administered by a monk, is too ill to take much comfort from the news. The rebellious lords, warned that neither of the contending monarchs will thank them for their treachery, hastily return to their true allegiance; but the promise of an English victory is blighted when the bulk of the Bastard's forces are drowned in the Wash. The situation is saved by the death of John, and Pandulph's mediation. Lewis agrees to disband his army and recognize the young Prince Henry as King. The Bastard, true to form, interposes

> He will the rather do it when he sees
> Ourselves well sinewed to our defence
>
> (V, vii, 87-8)

but it has been done already; and it only remains for the man whose stature towers above the divisions, at once historical and artistic, of the play, to read the lessons of an earlier 'discord of nobility'

> This England never did, nor never shall
> Lie at the proud foot of a conqueror
> But when it first did help wound itself.
>
> (V, vii, 112-14)

As Shakespeare returned to his tetralogy, and the curing of similar wounds, he must have had these words in mind. But his patriot King was never to engage our sympathies as closely as his patriot Commoner.

Chapter 9

The Prince of all Humours

1

There can be no reasonable doubt that the two parts of *Henry IV* were planned as a single work, for although there is duplication there is also development. History repeats itself, and the historical drama- tist must take his cue from it, whatever liberties of adaptation or compression he allows himself. Shakespeare needed space to enlarge his canvas, so that Gloucestershire as well as Eastcheap should have its place on the map. To have passed from the death of Hotspur to the coronation of Hal would have argued too abrupt a conversion, and too sudden a cure for the sickness in society and sickness on the throne which are so strongly emphasized in the later play. History — and human nature — take their time, and Shakespeare refuses to be hurried.

Yet how skilfully he varies his pace. The political scenes have the urgency of crisis; the Falstaff scenes the tempo of frivolity. 'Time must have a stop' when Hotspur looks death in the face at Shrewsbury; at the Boar's Head it seems to go on for ever, until Hal is summoned to the Court and Falstaff to the colours. The themes of public and private life are brought together on the battlefield when Falstaff is allowed the credit for the death of Hotspur, and again when he is rejected by the Prince who has come into his Kingdom. They are linked just as closely when the conflict between the King and the Heir Apparent is resolved by the reconciliation of the father and the son.

A Quarto edition of Part One was published in 1598. Five subsequent Quartos appeared before the play was included in the First Folio. It was probably written between 1596 and 1597, and there is some reason to believe that it was performed at Christmas in the latter year. When the Carrier observes that Robin Ostler 'never joyed since the price of oats rose' he may have been referring to the dearth of corn in 1596. When the Prince breaks the metre to warn Douglas that

> the spirits
> Of valiant Shirley, Stafford, Blunt, are in my arms
>
> (V, iv, 40-1)

Shakespeare may have insinuated a sly compliment to the Shirleys who were knighted by Elizabeth in 1597. Francis Meres mentions the play in his *Palladis Tamia* (1598); and in *The Return from Parnassus,* acted at St John's College, Cambridge, at Christmas of that year there are clear echoes of tapster Francis' 'Anon, anon, sir' when the Prince is talking to him in one room, and Poins is calling him from another.

Shakespeare sticks close to history except in one important particular. Since the conflict, and the competition, between Hotspur and Hal is a central motif of the play, they are shown of the same age, whereas in reality Hotspur was twenty-three years older. Also, Bolingbroke speaks of himself as 'shaken' and 'wan with care' only two years after he had ascended the throne, and of his 'old bones' encased in armour to meet the rebels. In fact, he was no more than thirty-seven at the time, just as Hal was only fourteen. The dramatist went to his usual sources, Hall and Holinshed, and the anonymous *Famous Victories of King Henry the Fifth,* altering and adding as he saw fit. Douglas challenges the King, thus provoking the prince to challenge Hotspur; and the Prince saves his father when Douglas is on the point of killing him. It is Shakespeare, again, who brings the rivalry of Hotspur and Hal to a climax when they meet at Shrewsbury, and Hotspur's 'mangled face' is all that is left of the 'Percy of the north'. (Audiences are generally spared this unpleasant sight, but it was shown in a recent production at Stratford.) Falstaff, as he comes to us here, is wholly Shakespeare's invention. A Sir John Oldcastle was one of Prince Hal's dissolute companions in the *Famous Victories,* and Shakespeare seems at first to have kept the name. At one point the Prince addresses Falstaff as 'my old lad of the castle'; and his line to Poins 'Away, good Ned, Falstaff sweats to death' would have preserved the metre if it had read 'Oldcastle sweats to death'. The historical Oldcastle was a notorious Lollard and the degradation of his character might well have offended Protestant opinion. Nicholas Rowe reports the tradition that 'this part of Falstaff is said to have been written originally under the name of Oldcastle' and that 'some of that family being then remaining, the Queen was pleased to command him to alter it'. In his search for an alternative Shakespeare evidently bethought him of the Sir John Falstolfe in *Henry VI, Part One* who is depicted as a coward at the siege of Orleans. The historical Falstaff was also a Lollard, and Fuller in his *Worthies of England* was among the Protestant critics who were not disarmed by the change of name. Shakespeare prudently refrained from any discussion of the Lollard controversy in treating the 'unquiet reign' of Henry IV. His most radical gloss on historical truth is in the characterization of 'the irregular and wild Glendower'

— a great soldier and patriot, educated in England at the Inns of
Court, to whom there was much more than Celtic superstition. If
Glendower failed to turn up at Shrewsbury he probably had good
reason for his delay; but Shakespeare could not resist the contrast
between Hotspur's impetuosity and the vaticinations of his Welsh
ally.

The play insistently looks back to *Richard II*. Worcester reminds
the King that his 'greatness' was

> that same greatness too which our hands
> Have holp to make so portly.
>
> (I, iii, 12-13)

Northumberland recalls Richard's proclamation of Mortimer as his
heir — not referred to in the preceding play

> And then it was when the unhappy King —
> Those wrongs in us God pardon! — did set forth
> Upon his Irish expedition.
>
> (I, iii, 148-50)

Hotspur reproaches his father and his uncle for their part in
Richard's deposition

> Shall it for shame be spoken in these days,
> Or fill up chronicles in time to come,
> That men of your nobility and power
> Did gage them both in an unjust behalf,
> As both of you — God pardon it — have done
> To put down Richard, that sweet lovely rose,
> And plant this thorn, this canker, Bolingbroke . . .
>
> (I, iii, 170-6)

Henry reminds his son of how carefully, as Bolingbroke, he had
economized his public appearances

> And then I stole all courtesy from heaven,
> And dress'd myself in such humility
> That I did pluck allegiance from men's hearts . . .
> Thus did I keep my person fresh and new;
> My presence, like a robe pontifical,
> Ne'er seen but wonder'd at.
>
> (III, ii, 50-2; 55-6)

Hotspur, receiving word of the King's profferred magnanimity, replies
that

> well we know the King
> Knows at what time to promise, when to pay
>
> (IV, iii, 52-3)

and relates at much length how

> A poor unminded outlaw sneaking home
>
> (IV, iii, 58)

and demanding no more than the restitution of his rights had climbed to the throne on the shoulders of the northern Percies. And Worcester, summoned before the King on the eve of the battle, recapitulates the story. All this gives an emotional excuse for the revolt, and reminds the audience of what they might have forgotten, or not have heard before.

Nevertheless Henry does not dominate the stage in the play that bears his name as he had come to dominate it in *Richard II*. He was a more formidable figure coaxing the crown to fall into his lap than wearing it uneasily upon his head. Remorse for the past, anxiety for the present and the future, leave him no grounds for comfort. The central, though not the most captivating, character is the Prince. It has been well said that the English give their warmest affections to a man when they can also laugh at him; Winston Churchill was a good example of this. But the sense of humour which is a form of moral courage can also be a cloak for mental cowardice. Prince Hal, and even for some people Henry V, have had a 'bad press'; and both Hotspur and Falstaff have been correspondingly sentimentalized. But the least one can do in reading an historical play is to read it in the light of history. Shakespeare may have wished, as we can reasonably wish, that he had been able to turn his patriot Commoner into his patriot King; all he could do, however, was to interpret the facts as he found them.

Some mitigation he allowed himself. We are told that the Prince had struck the Lord Chief Justice, but we are not shown him in the act. What a careful reading of the character corrects, although less often in performance, is the impression of a thoughtless playboy who suffers a miraculous conversion to kingship. The Prince is a thoroughly mixed-up young man, growing up in the shadow of his father's remorse, sensitive to his vocation, and straining at the restrictions of protocol. A comparison with Edward VIII springs plausibly to mind. But there was a steel and a subtlety in Hal quite lacking in his unfortunate successor. His father is neither tactful nor intelligent in constantly comparing him with Hotspur

> A son who is the theme of honour's tongue;
> Amongst a grove the very straightest plant . . .
>
> (I, i, 81-2)

The Prince is amused by Falstaff, and amuses himself in his company, but he is not for a moment taken in by him. If there is any love lost between them, it is on the side of Falstaff; and this makes the rejection of the private pleasure by the public duty as painful to the audience as it is to Falstaff himself. It may well have been just as painful to the dramatist, but Shakespeare knew as well as another man that duty, like truth, is hard and not infrequently hurts.

When Falstaff and Poins propose their plan for the robbery on Gadshill, the Prince exclaims: 'I, a thief? not I, by my faith . . . come what will, I'll tarry at home'; and he only joins the party to recover the money from Falstaff, and afterwards to restore it to its rightful owners. The soliloquy that follows shows the discrepancies of a divided life, but not the confusions of a divided mind. Hal knows exactly where he is going, even when he goes in opposite directions. Indeed he is already resolved that the ways shall meet

> I'll so offend to make offence a skill.
>
> (I, ii, 240)

This candour does not endear him to us, but explanation — not endearment — is here the dramatist's business. Presently the Prince lets us see what he means, as he tells Poins

> I have sounded the very base-string of humility. Sirrah, I am sworn brother to a leash of drawers; and can call them all by their christian names, as Tom, Dick, and Francis. They take it already upon their salvation, that though I be but Prince of Wales, yet I am the King of courtesy . . . I can drink with any tinker in his own language during my life.
>
> (II, iv, 5 *et seq.*)

The Prince of Wales was determined to be a prince of all seasons, for he later confesses

> I am now of all humours that have showed themselves humours since the old days of goodman Adam to the pupil age of this present twelve o'clock at midnight.
>
> (II, iv, 105-7)

There are worse recipes for royalty. But when, in reply to Falstaff's impersonation of the Prince whom he imagines on the carpet before the King

> banish not him thy Harry's company, banish not him thy Harry's company; banish plump Jack, and banish all the world
>
> (II, iv, 525-7)

the Prince replies 'I do, I will', there can be little doubt that he means what he says. This is playacting, but he is looking forward with one half of a subtle mind to the day when the play will be over. Falstaff can say to him: 'Thou owest me my love', little realizing that the debt will never be paid because it has never been acknowledged.

The test, when it comes, will be moral and political; the easier test is military, for Hotspur is a foeman worthy of his steel. When Hotspur inquires where is 'the nimble-footed madcap Prince of Wales', we see him through the eyes of Vernon — and some of the finest poetry in the play

> I saw young Harry, with his beaver on
> His cuisses on his thighs, gallantly arm'd,
> Rise from the ground like feather'd Mercury,
> And vaulted with such ease into his seat,
> As if an angel dropp'd down from the clouds,
> To turn and wind a fiery Pegasus,
> And witch the world with noble horsemanship.
>
> (IV, i, 104-10)

When the Prince tells Poins that he has 'sounded the base-string of humility' he means, of course, that he has proved his good fellowship with the humblest of his fellow-men. Now, in emulating his father's praise of Hotspur in his father's presence

> I do not think a braver gentleman,
> More active-valiant or more valiant-young
> More daring or more bold is now alive
> To grace this latter age with noble deeds

he goes on to admit

> For my part, I may speak it to my shame
> I have a truant been to chivalry . . .
>
> (V, i, 89-95)

This impression is confirmed, again by Vernon

> He made a blushing cital of himself;
> And chid his truant youth with such a grace
> As if he master'd there a double spirit
> Of teaching and of learning instantly.
> There did he pause; but let me tell the world,
> If he outlive the envy of this day,
> England did never owe so sweet a hope,
> So much misconstrued in his wantonness.
>
> (V, ii, 62-9)

We have seen the Prince as his father sees him, as Hotspur sees him, and as he sees himself; here is a first hint of how England will see him by the time that Shakespeare has completed the portrait. When Falstaff unsheaths a bottle of sack instead of a sword, he is not amused

> What, is it a time to jest and dally now?
>
> (V, iv, 57)

and the nearest we penetrate to his real feelings about Falstaff is when he finds him on the ground, apparently dead

> Poor Jack, farewell!
> I could have better spared a better man:
> O, I should have a heavy miss of thee
> If I were much in love with vanity

with the implication — a little premature — that his flirtation with vanity is over.

Falstaff's observation 'I live out of all order, out of all compass' applies to Hotspur as well as to himself. As a Canadian diplomat, who knows more of the world than the chanceries could teach him, has shrewdly written

> We know what Hotspur is at bed and at table, how he would make love, how he would flick impatiently through his morning paper, how he would drive a car, how he would bring up his children. Hotspur the falcon-eyed aviator, reckless skier is easy to imagine. The jesting, unsentimental tone when talking with his wife, and his quick come-backs are startlingly modern.[1]

His impatience with Glendower betrays the provincial and the philistine — the kind of Englishman, for whom it may be that Shakespeare had a sneaking regard, who believes that dagoes begin at Calais. Michael Redgrave, at Stratford in 1953, was right to give him a Northumbrian accent, just as Olivier was right to give him a stammer. Not to be able to get out his 'Ws' lent an intolerable pathos to his dying utterance — 'food for . . .', leaving Hal to complete the sentence. Hotspur is not, like his father and his uncle, or Bolingbroke and Hal for the matter of that, a political animal; and he is very much of an amateur strategist. His conception of honour is primitive, though he expresses it in sublime poetry

> By heaven, methinks it were an easy leap
> To pluck bright honour from the pale-faced moon,
> Or dive into the bottom of the deep
> Where fathom-line did never touch the ground
> And pluck up drownèd honour by the locks.
>
> (I, iii, 201-5)

Like Falstaff he is too exorbitant for the society he moves in; and just as it was said of Falstaff that he 'lards the lean earth as he goes along', so it might be said of Hotspur that the grass grows greener under the horse which is to bear him 'like a thunderbolt / Against the bosom of the Prince of Wales'. The cynicism of Falstaff's reflections upon honour matches the romanticism of Hotspur

> Can honour set to a leg? no; or an arm? no; or take away the grief of a

---

[1] Charles Ritchie, *The Siren Years* (1974), p. 17.

wound? no. Honour hath no skill in surgery, then? no. What is honour? a
word. What is in that word honour? What is that honour? air . . .

(V, i, 131-6)

and so on to the end of a catechism in which he parodies the political
ethics of his time. Hotspur is too one track-minded to achieve that
integrity that the Prince is fitfully searching for; the integrity of the
King which must assure the integrity of the commonwealth. He is
limited by his own exorbitance; the only person in the play who
loses his temper, and in the event that is something the commonwealth cannot afford. Though fighting (or pretending to fight) on
opposite sides, the political anarchy represented by Hotspur and the
moral anarchy represented by Falstaff join forces in a league of
dissolution which it is the Prince's duty to resist. In *Henry IV, Part
One*, the first part of that duty is discharged. It is not for the Prince
who is his adversary, but for Worcester who is his ally, to rebuke
Hotspur for his intemperance

> You must needs learn, lord, to amend this fault.
> Though sometimes it shows greatness, courage, blood —
> And that's the dearest grace it renders you —
> Yet often times it doth present harsh rage,
> Defect of manners, want of government,
> Pride, haughtiness, opinion and disdain:
> The least of which haunting a nobleman
> Loseth men's hearts, and leaves behind a stain
> Upon the beauty of all parts besides,
> Beguiling them of commendation.

(III, i, 180-9)

Hotspur may lose his temper, but he loses no one's heart, and the
Prince, as he stands over his body, reminds us that if something of
Falconbridge had gone into Hal, something had also gone into
Hotspur

> Ill-weaved ambition, how much art thou shrunk!
> When that this body did contain a spirit,
> A kingdom for it was too small a bound;
> But now two paces of the barren earth
> Is room enough: this earth that bears thee dead
> Bears not alive so stout a gentleman . . .

(V, iv, 88-93)

As Parolles says in *All's Well That Ends Well*, 'Simply the thing I am
shall made me live'; Hotspur might have said no less.

And so might Falstaff. He bestrides not only the two plays of
Henry IV, but the whole wide world of English comic characters.
The claim is a large one when you think of Dickens; but where the
characters in Dickens are fantastic individuals living by virtue of their
eccentricity, Falstaff is at once an individual and an archetype. In

plays which are at root Moralities, he is the old Vice writ new and very large; a catalyst for those human weaknesses without which a Morality would lose its point, and an audience its pleasure. He enlists our sympathies because he is meant to; because Shakespeare, in seeing all round a character, sees all round himself. J. B. Priestley, in a fascinating broadcast, caught the incandescence of poetry in Falstaff's exquisite prose, and in his rejection by the young King Henry V the rejection of Shakespeare the poet by Shakespeare the dramatist. If this is so, the gesture, aesthetically speaking, was an empty one. The last word was with poetry, and Falstaff's 'God, God, God' echoes in our ears long after the rhetoric of Agincourt has died away. In *Henry IV, Part One* Hotspur shares with him the honours of sheer vitality, and speaks in verse that has no need to disguise itself in prose

> But thought's the slave of life and life time's fool . . .
>
> (V, iv, 81)

Falstaff could not have put it better, though he would have put it differently. Elsewhere in the play, however, Falstaff enjoys a monopoly, if not of life itself, then at least of a commentary on life. The contrast is between the men who are dedicated to power — the King on one side, the rebels on the other — and the men who are dedicated to pleasure, with the Prince wavering between them and learning from the present enjoyment of pleasure something about the future exercise of power. Could he have talked as he did to William on the vigil of St Crispian if he had not learnt how to talk to Bardolph at the Boar's Head? Falstaff, in his own definition, is not only witty in himself, but the cause of the wit that is in other men. Like Hotspur, he is the voice of spontaneous anarchy opposed to calculating order. If his life style of pure hedonism is a defiance of political necessity, then he may be seen, as he undoubtedly sees himself, as the supreme realist in a world of colossal make-believe. And if you choose to regard the Prince as a hypocrite, then Falstaff may be seen as Vice enlisted to strip off the hypocritical mask of virtue; and his enjoyment of his own lies confers upon them the innocence of truth itself.

I am far from saying that this was Shakespeare's intention, or at least the whole of it. No great writer so readily resists simplification. Maurice Morgann, in his ingenious, if specious, acquittal of Falstaff on the charge of cowardice, writes of Shakespeare's 'comprehensive energy of mind', and goes on to argue that it was not enough for him 'to have found his characters with the most perfect truth and coherence; it was further necessary that he should possess a wonderful facility of compressing, as it were, his spirit into these images, and of giving alternate animation to the forms. This was not to be done *from without*; he must have *felt* every varied situation, and have spoken thro' the organ he found.' If we do not disapprove of Falstaff, it is because Shakespeare does not disapprove of him either; he simply makes him live by virtue of his own creative genius — which was a genius, not of judgment but of sympathy or, as Keats so memorably put it, of 'negative capability'. Falstaff robs an innocent traveller; refuses to pay his debts to Mistress Quickly; goes the round of the brothels; recruits a company of foot and allows them to buy off their services; and dishonours the corpse of Hotspur. He is the reverse of admirable, and we are not asked to admire him. But because he makes no bones about his sins we grant him absolution; and we should be disappointed if he expressed a purpose of amendment.

2

The Second Part of *Henry IV* has been unfairly rated lower than the First, for it is a rather different kind of play. The mood is autumnal, with the fall of leaves corresponding with the fall of life. The emphases and proportions have changed, and the landscape broadened. Northumberland, too sick to join forces at Shrewsbury, recovers on learning that his son is dead, and his cause momentarily lost, but afterwards he retires to Scotland, and we do not hear of him again. Worcester has been executed, and only the Archbishop is left to rekindle the fires of civil disobedience. The heart has gone out of conspiracy. The King does not appear until the beginning of the third act, and the political theme has lost a good deal of its interest now that Hotspur is no longer there to animate it, and Glendower has died among the Cymric mists. Falstaff has all his wits about him, but even he is suffering from gout and the pox — the one brought on by too much imbibing of sherris sack, the other by too assiduous frequentation of the stews. When he has Doll Tearsheet on his lap the shadow of mortality falls upon 'Saturn and Venus in conjunction'. The chimes of midnight echo sepulchrally when Justice Shallow reminds him of them; and if there is one line more than another that gives its motif to the first three-quarters of the play, it is Shallow's 'And is old Double dead?' Old Double is among the more significant characters that Shakespeare does not trouble to bring on to the stage, for he resumes the twin themes of sickness and senility. It will require the coronation of a young King to cure them.

The only Quarto version of Part Two was published in 1600, but there is no evidence that it was less popular than Part One. Its relative unpopularity appears to have grown through the eighteenth century when, as against a hundred performances of Part One in the

London theatres, there were less than a quarter as many of Part Two. The first scene of Act Three was at first omitted from the Quarto, possibly from fear of the censorship, since the references to Richard's deposition touched a sensitive nerve when the Essex revolt was still fresh in memory, and those to Northumberland's share in it might have offended the ninth Earl who was Essex's brother-in-law. The Percies' recent past was a stormy one, with Sir Thomas executed for his part in the Pilgrimage of Grace; and neither the seventh nor the eighth Earls died in their beds. The first perished on the scaffold, and the second was shot through the heart in the Tower. The play was probably written in 1597, and first performed in the following year.

Professor Bullough has written that 'Shakespeare deliberately departed from historical time and sequence to give dramatic force, concentration, and unity of tone to a sprawling series of events',[1] cramming five years of the reign into a few weeks. This led to a certain simplification, and perhaps to a loss of subtlety. There is no hint that the Prince has been actively engaged in state affairs. Like the Prince of Wales under Queen Victoria and George V, he has not been 'shown the papers'. The choice is still between the example he is given no opportunity to set in public, and the example he loses none to set in private; and it is only resolved when he realizes that a Prince's private life is also to some extent a public one, and the more public the nearer he approaches his accession. His gradual realization of this provides the development I have spoken of, although the progress is registered through the duplication of previous themes which are not staled by repetition. So long as Falstaff was alive, he was obliged, theatrically speaking, to be kicking.

As in Part One Shakespeare is mindful of those who may not have seen the preceding play; each part of the tetralogy shades into the next. In the opening scene conflicting rumour keeps the fate of Hotspur in suspense, and Northumberland's recovery of strength and resolution on learning of his death promises more excitement to the new conspiracy than it is able to generate when Northumberland has retired to Scotland

> Let heaven kiss earth! now let not Nature's hand
> Keep the wild flood confined! let order die.
>
> (I, i, 154-5)

But order must not be allowed to die: that is the lesson of *Henry IV*. Scrope is too faintly drawn to replace the Percies as a pivot of revolt, even though he

---

[1] See Bullough, Vol. IV, p. 253.

Doth enlarge his rising with the blood
Of fair King Richard, scraped from Pomfret stones . . .

                                                    (I, i, 204-5)

Mowbray, too, is eager to avenge his father's banishment, and death
in the Holy Land which Bolingbroke will never reach. It looks for a
moment as if the lesson of Shrewsbury has been learnt, for Lord
Bardolph reminds the Archbishop how Hotspur had

lined himself with hope
Eating the air on promise of supply,
Flattering himself in project of a power
Much smaller than the smallest of his thoughts:
And so, with great imagination
Proper to madmen, led his powers to death,
And winking leap'd into destruction.

                                                    (I, iii, 27-33)

The conspiracy founders on the treachery of Prince John of
Lancaster, and also maybe on the scepticism of the political ecclesi-
astic who leads it. Popular enthusiasm is a fragile basis for victory

An habitation giddy and unsure
Hath he that buildeth on the vulgar heart.
O thou fond many, with what loud applause
Did'st thou beat heaven with blessing Bolingbroke,
Before he was what thou would'st have him be.

                                                    (I, iii, 89-93)

The 'fond many' are compared to a 'common dog' disgorging its
'glutton bosom of the royal Richard'; the ghost of the Divine Right
walks again, and not for long are we allowed to forget it

They that, when Richard lived, would have him die,
Are now become enamour'd on his grave:
Thou that threw'st upon his goodly head
When through proud London he came sighing on
After the admiréd heels of Bolingbroke,
Criest now 'O earth, yield us that King again,
And take thou this.'

                                                    (III, i, 101-7)

I have no doubt that Shakespeare shared these anti-populist opinions,
for the time gave them proof

Past and to come seems best; things present worst . . .
                                                    (III, i, 108)

The Prince has lost a good deal of his resilience. 'Before God I am
exceeding weary' are his opening words to Poins, and he goes on to
ask: 'Doth it not show vilely in me to desire small beer?' — by which
he means low company. He admits that his 'heart bleeds inwardly
that my father is so sick', and that if he should weep, 'every man

would think me an hypocrite indeed' because, as Poins tells him, he
has 'been so lewd and so much engraffed to Falstaff'. He has indeed
supplied Falstaff with a pert young page, but the only time we see
them together is when he and Poins are disguised as bartenders at the
Boar's Head, and overhear no good of themselves. The old intimacy
has gone. As Peto brings word that 'a dozen captains' are knocking at
all the tavern doors in search of Falstaff — which lends some colour
to Morgann's special pleading — the transition from prose to verse
hints already at a change of heart

> By heaven, Poins, I feel me much to blame
> So idly to profane the precious time; . . .
> Give me my sword and cloak. Falstaff, good night.
>
> (II, iv, 390 *et seq.*)

He never speaks to Falstaff again until the day of his coronation, and
then it will be over the public address system.

The King in his first short scene with Warwick (III, i) does not
advert to the Prince's deliquencies — Shrewsbury must have given
him temporary reassurance; what afflicts him is the general ill health
of the Kingdom

> How foul it is; what rank diseases grow,
> And with what danger, near the heart of it!
>
> (III, i, 39-40)

and what particularly rankles is the defection of Northumberland

> 'Tis not ten years gone
> Since Richard and Northumberland, great friends
> Did feast together; and in two years often
> Were they at war; it is but eight years since
> This Percy was the man nearest my soul . . .
>
> (III, i, 57-61)

His disillusion echoes the Archbishop's 'What trust is in these times?'
(I, iii, 100). In the fourth act he commends the Prince to Clarence
with a shrewd eye to his mercurial temperament

> For he is gracious, if he be observed:
> He hath a tear for pity, and a hand
> Open as day for melting charity:
> Yet notwithstanding, being incensed, he's flint,
> As humorous as winter, and as sudden
> As flaws congealéd in the spring of day . . .
>
> (IV, iv, 30-7)

But when he learns that, so far from hunting at Windsor, the Prince is
dining in London 'with Poins and other his continual followers', all
his misgivings return, and it is left for Warwick to allay them very
much as the Prince himself might have spoken in his own defence

> The Prince but studies his companions
> Like a strange tongue, wherein, to gain the language
> 'Tis needful that the most immodest word
> Be look'd upon and learn'd
>
> (IV, iv, 61-71)

prophesying, truly enough, that he

> will in the perfectness of time
> Cast off his followers; and their memory
> Shall as a pattern or a measure live
> By which his grace must mete the lives of others
> Turning past evils to advantages . . .
>
> (IV, iv, 74-7)

The Prince's gesture in removing the crown from his father's pillow and leaving the room with it on his head — a detail Shakespeare had taken from his sources — should not be misconstrued, though it lent itself to misconstruction. It was a gesture, albeit indecently premature, of total dedication

> Lo, here it sits,
> Which God shall guard: and put the world's whole strength
> Into one giant arm, it shall not force
> This lineal honour from me: this from thee
> Will I to mine leave, as 'tis left to me.
>
> (IV, v, 43-7)

The Prince's mood is indicated by Warwick who explains to the King how he had found him

> in the next room
> Washing with kindly tears his gentle cheeks
>
> (IV, v, 83-4)

but more explanation than this is needed before father and son are reconciled, and Bolingbroke has once again confessed

> By what by-paths and indirect crook'd ways
> I met this crown.
>
> (IV, v, 185-6)

It falls upon Hal 'in a more fairer sort', but even so he will be well advised, with the late conspiracy's 'stings and teeth newly ta'en out', to 'busy giddy minds with foreign quarrels'. That he has in him the grace of magnanimity as well as the stuff of statesmanship is shown by his treatment of the Lord Chief Justice who had not forgotten that box on the ear, and feared that the Prince had not forgotten its consequences

> What! rate, rebuke, and roughly send to prison
> The immediate heir of England!
>
> (V, ii, 70-1)

But now he returns the sword of justice to its appointed custodian

> With this remembrance, that you use the same
> With the like bold, just, and impartial spirit
> As you have done 'gainst me.
>
> (V, ii, 115-17)

The test, however, will be Falstaff whom, in Part Two, we first meet replying to the Lord Chief's accusations with an invincible impudence. He is older now, and the doctor has warned him that he may have more diseases than he knows of. But though disreputable, he is not *déclassé*; the Lord Chief can still bid him 'commend me to my cousin Westmoreland', as if he were in the habit of dining with Westmoreland when he was not dining at the Boar's Head. Moreover he is engaged to march, as well as his legs will carry him, 'with Prince John of Lancaster against the Archbishop and the Earl of Northumberland'. His next meeting with the 'rusty arm of the law' is in the street where Mistress Quickly sues him for debt and breach of promise. We must not picture the Boar's Head as a seedy tavern, for Quickly refers to her 'parcel-gilt goblet', her plate, tapestries, and 'dining-chambers'. It may be in Eastcheap but it is not, so to speak, in the 'East End'. Here Pistol and Doll Tearsheet are new acquaintances. Pistol is wholly, and to us incomprehensibly, Elizabethan; Shakespeare must have met his like, returned bragging from the French or the Flemish wars. Doll might have exchanged the time of night with Mr Gladstone. James Agate wrote of this scene in a performance of the play at Oxford[1]

> There was a moment then when I became sensible of the greatest effect of which the art of the dramatist is capable — the Pisgah-like view of human life. The scene was the Eastcheap tavern; the musicians were playing; the Prince and Poins had entered in disguise; and Doll had asked her whoreson little Bartholomew boar-pig when he would leave fighting o' days and foining o'nights, and begin to patch up his old body for heaven. From the fat Knight's 'Peace, good Doll! Do not speak like a death's head; do not bid me remember mine end' down to his 'I am old, I am old', it seemed that night at Oxford as though the world stood still and the English centuries were spread beneath one like a map.

The English counties also, when Shallow asks Silence 'How a good yoke of bullocks at Stamford fair?'; and the Inns of Court when he boasts of fighting 'with one Sampson Stockfish, a fruiterer, behind Gray's Inn'. Old men forget, but insignificant proper names lodge in the memory, and here they give the incandescent particularity of poetry to Shakespeare's prose — 'little John Doit of Staffordshire, and black John Barnes, and Francis Pickbone, and Will Squele, a

---

[1] *Playgoing* (1927), pp. 73-4.

Cotswold man'. This is language that actors like to speak, and how wonderfully they have spoken it since the days when H. O. Nicholson quavered on the Bench with the Bensonians, and Olivier almost made us forget how, the night before, he had fought and died as Hotspur. Here is all the pathos — never less than excruciatingly funny — of a life which had been perfectly hollow since the small hours when he lay with Jane Nightwork, and listened to the chimes at midnight from Old St Paul's. Jane Nightwork is still alive, but 'old, old, Master Shallow' — like all those who had enjoyed her favours, and the many others who had not, in this play where age is already rotting the apples in the straw, as it is rotting the guts of the commonwealth. If Shallow was Shakespeare's sly dig at Justice Gardiner, who had tried to close the Swan, or a paying off of old scores against Sir Thomas Lucy, it was a remarkably good-humoured *riposte*.

Shallow remembers Falstaff as a 'good back-sword man' — he was evidently capable of stabbing worthier targets than Mistress Quickly, and we have already seen him chasing Pistol out of doors — and in recruiting his ragged army he nicely balances the occasion of duty with the opportunity of corruption. The mind is always in the ascendant. He remembers Shallow at Clement's Inn 'like a man made after supper of a cheese-paring; when a' was naked, he was, for all the world, like a forked radish, with a head fantastically carved upon it with a knife' — but still worth 'two philosopher's stones' to this Olympian buffoon for whom 'the great globe itself' is not too large for his comment. We understand Prince John's duplicity a little better when Falstaff tells us he is a teetotaller; and class relationships in the Cotswolds when he notes that Shallow's servants 'by observing of him, do bear themselves like foolish justices; he, by conversing with them, is turned into a justice-like serving-man'. Falstaff understands everything except the truth of his own situation.

Illusion is magnified six times over when Pistol swaggers in to that hilarious al fresco supper party with the news of the young King's accession. But parties will no longer be the same at the Boar's Head now that Doll Tearsheet, big with child, is on her way to the whipping-post because one or two men have been killed competing for her. The short little scene is a warning that the weather has changed in Eastcheap, and indicates the passage of time required for Falstaff, Shallow, and the rest to ride up from Gloucestershire. To understand the Rejection one must picture the scene. The streets more crowded than any stage is likely to show them; the population jubilant; the nobility in procession; the King anointed. And then, breaking out from the massed spectators, Falstaff emerges — a familiar figure to many of them. Henry, facing his future, is suddenly confronted with his past — and a past which has been the subject of public obloquy. It is the crucial test. If he wavers, rumour will again be rife. He dare not falter. Shakespeare certainly invites us to sympathize with Falstaff — and this we do readily enough — but I think he also invites us to sympathize with Hal. Having a difficult thing to do, he does it clumsily — even cruelly — but he also does it courageously. His victory over Hotspur, in an equal contest of valour, had been a victory of intelligence over temperament; his victory over Falstaff is a victory of conscience over compassion. Falstaff is not so lovable — is he indeed ever lovable? — that we cannot bear to see him go. Because he is so much larger than life, life no longer has room for him. And has he indeed really gone? 'If you be not cloyed with fat meat' the Epilogue tells us 'our humble author will continue the story with Sir John in it'. Evidently those Bankside audiences were in need of reassurance. Biding his time, Shakespeare would keep his options open, and they, no doubt, their fingers crossed.

Chapter 10

'The Great Globe Itself'

1

Among the warmest admirers of Falstaff, it appears, was the Queen herself. Shakespeare's first biographer, Nicholas Rowe, tells us that she 'was so well pleased with that admirable character of Falstaff that she commanded him to continue it for one play more, and to show him in love'. John Dennis, the literary critic, writing 105 years later, also noted that *The Merry Wives of Windsor* was written by royal command, and that the Queen was 'so eager to see it acted that she commanded it to be finished in fourteen days and was afterwards, as tradition tells us, very well pleased with the representation'. These traditions are respectable, although they may need correction in detail.

If Elizabeth gave Shakespeare a deadline, she obviously wanted the play for a special occasion. Now in April 1597 Lord Hunsdon, the Lord Chamberlain, was among the new Knights of the Garter elected at Westminster, and they were all invested in St George's Chapel, Windsor, on 24th May. Shakespeare, with the other Lord Chamberlain's Men, was certainly among the retinue of servants and retainers who rode down from London for the ceremony, 'in blue coats faced with orange-coloured taffeta, and orange-coloured feathers in their hats, most part having chains of gold'. Internal evidence from the play confirms this supposition. What does Dr Caius mean when he says that he will go to the Court for the 'grande affaire'? Anne Page gives us the answer when she bids the elves

> Search Windsor Castle, elves, within and out . . .
> The several chairs of order look you scour
> With juice of balm and every precious flower:
> Each fair instalment, coat, and several crest,
> With loyal blazon, evermore be blest!
> And nightly, meadow-fairies, look you sing
> Like to the Garter's compass, in a ring.

> (V, v, 59; 64-9)

Of course the elves do nothing of the sort; the speech is a clear reference to the annual ceremony at which the Knights take their places, each in his own stall and under his own canopy, in St George's Chapel.

The play gives us a further clue. In Act IV Scene III Bardolph rushes in to mine Host of the Garter with the following request

> Bard. Sir, the Germans desire to have three of your
>   horses: the duke himself will be tomorrow at
>   court, and they are going to meet him.
> Host   What duke should that be that comes so secretly?
>   I hear not of him in the court. Let me speak
>   with the gentlemen: they speak English?
> Bard. Ay, sir; I'll call them to you.
> Host   They shall have my horses; but I'll make them
>   pay; they have had my house a week at command;
>   I have turned away my other guests; they must
>   come off; I'll sauce them.
>
> (IV, iii, 1-11)

We hear no more of these mysterious Germans until Act IV Scene V, when Bardolph comes in to tell Mine Host that they have run away with the horses

> Bard. . . . for as soon as I came beyond Eton, they threw
>   me off, from behind one of them, in a slough of
>   mire; and set spurs and away, like three German
>   devils, three Doctor Faustuses.
> Host   They are gone but to meet the Duke, villain: do
>   not say they be fled: Germans are honest men.
>
> (IV, v, 65-71)

Then arrives Sir Hugh Evans with more precise information

> Evans Have a care of your entertainments: there is a
>   friend of mine come to town, tell me there is
>   three cozen-germans that has cozened all the hosts
>   of Reading, of Maidenhead, of Colebrook, of horses
>   and money.
>
> (IV, v, 72-5)

and he is followed by Dr Caius

> Caius It is a tell-a-me dat you make grand preparation
>   for a duke de Zamany: by my trot, der is no duke
>   dat the court is know to come.
>
> (IV, v, 82-5)

That is the last we hear of the Germans; reasonably enough, since they have nothing to do with the play. Why then did Shakespeare drag them in? Because Frederick, Duke of Württemberg, previously Count of Mömpelgart, was due to be invested with the Garter on that day. For years he had been plaguing Elizabeth to give him this honour, but she exercised her genius for procrastination until, at last for political reasons, she gave way. He was elected to the Order in *absentia*, but was not informed of the fact until after the ceremony of investiture had taken place. She even postponed the dispatch of his insignia; this was an expensive business, and Elizabeth was careful about money when it suited her. Since the rumour ran that his followers had misused a warrant for taking up post-horses free of charge, Shakespeare could not resist the topical allusion. The Duke of Württemberg was a popular figure of fun, like any other man who notoriously cadges for honours, and the dramatist's joke at his expense would appear to date the first performance either at Windsor on 24th May, or more probably a month earlier at Westminster where the election of the new Knights took place. If the Lord Chamberlain's singing boys were used for the masquerade, they could more conveniently have rehearsed in London.

This strange interpellation — for Shakespeare was not in the habit of leaving a theme, however subsidiary, hanging in the air — argues haste, or else a defective prompter's copy. Haste there must have been; for if we are right in supposing that *Henry IV, Part One* was performed at Christmas 1597, then the dramatist would have his hands full with *Part Two*, and his mind already on *Henry V*. He was unlikely to have thanked the Queen for the interruption. The play must have been written before *Henry V*, if only for the reason that Falstaff is still very much alive; and probably before *Henry IV, Part Two* had been completed, since there is no mention of his disgrace. This is a younger Falstaff, in the pink of health and with the means to hire a suite at the Garter Inn for himself and his hangers-on, and flying at higher game than Doll Tearsheet. He has all of the outer, but little of the inner, man. It was the secret of Falstaff to survive all his situations except the last, but in *The Merry Wives* he survives none of them. Shakespeare was so possessed with his decline and fall that he was too scrupulous an artist to transfer the same person, even under royal command, from London to Windsor, and from medieval to Elizabethan times. So he keeps the familiar name and figure, and brings along with them a number of the other characters that were in his mind at the moment, Pistol and Bardolph, Shallow and Nym. Master Fenton, we learn, had set the town alight with Prince Hal and Poins before his affections settled on Anne Page. Dr Caius was a convenient butt for the fashionable Francophobia that Shakespeare was presently to flatter in *Henry V*. Sir Hugh Evans may have been a kindly tilt at his old schoolmaster, Thomas Jenkins; and the part gave a further opportunity to the Welsh actor who had played Glendower and was afterwards to play Fluellen. The three strands of the plot — Falstaff and the Wives, Fenton and Slender in competition for Anne Page, the quarrel between Dr Caius and Sir Hugh — are neatly dovetailed; and in all the circumstances we should not complain if *The Merry Wives* does not rank with the greater Shakespearean comedies. It was, perhaps, the nearest he came to a pot-boiler – but this was no ordinary pot.

The play is interesting if it is seen as a parenthesis rather than a sequel; and more interesting still as an occasion to include the commercial middle classes in a social panorama from which they had hitherto been excluded. Ford is the kind of customer one would have preferred not to meet over a business deal – as suspicious, maybe, of his clients as he was suspicious of his wife. The hints are many of bourgeois comfort and recreation – coursing the hare; neighbours calling on one another and gathered round the 'country fire'; the picture conjured up of blazing logs, venison turning on the spit, and copper saucepans hanging in the inglenook – and all under the benevolent shadow of the Castle. It was the life that Shakespeare had known at Stratford, upon which he was never to turn his back, but of which he allows us so few hints elsewhere. The play can warm the heart if it is not pushed overboard into farce, but one's ears, unravished by poetry, are left wistfully longing for Verdi.

2

For some time James Burbage had been suffering from the hostility of the City fathers. This was increased with the appointment of the new Lord Chamberlain in 1596. Thomas Nashe writes to a friend in the summer of that year: 'Now the players . . . are piteously persecuted by the Lord Mayor and the aldermen, and however in their old Lord's time they thought their state settled, it is now so uncertain they cannot build upon it.'[1] Burbage died on 2 February 1596, and the 'Theatre' passed into the hands of his widow and his two sons, Cuthbert and Richard. The twenty-one years' lease of the land was due to run out in April 1597, and the building itself, no longer fashionable as it once had been, was in a poor state of repair. The landlord, feeling no doubt the ill wind that blew from the City, was unwilling to renew the tenancy; and the Burbage brothers, with Shakespeare and four others of the Lord Chamberlain's men – Augustine Phillips, Thomas Pope, John Heminge, and William Kempe – decided to transfer the theatre, lock, stock, and timbers, to a site on Bankside for which they secured a lease of thirty-one years. The original building was taken down, in defiance of the landlord, late in December 1598, and erected – much improved no doubt – in Southwark at some date between January and May 1599. The ground landlord of the 'Theatre' brought an action against the carpenter who supervised its removal, but lost his suit.

[1] See Hotson, *Shakespeare versus Shallow* (1931), p. 16.

In the year of his death James Burbage had bought the much smaller, indoors theatre in Blackfriars, which had been empty since 1584. It stood on what used to be the site of *The Times* publishing offices in Printing House Square. He considerably embellished the interior, but his son Richard was too busy with transplanting the 'Theatre', and playing leading parts in Shakespeare, to make himself responsible for its management. It was therefore handed over to the Children of the Chapel Royal. The exact site of the Globe, as the 'Theatre' was now rechristened, has given rise to much dispute. It appears to have stood either on the north or the south side of Maid Lane a street running parallel to the river and afterwards to be renamed Globe Alley. In 1909 a commemorative tablet was placed on the South side, on the wall of Barclay and Perkins' brewery; but Visscher's panoramic map of London (1616) indicates that it stood on the opposite side of the street.

If, as I think it plausible to suggest, the Globe opened its doors with the first performance of *Henry V*, that would have been the most historic occasion in the annals of the English theatre. The audience presumably had some idea of what the building would look like, and there is a hint in the opening chorus that Shakespeare thought it might have looked a little better, or at any rate a little bigger. Did he speak the Chorus himself? He might well have done so. Did the old timbers creak a little? How did they compare with what Henslowe had done with the Rose, or Langley with the Swan? We cannot tell. There is a hint also that the Lord Chamberlain's Men were a shade depressed. Did Richard Burbage feel that Henry V was small beer after Richard III as an acting part? Was Kempe sulking because Falstaff was dead, and he, like everyone else, 'must mourn therefore'? However that may be, Shakespeare felt he must apologize for all those

> flat unraiséd spirits that have dared
> On this unworthy scaffold to bring forth
> So great an object: can this cockpit hold
> The vasty fields of France? Or may we cram
> Within this wooden O the very casques
> That did affright the air at Agincourt?

(Chorus, Act I)

And so he appealed to the 'imaginary forces' to which he had already, in other plays, given a good deal of salutary exercise

> Think, when we talk of horses, that you see them
> Printing their proud hoofs in the receiving earth

(ibid.)

and here the Dauphin was certainly to do better than any hobby-horse that might have been allowed on the stage, or reluctant nag that might have shambled into the yard. But this was the least of the dramatist's appeals to the audience. Later on they must

> Suppose that you have seen
> The well-appointed King at Hampton pier
> Embark his royalty
>
> (Chorus, Act III)

and then at Southampton

> his brave fleet
> With silken streamers the young Phoebus fanning
>
> (ibid.)

they must imagine

> Upon the hempen tackle ship-boys climbing
>
> (ibid.)

and

> behold the threaden sails,
> Borne with the invisible and creeping wind
>
> (ibid.)

— providential weather for D-day —

> Draw the huge bottoms through the furrow'd sea
> Breasting the lofty surge
>
> (ibid.)

although one cannot help wondering how an 'invisible and creeping wind' would have created a 'lofty surge'. And so to the 'cripple tardy-gaited night' before Agincourt where poetry struggles, and not in vain, against a grey or glaring afternoon on the South Bank; and then finally to what we are not to see, even in the dumbest and most denuded show — the King's victorious return

> Behold, the English beach
> Pales in the flood with men, with wives and boys,
> Whose shouts and claps out-voice the deep-mouth'd sea
> (Chorus, Act V)

the nobility assembled on Blackheath, asking that

> His bruiséd helmet and his bendéd sword

should be carried before him into the city; his characteristic refusal

> Giving full trophy, signal and ostent
> Quite from himself to God
>
> (ibid.)

and the 'mayor and all his brethren in best sort' who

> Go forth and fetch their conquering Caesar in.
>
> (ibid.)

Now observe that all this precedes the wooing of the French princess, and that in fact we never get back to London at all. But Shakespeare feels obliged to squeeze it in, because the play was highly topical. On 27th March of that same year, 1599, Essex had ridden out from London to take command of an army, recruited for its time-dishonoured occupation of suppressing the Irish. We read that 'about two o'clock in the afternoon he took horse in Seeding Lane, and from thence being accompanied with divers noblemen, and many others, himself very plainly attired, rode through Grace-street, Cornhill, Cheapside, and other high streets, in all which places, and in the fields, the people pressed exceedingly to behold him.' *Henry V* was evidently produced while Essex was away, and in the same chorus Shakespeare imagines his return, comparing it with that of his patriot King

> Were now the general of our gracious empress,
> As in good time he may, from Ireland coming,
> Bringing rebellion broachéd on his sword,
> How many would the peaceful city quit
> To welcome him!
>
>   (ibid.)

But, of course, as we know, Essex's return had consequences both unfortunate and unforeseen.

The Lord Chamberlain's Men were among those to suffer from them. Two years later, on the eve of that insane insurrection, a number of Essex's partisans — doubtless Southampton was among them — offered Augustine Phillips, whose particular friendship with Shakespeare was well known, forty shillings to put on a performance of *Richard II*. Phillips replied that the play had been so long out of the repertory that it would be hard to attract an audience. Nevertheless the performance took place on Saturday, 7 February 1600-1. In August of that year the Queen complained that the play had been given 'forty times in open streets and houses'. This referred no doubt to the company's prudent absence on tour after the rising. It was stated at Essex's trial that he had often attended performances of the play 'with great applause giving countenance and liking to the same'. Phillips was called as a witness and explained the circumstances of its revival. But the Lord Chamberlain's Men passed unscathed through a ticklish ordeal. It is worth noting, however, that all reference to Richard's deposition was omitted from the Quartos of *Henry IV* until James I had succeeded to the throne. The Queen remained sensitive on the subject: 'I am Richard II, know ye not that?' she exclaimed.

The tensions that gave an abundant life and variety to *Henry IV* are absent from *Henry V*, which contains too many words for its matter. Shakespeare wisely decided to leave Falstaff out of the play, though not out of the picture, for nothing in his life became him like the leaving it. Mistress Quickly's account of his death is the summit of a work in which he does not appear. He dies, as he had lived, immortally. The field must be left clear for the 'Prince of all humours' to show his paces as the patriot King. Henry is the same man who had assumed the crown with confidence and humility at the close of *Henry IV*, but the Rejection of Falstaff would have been an unhappy note to end on. Thoughtful as we have seen him even in his 'thoughtlessness', he is now thoughtful in the preoccupations of sovereignty. 'Giddy minds' at home exercise him more than the 'foreign quarrels' which he hopes will restore their balance; and they are given short shrift before he embarks at Southampton. He listens patiently to Canterbury's pedantic exposition of the Salic law, though he probably understands it as little as the average audience, and wishes as fervently that it would come to an end. Still, if an Archbishop tells him he can wage a war of dynastic aggression, who is he to say him nay? He was not likely to suspect that the path to Hell is paved with canon lawyers. Moreover the right of a woman to succeed to the throne would readily have been conceded by a Tudor audience. There is no animus in Henry's challenge to the French, though a good deal of popular prejudice runs through Shakespeare's treatment of them. In the anonymous *Famous Victories*, to which he stuck more closely here than in *Henry IV*, the Archbishop advises the King to attack the Scots before he tackles the French. It was very much a case of 'Who shall we play on Saturday? Anything to keep the boys out of mischief.'

Heraldry is seldom lacking to productions of *Henry V*, and the great feudal names — Warwick and Talbot, Salisbury and Gloucester — resound in the rhetoric of Agincourt. But, for all that, this is an essentially democratic Henry at a time when democracy was not even a dirty word. He has discovered within himself the kingship he has inherited, and through his comradeship with other men. Always in the front line and always in command, he is on terms of common humanity with the least of his 'Old Contemptibles'. They are a mixed lot, to be sure. No shreds of romanticism, now that Falstaff's 'fuel is out', cling to the Bohemia of the Boar's Head. Bardolph swings on a gibbet after stealing a pyx, and Pistol, characteristically escaping with his life, returns home to boast of the wounds he had earned from Fluellen's cudgel. Fluellen is the most vital character in the play; and he speaks to the King with a Celtic instinct for equality. David Jones, whose *In Parenthesis* immortalized the experience of the 1914-18 War, described to me how, as a private in the Welsh Fusiliers, he saw a fellow-private cleaning out the latrines of a forward trench, and observed what a disagreeable job the man had on hand. The answer came pat, as it might have come from Fluellen himself: 'The army of Artaxerxes was utterly destroyed for lack of any sanitation whatever.' Dover Wilson was not alone in supposing the character to have been inspired by Sir Roger Williams of Penrhos, a gallant and eccentric Welshman who had fought with Sir Philip Sidney in the Low Countries, and later with Henry of Navarre. He was the author of *A Briefe Discourse of Warre* (1590), in which, though never niggard of theory, he upheld the priority of practice. Like Fluellen, he took Alexander the Great as his exemplar: 'What caused Alexander to overthrow Darius, with few men, considering his number?' The same valour, he argued, that enabled Henry V, despite a similar inferiority, to defeat his enemies.

It was, a little surprisingly, an army of all the nationalities at a time when the English were fighting the Scots, the Welsh, and the Irish at least as often as they were fighting the French. Captain Gower is a simple officer from any regiment of the line; Macmorris is eager to pick a quarrel, and Jamy to weigh the pros and cons of an argument; Williams and Bates are the voice of the 'poor bloody infantry', although they speak in prose that does not normally sweeten the vernacular of the barrack-room. It is they who remind the King of his humanity, just as the defection of the 'northern Percies' had reminded Richard II

> I think the King is but a man as I am: the violet smells to him as it doth to me; the element shows to him as it doth to me; all his senses have but human conditions: his ceremonies laid by, in his nakedness he appears but a man; and though his affections are higher mounted than ours, yet, when they stoop, they stoop with a like wing.
>
> (IV, i, 104-12)

The Elizabethans had a passion for ceremony and Shakespeare, conservative though he was, seems to have thought one could have too much of it. For this conversation, in the small hours of that dispiriting vigil, gave Henry his cue for reflection and, afterwards, for a vicarious remorse

> O ceremony, show me but thy worth!
> What is thy soul of adoration?
> Art thou aught else but place, degree, and form
> Creating awe and fear in other men?
> Wherein thou art less happy being fear'd
> Than they in fearing
>
> (IV, i, 261-6)

and this leads to the prayer in which, for the last time in the tetralogy, the ghost of Richard troubles his posterity

> Not today, O Lord,
> O, not today, think not upon the fault
> My father made in compassing the crown:
> I Richard's body have interréd new;
> And on it have bestow'd more contrite tears
> Than from it issued forcéd drops of blood:
> Five hundred poor I have in yearly pay,
> Who twice a-day their wither'd hands hold up
> Toward heaven, to pardon blood; and I have built
> Two chantries, where the sad and solemn priests
> Sing still for Richard's soul. More will I do;
> Though all that I can is nothing worth,
> Since that my penitence comes after all
> Imploring pardon.
>
> (IV, i, 309-22)

Only a perverse cynicism will discredit this as hypocrisy. The pathos of kingship, in Shakespeare's vision, lies in the inalienable humanity of kings. Chantries and requiems may, or may not, have wiped out the stains of murder and usurpation, but Henry at least felt the need of sending his father's sins to the laundry, though he makes no mention of his own. By the time Agincourt has been won, however, and policy has brought its crown to conquest in the alliance with Katharine of France, it seems that plenary absolution has at last been granted. But Shakespeare's audience knew better; the first tetralogy had told them how the conquests would all be lost, and how once again the 'giddy minds' would foster 'the discord of nobility'. *Henry V* is a patriotic parenthesis between one discord and another.

Yet the patriot King is not quite too good to be true, and at one point he loses his temper. Hearing that all the 'boys' who form part of his rag-bag of an army have been killed by the French, he gives orders that every soldier shall kill his prisoner. This retaliation is too often dishonestly cut in performance, and there is a hint that Shakespeare was none too happy about it. As Professor Bullough has pointed out,[1] Fluellen compares Henry to Alexander the Great not only in his victories, but in 'his rages, and his furies, and his displeasures, and his indignations'. An Elizabethan audience might have resented the Rejection of Falstaff rather more than the killing of the prisoners, for which the unexpected mustering of the French cavalry was the excuse; but here Fluellen maintains that the King was 'in his right wits and good judgements'. The impetuosity of the one action — in character with Henry IV's diagnosis of his son, 'being incens'd, he's flint' — is contrasted with the calculation of the other. Fluellen was too serious a soldier to nourish any sentimental illusions about Falstaff. Whatever Shakespeare thought about the killing of

---

[1] See Bullough, Vol. IV, p. 367.

the prisoners — and a lawyer[1] writing in 1599 thought it perfectly justified, since they might have joined up with the French counter-attack — he snatched at the opportunity to humanize a man whom Holinshed had described as 'a majestie . . . that both lived and died a paterne in princehood, a lode-starre in honour, and mirrour of magnificence'. In the wooing of Katharine he even credits him with a sense of humour which an insensitive performance can easily translate into vulgarity.

The chauvinism of the play is unblushing and this makes much of it distasteful to a modern audience. Mountjoy has dignity both in challenge and defeat; Burgundy speaks nobly of the havoc wrought in the countryside when the 'dogs of war' are unleashed upon it; and Charles VI is quite unwarrantably presented on the stage as certifiably insane. But of the French army we only see the aristocracy languid or boasting at their headquarters, and only a single *poilu* who cowers before Pistol. The English casualties are ridiculously light, although Shakespeare got them from Holinshed, and 'Davy Gam Esquire' is another example of his genius for proper names, for which, in this case, he had historical warrant.

Henry V is a military progress, a demonstration of men and monarchy under arms rather than an action dramatic in its own right. Other writers of the time were hankering after the epic form, of which there was no example in English literature. Daniel, in the fourth book of his *Civil Wars*, had lamented

> O what external matter here is found!
> Whence new immortal *Iliads* might proceed

and by his use of a Chorus, as well as by the narrative structure of the play, Shakespeare went some way to meet the demand. The conflict is extrinsic to the characters; the Scots or the Welsh or the Irish would have served as usefully as the French. It should be seen as a coda rather than a climax to the second historical tetralogy. But in its fluent prosody, and easy alternations of verse and prose, its adroit use of material, and in certain of its characterizations it shows Shakespeare's technical powers at their height. The stage lights up whenever Fluellen is in full spate of classical analogy, and the shadows fall when Mistress Quickly, on hearing that Falstaff is ill, declares with a piercing simplicity that 'the King has killed his heart'. But the stiffer challenge to that limitless imagination was yet to come.

---

[1] R. Crompton, *The Mansion of Magnanimitie.*

Chapter 11

The Uses of Adversity

1

We must retrace our steps a little. Of the works considered up to now
— seventeen plays, two long narrative poems, and the *Sonnets* — all
were written within the eleven years from 1588 to 1599. It was an
astonishing achievement, the output of a lifetime for another man;
yet Shakespeare was only thirty-five years old. Nor was this all, for
he was still able to turn out three comedies of which no account has
as yet been given, written concurrently, one must suppose, with the
last three plays of the second tetralogy. Comedy was his natural vein
during these later years of the 1590s, though chequered as comedy
generally is in real life. When the skies are clear — as they are in *The
Taming of the Shrew* and *The Merry Wives of Windsor* — he is writing
below his best; competently enough, to be sure, but not as we prefer
to remember him. Shakespeare was an inclusive dramatist, with all
life as his subject, whatever his particular theme; and here there was
too much left out.

Reference has been made to the trial and execution of Dr Lopez in
1594. A Portuguese Jew, he was the Queen's personal physician. For
a time he had been attached to the household of the Earl of
Leicester, who may well have introduced him to the Queen. Here he
must have been known to James Burbage when Burbage was a
member of Leicester's company; it is possible that Shakespeare
himself may have met him. Accused of a plot, fostered by Spanish
agents, to poison the Queen and Antonio Perez, a victim of Philip II's
persecution, whom Essex had brought over to England, he was
convicted on evidence that many people, and notably the Queen
herself, regarded as insufficient. Nevertheless his disgrace and execution were a more than nine days' sensation at the time. They inspired
the revival of Marlowe's *The Jew of Malta* by the Lord Admiral's
Men, and fifteen performances of this were recorded between the
Lopez trial and the end of 1594. A wave of anti-Semitism swept the
country which Marlowe's colossal caricature did much to flatter.

The Merchant of Venice, written two years later, flattered it only
slightly less. There can be no doubt that Shakespeare intended

Shylock to be the villain of the piece — and so, to a great extent, he is although he is equally its victim. Look at him closely, and you will not find in him a single likeable characteristic. He is ruthless, avaricious, vindictive, and his thrift is hardly to be distinguished from parsimony. Both his daughter and his servant detest him. He is far less likeable than the unfortunate Lopez, who was an 'accomplished linguist with friends in all parts of Europe'.[1] This, no doubt, is the way he was presented by Burbage, whose funeral elegy speaks of

> the red-haired Jew
> Which sought the bankrupt merchant's pound of flesh
> By woman-lawyer caught in his own mesh.

The red wig was canonical until Macklin exchanged it for a dark one, but it was only when Irving took the Lyceum by storm with his offended patriarch that the traditional interpretation was challenged. Audiences today are no longer anti-Semitic, but they are resolutely unsentimental, and Macklin's 'Jew that Shakespeare drew' has looked like coming into his own again. Yet this was a case where the dramatist drew deeper than he knew, or perhaps intended. Heinrich Heine, watching a performance at Drury Lane long before Irving reigned at the Lyceum, could write afterwards

> There stood behind me in the box a pale, fair Briton, who at the end of the Fourth Act, fell a-weeping passionately, several times exclaiming: 'The poor man is wronged' . . . When I think of those tears I have to rank *The Merchant of Venice* with the Tragedies, although the frame of the piece is decorated with the merriest figures of Masks, of Satyrs, and of Cupids, and the Poet meant the play for a Comedy.

Heine looked for Shylock on the Rialto, but found him in the synagogue on the Day of Atonement. Here he heard a voice which seemed 'the death-rattle of a soul sinking down dead-tired at heaven's gates. And I seemed to know the voice, and I felt that I had heard it long ago, when, in utter despair, it moaned out, then as now, "Jessica, my child".' Nevertheless Heine was right in acknowledging that Shakespeare meant the play to be a comedy, and as such it must be judged. The fatal bond is all but forgotten while another bond is being sealed with a kiss at Belmont; and forgotten altogether when 'the moon sleeps with Endymion' in the same enchanted garden, and wedding rings are seen to be absent from the fingers they should adorn.

It seems at least possible that Shakespeare knew of an earlier play, *The Jew*, to which reference is made by Stephen Gosson in his *Schoole of Abuse* (1578) representing 'the greedinesse of worldly chusers and bloody minds of Usurers'. Portia's suitors may have been

---

[1] Sidney Lee, *A Life of William Shakespeare* (1916), pp. 133-4n.

inspired by the first, and Shylock by the second, although many versions of a trusting debtor engaging himself to forfeit a part of his body to a usurer were current in the later Middle Ages. We miss the point of *The Merchant of Venice* if we forget the medieval doctrine that usury was a mortal sin; the Christians offer generosity before their advocate pleads for mercy. The theme of Jessica's elopement with Lorenzo came from a fifteenth-century *Novellino* by Masuccio di Salino, evidently at second hand since this had not been translated into English; and that of the caskets is variously treated by Boccaccio in the *Decameron* (Day X, Story I), by the *Gesta Romanorum*, and by Gower in the *Confessio Amantis*. Its prototype was a story by a Greek monk in the ninth century. Here a King invites his courtiers to choose between four chests of which two are encrusted with gold but contain human bones, and two are overlaid with pitch but contain 'exquisite gems and ointments of the richest colour'. Naturally they choose the chests which are most attractive to the eye, but the King reminds them that they should have chosen with the eye of the mind.

The parallel plots of *The Merchant of Venice* can be labelled Realism and Romance, and both of them — as Granville-Barker called them — fairy-tales. Now it is of the essence of a fairy-tale that it compels a 'willing suspension of disbelief'. We believe in the preposterous will that determines the choice of Portia's suitors; we believe in her submission to it, high-spirited and resourceful as she is; we believe that Bassanio will not recognize his own wife in cap and gown, and old Gobbo the voice of his own son; we believe in the bizarre legal procedure of the Venetian court; we believe that the Doge will have asked for 'old Bellario's' advice at the same time as Portia is borrowing his cap and gown. We can even ask ourselves what Jessica is doing in Genoa on her way to Belmont, and not wait for the answer. We can believe in Shylock's 'pound of flesh'. But Shylock himself has outstripped the dimension of fairy-tale. He belongs to another kind of play which might, as Heine suggested, have been a tragedy; and he turns *The Merchant of Venice* into something very like an allegory, although it does not say so.

This is the Venice of the High Renaissance; Titian might have been painting next door to Antonio's counting-house — or so it must have seemed when Reinhardt produced the play in the Campo San Trovaso, and Shylock came strolling with Bassanio across the bridge. Money and love are the reigning absolutes — money jealously hoarded or prodigally spent, romantic love or passionate friendship. The sense is vivid of new liveries and long overdrafts. Bassanio needs money to go a-wooing, and Lorenzo will live happily on a substantial private income. Much of the poetry has the mellow glitter, and the occasional heaviness, of gold. Gratiano is something of a Mercutio *manqué,* and the talk of 'masks and torchbearers' reminds one of the streets of Verona on the night of Capulet's ball. Shakespeare's Venice, like Shakespeare's England, is a commercial and seafaring aristocracy. Salarino speaks of

> dangerous rocks,
> Which touching but my gentle vessel's side
> Would scatter all her spices on the stream,
> Enrobe the roaring waters with my silks . . .
>
> (I, i, 31-4)

To an audience on Bankside this would recall the bustle and pageantry of the Thames no less than the piracy of Drake and Hawkins

> Elizabeth and Leicester
> Beating oars
> The stern was formed
> A gilded shell
> Red and gold
> The brisk swell
> Rippled both shores
> South-west wind
> Carried down stream
> The peal of bells
> White towers[1]

The bells of the Salute mingle with those of Old St Paul's, and Shylock's objection to the 'vile squealing of the wry-necked fife' echoes with a Puritan rancour.

In this society dedicated to the pursuit of happiness he is an outsider. As a Jew in a Christian community he is a natural outsider. The money which for others is a means to pleasure is for him a means to power. The irony of the play lies in this, that the letter of the law on which he takes his stand proves his undoing. The conflict, in both the fairy-tales, is between legalism and justice. Bassanio breaks through the letter of the law, without infringing it, by his choice of the right casket, for it is just that a man and woman who love each other should be free to marry. That, at least, is the Shakespearean ethic. It is just that a good man should escape the malevolence of a man whose vindictiveness will stop at nothing, whatever excuse he may think he has for it. Law is not broken in *The Merchant of Venice*, but it is reconciled with justice.

Shakespeare does not invite our sympathy for Shylock, and except in one passage Shylock does not invite it either

> Hath not a Jew eyes? hath not a Jew hands, organs, dimensions, affections,

[1] T. S. Eliot, 'The Waste Land'.

passions? fed with the same food, hurt with the same weapons, subject to the same diseases, healed by the same means, warmed and cooled by the same winter and summer as a Christian is?

(III, i, 61-6)

True enough, but these similarities are material; he does not add, as Richard II had done: 'taste grief, need friends'. Moreover the subsequent equation of the loss of his ducats with the loss of his daughter neutralizes whatever sympathy he may have aroused. Pride, not pathos, is his *forte*. I do not see him leave the court as a broken man; the terse, monosyllabic, 'I am not well' indicates, surely, not collapse but self-control. The tragedy of Shylock — for tragic he remains, and just beyond the limits of a comedy — lies in his character, not in his situation. This outsider is helplessly, incurably, circumscribed — whereas Jessica by marrying Lorenzo, and robbing her father into the bargain, breaks the barriers of history. An Elizabethan audience would have taken the point more kindly than we do.

Nonsensical attempts have been made to suggest a homosexual relationship between Antonio and Bassanio

> I saw Bassanio and Antonio part:
> Bassanio told him he would make some speed
> Of his return: he answer'd 'Do not so;
> Slubber not business for my sake, Bassanio,
> But stay the very riping of the time;
> And for the Jew's bond which he hath of me,
> Let it not enter in your mind of love:
> Be merry; and employ your chiefest thoughts
> To courtship, and such fair ostents of love
> As shall conveniently become you there.'
> And even there, his eye being big with tears,
> Turning his face, he put his hand behind him,
> And with affection wondrous sensible
> He wrung Bassanio's hand; and so they parted.

(II, viii, 36-49)

When Antonio says he 'knows not why I am so sad', the reason may have been that he felt himself to be one of nature's bachelors; but is not this exactly how two very close friends would say good-bye when the one realizes that marriage may separate him from the other? There is no need to saddle intimacy with ambivalence.

There was a time when stately performances of Portia turned her into something of a schoolmistress, and very much of a *châtelaine*. Of course, there is no doubt about the *château*, and Bassanio is well aware of it, 'In Belmont is a lady richly left'. But it has been left for Dorothy Tutin and Peggy Ashcroft to restore the 'unlesson'd girl, unschool'd, unpractis'd'. She is witty and resilient even when she is threatened by the success of an unwelcome suitor. Released from her gilded cage into the plenitude of love's fulfilment, she adventures as boldly and as far as any other heroine in the Shakespearean canon. If her heart is of gold, though the lucky casket be of lead, she is very far from leaving her 'other elements to grosser life'; the comedy of the rings is spiced with uninhibited allusions to the marriage bed. There is nothing wanting to her — beauty, humour, dignity, intelligence, and courage. The Prince of Morocco and the Prince of Aragon are the only threat to her good estate, and when she is rescued by Bassanio's choice of the right casket, she shows her mettle both of mind and heart by the resourceful rescue of Bassanio's best friend. No tears, only a pervading seriousness, cloud the still sunshine or the moonlit calm of *The Merchant of Venice*, and music reinforces its gravity. This is not lightened by Launcelot Gobbo, who is chiefly interesting for the coincidence of his surname with that of a servant at Southampton House. The play is of more solid substance than *A Midsummer Night's Dream* or *Love's Labour's Lost*, and for that reason less endearing to us. Belsen and Ravensbruck have made it harder to appreciate; and nothing Shakespeare wrote is more difficult to look at through Elizabethan eyes, for Shylock in one way, and the gilded youth of the Serene Republic in another, present the 'less acceptable faces of capitalism'. But it is the play in which Shakespearean Woman comes irresistibly of age, and her future will dazzle us for some years to come.

2

Just as *The Merchant of Venice* mingles melodrama and high romance, *Much Ado About Nothing* mingles melodrama and comedy of manners. Written for the greater part in prose, although it canters along 'the even road of a blank verse' when the dramatic tension heightens, it communicates a lightness of heart and labour, now that, in 1599, the effort of the tetralogy can be relaxed. Shakespeare is evidently worried by Essex's ambitions, and more particularly, one suspects, by Southampton's engagement in that *galère*

> favourites
> Made proud by princes, that advance their pride
> Against the power that bred it
>
> (III, i, 9-11)

but in general the mood, like the writing, is easy. As in *The Merchant* two plots are run in tandem, again brought together in the fourth act. One of them — the false suspicion that falls on Hero, with its potentially tragic consequence — is taken from Bandello's *Novelli* (no. xxii), translated into French by Belleforest in *Les Histoires*

Tragiques. It had also been used by Ariosto in *Orlando Furioso* (Canto V). This had been dramatized in English during Shakespeare's boyhood, and translated by Sir John Harington; and a variation of the story found its way into Spenser's *Faerie Queene*. All these sources were open to the dramatist, but it was not for nothing that Charles I inscribed 'Benedick and Beatrice' on his copy of the play, and that Berlioz composed an opera under the title. *Much Ado About Nothing* lives by virtue of what Shakespeare invented, not of what he found.

No one has invited us to treat the play as a fairy-tale, and here one meets a difficulty. Is it conceivable that Margaret, having learnt how her midnight conversation with Borachio had been misinterpreted, would not immediately have come forward with an explanation? Although she was on terms of nocturnal assignation with Borachio, how came she, in any case, to be in occupation of Hero's room? Shakespeare could have shown us Claudio and Don Pedro over-looking (if not overhearing) the scene, as he was later to show us Troilus and Ulysses eavesdropping on Cressida and Diomede. That he did not do so was due, no doubt, to the demands of plausibility, and because he was reserving Claudio's recriminations for the church scene. He was generally too cunning a playwright to repeat an effect. But it was also due, I think, to a technique of dramaturgy peculiar to this play, where nearly everything important is overheard, or heard about, before it is acted upon.

In the opening scene we hear that Claudio has 'borne himself beyond the promise of his age' — Shakespeare is anxious from the start to let him off as easily as he can; and that Benedick has 'done good service . . . in these wars'. In Act I, Scene 2, a servant of Antonio has misheard Don Pedro and Claudio 'walking in a thick-pleached alley' and gathered that the Prince was in love with Hero. Benedick overhears the conversation designed to make him think that Beatrice is in love with him, and Beatrice the conversation similarly designed to make her think that he is in love with her. The officers of the watch overhear Borachio's narration of the plot to entrap Hero. Benedick hears from Don Pedro how Beatrice 'did . . . one hour together trans-shape thy particular virtues; yet at last she concluded with a sigh, thou wast the properest man in Italy'. In other respects also, in this play, Shakespeare follows the technique of Polonius, and 'by indirection finds direction out'. It cannot be called anti-romantic since it ends with a double wedding; but it does suggest that romanticism has two faces, and that if one of them could wear a sleeve it would be laughing up it.

The verbal fencing between Benedick and Beatrice had been prefigured in *Love's Labour's Lost*. There is, indeed, much of

Berowne in Benedick, but Beatrice is no Dark Lady. She is closer to
Rosalind than to Rosaline, and she is also first cousin to Portia,
taking over, so to speak, from Portia's candid comments on her
suitors, and exchanging a wink over the comedy of the rings; but
Portia's 'How all the other passions fleet to air' would have been
beyond her. Portia is a heroine of high romance, where Beatrice is a
woman of the world — and of a world very remote from Belmont.
Both have the instinct of chivalry; 'Tarry a little, Jew' has the
authority of 'Kill Claudio'. But Portia moves in the element of
poetry, and Beatrice in that of prose — a prose as finely tempered as
any that Shakespeare was to write. Was the kinship between the
heroines in Shakespearean comedy inspired by a particular boy actor
exceptionally qualified to play them, or by a woman whom he loved
but whose identity we shall never know? It is a tempting, though
vain, conjecture.

The Claudio-Hero theme would be treated in more tragic depth in
The Winter's Tale. In each case a woman is wrongfully accused; is
presumed to die under the accusation; subsequently comes to life;
and is reconciled with her accuser. But where Claudio is an impetuous young man, behaving like a cad under the stress of emotion,
Leontes is a psychopath. Shakespeare returned to the same theme of
resurrection in *Pericles,* but in *Much Ado* he is careful not to give it
more weight than it will bear. He brilliantly contrives that Claudio's
denunciation of Hero shall be the occasion of Benedick and Beatrice
declaring their love, just as Bassanio's winning of Portia had led to
Antonio's salvation and Shylock's discomfiture. In both cases the
two plots are brought together in the climactic scene of the play;
and in *Much Ado* there is no need for a 'willing suspension of
disbelief'. Don John who causes all the trouble remains a very
summary sketch of a familiar Renaissance type — the malcontent
whose melancholy is a form of mental illness. When he has set the
conspiracy afoot he is expendable until, in the last lines of the play,
we learn of his arrest.

Dogberry and Verges at once lighten and tighten the melodrama,
for here the simplicity of fools unmasks the sophistication of knaves.
Aubrey had it that Dogberry was taken from the village constable at
Long Crendon where, as Dr Rowse reminds us, Shakespeare would
have passed on his way from Stratford to London. If so, he bettered
the acquaintance to marvellous effect. Dogberry stands with Bottom
and Falstaff among his greater creations in comedy that combine
breadth and delicacy. Note that the law which Falstaff set at
defiance and that the Lord Chief Justice represented with the dry
dignity of officialdom, finds its spokesman in a character which
excites both laughter and applause. Dogberry has an uncertain

command of the English language — he speaks beyond his schooling, confusing 'damnation' with 'salvation', 'sensible' with 'senseless', 'assembly' with 'dissembly', 'opinioned' with 'pinioned', and so forth — but in calling him an 'ass' Borachio is at once insulting and inaccurate. Such 'asses' are to the internal security of the commonwealth what the balance of payments is to its good housekeeping. Of all Shakespeare's characters it is Dogberry who makes anarchy indecent. The part was the last played by Will Kempe for the Lord Chamberlain's Men before he left on his solo dance to Norwich. On his return he joined the Earl of Worcester's troupe, and died in the same year as the Queen. He was replaced as principal comedian by Robert Arnim, and his share in the company, equivalent to a tenth part of the whole, was distributed in four equal parts between those who had been his partners in the second moiety, the first being in the hands of Cuthbert and Richard Burbage. As a result of Kempe's departure, Shakespeare came to own an eighth instead of a tenth part of the theatre estate.

The Messina of *Much Ado* is as far from Sicily as it is from Belmont. Dogberry and Verges root it firmly in a native landscape, and Antonio's reference to the 'thick-pleached alley' in his orchard sets us down in the Vale of Evesham or the Weald of Kent.

3

Dame Helen Gardner has described *As You Like It* as 'a Mozartian comedy'. I gladly endorse the comparison, although I think it might be even more pertinent to *Twelfth Night*. The last thing that you would say about any of Mozart's operas is that they are just comic operas; yet there is not one of them, with the exception of *Idomeneo* and *La Clemenza di Tito*, which you would scruple to describe as a comedy. Even the damnation of Don Giovanni is the cue for a sextet almost cynical in its high spirits; but there does not exist an opera more essentially *serious* than *Don Giovanni*. In the same way Shakespeare's comedies create a world of harmony out of a world of discord; a world in which virtue is rewarded and vice punished or repented of; a world of laughter and tears and strange initiations. The characters in comedy are generally fulfilled, the characters in tragedy are generally frustrated — often by their own fault, sometimes by other people's. Comedy is completion, tragedy is fragmentation and loss; and what differentiates one Shakespearean comedy from another is the degree to which the clouds are dissipated.

There are no clouds in *The Comedy of Errors* or *The Taming of the Shrew*. In *The Two Gentlemen of Verona* Valentine's treachery demands foregiveness, and in *A Midsummer Night's Dream* the misunderstandings are a variation on midsummer madness. In *Love's*

Labour's Lost a King dies, marriages must be earned by long engagements, and Don Armado must hold 'the plough for three years' — a task for which his hands are ill accustomed. In *The Merchant of Venice* Shylock is the only casualty, albeit a serious one. In *Much Ado*, the dramatist escaped from Bandello's plot to elaborate the two characters that had seized his imagination. Now, in *As You Like It,* the plot — taken pretty faithfully from Thomas Lodge's *Rosalynde* — is auxiliary to the characters, two of whom — Jaques and Touchstone — are wholly the dramatist's invention. There is actual drama at the beginning, and reported drama at the end — and there are no casualties, only a couple of somewhat arbitrary conversions. Jaques, too, has his mind on moral improvement, but his will take a little longer. It will all depend on the 'convertite' from whom there was 'much matter to be heard and learned'.

The play is a quadrille of conversations about the folly and sublimity, the paradox and the necessity, of love. It also states the pros and cons of life in the country and at the court. Shakespeare knew as much as he needed to know about both. We have two brothers, Duke Senior and Duke Frederick, of whom the former has been deprived of his rights and banished from the court to the countryside. We shall find a parallel situation in *The Tempest*, although there is no suggestion that Duke Senior has been neglecting his studies. Where Prospero had found his books in the Ambrosianum, the Duke finds them in 'running brooks', and the uses of adversity are sweet. We have a second pair of brothers, Orlando and Oliver, of whom the former is also deprived of his natural rights. Orlando, too, is banished, like Rosalind who has fallen in love with him at first sight, as he with her. The countryside is the refuge from misfortune; moreover it is here that both Oliver and Duke Frederick repent of their misdeeds. But this is not the end of the story. Arden is not Utopia; snakes lurk in the grass and lions in the brushwood; the winds blow, albeit less keenly than man's ingratitude; and when the Duke has recovered his dukedom, and Hymen has sealed the bonds of matrimony, those who have sought refuge in the country are glad to return to the court where they belong. As in *The Tempest* the court may be corrupt, but we are not to suppose it past redemption; and Le Beau, who has something in common with Boyet, will be there to welcome them back, as he had warned them to go away

> Hereafter, in a better world than this,
> I shall desire more love and knowledge of you . . .
>
> (I, ii, 274-5)

There is promise that the hereafter will be the here and now.

Shakespeare: from the engraving by Martin Droeshout for the title page
of the First Folio, 1623

Shakespeare's birthplace in Stratford-upon-Avon

Entry of Shakespeare's baptism in the register of Holy Trinity Church, Stratford, 26 April 1564

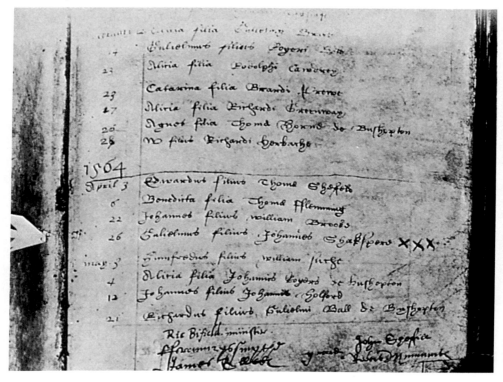

Holy Trinity, Stratford

Grammar School and Gild Chapel, Stratford

Queen Elizabeth I: the Ermine portrait by Nicholas Hilliard

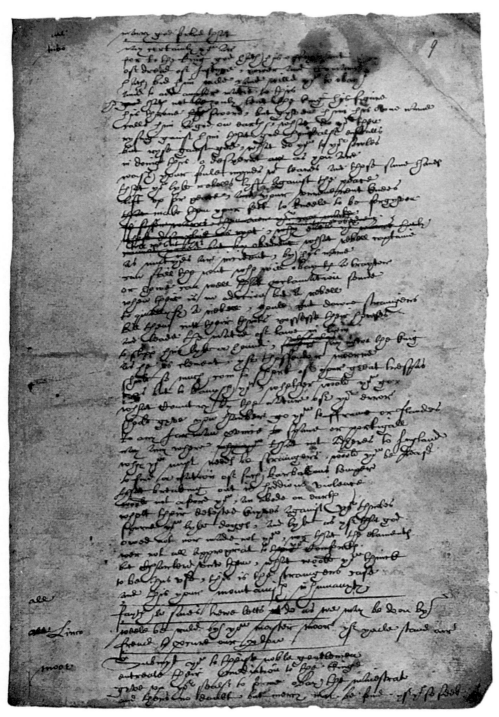

Shakespeare's handwriting from *The Booke of Sir Thomas More*

Southampton at the period of the *Sonnets,* a miniature by Nicholas Hilliard

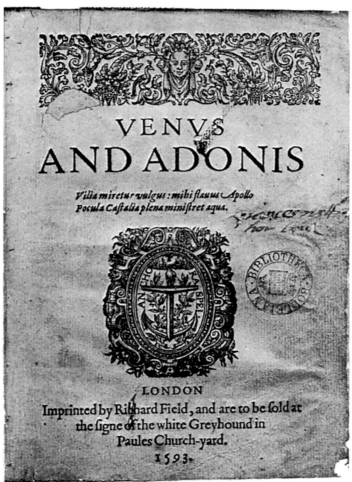

Title page of *Venus and Adonis.* Shakespeare dedicated the poem to his patron, the Earl of Southampton

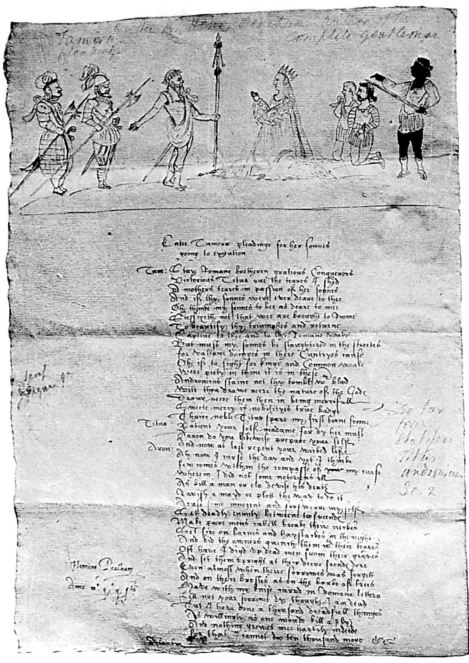

Sketch for *Titus Andronicus* by Henry Peacham, *c.* 1594

The Swan Theatre from a drawing of 1596 by Johannes de Witt

Travelling players visiting a
manor from Moyses Walens'
Album Amicorum, 1610

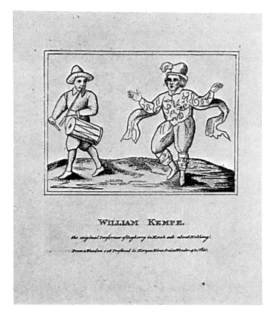

William Kempe: from a
woodcut, *c.* 1600

A section of Hollar's *Long View* of 1647 showing the two south bank theatres, which are incorrectly named on the engraving. The more southerly should be the Globe, not the 'Beere bayting', while the more northerly should be the Hope

Richard Burbage

John Lowin

William Sly

Shakespeare: the 'Chandos'
portrait

Where Shakespeare lodged with
the Mountjoys: part of the
Aggas map, *c.* 1560. (The house
at the corner of Monkswell
(Mugle) Street and Silver Street)

(Left) James I: portrait by Daniel Mytens

Reconstruction of New Place, Shakespeare's Stratford home, from Vertue's sketch

Entry of Shakespeare's death in the register of Holy Trinity church, Stratford, 25 April 1616

Mr. WILLIAM

SHAKESPEARES

COMEDIES,
HISTORIES, &
TRAGEDIES.

Published according to the True Originall Copies.

LONDON
Printed by Isaac Iaggard, and Ed. Blount. 1623.

Title page of the First Folio, 1623

The characters vary from the conventional to the fully developed. The motive of Oliver's jealousy of Orlando hints, already, at Iago's jealousy of Cassio

> My soul, yet I know not why, hates nothing more than he. Yet he's gentle, never school'd and yet learned, full of noble device, of all sorts enchantingly beloved; and indeed so much in the heart of the world, and especially of my own people, who best know him, that I am altogether misprized.
>
> (I, i, 159-64)

This looks forward to Iago's

> He hath a daily beauty in his life
> That makes me ugly
>
> (*Othello*, V, i, 19-20)

Shakespeare knew that hatred, like love, defies rational explanation. Nevertheless this is a play about love, and about little else. For Touchstone love is a necessity, and even the hoydenish Audrey may fill the need

> As the ox hath his bow, sir, the horse his curb, and the falcon her bells, so man hath his desires; and as pigeons coo, so wedlock would be nibbling.
>
> (III, iii, 76-9)

Yet he is not quite sure whether he is right to follow Jaques' advice to get married by a priest whose credentials are less dubious than those of Sir Oliver Martext

> Not being well married, it will be a good excuse for me hereafter to leave my wife.
>
> (III, iii, 88-90)

For Silvius love is abject and humourless romanticism, and Phoebe, though she may not 'thank heaven for a good man's love', settles for a sensible second-best. Is there not a reminiscence of the Dark Lady, and of Rosaline, in her 'inky brows', her 'black silk hair', her 'bugle eyebrows', and her 'cheek of cream'? Doubts persist, however, as to how either of these marriages will work out. Shakespeare invites us — and the invitation is fairly breathtaking — to accept the alliance of Oliver and Celia as a *fait accompli*. So there remains Rosalind who sees all round the problem, and Orlando who sees only Rosalind; and Rosalind, when she has had her say and pitted her wits against her heart, sees only Orlando. By the time she has finished — and we never want her to finish — she has said all that can be said on the subject, at least in prose. She justifies T. S. Eliot's contention that Shakespeare is not only our greatest poet, but also our greatest writer of prose; and she illustrates more vividly than any other of his heroines the Pascalian aphorism that 'the heart has its reasons that the reason knows not of'.

Just as Portia shades into Beatrice, so Beatrice shades into Rosalind. But Rosalind (one thinks) is younger, less apparently independent, and, unlike her cousins once or twice removed, she meets the challenge of adversity. M. C. Bradbrook has observed[1] how Shakespeare's women mature when they put on doublet and hose; Portia had grown considerably on the short journey from Belmont to Venice, with the stop at Padua *en route*. No doubt there was a practical reason for this; the boy actor had a greater freedom when he no longer had to think about his farthingale. Rosalind is depressed in her opening scene with Celia for, with her father banished, Fortune's 'benefits are mightily misplaced'. Yet she falls in love with Orlando at first sight. How different, though, from the liturgical sonneteering of Romeo and Juliet! She gives him a chain, and then it is simply 'Shall we go, coz?'; the single line murmured to herself 'My pride fell with my fortunes'; and the enigmatic

> Sir, you have wrestled well, and overthrown
> More than your enemies.
>
> (I, ii, 244-5)

This — and Shakespeare knew it by now — is how people behave in real life; and no less real is Orlando's impassioned 'But heavenly Rosalind!'

Depression settles again, for melancholy is the 'natural food' of those who 'trade in love', but the combination of adventure and adversity dispels it. Reality defies convention — and a more improbable convention the dramatist never asked us to accept — when Rosalind meets Orlando in the forest, and he does not recognize her. She is most characteristically herself when her lover does not know who she is. Another woman might have exclaimed to Celia

> What did he when thou saw'st him? What said he? How looked he? Wherein went he? What makes he here? Did he ask for me? Where remains he? How parted he with thee? And when shalt thou see him again? Answer me in one word
>
> (III, ii, 218-23)

or again 'Do you not know I am a woman? When I think, I must speak.' But when she meets Orlando the convention gives her leave to speak about love in general; she can bide her time to speak about love in particular, since she knows that Orlando has hung his 'odes upon hawthorns and elegies on brambles'. She can tease him and test him because she is sure of him — 'Love is merely a madness' — and when Orlando wishes 'I could make thee believe I love', she snatches at the cue for a moment of truth

---

[1] *The Growth and Structure of Elizabethan Comedy* (1955), p. 89.

Me believe it? You may as soon make her that you love believe it, which I warrant she is apter to do than confess she does; that is one of the points in the which women still give the lie to their consciences.

(III, ii, 379-84)

But she will confess it, candidly enough, to Celia; 'But why talk we of fathers when there is such a man as Orlando?'; or again 'O coz, coz, coz, my pretty little coz, that thou did'st know how many fathom deep I am in love!' Love is still 'that same wicked bastard of Venus that was begot of thought, conceived of spleen, and born of madness' — but all the same 'I'll tell thee, Aliena, I cannot be out of the sight of Orlando'.

Rosalind is Shakespeare's most complete treatment of a love that is at once romantic and realistic. Even in the mock wedding with Orlando realism keeps its end up with romance

> *Ros.* Now tell me how long you would have her after
> you have possessed her.
> *Orl.* For ever and a day
> *Ros.* Say 'a day' without the 'ever'. No, no, Orlando.
> Men are April when they woo, December when they
> wed. Maids are May when they are maids, but
> the sky changes when they are wives.

(IV, i, 136-41)

If you had to choose a wife from Shakespeare's heroines, the choice would be difficult. But once again one has the impression that a star had danced over Shakespeare's invention, and that Beatrice was not alone to be born under it.

Touchstone was among the first parts played by Robert Arnim after he had joined the Lord Chamberlain's Men. He was himself a dramatist, and although, as Miss Bradbrook suggests, *Two Maids of Moreclacke* may represent a 'low water mark' in hack playwriting,[1] his accession to the company might have contributed to the sudden maturity of Touchstone, compared with previous Shakespearean clowns. Launce and his dog are a superb music-hall turn; Launcelot Gobbo and his father are music-hall turns on a very off night; Costard is a village simpleton, although he speaks eleven words of immortal wisdom. But Touchstone is employed at the Court — and in the play — for the sake of his intelligence. He speaks for the Court, as Corin speaks for the countryside. 'Why, if thou wast never at court, thou never said'st good manners' — to which Corin replies: 'Those that are good manners at the court are as ridiculous in the country as the behaviour of the country is most mockable at the court.' Touchstone is your incorrigible townsman, while Corin, alone

---

[1] ibid., p. 56.

of all the characters in the play, is a citizen of Arcadia

> I earn that I eat, get that I wear, owe no man hate, envy no man's
> happiness, glad of other men's good, content with my harm; and the
> greatest of my pride is to see my ewes graze, and my lambs suck.
>
> (III, ii, 73-7)

If Shakespeare was thinking of Warwickshire when he wrote that, he
was looking at it through rosy spectacles.

There remains Jaques; and in a sense Jaques is Touchstone's
double, for Touchstone is the only person whose company he enjoys.
The conventional malcontent, of whom we caught a casual glimpse in
Don John, has developed into the *raisonneur*. Hints are thrown out
of a profligate past, for which the woodland 'uses of adversity' and
the conversation of the 'convertite' are presumably a cure. He
belongs to neither court nor countryside, though he has learnt his
manners from the one and his observation from the other. He tells us
what he sees, but he tells us little about himself. He is solitary even
when he is sociable; and in the end he takes no partner in the nuptial
dance, wandering off through the trees like Marcel Proust retiring to
a monastery.

Granville-Barker was wrong to underestimate this play; it lacks the
qualities of drama, of theatrical challenge, he was looking for. The
drama is in the dialogue, and the dialogue springs from the characters. What Mr Barber has said in reference to *Twelfth Night* is equally
applicable to *As You Like It*, or even more so. 'Shakespeare is so
skilful by now in rendering attitudes by the gestures of easy
conversation that when it suits him he can almost do without
events.'[1] Fortune and Nature fight it out in *As You Like It*, and the
last word is not with Fortune. Above all, the play is an example of
how the bold use of convention can lay bare the rock-bottom of
reality.

4

Professor Leslie Hotson is the Sherlock Holmes of Shakespeare
criticism, and nearly as readable. Quoting Quiller-Couch to his
purpose: 'We can immensely increase our delight in Shakespeare, and
strengthen our understanding of him if . . . we keep asking ourselves
how the thing was done', he has no doubts, in *The First Night of
Twelfth Night* (1954), as to how it was done, and when, why, and
for whom. He argues, persuasively enough, that the play was
commissioned by the Master of the Revels, on behalf of the Queen,
to entertain Duke Orsino Bracciano, then out of favour with both
France and Italy; that it was performed at Whitehall on 6 January

[1] C. L. Barber, *Shakespeare's Festive Comedy* (1959), p. 242.

1600-1; and that it was preferred to Ben Jonson's more satirical *Cynthia's Revels*. Whether the Duke on the dais would have been flattered by the assimilation of his name to the Duke in the play seems to me rather more doubtful. Shakespeare's Orsino has been evidently reading too much Spenser and Sidney for the good of his soul; and if, as Professor Hotson suggests, the Queen was intended to see an oblique reference to herself in the Lady Olivia she was unlikely to have been flattered at all. Olivia has too much time on her hands, and too much money; nor is it easy to imagine Elizabeth, whose taste in dress challenged sartorial ingenuity, going about for seven years in deep mourning. Professor Hotson proposes Sir Francis Knollys, the unpopular and Puritanical Comptroller of the Royal Household as the model for Malvolio, but Dr Rowse has a more promising candidate. Sir Thomas Posthumus Hoby 'had made himself obnoxious in Yorkshire by interfering with the jollities of his Catholic neighbours. In Posthumus' absence from home a party of these good fellows entertained themselves in his house, helped themselves liberally to his cakes and ale, especially the latter, made a perfect uproar all night and next day, much interfering with the devotions of his religious lady.'[1] Professor Hotson thinks that Sir Andrew Aguecheek was a Spaniard, and that his name was a corruption of 'Agu-chica', meaning Little Wit. 'We might have known,' he argues 'that the English "ague-cheek" could not be right.' I hope I am not unduly dense in maintaining that, for the character in question, it could not be righter.

It was of the essence of an Elizabethan play that it could be produced pretty well anywhere, and *Twelfth Night* at Whitehall would have looked very different from *Twelfth Night* at the Globe. If it was presented, like the early Tudor Court plays, with spectator-scaffolds 'all Round abowte', 'on all sides' and 'on every side', then here indeed was the arena stage which Professor Hotson has postulated for the Globe and elsewhere — except that it was not a stage at all, but an open space. In a hall ninety feet long the acting could most conveniently have taken place in the middle. A couple of scenic elements to represent Orsino's palace and Olivia's house, with the indispensable box hedge, would have assisted illusion. So much may be granted to our Sherlock Holmes. But *Twelfth Night* was destined for the popular stage as well, and later for the intimate Blackfriars. It is going beyond the evidence to assume that what was an arena in Whitehall was also an arena on Bankside.

Twelfth Night is generally considered Shakespeare's most perfect comedy; the one that best illustrates Henry Belayse's definition of

---

[1] See Rowse, p. 335.

English humour as 'somewhat like unto that of the Italians, and a middling humour between too much of the French and the too little of the Spaniard. It neither melts away like a snowball, nor stands out dully like a stone.' Let us agree with John Wain and call its melodies Mozartian. John Manningham, a member of the Middle Temple from January 1601-2 to April 1603, recorded in his diary that for their feast at Candlemas (1601-2) 'We had a play called Twelfth Night, or What you Will. Much like the Comedy of Errors, or Menechmi in Plautus; but most like and near to that in Italian called Inganni. A good practice in it to make the steward believe his lady widowe was in love with him' — and more to the same purpose. Manningham had got it wrong, of course; Olivia was not a widow and only towards the end of the play becomes a wife. But the suggestion is clear that Malvolio 'stole the show' at the Middle Temple; as he did for some time afterwards, for Charles I inscribed 'Malvolio' at the head of his copy of the play. Its popularity must have been immediate if it had been acted at Court less than a month before; and no doubt Charles Knight, writing in the nineteenth century, was right in thinking that its more boisterous humours 'taught the swaggering, roaring, over-grown boy, miscalled student, that there were higher sources of mirth than affrays in Fleet Street, or drunkenness in Whitefriars'. Did the *ingannati* — or twins — stand somewhat in the shade under the soft candlelight of the Middle Temple?

Professor Hotson deduces that the play was written in eight days — a not impossible feat when *The Knight of the Burning Pestle* was written in less, and some of Lope de Vega's comedies in twenty-four hours. One way or another, the play appears to have been com-missioned for a performance on Twelfth Night, and so for a festive occasion. Comedy must predominate, but comedy in the dramatist's present vein with *As You Like It* just behind him, and *Hamlet*, *Troilus and Cressida*, and *Measure for Measure* not far ahead, or even already nudging his elbow. Shakespeare's imagination was capable of entertaining many more than one thing at a time. The theme of identical twins, not of the same sex, was a promising one, and the death of Hamnet only four years earlier would have suggested a treatment not wholly farcical. Twins had been shipwrecked and separated in *The Comedy of Errors*, and that too had pleased the Inns of Court. The variation by which the girl takes service as a page with the man she loves could be found in a number of plays and prose stories published on the continent, many of them derived from *Gl' Ingannati* (1537), a play written for the Academy of the Intronati at Siena. Shakespeare's principal debt appears to have been to the second story, 'Apolonius and Silla', in *Barnaby Riche's*

Farewell to Militarie Profession (1581).[1] But Malvolio was entirely his own invention.

The *Ingannati* do not stand in the shade today, whatever exits and entrances may be contrived for Malvolio — and these are never less than effective. Shakespeare holds his two plots in even balance, and we judge a production of the play by the tact with which the director keeps them so. But the theme of the two plots is the same — the impact of truth upon fantasy. Orsino imagines he is in love with Olivia; Olivia imagines she is in love with Viola; Malvolio imagines he is in love with Olivia, and she with him. The play is a drama of discovery. Orsino discovers that he is really in love with Viola, whose assumed masculinity elicits his own; Olivia discovers that Sebastian will do just as well as Viola, because all she really wants is a man so long as he is not Orsino; and Malvolio discovers that he is in love with no one but himself — for what excites his fantasy is 'To be Count Malvolio'. This explains why he is the only character to be left unhappy at the end — although we cannot help wondering what will become of Antonio. Is he, like his namesake in *The Merchant of Venice*, invited to the wedding breakfast? One would like to think so. Or is he left to pursue his piracy on the Adriatic? For there is something in common between his passionate affection for Sebastian, and his namesake's affection for Bassanio. In the same way, we wonder what will happen to Malvolio. Unrepentant and absurd, he is still a bigger man than his persecutors; and, as Mr Barber points out, he and his like will be 'revenged on the whole pack of them' when the Puritans have closed the theatres, and there are no more 'cakes and ale'. Our pity has already been aroused for him — many practical jokes are disastrous in proportion to their success — and in this autumnal comedy his exit strikes a wintry chill. Unless Shakespeare's characters die upon the stage, they live long after they have left it, and continue to abide our question.

In *Twelfth Night* the insiders live in a privileged enclave of fantasy and frivolity, while the outsiders are the instruments of truth. Viola, like Rosalind, meets adversity with courage and resource, and conquers it with the familiar transvestite trick. The disguise is thinner, however. Not even Orlando in his mock wooing would have gone to the length of

> Dian's lip
> Is not more smooth and rubious; thy small pipe
> Is as the maiden's organ, shrill and sound,
> And all is semblable a woman's part . . .
>
> (I, iv, 30-4)

[1] See for an exhaustive discussion Bullough, Vol. II, pp. 270-85.

But if Viola finds her part more difficult, it is because her predicament is more acute. Rosalind was certain of her man; Viola is certain
of nothing but her bed and board. Nevertheless disguise enables her
to speak to Orsino and Olivia as she would hardly have spoken to
them if they had taken her for a woman; 'I see you what you are,
you are too proud' to Olivia, and she invents a sister to speak her
mind to Orsino. She enters their security from shipwreck, and
separation from a brother whom she loves at least as dearly as Olivia
had loved hers. When Dorothy Tutin played the part at Stratford, she
went to the astonishing length of wearing two wigs, one of which,
like her clothes, showed distinct signs of having been touched by salt
water; and instead of landing in Illyria like a leading lady, she
actually clambered ashore as if she were in some doubt as to whether
she would get there. Feste, too, is something of an outsider, with a
foot in either camp, singing for Orsino and cracking his jokes for
Olivia. A clue to his status is found in his remark to Viola: 'I live by
the church.' He is neither altogether of Olivia's world, nor of
Orsino's. Professional but a little *passé*, he inhabits a world — as he
inhabits a house — wholly of his own. In the end he is left alone to
sing his melancholy *envoi*, casting a shadow behind him on to the
nuptial pavane; and perhaps a lingering doubt as to how a character
at once so adventurous and so vulnerable as Viola will settle down
with a husband who is not conspicuous for his sense of humour. The
saddest but one of Shakespeare's clowns, Feste is the nexus of the
play; and it was a great part for Robert Arnim. With 'Come away,
death', 'Youth's a stuff will not endure', and 'the rain it raineth every
day' he sings farewell to a certain kind of comedy, just as Viola is the
last, and perhaps the loveliest, in a certain line of comédienne. John
Wain has described him standing at the 'exit of this garden of
Shakespearean comedy. And as he sings us out, he closes the gate
behind us.'[1]

If 'I live by the church' gives us a clue to Feste, so Sir Toby's
hiccuping 'There's one at the gate' gives us a clue to the play's
geography. I have yet to see a production of the play where the gate
is allowed its due importance, for it is through the gate that reality in
the guise of make-believe enters the domain of delusion; through the
gate that Orsino enters at last to recognize what his subconscious had
recognized already; through the gate that Malvolio storms out to
nurse his incurable self-love. The other invasion of reality from the
wind-swept shore into some wainscoted interior out of one of Nash's
'*English Mansions*' we can easily imagine. More than this, the gate
gives the entry of poetry into prose, and onto the terrain of resolved

---

[1] *The Living World of Shakespeare* (1964), p. 92.

misunderstandings where poetry is the language of love. Sir Toby and his fellow-lords of misrule — the ineffable Aguecheek and the mischievous Maria; the infatuated Malvolio; and the self-satisfied Olivia — these are all creatures of prose until poetry comes through the gate with Viola, and Olivia can plead 'Cesario, by the roses of the spring'. At the court of Orsino, on the other hand, love is the only topic of conversation, and verse its natural accompaniment. Verse and prose are not varied in *Twelfth Night*, as in *A Midsummer Night's Dream*, to illustrate distinctions of class but difference of character; to initiate a mood and modulate an emotion. The play begins and ends with music; but whether sentiment or satire is the predominating key, it could only have been written by a man for whom music may well have been the food of love, and was certainly the food of literature. When the play is over, Anne Barton has written, 'we have been dismissed to a world beyond holiday'.[1] Shakespeare would presently be writing plays which he described as comedies, and which others have described as problems or romances; but *Twelfth Night* was the end of his Long Vacation.

---

[1] Programme note, Royal Shakespeare Theatre, 1969.

Chapter 12

The Grandeur that was Rome

1

In 1596 John Shakespeare, no doubt encouraged by his son, had applied to the College of Heralds for the grant of a coat-of-arms. The application was successful on the grounds, not strictly verifiable, that the Shakespeares' 'parents and late ancestors were for their valiant and faithful service advanced and rewarded by the most prudent prince Henry the Seventh of famous memory, since which time they have continued at those parts (Warwickshire) in good reputation and credit.' John's credit had fallen somewhat, however, and the draft in principle agreed to was not exemplified until 1599. Essex — the friend of Southampton, if not of Shakespeare himself — was then Earl Marshal and chief of the Heralds College; and William Camden, the eminent scholar and antiquary, was Clarenceux King-of-Arms. The arms were impaled with those of the Ardens of Alvanley in Cheshire; they were no relations to the family of Shakespeare's mother. Certain officials of the Heralds College disapproved of such honours being bestowed on actors; Augustine Phillips and Thomas Pope, who were among the shareholders of the Globe, incurred their particular censure. The York Herald, Ralph Brooke, included Shakespeare's name among twenty-three persons whom he accused of obtaining coats-of-arms on dubious pretences.

This was not likely to have troubled the dramatist, who had more material business on his mind. On 4 May 1597, he purchased New Place in Chapel Street, at Stratford-upon-Avon. Described as a 'pretty house of brick and timber', this had been built by Sir Hugh Clopton towards the end of the fourteenth century. He called it 'my great house at Stratford-on-Avon', and that was no idle boast. It was thirty yards long and stood thirty feet high. The gabled roof with its five dormer windows looked on to the street, and faced the recreation ground of the grammar school. Here were the servants' quarters, and below them the long gallery. Through the gate a passer-by would have caught a glimpse of the grassed courtyard, and the main body of the house beyond, with its central hall, ten rooms, and staircase of carved oak. New Place was pulled down in 1702 and another building put up in its place. It was here that George Vertue, passing through Stratford in 1737, learnt from Shakespeare Hart, who was living there, what the original building had looked like — more suggestive of a manor house in the country than even the most substantial urban dwelling. Shakespeare had restored it with its adjacent barns, and laid out the gardens; later he added an orchard. These stretched down to the river bank, where the Royal Shakespeare Theatre now stands. The College, previously the home of the parochial clergy and later confiscated by the Crown, was the only house in Stratford larger than New Place. This was bought in 1596 by Thomas Combe with whom Shakespeare had renewed contact when he came to London, and who was now a welcome neighbour on his visits to Stratford. It is tempting to suppose, however, if we admit the prototype of Justice Shallow, that he 'regretted' — or rather did not regret — his absence from the elaborate funeral of Sir Thomas Lucy at Charlecote on 7 August 1600. The purchase and restoration of so substantial a property argued a substantial income. Although his plays, once they had been acted, were the property of the theatre, his narrative poems had lost nothing of their popularity. Their dedication to a wealthy patron may well have been rewarded with something more than a word of thanks. He earned his share in the profits of the Globe, and of the company when they were on tour; and as an actor he was extremely well paid. In *The Return from Parnassus* (1601) a penurious student envies the affluence of the theatrical profession

> England affords those glorious vagabonds
> That carried erst their fardles on their backs,
> Coursers to ride on through the gazing streets,
> Sweeping it in their glaring satin suits,
> And pages to attend their masterships;
> With mouthing words that better wits had framed,
> They purchase lands and now esquires are named.

Shakespeare and his fellow-players, in so far as they strolled at all, evidently strolled in style, for they represented the élite of their calling. Will Kempe could assure stage-struck undergraduates that 'You have happened upon the most excellent vocation in the world for money: they come north and south to bring it to our playhouse, and for honours, who of more report, than Dick Burbage and Will Kempe?' Kempe obviously thought no small beer of himself; and it may be that Burbage and Shakespeare wished the beer were smaller. Sir Sidney Lee reckons that Shakespeare's average annual income before 1599 cannot have been less than £150 — roughly £5,000 in present day money. For a man not noted for extravagant living it should not have been difficult to save enough out of this to acquire

New Place. Stratford had fallen on hard times, with much local unemployment, when only farmers were allowed to grow barley for the brewing of beer; and by the turn of the century Shakespeare, reputed to have eighty bushels of corn and malt in his barns, could have passed for a relatively rich man.[1]

2

This same year of 1599 was something of an *annus mirabilis*; as in the case of 1594 the scholars cannot be right about *all* the plays written or produced within twelve calendar months. Nevertheless Shakespeare needed, it appears, to ride not only two plots but two or more plays in tandem. There is no record of a tour by the Lord Chamberlain's Men in 1599, although two years earlier they had visited Faversham, Rye, Dover, Marlborough, Bristol and Bath. The building of the Globe kept them busy, and Shakespeare was now living nearby. With the tetralogy completed and the Globe now open for regular performances, it seems that *Julius Caesar* was seen there by a Swiss traveller in the autumn of the same year. Shortly afterwards Jonson has 'Et tu, Brute' in *Every Man out of his Humour* (V, vi, 79), and Samuel Nicholson the same quotation in *Acolastus his Afterwitte* (1600). Weever's *Mirror of Martyrs* (1601) tells us that

> The many-headed multitude were drawn
> By Brutus' speech, that Caesar was ambitious.
> When eloquent Mark Antonie had shown
> His virtues, who but Brutus then was vicious?

T. S. Eliot wrote that 'bad poets borrow; good poets steal'; Shakespeare's thefts were unashamed, but his innovations were just as remarkable. Having brought to perfection — and *Twelfth Night* was yet to come — a new genre of comedy, he now turned to Roman history. Caesar had hitherto been a subject for historians, not for playwrights; but Shakespeare already has his eye on him in the last chorus of *Henry V* when he evokes the London crowds that 'fetch their conquering Caesar in'. Jonson was quick to follow suit, but *Sejanus* and *Catiline* fell flat, where *Julius Caesar* was immediately popular. And its popularity was lasting. Some few years later Leonard Digges recalled his recent playgoing

> So have I seen when Caesar would appear,
> And on the stage at half-sword parley were
> Brutus and Cassius — O, how the audience
> Were ravished! With what wonder they went thence,
> When some new day they would not brook a line
> Of tedious, though well-laboured, Catiline.

[1] See Lee, pp. 298-300.

> Sejanus too was irksome, they prized more
> Honest Iago, or the jealous Moor.

The classicist had failed with classical themes where the romantic was brilliantly successful with them — although in the case of Shakespeare these categories should be sparingly used. Within his own very different conventions, Shakespeare could be as 'classical' as Corneille if he chose.

The subject, though tempting, was a tricky one. The Elizabethan age has been called the age of expansion; it might equally be called the age of conspiracy. Essex was under a cloud after the fiasco of his Irish expedition. To exhibit an absolute ruler, whom absolute rule had not corrupted absolutely — one, moreover, whom history had placed on a pedestal — murdered by a man for whom the dramatist intended to gain our sympathies, if not our approval, craved wary walking. The last word but one, though not spoken by Brutus, is spoken about him; and he could not have wished for a nobler epitaph. It is true that the play would have taught its audience what is liable to happen when a *pur et dur* republican takes to regicide; but it would also have taught them some unpleasant truths about the *parvenus* imperialists, and how easily an angry mob may get its teeth into the wrong man. Caesar's death is duly avenged, but the political arena is the dirtier for his disappearance. Civil war is the result, and there is not much sign of civil liberty.

It is important to picture how contemporary the appearance of the play, quite apart from its carefully balanced motivations, must have seemed to that Elizabethan audience. Granville-Barker has suggested that 'quite possibly the Roman Senate assembled did *not* look like the cooling-room of a Turkish bath'.[1] Indications are clear that when the conspirators meet in Brutus' orchard they were not costumed in togas newly come back from the laundry. We are told that

> their hats are pluck'd about their ears
> And half their faces buried in their cloaks.

Nowhere in the play is there any reference to classical accoutrements, and the Globe bore no resemblance whatever to a setting by Sir Laurence Alma-Tadema. Of course the myth of ancient Rome is all-pervasive in the play, but it was a myth in modern dress — very much as Orson Welles presented it many years ago at the Mercury Theatre in New York. Quite legitimately, and for the most part very effectively, except that, in the fashion of the time, he was under the delusion that *Julius Caesar* is an 'anti-fascist' play. On the contrary, it is well calculated to give second thoughts to anyone who supposes

[1] *Prefaces of Shakespeare,* First series (1927), p. 126.

that you get rid of dictatorship by simply getting rid of the dictator. Inevitably, there clings about *Julius Caesar* a certain air of the class-room, and we do well to forget those depressing illustrations of the Forum that used to hang upon its walls. This is actuality, not archaeology; those 'hats about their ears' looked back to Babington, and a few years onward to Guy Fawkes.

The difficulty was Caesar himself; he must be the centre of the play, but not its principal character. The play is about Caesarism rather than about Caesar. We must never lose sight of him, and Shakespeare takes care that we shall not; but he keeps him, so to speak, in the middle distance showing us a man not corrupted, but somehow petrified, by power. He is majestic and indispensable, but remote. His first two entrances tell us much, if not all, that we need to know; that he has sized up Cassius, and is not to be put off his stroke by soothsayers. Calpurnia's ill-omened dreams leave him unaffected, but he decides to stay at home to please her, and only changes his mind when Decius Brutus gives them a different interpretation. When the other conspirators arrive to fetch him he relaxes into geniality and bids them 'go in and taste some wine with me'. This is the closest we ever get to Caesar the man; it is Caesar the monolith who is struck down in the Capitol, and his fate, though not foreseen, has already been accepted

> What can be avoided
> Whose end is purposed by the mighty gods?
>
> (II, ii, 27-8)

Shakespeare was concerned with purposes more mundane, though no less momentous. At another stage of his career Caesar might have tempted him, as Antony was already tempting him, and as Coriolanus tempted him later on. He could have shown us Caesar at war with Pompey or in the toils of Cleopatra; and the man who 'unassailable holds on his rank / Unshaked of motion' would have stood up unsteadily against the murder of Vercingetorix. But Shakespeare's mind had long been playing with a different kind of man, foreshadowed in Richard II and Jaques, whose capacity for action was modified by 'the pale cast of thought'. He found him and developed him in Brutus; he created him for all time in Hamlet. But in *Julius Caesar* he did not allow him to run away with the play, and this, one feels, must have been something of a self-denying ordinance. You will search in vain through the swiftly moving five acts for a syllable of digression. Variety is there, but it is the variety of mood and character and situation. Everything hinges on the preparation of a single act, and its consequences. Nor, with the steely Octavius — every word of his small part incised, as it were, on stone

— proving already stronger than his ally, are the further consequences unforeseen. Here, then, was something new. No time for comedy or charm, and only a few notes of music. Neither ale in the tavern, nor apples in the orchard; not the crumb of a part for Robert Arnim; Burbage to take his pick between Brutus and Antony; mixed motivation and simple language; just the bare bedrock of dramatic conflict. Shakespeare was to write greater plays than *Julius Caesar*, but none more solidly built and scrupulously balanced. We miss the peripheral splendours, but the centre holds firm.

He had abundant material to work on with North's *Plutarch* at his elbow; he had had it by him since the days of the Stratford grammar school. There was Cicero's observation that 'Stoic oratory is too closely knit and too compact for a popular audience' — a clear hint for Brutus when he ascends the tribune; and Cicero's later admission to his fellow-republicans; 'It would seem that we have been delivered, not from a tyranny, but only from a tyrant.' There was Tacitus on Octavius who 'little by little . . . drew to himself the affairs of Senate, the duty of magistrates and laws, without contradiction of any'. There was Appian who shrewdly judged the motives of those who killed Caesar 'either for envy . . . or, as they said, for love of their country's liberty'; and Antony who combined 'boldness vehement' with 'dissimulation extreme'. Shakespeare's verdict was that of the ancient historians, most of whom, Professor Bullough reminds us, considered the assassination 'a gross mistake fraught with evil consequences . . . Brutus shared the double reputation of Caesar. He was noble in his Republican and Stoic principles, yet he killed his benefactor, and though he did it for the best political motives the result proved him wrong.'[1] There was also Sir Thomas Elyot's ascription of Caesar's unpopularity to his want of 'affability', of which he shows little enough in the play; and the fate of his assassins would certainly have been seen by an Elizabethan audience as an example, in the words of Appian's translator, of 'How God plagueth them that conspire against their Prince'. Shakespeare may not have seen it in quite such simple terms, for he had a way of seeing all round his subject; but if other people saw it like that, he would have no trouble with the censor.

The clue to the conspiracy is the friendship between Brutus and Cassius. Without Cassius to excite him, Brutus would not have acted, and the others would not have acted without him. Cicero hesitates, and Casca is the kind of thug that is glad to be in upon any night of the long knives. (It is an artistic flaw that when he meets Cassius in the storm they speak in the same idiom. The scene is descriptive and

[1] See Bullough, Vol. V, p. 18.

atmospheric, not psychological. The storm scenes in *Lear* are both.) Brutus and Cassius, though so different, are mutually dependent; the volatility of the one strikes like flint on the granite of the other. Yet the integrity of Brutus is betrayed by an awareness of itself, and his dispassionate reasoning by a fallacy that does no credit either to his heart or to his head

> Fashion it thus; that what he is, augmented,
> Would run to these and these extremities:
> And therefore think him as a serpent's egg
> Which hatch'd would as his kind grow mischievous,
> And kill him in the shell.
>
> (II, i, 30-4)

Preventive murder has based itself on better arguments than these; and they would have carried no conviction to an audience which already knows that Caesar has three times refused the crown.

Most tragic destinies are the penalty of pride; and *Julius Caesar*, though it is a play about politics, is also a play about pride. The moral failure of Brutus is that of self-righteousness. He thinks he is better than the other men around him, as no doubt he is; but he has no right to be so sure of it. His intellectual failure is that of a man who cannot recognize his mistakes; he lives, acts, and dies, but he does not develop. His political failure is that of a man who knows nothing about politics. All politics are *Realpolitik*, and Cassius who knows about men — which means knowing about mobs — sees the menace of Antony's proposed oration. Brutus is the idealist intellectual; Cassius and Antony are the realists — sincerity and opportunism too mixed to know which is which. Only Octavius is the pure political animal; and Octavius, though we hear and see so little of him, is the winner and eventually takes all.

Shakespeare achieves his balance by switching our attention from one protagonist to another. In the first scene the mob — decent enough fellows they seem — are in Bank Holiday mood. It will take more than a reminder of Pompey's erstwhile popularity to bring them to the barricades. Just so, and just as unsuccessfully, might an anti-Gaullist agitator have reminded a merry crowd of Parisians on the *quatorze juillet* that they had once applauded a man called Pétain. But it was useful to remind the audience that an absolute ruler rarely comes to power except by the *fil de l'épée*,[1] and that Caesar was no exception. Marullus and Flavius are left alone to pull down the flags and, not unexpectedly, are 'put to silence'. The second scene belongs to Cassius, private envy and public spirit giving an alternate edge to his persuasion. By the end of it his battle is half

---

[1] The title of General de Gaulle's first published work.

won — although Casca's dry narration of the Lupercalia, appropriately in prose, gives slender support to his rhetoric. The short glimpse of Antony is enough to show us the sportsman and the *bon viveur* — had Caesar whetted his appetite for Cleopatra? He would like to be a kingmaker, but ends up as 'the triple pillar of the world / Transformed into a strumpet's fool'. This is in the future, but Shakespeare — we can hardly doubt — already has his eye on it. The mutual attraction of Caesar and Antony is the attraction of maturity and youth, of the powerful and the patronized. Antony lacks the genius, though not the eloquence, to be Caesar's Malraux; but he might have been his Palewski.[1]

The interest shifts to Brutus, and then to Caesar; domestic interiors (even though one be an orchard) where politics are in conflict with the private life. Conspiracy is sealed, but doubts persist as to whether Caesar will keep the appointment. Who is Artemidorus, and how has the secret leaked out to him? There is here an opportunity for the stage director which I have yet to see turned to advantage, for occasions have not been wanting to an eavesdropper. Might not somebody have been passing by Brutus' orchard, and one of the conspirators have left the gate ajar? No sooner is Caesar dead than the camera moves to Antony. First, the question: 'Where is Antony?' and the answer: 'fled to his house amazed'. Then, Antony's servant with his master's promise to

> follow
> The fortunes and affairs of noble Brutus
> Through the hazards of his untrod state
> With all true faith
>
> (III, i, 134-7)

which Brutus takes on trust and Cassius suspects. When Antony appears we do not question — and are not, I think, meant to question — the sincerity of his grief and indignation. In his offer of a pact with the assassins they struggle with diplomacy, and diplomacy prevails — but only just — against Cassius' objections. The camera closes on Antony alone with Caesar's body, and his prophecy of 'domestic fury and fierce civil strife'. An effective curtain in a theatre where curtains go up and down; but Caesar's body has to be removed, and Shakespeare turns inconvenience to commodity. For the first time the name of Octavius is spoken, for his servant, all unsuspecting, comes in with a message. Caesar's body can be removed with dignity, and the camera, though shifting only an inch or two, can hint at what it will presently disclose.

The forum scene shows how a citizenry can be turned into a mob,

---

[1] Gaston Palewski: an early and faithful adherent of General de Gaulle.

for this is not a rabble that gathers round Caesar's corpse. They are prepared to listen to argument before they surrender to emotion. Antony's triumph is complete, but note the sequel as a messenger informs him

> Sir, Octavius is already come to Rome
>
> (III, ii, 264)

and Antony's final word in a scene where his words have sown the whirlwind: 'Bring me to Octavius'. The dramatist, however, has another word to say, and it is loaded with irony. The mob has gone berserk and will not believe that Cinna the poet is not Cinna the conspirator. It is like assuming that the Smith you meet in Trafalgar Square is necessarily the Smith you are looking out for. Many people come to a violent end in Shakespeare's plays, but this is the only one to be lynched.

Antony is still in command when he meets Octavius — 'Octavius, I have seen more days than you' — and the younger man agrees, albeit reluctantly, that Lepidus shall be treated 'but as a property'. The stagecraft of the fourth and fifth acts has been absurdly undervalued. Their comings and goings make perfect sense on a stage that has no need to be localized. Moreover the interest has shifted from politics to people, and from conspiracy to tactics. In their quarrel and reconciliation the characters of Brutus and Cassius are fully revealed. Cassius has taken bribes like another man, and Brutus makes it too plain that he does not regard himself like other men. Having alienated our sympathies from his hero, Shakespeare brings them back again in a passage where the dialogue has the exactitude of musical notation

> *Bru.* O Cassius, I am sick of many griefs.
> *Cas.* Of your philosophy you make no use
>   If you give place to accidental evils.
> *Bru.* No man bears sorrow better; Portia is dead.
> *Cas.* Ha! Portia!
> *Bru.* She is dead.
> *Cas.* How 'scaped I killing when I cross'd you so? . . .
>   Upon what sickness?
> *Bru.*   Impatient of my absence
>   And grief that young Octavius with Mark Antony
>   Have made themselves so strong: for with her death
>   That tidings came: with this she fell distract,
>   And, her attendants absent, swallow'd fire.
> *Cas.* And died so?
> *Bru.*   Even so.
> *Cas.*   O ye immortal gods!
>
> (IV, iii, 143-57)

There is not much left of the private life in *Julius Caesar*; the rest is retribution. Octavius is now asserting himself

> *Ant.* Octavius, lead your battle softly on,
>   Upon the left hand of the even field,
> *Oct.* Upon the right hand I; keep thou the left.
> *Ant.* Why do you cross me in this exigent?
> *Oct.* I do not cross you; but I will do so.
>
> (V, i, 16-20)

When the leaders of the two armies meet, Cassius is 'Old Cassius still'. If Antony can now recall the butchery on the Capitol, Brutus has only himself to thank for it

> This tongue had not offended so today,
> If Cassius might have ruled . . .
>
> (V, i, 46-7)

Omens have suggested that their 'army lies ready to give up the ghost'. What will they do if it is defeated? Brutus finds it

> cowardly and vile,
> For fear of what might fall, so to prevent
> The time of life.
>
> (V, i, 104-6)

He had not found it 'cowardly and vile, for fear of what might fall' to prevent the time of Caesar's life. Yet he will fall upon his sword sooner than be the victim of a Roman triumph, and so will Cassius. A fatalist to the end, Brutus had received the apparition of Caesar's ghost without emotion; to the warning that he would see it again at Philippi he had the Stoic answer, 'Why I will see thee at Philippi then'. It is not thus that Hamlet will reply to the 'majesty of buried Denmark' when he receives the visitation of another murdered monarch. Yet the similarity is striking between

> O that a man might know
> The end of this day's business ere it come.
> But it sufficeth that the day will end,
> And then the end is known
>
> (V, i, 123-5)

and Hamlet's

> there is special providence in the fall of a sparrow. If it be now, 'tis not to come; if it be not to come, it will be now; if it be not now, yet it will come; the readiness is all
>
> (V, ii, 230-4)

— the Stoic philosophy, the one in a pagan, the other in a Christian, context. The hero as victim has taken hold of the poet's imagination after the heroics of the patriot King.

Every art that achieves permanence must refer to something

greater than itself. The immediate purpose of the theatre is to hold an audience to its seats, but in his later histories and comedies Shakespeare had been concerned, though tentatively as yet, with 'the mystery of things'. They now awaited his exploration.

3

Shortly after the collapse of the Essex revolt in 1601 a strange volume of verse entitled *Love's Martyr*, or *Rosalyn's Complaint*, was published under the name of Robert Chester, who claimed to have translated the poems from the Italian of Torquato Calleano. Neither Chester nor Calleano are known to the literature of the time; both were obviously pseudonyms (supposing that the Italian original existed at all) for an author who for good reasons preferred to remain anonymous. The first edition of the book was denounced as 'seditious', never entered in the Stationers Register, and clandestinely printed and sold. This suggests that the verses, as apparently innocuous as they were inept, concealed a reference to some contemporary happening which would have been clear to any reader at the time. Chester's verses were followed by poems 'by the best and chiefest of our modern writers', dedicated to Sir John Salisbury under the printer's device of John Field. The first of these was Shakespeare's *The Phoenix and the Turtle*; it preceded others by Chapman, Marston, and Ben Jonson. A second edition of *Love's Martyr* was published without let or hindrance in 1611. Ralph Waldo Emerson, who showed his critical judgement in appreciating *The Phoenix and the Turtle* as one of the most beautiful poems in the English language, wished that some academy would offer a prize to anyone who could 'explain by historical research the frame and allusions of the poem'. The attempt has been made by Clara Longworth de Chambrun,[1] and although the evidence she has unearthed is not coercive, it deserves examination. On 27 February 1601, Anne Line and Mark Barkworth were among six persons executed at Tyburn; the others had been involved in the Essex conspiracy, but these two paid the penalty of adherence to the Catholic religion. Both were eventually beatified. While Anne Line's body was still hanging from the gibbet, Barkworth embraced it with the words: 'O blessed Mrs Line, who hast now happily received thy reward: Thou are gone before us, but we shall quickly follow thee to bliss, if it please the Almighty.'

It was not only necessary, but natural at this stage of his development, that Shakespeare should have celebrated this event in allegory, if he wished to celebrate it at all. The poem is quite unlike

---

[1] *Shakespeare — a Portrait Restored* (1957), pp. 237-47.

anything he had written before, or was to write again. In its strictly linear beauty and impersonal, though profound, emotion it stands, uniquely, by itself. The phoenix and the turtle are the emblems of Faith and Constancy — and also of 'married chastity', a subject obsessively on Shakespeare's mind at a moment when *Hamlet* was in the act of composition. After inviting the 'bird of loudest lay' to summon the other 'chaste wings' to welcome the phoenix and the turtle — 'fled in a mutual flame from hence' — he warns the 'shrieking harbinger . . . augur of the fever's end' to keep away. This reminds one of Macbeth's 'after life's fitful fever'; and the reference may well have been to Richard Topcliffe, the most notorious of Walsingham's agents, or to Chief Justice Popham who had sentenced Barkworth to the gallows.

Only two 'outsiders' are admitted to the requiem. One is the 'eagle feathered King' — a reminder that James VI of Scotland, whom the Essex faction had plotted to put on the throne, had promised toleration to the Catholics — a promise he was afterwards forced to go back upon. The other is the

> treble dated crow
> That thy sable gender makest
> With the breath thou giv'st and takest.

This plausibly refers to Archbishop Whitgift, whom Elizabeth habitually called her 'little black husband'. He perpetuated his own order by the laying on of hands; and he had also, as Bishop of Worcester, shown his sympathy for Shakespeare by issuing a licence for the shot-gun marriage to Anne Hathaway, and for at least three other Catholic unions. Later, as Archbishop of Canterbury, he had authorized the publication of *Venus and Adonis*, a poem that might well have proved offensive to episcopal ears. Topcliffe knew him for his enemy, and on one occasion offered to release a prisoner if the man would confess to being Whitgift's bastard. It remains to note that a properly ordained priest is required for this feathered requiem

> Let the Priest in surplice white
> That defunctive music can
> Be the death-divining swan,
> Lest the requiem lack his right

for Sonnet 51 had shown that Shakespeare had no scruples in praying for the faithful departed

> How many a holy and obsequious tear
> Hath dear religious love stolen from mine eye
> As interest to the dead . . .

The significance of the poem far transcends the occasion of its

composition, assuming this to have been such as I have outlined it
here on the basis of Clara de Chambrun's plausible, though unproved,
hypothesis. It is a hymn to the paradox of perfect love; identity in
difference, gain in giving, unity in separation, fulfilment in self-denial

> So they loved, as love in train
> Had the essence but of one;
> Two distincts, division none:
> Number there in love was slain
>
> Hearts remote, yet not asunder:
> Distance, and no space was seen
> Twixt the Turtle and his queen;
> But in them it was a wonder . . .

Towards the end of the poem the trochaics give way to a *terza rima*,
which is found nowhere else in the verse of the period

> Beauty, Truth and Rarity,
> Grace in all simplicity
> Here enclosed in cinders lie . . .

The Phoenix and the Turtle is the sketch for a Paradiso of which we
catch glimpses in the later plays. Here, to quote Middleton Murry,
'an immediate intuition into the nature of things'[1] is conveyed, not
by description or dithyramb, but in a diagram almost mathematical
in its dense, translucent purity, and in a poetry so absolute that one
is tempted to wonder whether it is poetry at all. As a perfect
definition of perfect love it leaves us, however, with a question to
which the answer remains folded beneath those enigmatic wings: was
this a love that Shakespeare had himself experienced? Like Dante's
vision at the end of the *Divina Commedia*, it was enough to have
imagined it.

---

[1] *Discoveries* (1924).

Chapter 13

The Pale Cast of Thought

1

At the risk of 'thinking too precisely on the event', it is as an 'event' that I wish first to look at *Hamlet* before going on to discuss it as a play and as a problem. Tillyard was right to place it first among the 'problem' plays[1] rather than first among the major tragedies, though a tragedy in some sense it unquestionably is. But he did not discuss its genesis in the poet's mind, or the process of its composition. On this 'event', as I choose to call it, one cannot speak 'precisely'. Nevertheless the problems it raises are relevant to the problem of the play as a whole. Here, more significantly than elsewhere, Shakespeare does not answer our questions; he articulates them.

The play was not mentioned by Meres in *Palladis Tamia* (1598). The first, and garbled, Quarto, to judge from its entry in the Stationers' Books, was evidently patched together and pirated in 1601; and the Second Quarto, substantially the same text that appears in the First Folio, may be dated not later than 1603. Since the Children of the Chapel Royal — 'the little eyases' of Hamlet's conversation with Rosencrantz and Guildenstern — were playing at Blackfriars during 1601, when the Lord Chamberlain's Men were prudently on tour after the failure of the Essex conspiracy, it seems likely that Shakespeare was at work on the play during that year — immediately, that is to say, after the production of *Twelfth Night* during the previous Christmas festivities. But it is with *Julius Caesar* that *Hamlet* invites comparison and contrast. If *Twelfth Night* was hastily commissioned and hastily composed, it was probably an interruption of work already for some time in progress. We do not know any details about its first performance, except that Burbage played the title role.

It has become a cliché of criticism to see in Brutus a foreshadowing of Hamlet. But Brutus is not the centre of *Julius Caesar*, as Hamlet is the centre of *Hamlet*. The question I am asking is this: was

---

[1] *Shakespeare's Problem Plays* (1951)

the Hamlet that comes to us in performance or on the printed page the character that Shakespeare conceived in the beginning, or did he become the character during the writing of the play? Was the play itself the play that he set out to write, or did it become something different — something quite exceptional in the whole body of his work? The plan of *Julius Caesar* was obviously clear in his mind from the start, although its characterization and structure were organically, not mechanically, developed. Shakespeare was too creative a dramatist not to let his characters answer back — sometimes inconsistently. But the sense of design that we get in *Julius Caesar* is very different from the sense of improvisation that we get in *Hamlet*; that the dramatist is sometimes wondering, like his hero, what he is going to do next. Of course, the improvisations — if such we allow them to be — contribute to the perennial fascination of the play, and to its stunning theatrical effect. But *Julius Caesar*, in its own way, is just as theatrically effective. So why, we ask, the extraordinary — and indeed excessive — length of *Hamlet*; the longest, by 300 lines, of any play that Shakespeare was to write? No one in his senses cuts a syllable of *Julius Caesar*, except the repetition to Messala of Portia's death — which is almost certainly the result of defective copying. So why can *Hamlet* be abridged with advantage, and not only because it normally has to be? *Julius Caesar* is the most classical, *Hamlet* the least classical, of Shakespeare's plays, although it is also the most popular. I can only conclude that he had many other things besides playwriting on his mind when he wrote it, and that he did not deny himself the distraction.

Two subjects had hitherto preoccupied him — romantic love and politics. The latter preoccupied him still. He had found it illustrated in the history of England and Rome; and now, with the Essex conspiracy frustrated, and the Queen still on the throne, but with the end of the reign and the eclipse of the dynasty shortly to be foreseen, politics were the talk of the town and the anxiety of the hour. The Icelandic saga of Amleth entered Elizabethan drama through Belleforest's *Histoires Tragiques*, and was the origin of an 'Ur-Hamlet', of which all trace is lost. This was known in 1589, when Nashe was warning the students of Oxford and Cambridge against bad dramatists who 'will afford you whole Hamlets, I should say handfuls of Tragical Speeches'. Other passages in Nashe's admonition seem to refer to Kyd, and *The Spanish Tragedy*; and although he does not name Kyd as the author of the 'Ur-Hamlet', it appears likely that Shakespeare was working on a play written by Kyd or by one of his imitators. The Senecan overtones are very audible. That he was well acquainted with *The Spanish Tragedy* is clear from internal evidence. Among the resemblances cited by Professor Bullough[1] I pick out the following.

A Ghost demands revenge; a secret crime has to be verified; an oath is taken on a sword; the avenger pretends to be mad, and a woman actually goes mad; the revenge is postponed, for which the avenger reproaches himself; the avenger contemplates suicide, and the woman he loves is warned off him by her father and brother; he discusses the art of the theatre, and a play-within-the-play furnishes a dramatic climax; in each play Horatio is the faithful friend and confidant; in each play the lovers are spied upon, a brother hates his sister's lover and treacherously contrives his death, a woman dies by suicide, and there are embassies between one kingdom and another. Whether the 'Ur-Hamlet' preceded or followed *The Spanish Tragedy* it is impossible to determine. The 'Ur-Hamlet' was produced for Henslowe in 1594, and Thomas Lodge referred to it in 1596. *The Spanish Tragedy* was more popular, and Ben Jonson refurbished it in 1602. That Shakespeare drew upon them both can hardly be questioned. Why he did so is equally clear; they provided him with a theme in which the nature of sex and the nature of politics could both be explored. In the 'event' a good many other things were explored as well.

Shakespeare never contrived a finer opening; the midnight chill; the guard strenthened against the landing of Norwegian commandos. Between the two appearances of the Ghost, Horatio expounds the delicate political situation. Young Fortinbras of Norway is claiming back the lands which his uncle had forfeited to Hamlet's father, and this is the excuse for an intensive rearmament. The exposition occupies nearly thirty lines. In the second scene Claudius recapitulates what the audience already knows, and dispatches Voltimand and Cornelius on a mission to settle the dispute by diplomacy. A further twenty-three lines. In Act II, Scene 2, the ambassadors return with the news that the King of Norway has called his nephew to order with instructions to direct his levies against Poland. For this purpose he requests a free passage through Danish territory, and Claudius will give the matter his attention. Another twenty-four lines. But we hear nothing more of Fortinbras until Hamlet meets him, with his army, en route for Poland, in Act IV, Scene 4, and gets his cue for the last of his soliloquies — 'How all occasions do inform against me'. But this is not the end of Fortinbras; he reappears to 'claim some rights of memory in this Kingdom' — the first we have heard of them — and to assure us that Hamlet

---

[1] See Bullough, Vol. VII, p. 17.

> was likely, had he been put on,
> To have proved most royally.
>
> (V, ii, 408-9)

Is Fortinbras the image of political virginity in a state of grace to espouse society? George Pitoeff thought so when he produced the play in Paris, and had him dressed in white. Jean-Louis Barrault had seen him in his white and green cloak as the Angel of the Last Judgement — the messenger of life redeemed. 'Every year' he has written 'towards the end of January, in midwinter, you have one or two days of false spring. The air is pale and green, and the sun is all white, like a mirage of the first leaf. When I hear this brief explosion in the air and in nature I now say "There are the trumpets of Fortinbras".'[1] But will a true spring follow the false one? Is Fortinbras no more than the latest exponent of *Realpolitik*, invading Poland to

> gain a little patch of ground
> That hath in it no profit but the name
>
> (IV, iv, 18-19)

and returning through Elsinore at a lucky moment? Since he has Hamlet's 'dying voice', I am inclined to think that Pitoeff and Barrault were right. But judging from the amount of attention given to Fortinbras and his affairs at the beginning of the play, and his prolonged disappearance from it thereafter, I think that Shakespeare may have destined him for a larger role. It had looked for a moment as if *Hamlet* were going to be a play about foreign policy. Most of the political matter concerning Fortinbras is usually cut in performance, and in modern times he was not even allowed to appear until Forbes-Robertson restored him. The restoration was long overdue, but one can understand why stage directors, pressed for playing time and possibly short of actors, thought he was expendable. The part is most appropriately doubled with that of the Ghost — political virginity violated and then restored; the voice that comes from Poland reminding us of the voice that came from Purgatory.

Now consider Polonius. Here it appears that Shakespeare was poking his fun at Burghley, the main architect of such 'deep consent' as the reign had achieved. He had died in 1598, and like a good many other elder statesmen had become something of a bore to the younger generation. His services and ability were immense, but he was not popular at Southampton House. Moreover he had left to his son Robert a set of Precepts designed to show how a young man could make the best of this world and the next without offence to either. Polonius, it is true, is not concerned with the next world at

[1] *Souvenirs pour demain* (1972), p. 194.

all, but his sensible advice to Laertes, if followed, would gain a man entrance to the most exclusive club, not to mention a commission in the Brigade of Guards. Up to this point he is presented as a perfectly serious person, and indeed his further advice to Ophelia would have been taken seriously — if perhaps with a smile — by an audience for whom the alliance of the heir to the throne with a commoner was unthinkable. Nor, of course, are these admonitions irrelevant to Shakespeare's deeper dramatic purposes. But then what happens? When we meet him again, we are treated to a scene of admirable comedy in which he instructs Reynaldo to discover how Laertes is behaving on Montmartre; and this usefully conveys the passage of time between Hamlet's colloquy with the Ghost and his distraught appearance before Ophelia. Shakespeare cannot resist the truth that has dawned upon him. He knew that politicians could be dangerous; he now sees that they can be ridiculous. And ridiculous Polonius remains until he is killed behind the arras; but the dramatist has devoted seventy-five lines to an illustration of his absurdity in a context which has nothing whatever to do with the main plot. It serves merely to satirize those methods of espionage in which Elizabeth's chief minister had been so adept. The scene is usually cut, for we shall presently have clear evidence of how Polonius 'by indirection' tries so fatuously to 'find direction out'. I draw attention to it here because it shows how willingly Shakespeare allowed himself to be diverted by a political character, so that the Prime Minister we first meet in attendance on Claudius' Privy Council becomes a preposterous busybody whom a ruler as astute as Claudius would very soon have dismissed into retirement. Polonius cannot run away with the play, but he does run away with the part. This is a case where one of Shakespeare's characters has no hesitation in 'answering back'.

Claudius is far more than the villain of the piece; the role is a brilliant study in Machiavellian amorality. Denmark is an elective monarchy, and Claudius times the murder of his brother to coincide with Hamlet's absence at Wittenburg. It was reasonable, in any event, that the electors should prefer him to a graduate student of no political experience or capacity. If Claudius is the pure political animal as well as the *homme plus que moyen sensuel*, Hamlet is the non-political man *par excellence*. His celebrated outcry

> The world is out of joint; O curséd spite
> That ever I was born to set it right

> (II, i, 188-9)

is the admission of one who knows that he is unfitted for public life, and *a fortiori* for the task which has just been laid upon him. The latter, as I shall presently argue, would not have been easy for anyone. Claudius, on the other hand, shows at every point his political sagacity, and he evidently enjoys the confidence of the court. He is sceptical of Polonius' diagnosis of Hamlet's strange behaviour, and his scepticism is confirmed by what he overhears of Hamlet's scene with Ophelia (III, i). He is vulnerable only in his conscience, and it was subtle on Shakespeare's part to give him one

> The harlot's cheek, beautied with plastering art,
> Is not more ugly to the thing that helps it
> Than is my deed to my most painted word.
>
> (III, i, 51-3)

But in Hamlet's 'Those that are married — all but one — shall live' he has scented danger, and concludes that a diplomatic mission to England may 'expel the something-settled matter in his heart'. The danger comes closer as he watches 'The Murder of Gonzago', taking — and here I agree with Granville-Barker as against Dover Wilson — the Dumb Show on the chin; but when Lucianus pours the poison into the ear of the Player King, the memory of that sultry afternoon in the orchard is too much for him, and he interrupts the performance. If it proceeds — and indeed it has already proceeded too far — Gertrude will know that he has killed her husband. Her astonished 'As kill a King!' in the Closet scene surely indicates that she was unaware of it. But Claudius does not lose his self-control — as he too often is made to do on the stage; he simply calls for lights and is away. Only Hamlet is excited: the others think — and not for the first time — that he has made a fool of himself. It is not an impression that he subsequently does anything to discourage.

In the following scene the Divine Right is articulated in accents more proper to Richard II than to Rosencrantz. I quote it here in full because it shows, once again, that this is a profoundly political play, and because in performance it is generally omitted. It is what everyone, except a few malcontents, would have said about Elizabeth

> The single and peculiar life is bound
> With all the strength and armour of the mind
> To keep itself from noyance; but much more
> That spirit upon whose weal depends and rests
> The lives of many. The cease of majesty
> Dies not alone, but like a gulf doth draw
> What's near it with it: it is a massy wheel,
> Fixed on the summit of the highest mount,
> To whose huge spokes ten thousand lesser things
> Are mortised and adjoined; which, when it falls,
> Each small annexment, petty consequence,
> Attends the boisterous ruin. Never alone
> Did the King sigh, but with a general groan.
>
> (III, iii, 11-23)

How such words must have reverberated in 1602! Nevertheless the dramatist can spare twelve lines of political theory at a moment of high theatrical tension. Claudius opens his soul in the ensuing soliloquy. He knows what he has done, but there is no going back; he cannot restore the life that he has taken away. He is a better man than Macbeth, although he lacks Macbeth's imagination; but just as Macbeth was in fear of Banquo, Claudius is in fear of Hamlet, and so Hamlet too must die

> For like the hectic in my blood he rages . . .
>
> (IV, iv, 68)

England will do what Denmark dare not do, but the plot miscarries. The opportune return of Laertes to avenge his father's death gives Claudius a second chance. This, too, miscarries — but right up to the final sword-thrust Claudius' control never falters. Not for a moment has his political sense deserted him; he has played the game according to the rules of a world which is 'out of joint'. If political genius consists in a nice balance of calculation and courage, Claudius was lacking in neither. If Hamlet was in all respects the Renaissance man, Claudius was in many respects the Renaissance ruler.

Both the sexual and political themes of the play are gathered up in what is generally known as the Closet scene. (Let stage directors take note that this is *not* Gertrude's bedroom.) The total design of *Hamlet* can be summed up in the reiterated leitmotiv — the killing of the King. The King is the husband, the father, and the brother. Any king is, by definition, the father of his people; he is also their husband, bound to them in a kind of mystical alliance, analogous to what theologians call the mystical marriage of Christ and His Church. The family drama of *Hamlet* — father, mother, brother, and son — is a microcosm of the political drama; and the political drama is familial also. Society, as Shakespeare sees it, is a natural organism; in this it is like the family, and every crime against the natural authority of the State is a parricide. To understand *Hamlet* we must reckon with this social adultery, and it is the vocation of Hamlet himself to smell it out. For the corrupted and unnatural society of Elsinore yields to the political lust of Claudius, as Gertrude yields to his carnal importunity. Each of the two Kings plays a dual role. Hamlet *père* was the faithful husband both to his Queen and of his Kingdom. He was also the dutiful father of his people and of his son. Claudius, on the other hand, is the ravisher of his Kingdom and of his Queen; and both are corrupted in proportion as they consent to his desires. He usurps the authority of a father towards Hamlet

> Our chiefest courtier, cousin and our son
>
> (I, ii, 117)

as he had already usurped the authority of a father over the people that Hamlet might have ruled. The good father had been supplanted by the wicked step-father, both in the family and the State. Hamlet, despite his vacillation — and which of us might not have vacillated? — is the witness and imperfect instrument of outraged nature. Here, at least, the Freudian complexity of filial love comes into play. In a profound sense Hamlet the son *is* Hamlet the father. It is against *him* that Claudius and Gertrude have committed their adultery, and in so far as society — Rosencrantz, Guildenstern, Polonius, and Laertes — approve the unholy alliance, society also sins against him. And the sin is not only political; within the terms of the analogy I have been tracing here, it is sexual also. Hamlet replaces his father, assuming both his personal and political wrongs. He falls under the burden, as such people usually do, and the avenger becomes the victim in the act of accomplishing his revenge. It is in him, no less than in those who lie dead around him, that those wrongs are expiated.

You will hear it said that Hamlet is Everyman. This is nonsense; Hamlet is a recognizable youth living at a particular moment of history in a somewhat ambiguous mental climate of Renaissance thought and medieval eschatology. He has also been taken as a portrait in a mirror of Shakespeare himself. More to the point is the suggestion that he is the only one of Shakepeare's characters who could have written Shakespeare's plays. None of these hypotheses, however, brings us to the heart of his problem. This has been perceptively analysed in a remarkable essay by John Vyvyan.[1] Hamlet is a nature made for love, whom circumstances divert to hate. Beneath the external conflict with Claudius there is the conflict within himself. I suspect that this division only became apparent to Shakespeare in the course of writing the play, and it may have been partly responsible for its length. *Hamlet* is about man in society and man in solitude, and about both of them simultaneously. This is why it appeals to everyone, although Hamlet is not Everyman.

The nature made for love reels under three successive shocks. Tillyard is unquestionably right in seeing Gertrude's precipitate remarriage as the most severe of these. Nothing in the play is more violent in its outburst than the opening soliloquy. Notice how the verse changes in tune with it — urgent and loquitive, the words tread on each other's heels. Jean-Louis Barrault once suggested to me that Gertrude had not enjoyed physical satisfaction with Hamlet's father, but I do not think that this suggestion holds good

> why, she would hang on him
> As if increase of appetite had grown

[1] *The Shakespearean Ethic* (1959).

By what it fed on.

(I, ii, 143-5)

Hamlet had seen them together, and his was not an eye that much escaped. So much was knowledge; what he says of Claudius is divination. When I say that Hamlet was a nature made for love, I mean that it was also made for friendship. This is evident when he meets Horatio, and of all the characters in the play Horatio is the only one who does not let him down

> Since my dear soul was mistress of her choice
> And could of men distinguish, her election
> Hath seal'd thee for herself

(III, ii, 68-70)

and so on for eleven more lines when we are on tenterhooks to know how Claudius will stand up to 'The Murder of Gonzago'. But Shakespeare is not to be hustled by an impatient audience if Hamlet has something to get off his mind, no matter when or where.

The second shock comes with the revelation brought by the Ghost; a shock but not altogether a surprise — 'O my prophetic soul! my uncle'. This raises several questions. Is what the Ghost has told him true? Can he be sure that the voice of a soul expiating its sins in Purgatory carries the authority of a Divine command? When the voice comes to him from underground — 'you hear this fellow in the cellarage' — can he be sure that it comes to him from Purgatory and not from Hell? Did Shakespeare intend to convey that the command was mandatory? The last question, like so many other Shakespearean questions, is left open; but that Hamlet has a few doubts as to the Ghost's provenance is shown later, and he relies upon 'The Murder of Gonzago' to resolve them. A few, but not many; he will act, or try to act, as if he had none. What remains certain is that the nature made for love is further deflected into the way of hatred, and the inward fissure deepens.

Why, then, does he act as he did? His pantomime after the Ghost has vanished may be put down to hysteria; but since he explains to Horatio and Marcellus that he is going to affect a lunatic behaviour, this surely settles the question as to whether he is mad or sane. The last thing a mad person does is to explain to his friends that he is going to pretend to be mad. Let us ask ourselves how a sane person, even suffering a severe psychological shock, would have reacted to the Ghost's revelation and command, presuming that he believed the one and was prepared to obey the other. A weaker character might have wilted under the weight of so fearful a disclosure. His melancholy would have deepened with the creeping paralysis of his will, and he would have dragged about with him at the Court or the

University a secret that he had not the courage to get rid of. A stronger character would have bidden his time, and seized some moment propitious to a palace revolution — declaring to the world his reasons for acting as he did. Of course, the world might not have believed him; Horatio, Marcellus, and Bernardo were witnesses to the Ghost's appearance, but not to what the Ghost had said. A certain risk was inherent in any execution of the Ghost's command. In fact, however, Hamlet's behaviour responds to no conceivable test of reason. How did he expect to gain from it? What was the object of drawing an anxious and universal attention upon himself? His security lay in obscurity, not in ostentation. If he thought that the slaying of the King, when he brought himself to accomplish it, would be ascribed to lunacy, how was that going to help him? It was important that the world should know *why* he had killed the King, and the world would not believe the word of a homicidal maniac. If the assumption of lunacy gave him a certain freedom of insult and innuendo in his dealings with the Court, it brought immediate suspicion upon him as a man who knew more than he had any right to. No, the reason for Hamlet's 'madness' was, in the strict understanding of the word, theatrical; not for nothing was he a keen playgoer. Cast for a part for which he felt himself unsuited, he chose to play another. It was an excellent performance, but he gave it in the wrong play.

This love of acting for acting's sake is adumbrated in the 'customary suits of solemn black', the 'windy suspiration of forced breath' and 'the fruitful river in the eye' that mark his first appearance. It comes out into the open with the arrival of the Players to Elsinore, his own memory of the 'Pyrrhus' speech, and his subsequent advice. Here, again, Shakespeare seizes the chance to speak his mind upon theatrical matters; and we have already heard the discussion about the 'little eyases'. The whole theatrical section of this scene occupies no less than 240 lines; and the Play scene is still to come, where the Player King and Queen take 73 to exchange their mutual protestations of fidelity — not to mention the Dumb Show which threatens to give the show away before anyone has spoken a word. Shakespeare has used one aspect of Hamlet's character to demonstrate, and dilate upon, a subject in which he was passionately interested. But I do not imagine that he foresaw this divagation when the 'Ur-Hamlet' or *The Spanish Tragedy* first excited his interest in the Killing of the King.

The third shock was Hamlet's repudiation by Ophelia. I do not believe for a moment that Ophelia had been his mistress; her bawdy snatches in the mad scene might have come from the subconscious of a schoolgirl or a nun. To think otherwise is to confuse the parallelism of love and lust that runs through the play. Whatever Polonius and Laertes may have thought, Gertrude, over Ophelia's grave, admits that she had 'hoped thou should'st have been my Hamlet's wife'. The match was evidently not thought impossible, and there is no reason to doubt Ophelia's assurance that Hamlet had 'given countenance to his speech . . . with almost all the holy vows of heaven'. Barrault discerned in Hamlet an example of heroic chastity as well as 'superior doubt'. That he is sexually aware is nothing to the point; without sexual awareness chastity is not worth its name. Hamlet expiates with his own chastity the unchastity of those around him. So what had happened? Ophelia was too weak a character to withstand the family pressures, and she gave in. At this point we must reconstruct. Hamlet *may* have wished to take her into his confidence, and been met with the rupture of their relationship; or she may herself have sought him out. All we know is that Ophelia is the person before whom he first chooses to demonstrate his assumed lunacy. From now on it is a case of 'man delights not me — no, nor woman neither'.

The double betrayal by Gertrude and Ophelia coarsens his naturally sensitive nature. What is the use of a nature made for love, if love betrays you? He next meets Ophelia when she is set to spy upon him. The dramatist of the 'well-made play' — even the Shakespeare of *Julius Caesar* or *Othello* — would have brought Hamlet straight on to 'Nymph, in thy orisons be all my sins remembered!' Suicide would naturally be the last thing in his mind when he is excited to fever pitch by the composition of that 'speech of a dozen or sixteen lines' which will settle his own doubts, and betray Claudius into an admission of his crime. On the other hand, in this play which obeys no rules, a sudden thought may have struck the dramatist, and down it went on to the paper where he was reputed (falsely no doubt) scarcely to have blotted a line. Ophelia at her prayers at that hour of the afternoon probably surprises him, but he fences with her politely, and then, as she returns his gifts, with enigmatical self-reproach. What stings him to fury is her lie direct: 'Where's your father?' 'At home, my lord.' There is here no need, I think, to suppose an incautious movement of the arras; Hamlet has been on his guard throughout the scene, and drops it just when he should have been at pains to strengthen it. For if Polonius is eavesdropping. Claudius may be eavesdropping too; and in any case whatever Hamlet says will certainly be reported to him. The wound of Ophelia's complicity inspires the brutal repartee before the play

Ham. Lady, shall I lie in your lap?
Oph. No, my lord.

Ham. I mean, my head upon your lap
Oph. Ay, my lord
Ham. Do you think I meant country matters?
Oph. I think nothing, my lord
Ham. That's a fair thought to lie between maids' legs.
Oph. What is, my lord?
Ham. Nothing.

(III, ii, 119-28)

We have come a long way from 'the glass of fashion and the mould of form', although now, for very different reasons, Hamlet is still 'the observed of all observers'. He never sees Ophelia again until he fights with Laertes over her body. It is certainly a changed, a calmer, a more philosophic, and a more fatalistic Hamlet that returns to Elsinore with Horatio. He seems to be an older, but is he a wiser man? There is no talk of his unaccomplished mission, and bare mention of his mother, although his resourcefulness in getting rid of Rosencrantz and Guildenstern, like his subsequent fencing with Laertes, should dispose of the idea that Hamlet is not a man of action. But there were

more things in heaven and earth, Horatio,
Than are dreamt of in your philosophy

(I, v, 166-7)

and love was one of them. What could have excited that extra-ordinary outburst over the grave but the memory, perhaps the obsession, of a love that went deeper than Shakespeare, even in a play where he had time for so much, had allowed himself the space to show?

It is, however, in the scenes following the Pyrrhic victory of the play-within-the-play that the civil war between love and hate is most luridly revealed. His repartee with Polonius and Rosencrantz had never been so mordant; his excitement is at its height

Now could I drink hot blood
And do such bitter business as the day
Would quake to look on.

(III, ii, 408-10)

Yet he remembers the Ghost's injunction to 'speak daggers' to his mother, but 'use none'. Then he comes upon the King at prayer; here is his opportunity. It has been argued that his reason for sparing Claudius on his way to Purgatory, in order to be sure of sending him to Hell a little later on, is only a rationalization of his general reluctance to act. The motive of the soliloquy is, of course, ironical, because he has not heard Claudius' admission that he 'cannot repent'. But I am convinced that Hamlet's reasoning is a genuine refinement of his hatred, for a few minutes later he will not hesitate to plunge his sword through the arras behind which he suspects that Claudius is hiding. To his mother he does indeed speak daggers; he spares her nothing, not even the sexual nausea that has been stifling him for so long

> Nay, but to live
> In the rank sweat of an enseaméd bed
> Stew'd in corruption, honeying and making love
> Over the nasty sty . . .
>
> (III, iv, 191-4)

But when the Ghost has come and gone he softens a little

> Mother, for love of grace,
> Lay not that flattering unction to your soul
> That not your trespass but my madness speaks . . .
> Confess yourself to heaven;
> Repent what's past, avoid what is to come
> And do not spread the compost on the weeds
> To make them ranker. Forgive me this my virtue,
> For in the fatness of these pursy times
> Virtue itself of vice must pardon beg . . .
>
> (III, iv, 149-54)

He bids her gently good-night; but he knows that the bed of 'luxury and damn'd incest' waits next door for its partners, and the nausea rises in him again. The Queen asks, helplessly, 'What shall I do?'

> Not this, by no means, that I bid you do;
> Let the bloat King tempt you again to bed;
> Pinch wanton on your cheek, call you his mouse;
> And let him, for a pair of reechy kisses,
> Or paddling in your neck with his damn'd fingers,
> Make you to ravel all this matter out,
> That I essentially am not in madness,
> But mad in craft.
>
> (III, iv, 181-8)

He knows that he must go to England, with Rosencrantz and Guildenstern as escort, and he will trust them as he would 'adders fang'd'. As for Polonius, he will 'lug the guts into the neighbour room'. Although he promises Gertrude to 'answer well the death I gave him', the answer will be somewhat dusty

> *King* Now, Hamlet, where's Polonius?
> *Ham.* At supper . . . not where he eats, but where he
>   is eaten. A certain convocation of public
>   worms are e'en at him.
>
> (IV, iii, 18-22)

Hatred has at once coarsened Hamlet's feelings and sharpened his wits. To his sentence of exile he replies

Ham. Good.
King So is it, if you knew'st our purposes
Ham. I see a cherub that sees them

(IV, iii, 48-50)

for it is Hamlet's vocation in the play to see more than anybody else. The scene with Gertrude has almost extinguished pity, but it has not quite extinguished love. Hamlet is not Everyman; yet he has something of every man inside him — much of the beauty and something of the beast.

Up to the moment of his exile he has been a man of feeling rather than of thought, except when theatrical 'shop' diverts him, and the temptation of suicide presents an escape from the 'prison' that Denmark has become. Of the soliloquies all but 'To be or not to be' are passionate. But in 'How all occasions' feeling is tempered by thought, even by abstract thought

> Rightly to be great
> Is not to stir without great argument
> But greatly to find quarrel in a straw
> When honour's at the stake.

(IV, iv, 53-6)

What then has happened to alter Hamlet when he meets the Gravedigger and Yorick's skull? What has turned the man of passion into the man of thought and resignation? Whence comes this new-found serenity? The answer is, I think, supremely important. For the first time in his life Hamlet has acted effectively; he has sent Rosencrantz and Guildenstern to their deaths, and their deaths are not 'near his conscience'. They have no need to be. As for Claudius, he will bide his time, and he can quietly ask Horatio 'is't not perfect conscience to quit him with this arm?' At last he sees that he has been acting a part in the wrong play, for he has proved that he could act another part in the right one. In the meanwhile here is death in the graveyard, and he can face it calmly; even the process of decomposition excites his curiosity. Mortality was never less high-flown than here, as the gravedigger bids his assistant: 'Get thee to Yaughan; fetch me a stoup of liquor'. From what Bankside tavern did Shakespeare cull that inimitable name? One can hear the ale being quaffed down the gullet of its open vowels, just as throughout the racy, relaxed dialogue one can hear the muffled, melancholy thud of the upturned sod. But the man of thought, and now the man of action, is still the man of feeling. George Rylands once said that the only adequate translation of Virgil's *'lacrimae rerum'* was Hamlet's 'Alas, poor Yorick!' Hamlet is the most intelligent character in Shakespeare, but no one would accuse him of cerebration.

Only the appearance of Ophelia's sad little funeral *cortège*, and

Laertes' fraternal rivalry, break down 'the forts and pales of reason'. He is generous in apology to Laertes, and courteously amused with Osric. So indeed is Shakespeare; he can afford more than a hundred lines of satire at the expense of the 'lapwings' of the Court, just when the play is moving to its climax. But Hamlet's high spirits conceal a presentiment that does not ruffle his Stoic calm: 'Thou would'st not think how ill all's here about my heart', and a little later 'the readiness is all'. He accomplishes his mission in the confusion of a conspiracy not of his own devising; for the moment it is more important to win his match against Laertes than to avenge his father's murder and wipe out his mother's shame. Like his author, Hamlet is interested in everything, and that is one reason why everyone is interested in Hamlet. I have described the play as an 'event' rather than a masterpiece, because the latter suggests a more deliberate ordering than is apparent here. *Hamlet* belongs to life as much as to literature, for it opened up — like the essays of Montaigne and the *pensées* of Pascal — the consciousness of post-Renaissance man. Hamlet has become a synonym for anyone whose capacity for action is paralysed by 'the pale cast of thought', and whose nature is too frail for the burdens that are laid upon it. As I hope to have shown, the case is not so simple as that; the 'state of Denmark' is as important for an understanding of the play as the man — fallible as all men are — who nevertheless redeems its rottenness. Hamlet is Shakespeare's contemporary, and ours; and the play to which he gives his name has never been more contemporary than in our own time — present it how you will — when violence and lust lurk behind the façade of Establishment, as they did at Elsinore, and absolute power is liable to corrupt absolutely. By what process of trial and error, and by what lightning intuitions, Shakespeare turned a melodrama into a tragedy of the divided mind, and left it no whit less melodramatic, is a secret of the workshop. But that the work in the study was as eventful in the life of the workman as the work on the stage has become in the lives of his audience, there can surely be no doubt whatever.

Part Two

Jacobean

Chapter 14

Wars and Lechery

1

The death of John Shakespeare in 1601 must have been on William's mind when he was composing *Hamlet,* and done something to inspire the filial piety of its protagonist. For the play is not only about death, but about what happens after death. Hamlet's father is expiating his sins in purgatory, and the crime of his murder is all the worse because he has been taken

> grossly, full of bread
> With all his crimes broad blown, as flush as May . . .
>
> (III, iii, 80-1)

Ophelia is denied the proper rites of Christian burial, because she is supposed to have committed suicide. Hamlet wishes

> that the Everlasting had not fix'd
> His canon 'gainst self-slaughter
>
> (I, ii, 131-2)

and what deters him from suicide himself is 'the dread of something after death'. No such apprehension had troubled the *Liebestod* of Romeo and Juliet, or the Stoic suicides of Brutus and Cassius. John Shakespeare was buried in the Stratford churchyard on 8 September 1601. He left no will, and the two houses in Henley Street passed to William as his eldest son. His widow continued to live in one of them until her death seven years later. Any other properties of John and Mary Shakespeare had been forfeited to creditors, but it seems that John was still respected in the borough; his son's reputation had done much to compensate for the decline in his own fortunes.

In 1794 a Spiritual Testament, drawn up in the name of John Shakespeare, was discovered by a bricklayer at work on his house in Henley Street. This was a profession of faith in the Catholic religion composed by St Charles Borromeo, Archbishop of Milan. Copies had been distributed by the missionary Jesuit priests, Edmund Campion and Robert Persons, among the Catholic gentry of Warwickshire; and it may well have happened that this one had been given to John by Edmund Campion himself at the house of Sir William Catesby who was related to Mary Shakespeare. To possess such a document was extremely risky, and no doubt it had been walled up to escape detection. It was reported to Walsingham that 'the papists in this country (Warwickshire) do greatly work upon the advantage of clearing their houses of all suspicion'. The discovery tells us nothing about Shakespeare's personal beliefs, but it throws an important light on the religious background of his boyhood. Nor do we know whether his father died in the faith that he had formerly professed.[1]

Much ink has been spilt on the supposition that *Hamlet*, the 'problem' plays, and the Tragedies that followed them, were due to some unspecified emotional crisis in the poet's life. There is no evidence for this belief; moreover it contradicts what we may guess to have been Shakespeare's way of working. As a dramatist he was concerned with other people, not with himself. If we are correct in dating the *Sonnets* between 1593 and 1595, then he was engaged upon *Love's Labour's Lost* and *A Midsummer Night's Dream* at the same time. He knew all that he needed to know about 'the marriage of true minds' and 'the expense of spirit in a waste of shame'. There is no reason to suppose that because he chose to treat the wantonness of Cressida, he had therefore come to doubt the fidelity of Juliet; or that because he allowed Thersites to call a plague on the heroes of the Trojan War, he was unsaying what he had so recently said about his patriot King. He took life and history as he found them, and being a realist as well as a romantic he found them as many-sided as he was himself. What separates his work in the period now under discussion from what had gone before it is a far greater intellectual curiosity. Themes are as important as people, although the people remain very much alive; stories turn into allegories; complexities of language match complexity of thought and character. A man does not need to be in a state of neurosis to write a tragedy, or of mental confusion to write a play which posterity may regard as a problem. All that matters for the work in question is the degree of artistic control.

The accession of James I in 1603 brought marked favours to what were now designated as the King's Men. In the ten years preceding his accession they had given three performances a year at Court; in the ten years following his accession these had risen to thirteen, more than all the other London companies combined. Between 1594 and 1602 they drew an average of £35 a year from Court performances; between 1603 and 1607 the average had risen to £131.[2] On 19 May 1603, they were granted permission to play whatever they liked and

---

[1] See P. Milward, *Shakespeare's Religious Background* (1973), p. 44.
[2] See G. E. Bentley, *Shakespeare Survey I* (1948), pp. 38-49.

wherever they liked. They no longer depended on the good, or ill, will of municipal authorities. Shakespeare's name stood second, before that of Burbage, on this charter of privilege and freedom. Their title of Grooms of the Chamber was renewed, and when they were on duty as Court ushers they were given money for their keep. In the winter of 1603, when an outbreak of plague had closed the London theatres, the Court was at Wilton, and here, on 2nd December, the company was performing – probably *As You Like It*. In January they were at Hampton Court – short of cash, it appears, for in February the King contributed £30 to Richard Burbage 'for the maintenance and relief of himself and his company'. The royal progress through the City took place on 15 March 1603-4, and although the King's Men did not apparently take part in this, they were each provided with four and a half yards of red cloth to make themselves suits for the occasion. Shakespeare's name now headed the list of the beneficiaries. When the plague had abated, a letter from the Privy Council instructed – or warned – the Lord Mayor of London and the Justices of the Peace for Middlesex and Surrey to permit the King's Players to perform at their 'usual house'.

In August 1604 the Constable of Castille, with two other Spanish statesmen and three representatives of the Governor of the Spanish province of the Netherlands, came to London on a diplomatic mission and were lodged at Somerset House. Shakespeare and eleven other members of the company were in attendance on them for eighteen days. At the ceremonial banquet Southampton – now released from prison – and Pembroke both acted as Stewards. Later in the year the new Queen, Anne of Denmark, wished to see a performance elsewhere than under a royal roof. Southampton House was chosen, but Burbage – who had been asked to provide the entertainment – replied that he had in his repertoire 'no new play that the Queen had not seen'. He suggested *Love's Labour's Lost*, recently revived, as a play which 'for wit and mirth would please the Queen'. Obviously it did so, for between All Saints Day 1604 (1 November) and Shrove Tuesday (12 February 1604-5) seven performances of plays by Shakespeare were given at Whitehall: one each of *Othello, The Merry Wives of Windsor, Measure for Measure, The Comedy of Errors, Love's Labour's Lost*, and *Henry V*, and two of *The Merchant of Venice*. The King particularly enjoyed *The Merchant*.

The same year saw the heyday of the Mermaid Club in Bread Street, off Cheapside. It met on the first Friday evening of the month, and we learn that the vintner was had up for selling meat on twenty-nine successive Fridays. The prohibition was not inspired by piety, but by the protests of the fishermen who feared that laxity in observing the regulations would lose them their trade. Ben Jonson presided at these ordinaries

> That which most doth take my Muse and me
> Is a pure cup of rich Canary wine
> Which is the Mermaid's now, and shall be mine.

Shakespeare was so prominent among the revellers that Jonson could write

> That such thy drought was and so great thy thirst
> That all thy plays were drawn at the Mermaid first.

Fuller, in his *Worthies* (1662), recalled 'the wit-combats betwixt him and Ben Jonson, which two I behold like a Spanish great galleon and an English man of war; Master Jonson (like the former) was built far higher in learning, solid but slow in his performance. Shakespeare, with the English man of war, lesser in bulk, but lighter in sailing, could turn with all tides, tack about, and take advantage of all winds by the quickness of his wit and invention.' This is excellent literary criticism as well as vivid reminiscence. But the most colourful impression of those *convivia* comes from Francis Beaumont who dreamt of 'your full Mermaid wine'

> What things have we seen
> Done at the Mermaid! heard words that have been
> So nimble, and so full of subtill flame,
> As if that everyone from whence they came
> Had meant to put his whole wit in a jest
> And had resolv'd to live like a fool, the rest
> Of his dull life. Then, when there had been thrown
> Wit able enough to justify the town
> For three days past — wit that might warrant be
> For the whole city to talk foolishly
> Till that were cancel'd — and, when that was gone,
> We left an Aire behind us, which alone
> Was able to make the two next companies
> Right witty; though but downright fools, were wise.

Surely all this disposes of a Shakespeare who had lost either his sense of humour, or his *joie de vivre.*

It was about this time that he went to lodge with Christopher Mountjoy, a French Huguenot, who lived at the corner of Monkwell and Silver Street, near St Olave's Church in Cripplegate, within the north-west corner of the city walls. Mountjoy made ornamental head-dresses for women, and the Queen had favoured him with her custom. His shop was on the ground floor, with living quarters above. He had two apprentices, one of whom, Stephen Belott, fell in love with his daughter Mary, and Shakespeare, at the request of Madame Mountjoy, encouraged him in his suit. They were married at St

Olave's Church on the 19 November 1604, and it is reasonable to suppose that Shakespeare attended the wedding if he were not professionally engaged elsewhere. This was close to the heart of literary London, where the new publications were on sale in St Paul's Churchyard. The district was more salubrious, both physically and morally, than Southwark, and Shakespeare may have welcomed the opportunity to get away from theatrical 'shop', as well as to improve his French in conversation with the Mountjoy family with whom he was evidently on extremely friendly terms.

He had always, in comparison with other Elizabethan poets — Sidney, Spenser, Raleigh and Jonson — economized his flattery of the Queen. To them she was 'Astraea', but the nearest Shakespeare comes to Astraea is to allow the Dauphin in *Henry VI, Part One,* to salute Joan of Arc as 'Astraea's daughter'. Considering the treatment meted out to Joan of Arc, the Queen was unlikely to have taken this as a compliment. Titus Andronicus persuades his brother to shoot his arrow at a star called Astraea, and exclaims: *'Terras Astraea reliquit'.* But Titus is clearly out of his mind, and it was again no compliment to Elizabeth to assimilate her — if such were the intention — to a star shot out of the sky at the behest of a madman. Nor is there the slightest evidence of a nation softening into decadence under the new reign. The accession of James VI of Scotland had been welcomed with relief; the King did much to settle what Elizabeth, Mary Stuart, and Philip of Spain between them had disturbed. As Richard Burton, the shrewd anatomist of Melancholy, was to write in 1621

> We have besides many particular blessings, which our neighbours want, the Gospel truly preached, Church discipline established, long peace and quietness, free from exactions, foreign fears, invasions, domestic seditions, well mannered, fortified by art and nature, and now most happy, in that fortunate union of England and Scotland, which our forefathers have laboured to effect, and desired to see.

James has had as 'bad a press' as Elizabeth has had a good one. Yet John Donne was preaching at St Paul's; the prayers of Lancelot Andrewes and the poems of George Herbert entered the main stream of Anglican piety; and the Bible was collectively translated in a masterpiece of English prose which has held its own — to say the least — against any alternative version before or since. Inigo Jones in architecture brought the classicism of Palladio to challenge the Tudor exuberance, and Francis Bacon's *The Advancement of Learning* proved that men now had time to think. Patriotism was no longer equated with piracy, and for a brief period it was true to say that 'peace proclaims olives of endless age'. James' personal motto was *Beati Pacifici.* England was far from a miserable place during the first decade of the Jacobean reign, when Shakespeare was writing his

tragedies and 'problem' plays; and there is no evidence that
Shakespeare was a miserable man. The trouble arises from too
literally reading his biography into his plays. His plays *are* his
biography; which is not at all the same thing.

2

When Cézanne decided to break with Impressionism, and the Cubists
to break with figurative painting altogether, it was because they
wanted to paint a different kind of picture. We have no right to
assume that the apples and the violins were the consequence of a
private trauma. So it was with Shakespeare. His innovations need
have meant no more (and no less) than a decision to write a different
kind of play, of which *Hamlet* has already given us a foretaste. Their
proper reference is to the world of dramatic art, not of emotional
experience. *Troilus and Cressida* was such a novelty that
Shakespeare's contemporaries were as puzzled as we are to know
how to describe it. Two Quarto editions were published in 1609. The
first described the play as 'The Historie of Troilus and Cressida, as it
was acted by the King's Majesties servants at the Globe'. Shortly
afterwards this title page was suppressed and another one inserted
with no mention of the Globe performance, thus denying to the
Globe managers any rights in the play. On the back of the new title
page there also appeared a new preface telling the reader that 'you
have here a new play, never staled with the stage, never clapper-
clawed with the palms of the vulgar, and yet passing full of the palm
comical'. It emphasized that 'this author's comedies . . . are so
framed to the life, that they serve for the most common commentaries of all the actions of our lives, showing such a dexterity and
power of wit, that the most displeased with plays are pleased with his
comedies', and declared that among all of them 'there is none more
witty than this'.

The play was commended all the more 'for not being sullied with
the smoky breath of the multitude'. We may infer from this that it
had not been acted at the Globe for some years; had perhaps been
withdrawn from the repertoire for political reasons; but may have
been presented at the Inns of Court, where its satire and sophistication would have found a congenial public. If that were so we can
more safely assert that it was designed to flatter the taste of its
audience than suggest that it echoed the hypothetical *angst* of its
author. Satire had become so fashionable that it was forbidden by
law to indulge it at the expense of living persons; but mythical
characters were immune, and audiences were left to fit the cap to
whatever heads might be in danger of rolling. Achilles sulking in his
tent was a distant parallel to Essex sulking in his mansion, before he

so rashly emerged from it. Hector's challenge to Achilles is almost identical with Essex's challenge to the Governor of Rouen in 1591. *'Si vous voulez combattre vous-même à cheval ou à pied, je maintiendrai que la querelle du roi est plus juste que celle de la ligue, et que ma maitresse est plus belle que la votre.'* The publishers evidently wished the play to be regarded as a comedy, but the Folio editors were apparently in some doubt as to how it should be classified. It has no place in their table of contents, and the first three pages of the text were originally set to follow *Romeo and Juliet*. Finally it was left to stand between *Coriolanus* and *Henry VIII*. This was the best available compromise between Heminge and Condell who regarded it as a tragedy, the Quarto preface which insisted it was a comedy, and the title-page of both Quartos which stated it was a history. It provoked a subsequent definition of the play as 'a History in which historical verisimilitude is openly set at nought, a Comedy without genuine laughter, a Tragedy without pathos'. This is facile enough, but it forgets Troilus.

It is clear that already in 1599 Shakespeare had produced a version of the play we know, for in that year he was parodied in *Histrio-mastix,* and the date of the play eventually published in Quarto cannot be determined. The unevenness of style suggests that it was composed, perhaps at different times, at the turn of the century, and while Shakespeare was already at work on *Hamlet*. Troilus' 'Even in the fan and wind of your fair sword' closely parallels 'But with the whiff and wind of his fell sword' of the First Player; just as the long description of Priam's death indicates that the dramatist's mind was already upon the Trojan War. Certainly the play was well known by 1603, for a poem, *Saint Marie Magdalen's Conversion*, printed in that year, has references that could only apply to Shakespeare

> Of Helen's rape and Troy's besieged town,
> Of Troilus' faith, and Cressid's falsity,
> Of Richard's stratagems for the English crown,
> Of Tarquin's lust, and Lucrece chastity . . .

More often than not Shakespeare's sources were a convenience; in the case of *Troilus and Cressida* they were an inspiration. In 1598 Chapman produced his first translation of the Iliad, dedicated to Essex as 'Most true Achilles', and praising his 'Achillean virtues'. In Shakespeare's treatment of the character they are not conspicuous. If he had Essex in mind he cannot have been goading him to revolt, for the killing of Hector by Achilles' Myrmidons — for which there was no Homeric warrant — was far removed from flattery. This may have been suggested by Homer's picture of Achilles — 'a work not worthy him' — dragging Hector at the tail of his chariot through a 'whirlwind . . . of startled dust'

by Jupiter exil'd
To all disgrace, in his own land, and by his parents seen.

Moreover Achilles' friendship for Patroclus did not, in Homer, have the homosexual overtones which Shakespeare allows it; and Ulysses' plan to use Ajax as a pawn to get Achilles out of his tent is equally the dramatist's invention. Ulysses remains the most intelligent of the Greek leaders, getting the cue from Homer for his great speech on 'degree'

nor must Greeks be so irregular
To live as every man may take the sceptre from the King;
The rule of many is absurd, one Lord must lead the ring
Of far resounding government . . .

From Homer, too, came Thersites

A man of tongue, whose ravenlike voice a timeless
        jarring kept . . .
The filthiest Greek that came to Troy; he had a goggle eye;
Stark-lame he was of either foot: his shoulders were contract
Into his breast and crookt withal: his head was sharp compact,
And here and there it had a hair.

Shakespeare turns the character into a kind of private jester to Achilles, and to a chorus on the follies of 'wars and lechery'. Here is yet a further transformation of the Shakespearean fool; no longer the 'funny man', he neither laughs himself, nor is the cause of laughter in other people.

Ajax's 'blockish wit' could have been found in Arthur Golding's translation of Ovid's *Metamorphoses,* and other features of his character and person in John Lydgate's *The History, Siege, and Destruction of Troy* (1513), which Shakespeare must certainly have known. Here he is 'right corpulent . . . high of stature . . . and of his speech rude and reckeless . . . and but a coward was he of his heart'. Shakespeare acquits him of cowardice, but allows him the rest. Of the other characters Ulysses is 'in counselling discreet and full prudent'; Diomede 'lecherous of complexion'; Cressida 'in love variable, of tender heart and unsteadfastness'; and Troilus

He was alway faithful, just and stable
Perseverant and of will immutable.

Lydgate had described how Cressida kept Diomede on tenterhooks.

Day by day to put him in delays
To stand unsure betwixe hope and dread.

Shakespeare took Pandarus from Chaucer's *Troilus and Criseyde,* and much else in the love story besides, but Pandarus has changed from a brother-in-arms into a salacious pimp. If *Troilus and Cressida*

is a tragedy because Troilus is Romeo and Cressida is not Juliet, it is
a comedy because Pandarus is not Friar Lawrence.

In brief, the dramatist used Homeric and Chaucerian material to
construct a counterpoint of his own devising. His approach is
anti-mythic, as he deliberately deflates the romanticism both of
Romeo and Juliet and *Henry V.* There is a reminiscence of
Mercutio's teasing of Romeo in Pandarus' teasing of Troilus in the
opening scene; here the counterpoint is emphasized by the alternation of verse and prose. And in Pandarus there is also something of
the Nurse's worldly cynicism mixed with her earthy realism and good
nature. Troilus is more mature than Romeo — twenty-three, we are
told — and as direct as Cressida is devious. She is not a young widow,
as she had been in Chaucer, but she clearly has experience of men

> Yet hold I off. Women are angels, wooing;
> Things won are done; joy's soul lies in the doing
> That she beloved knows nought that knows not this:
> Men prize the thing ungain'd more than it is.
>
> (I, ii, 312-15)

The character is brilliantly drawn. Cressida is as truly in love as her
nature allows her to be; yet she knows her frailty

> I have a kind of self resides with you,
> But an unkind self that itself will leave
> To be another's fool. I would be gone:
> Where is my wit? I know not what I speak.
>
> (III, ii, 155-9)

And how different is this marriage contract, ratified though it be by
a twofold 'Amen', from the sacramental union in the Friar's cell!
Instead of a nuptial blessing we have Pandarus' voyeuristic glee

> I will show you a chamber with a bed: which bed, because it shall not
> speak of your pretty encounters, press it to death. Away!
>
> (III, ii, 215-18)

Another significant parallel is the 'morning after'; the realism of
Cressida's

> Prithee, tarry:
> You men will never tarry.
> O foolish Cressid! I might have still held off,
> And then you would have tarried
>
> (IV, ii, 15-18)

reminding us of Juliet's 'Wilt thou begone, it is not yet near day'. And
her very different reasons for begging Romeo to tarry. There is no
doubting the sincerity of Cressida's despair when she learns that she
must be handed over to the Greeks in exchange for Antenor, or of

her impatience when Troilus asks for a double assurance of her fidelity. He knows the dangers — 'The Grecian youths are full of quality' — and he is prompted, as he admits, by 'a kind of godly jealousy'

> But something may be done that we will not:
> And sometimes we are devils to ourselves,
> When we will tempt the frailty of our powers,
> Presuming on their changeful potency.
>
> (IV, iv, 95-9)

Diomed, when he comes as Cressida's escort, hints that he has entered the lists — 'when I am hence, I'll answer to my lust'; and how evocative is Ulysses' description of his return — 'he rises on the toe' — and of Cressida's provocative self-possession as she bestows her kisses on the Greek generals

> There's language in her eye, her cheek, her lip.
> Nay, her foot speaks; her wanton spirits look out
> At every joint and motive of her body.
>
> (IV, v, 55-7)

Better than anyone else on either side in this war over another wanton, Ulysses knows the world; and proof will soon be positive that Cressida, like Helen, is a 'daughter of the game'.

But not as like as all that. Helen drifts through her single scene, vacant of expression and personality as the model at a dress show, and we have no curiosity to meet her again. She too has been devalued from the day when she appeared to Faustus; the light has gone out from 'the face that launched a thousand ships' — though Shakespeare allows Troilus to steal the line. Cressida, despite her frailty, would have been better worth a war. Even in the torchlight of Calchas' tent her heart is more than half with Troilus; but, as Ulysses puts it, it is in her nature to 'sing any man at first sight'. Even in the act of giving Diomed the sleeve, she knows, like Goneril in *King Lear,* 'the difference of man and man'. The surrendered token was 'one's that loved me better than you will'. Cressida's saving grace is to have no illusions about herself

> Ah, poor our sex: this fault in us I find
> The error of our eye directs our mind:
> What error leads must err; O, then conclude
> Minds swayed by eyes are full of turpitude.
>
> (V, ii, 109-12)

When Ulysses and Troilus are left alone, the scene touches tragedy

> Let it not be believed for womanhood.
> Think, we had mothers . . .
>
> (V, ii, 129-30)

Troilus' disillusionment is akin to Hamlet's; we think of Claudius and Gertrude. But there is more stuff in Cressida than in Gertrude, and more subtlety in Shakespeare's portrait of her. Weak as she may be, she has none of Gertrude's lymphatic passivity; to put it bluntly, she would have been more fun to seduce. And even when she has gone her way with Diomed, she can still write to Troilus. What did she say? We do not know, because he does not read the letter. This is one of the several unanswered questions in what have been called the 'problem' plays.

Shakespeare preserves an ironic detachment between the rights and wrongs of the Trojan war. The Greeks are concerned with how the war can be won; the Trojans debate their moral right to win it. The Greeks have the better case, the Trojans the better men. Neither Shakespeare nor his audience would have forgotten the pious belief that the English were descended from the Trojans. The dramatist is more original in his treatment of Hector in whom he shows a mixture of 'Socratic insight and Quixotic behaviour'[1] — than in his treatment of Achilles. It is Hector — the noblest Trojan of them all — who argues, 'Let Helen go'

> If we have lost so many tenths of ours,
> To guard a thing not ours, nor worth to us,
> Had it our name, the value of one ten,
> What merit's in that reason which denies
> The yielding of her up?

(II, ii, 21-5)

or again

> If Helen then be wife to Sparta's King,
> As it is known she is, these moral laws
> Of nature and of nations speak alone
> To have her back returned.

(II, ii, 183-6)

Yet it is Hector who weakly surrenders the strength of his own argument

> I propend to you
> In resolution to keep Helen still;
> For 'tis a cause that hath no mean dependance
> Upon our joint and several dignities.

(II, ii, 190-3)

His sense of honour and his 'vice of mercy' with Ajax are equally sportive; here, one feels, are public schoolboys on the playing field, not Homeric heroes on the field of battle. 'My country, right or

---

[1] Nicholas Brooke, International Shakespeare Association Congress, 1976.

wrong' combines with Troilus' specious appeal to 'honour'. If the
Trojans had applauded the rape of Helen

> a pearl
> Whose price hath launch'd above a thousand ships
> And turn'd crown'd kings to merchants
>
> (II, ii, 81-3)

why should they now

> Beggar the estimation which you priz'd
> Richer than sea and land?
>
> (II, ii, 91-2)

or

> how may I avoid
> Although my will distaste what is elected,
> The wife I chose?
>
> (II, ii, 65-7)

Troilus conveniently forgets that Helen was someone else's wife; just
as Hector appeals to reason only to dismiss it, Troilus will not allow
reason to enter the argument at all

> Nay, if we talk of reason,
> Let's shut our gates, and sleep . . .
> reason and respect
> Make livers pale and lustihood deject . . .
>
> (II, ii, 46 *et seq.*)

and his resolution is not affected by Cressida's infidelity. Helen is
still worth a war.

The Greeks, sparing of the noble sentiments to which they have a
right, prevail by intelligence and cunning; Achilles is tempted from
his day-bed and his 'masculine whore', and the Myrmidons do his
dirty work. Hector, reluctant to shed the blood of Ajax because
some of it is Trojan, is murdered while his back is turned and 'in
beastly sort dragg'd through the shameful field'. It is left for Troilus
to avenge him, if he can, and

> dare all imminence that gods and men
> Address their dangers in . . .
>
> (V, x, 13-14)

The issue of the war is not determined in *Troilus and Cressida*, but it
is foreshadowed in Thersites' comment to a bastard son of Priam's:
'If the son of a whore fight for a whore, he tempts judgement'.

The play perplexes because it does not quite hold together. The
Prologue — omitted in the Folio, and perhaps not by Shakespeare's
hand — sounds a bombastic fanfare to what we expect to be a war of
gods and heroes. The strange return of Pandarus at the close has no

relevance to what has immediately gone before. We have finished with Pandarus; he has been no more than the middle-man of what Troilus believed was love, and Pandarus believed was lechery. The speech looks very like a sop to an insatiable comedian. As in *Hamlet,* when Shakespeare gets hold of an idea — Ulysses on 'degree' to the council of war, and on 'emulation' to Achilles — he lets it take him as far as it will go; and this is a little further than the average audience finds it easy to keep him company. The play gains by discreet abridgement. The writing varies from the complicated to the pithy and the crystal clear; and the frequency of rhymed couplets suggests a tired harking back to a style by now outgrown. When the attrition of time challenges the durability of love, the verse takes wing and glows with the deep Shakespearean essence

> Injurious time now with a robber's haste
> Crams his rich thievery up, he knows not how:
> As many farewells as be stars in heaven,
> With distinct breath and consign'd kisses to them
> He fumbles up into a loose adieu
>
> (IV, iv, 44-8)

and accommodates itself just as well to the needling of Ulysses' dialectic. But the triumph of the play is Cressida; viewed with imperturbable compasion and unflinching insight, she marks the furthest point that Shakespeare had yet reached in the exploration of a woman's character. The Folio editors were justified in not including this play among the comedies; for in so far as it laughs at all, it laughs entirely at its own expense.

Chapter 15

Bed-Tricks

1

All's Well That Ends Well is no one's favourite play, although Helena
was Bernard Shaw's favourite heroine — because here the wooing was
on the female foot. The title proclaims it to be a comedy, and in
itself links it with *As You Like It, Much Ado* and *Twelfth Night* or
'what you will', titles which all suggest a light-heartedness that in fact
it belies. There is no record of its performance in Shakespeare's
life-time, and it did not appear in print until the publication of the
First Folio. The style, and treatment of the story, with the characters
that the dramatist invented — the Countess, Parolles, and Lafeu —
would seem to place its composition at the turn of the century, or
shortly afterwards. But the unusual number of rhymed couplets, and
the laboured word-play, suggest that Shakespeare had had a version
of it in his drawer for some time; and it may well have been the
Love's Labour Won, mentioned by Francis Meres in 1598. The
indications are clear of second thoughts; if not exactly of a second
wind.

The editors of the New Cambridge Shakespeare roundly declare it
to be Shakespeare's 'worst play'. Tillyard[1] endorsed the general view
that it is a failure, while admitting that he has never seen it acted, nor
was likely to. In fact, it has been produced with much effect in
recent years — notably by Tyrone Guthrie at Stratford-upon-Avon
and Stratford, Ontario. It has been saved by its plot, which Tillyard
shrewdly picked out, with the character of Helena, as its strongest
feature. That the plot is unpleasant to the modern mind should not
be held against it; one would have thought, by now, that nothing was
too unpleasant for the modern mind. That the plot is impossible is an
accusation that you can bring with equal justice against *Twelfth
Night* or *As You Like It.* Shakespeare knew that impossibilities are
the stuff of fairy-tales or folk-legend or popular romance, and may
serve either to entertain or to instruct. In *All's Well* he was concerned

[1] *Shakespeare's Problem Plays* (1951).

to do both, relating naturalism to myth, and it may be argued that he did the second better than the first.

It is not a young man's play. Shakespeare seems no longer to have a very high opinion of young men. He had seen too much of them hanging around Southampton House; perhaps he had seen too much of Southampton himself, so foolishly compromised in the Essex conspiracy. But Lady Southampton, as Dr Rowse reminds us, may have given him his cue for the Countess; a cue that he did not take from Boccaccio. She illustrates the relaxed protocol and quiet courtesies of a life lived deep in the country; an aristocrat with a quick eye for the *arriviste*. She has been compared to 'one of Titian's old ladies, reminding us still amid their wrinkles of that soul of beauty and sensibility which must have animated them when young'. This is what Edith Evans gave us at Stratford and, on a smaller scale, Sylvia Coleridge at Greenwich. Helena, a doctor's daughter, is the only one of Shakespeare's heroines of whom it can be said that she came from the middle classes; and like the Countess, he thinks no worse of her for that. Indeed *All's Well* disposes of the idea that Shakespeare, once he had seen deeper into the ways of the world, was a snob. The King of France is no cardboard monarch, like the Dukes who preside over the earlier comedies, but active in mind, though invalid in body. It is he who tells young Bertram that he has no right to think himself too good for the hand of a physician's daughter

> She is young, wise, fair;
> In these to nature she's immediate heir,
> And these breed honour . . .
> . . . honours thrive,
> When rather from our acts we them derive
> Than our foregoers: the mere word's a slave
> Debosh'd on every tomb, on every grave
> A lying trophy; and as oft is dumb
> When dust and damn'd oblivion is the tomb
> Of honour'd bones indeed.
>
> (II, iii, 138-48)

We have heard much about honour from Hotspur, and again from Troilus. Shakespeare sets the record straight; he was perhaps less impressed than we are by tombs that look like trophies, although he was to be given a fairly handsome one of his own.

The relationship between the Countess and her clown — Monsieur Lavache — is not unlike that between Olivia and Feste, except that the Countess is more real as a person and Lavache less entertaining as a clown. Indeed his prolixity is a theatrical embarrassment, and he is not, like Feste, integral to the structure of the play. Lefeu, the mellow courtier, has something of the Countess's charm; a less sprightly Boyet, his function as an urbane go-between is similar.

These older characters are all representative of an 'antique world' to which the dramatist seems to be looking back with a regretful nostalgia. Of their juniors Bertram is what used to be described in the Officers' Mess as a 'young puppy'; immaturity is his only excuse. Shakespeare does his best for him by subjecting him to the bad influence of Parolles, introduced not only for the purpose of comic relief — excellent as most of it is. Parolles is described as 'a follower of Bertram'. No doubt he follows him because he is of good birth, breeding, and fortune — and, above all, impressionable to everything but Helena's charm. We are left to guess at Parolles' age, where he comes from, and how they met. He is probably younger than he usually appears on the stage. As Dr Jonathan Miller has put it, he is 'the kind of young man the Countess wishes her son would not bring back to the house'.[1] His importance to the scheme of the play, and its theatrical effectiveness, was recognized by Charles I who inscribed 'Parolles' on the title page of his copy of the Second Folio. In exposing his cowardice, deceitfulness, and treachery, Shakespeare brings Bertram a step nearer to responsible manhood; and it is Parolles who gives the necessary evidence of Bertram's supposed seduction of Diana. *All's Well* is essentially a play of exposure. Parolles speaks of virginity very much as Falstaff speaks of honour. 'It is not politic in the commonwealth of nature to preserve virginity. Loss of virginity is rational increase, and there was never virgin got till virginity was first lost.' Parolles is very far from being a Falstaff — for one thing he inspires in us no spark of affection — but he might be speaking for Falstaff when he declares 'Simply the thing I am shall make me live'.

All's Well can only be understood in terms of a Morality. Helena has the right to be in love with Bertram despite her lower rank in society; the right to claim him because this will be for his greater good; and the right to recover him by the bed-trick

> which, if it speed,
> Is wicked meaning in a lawful deed,
> And lawful meaning in a lawful act,
> Where both not sin, and yet a sinful fact.

(III, vii, 45-7)

In other words, Betram will still, subjectively, be the sinner. Helena has earned these rights not alone by virtue of her intrinsic goodness, but because she has cured the King of his infirmity. This, of course, she does for reasons far from altruistic; the cure is the first stage in her strategy. Nevertheless we are meant to believe — and the long passage of rhymed couplets puts the scene in a liturgical context —

[1] In conversation with the author.

that the powers, inherited from her father whom the King had known and admired, are quasi-supernatural

> Methinks in thee some blessèd spirit doth speak
> His powerful sound within an organ weak
>
> (II, i, 188-9)

and the contrast is all the more striking with the purely natural spontaneity of her love for Bertram, when the callow youth has left Roussillon to enlist in the war. Here she speaks with the directness of Imogen, and the verse obeys it

> 'Twas pretty, though a plague,
> To see him every hour; to sit and draw
> His archèd brows, his hawking-eye, his curls,
> In our heart's table; heart too capable
> Of every line and trick of his sweet favour:
> But now he's gone, and my idolatrous fancy
> Must sanctify his reliques.
>
> (I, i, 103-9)

It is not often, in this play, that Shakespeare's imagination works at an equal pitch. He is searching for a formula that he will only discover in the later plays — commonly called romances — where romance and realism are perfectly combined, with a theophany to bless the alliance. *All's Well* is a hesitant step in this direction, uneven and unsatisfying as a whole, illuminating in parts, and successfully claiming our sympathy — the bed-trick notwithstanding — for what Coleridge called Shakespeare's 'loveliest character'. The play is held together not only by its plot, but by its theme — which is charity that forgiveth all things, and contrition that cannot come too late. The dramatist's view of Bertram — and through Bertram of sinful human nature — is seen in the colloquy of the two Lords, acting here as a moralizing chorus very much as the four Gentlemen in *The Winter's Tale* act as a narrative chorus

> *First Lord* Now God delay our rebellion! as
> we are ourselves, what things we are!
> *Sec. Lord* Merely our own traitors. And as in the
> common course of all treasons, we see them
> reveal themselves, till they attain to
> their abhorred ends, so he that in this
> action contrives against his own nobility,
> in his proper stream o'erflows himself.
>
> (IV, iii, 19-24)

In short, treason to oneself or to other people will always give itself away in the end.

2

Walter Pater described *Measure for Measure* as 'an epitome of
Shakespeare's moral judgements',[1] and the definition may stand. As
in the case of *All's Well,* no text of the play was published before the
First Folio, but the style and theme both suggest 1603-4 as a likely
date of composition. We know that in the latter year it was played
before the King, whose character and quirks are mildly hinted at in
the character of the Duke. In 1607 William Barksted, an actor who
had played with the Children of the Chapel Royal, published a poem
where the following lines

> And like as when some sudden extasy
>   Seizeth the stature of a sickly man;
> When he's discern'd to swoon, straight by and by
>   Folk to his help confusedly have ran;
> And seeking with their art to fetch him back,
>   So many throng that he the air doth lack

clearly echo Angelo's

> So play the foolish throngs with one that swoons;
> Come all to help him, and so stop the air
> By which he should revive.

                                                        (II, iv, 24-6)

It has been conjectured[2] that Barksted may have been the original
Isabella; he would have been just the right age. Shakespeare took his
plot from Giraldi Cinthio's *Heccammothi* (1565), which he could
have read in a French translation. Cinthio dramatized the tale in
Epitia which, like *Measure for Measure,* is a tragi-comedy about
Justice and Mercy; and five years before this was published George
Whetstone, using the same themes, produced his tedious *Promos and
Cassandra.* This was never acted, but it provided Shakespeare with his
raw material, and a broader view of society than he would have got
from Cinthio. At the same time he ennobled the theme; added the
characters of Escalus, Lucio, Mariana, and most of the Duke; and left
the characters of low life no higher than he found them.

He had always been interested in the workings of politics, but
hitherto politics had been about power. In *Henry IV* he had given a
fairly complete picture of society. Now he was preoccupied by the
ethics of public and private life, and the interaction of one with the
other. He had shown this in *Hamlet*: but although the 'state of
Denmark' is an important element in the play, it is overshadowed, as
Pater wrote, by 'the problems which beset one of exceptional
temperament', whereas in *Measure for Measure* the subject is 'mere

[1] *Appreciations.*
[2] See H. P. Stokes, *The Chronological Order of Shakespeare's Plays*, pp. 106-9.

human nature'. The play, nearly contemporary with *Hamlet*, is as universal in its theme, though far less so in its appeal. A restricted popularity is the price of tragi-comedy; audiences like to know where they are sitting.

If a dramatist is unable, or unwilling, to invent his own plots, he must make the best of what he is given. The plot of *Measure for Measure* is a strong one, and brilliantly sustained. It accommodates philosophy, but philosophy does not hold it up. The play does not suffer from the prolixity of *Hamlet* or *Troilus and Cressida*; there is hardly a line that you can cut without damage. Nevertheless the plot is worked out on two levels, one realistic, the other allegorical. The first two acts, and the first scene of the third, reveal Shakespeare at the height of his powers. We are interested in the plot because we are interested in the people; and the minor characters are vividly developed, Barnardine with only 111 words in his part, and Froth with only 57. In the second half of the play they turn what might have been a tragedy into a tragi-comedy instead. Even if you take the view — and in my opinion it is the right one — that everything is ordained to Isabella's plea that Angelo shall be pardoned, this is the climax of a Morality, not of a study in human psychology. More exactly, as Nevill Coghill has pointed out in a brilliant essay, *Measure for Measure* is an allegory. 'Morality plays are the one-stringed fiddles of allegory, deficient in all other tones'[1] — and no one can deny that here the full Shakespearean orchestra is at work. If the play had continued on the realistic level, the Duke would have given short shrift to Angelo, once he had learnt of his infamous proposal; Isabella would have taken the veil; and wedding bells would have rung for Claudio and Julietta. But this would have reduced the play to three acts, and Elizabethan audiences liked their money's worth. They liked particularly a final scene where everything crooked is made straight, true identities are revealed, and there is some prospect that everyone will live more or less happily ever after.

This popular prejudice suited the design of an allegory. The Duke is something less than Almighty God, but something more than the 'fantastical Duke of dark corners'. Even if he is a first sketch for Prospero — as Wilson Knight has argued[2] — he feels no need to abdicate. To pardon his enemies costs him no inward struggle. He enjoys manipulating the plot of *Measure for Measure*, as Prospero enjoys gathering his 'projects to a head'. He puts other people to the test, as Prospero tests Ferdinand and Miranda. As a stage-manager there is nothing to reproach him with. The figure of the ruler moving disguised among his subjects in order to know them better had been

---

[1] *Shakespeare Survey*, 8.
[2] *The Wheel of Fire* (1969).

made familiar by Haroun al Raschid. We have seen it in Henry V among his soldiers on the eve of Agincourt. But how much did the Duke know of Angelo — who, we learn later, was his cousin — and how much did he suspect? Surely he had his doubts

> Lord Angelo is precise;
> Stands at a guard with envy; scarce confesses
> That his blood flows, or that his appetite
> Is more to bread than stone; hence shall we see
> If power change purpose, what our seemers be . . .
>
> (I, iv, 50-4)

Moreover he knew that, for the basest reasons, he had left Mariana inconsolable in her moated grange. Yet we have the word of Escalus that

> If any in Vienna be of worth
> To undergo such ample grace and honour
> It is Lord Angelo.
>
> (I, i, 23-5)

Probably Escalus knew nothing of that strangely Tennysonian heroine shedding her tears into the moat.

We may take the Duke at his word when he speaks of his distaste for publicity

> I love the people
> But do not like to stage me to their eyes
>
> (I, i, 68-9)

and plausibly assume him to be shy — we have Lucio's word for this — bookish, with a fair smattering of Stoic philosophy, not over-endowed with a sense of humour, and a contented bachelor until he fancies that Isabella would make him a good wife. This is altogether too much for a modern audience, however neatly it may have rounded off the play for the Jacobeans. There is reason to think that Shakespeare left the options ajar, if not exactly open. 'If you'll a willing ear incline' says the Duke; but Isabella says nothing to indicate whether her ear is willing or not. In his riveting production of the play at the Greenwich Theatre, Dr Jonathan Miller had her abruptly return to her convent — which is, of course, exactly what she would have done in real life, if real life had brought her into that improbable situation. The final scene presents other problems. Is Isabella's plea for Angelo to be construed as an act of perfect forgiveness, remembering that she only pleads because Mariana begs her to? For not even *that* bed-trick had cured Mariana's infatuation. The Duke is not encouraging

> Against all sense you do importune her:
> Should she kneel down in mercy of this fact,

> Her brother's ghost his pavéd bed would break
> And take her hence in horror.
>
> (V, i, 438-41)

For the Duke, stage-managing up to the last moment, has not yet disclosed that Claudio is still alive. Moreover — and this is the greatest puzzle — when Claudio is revealed neither he nor Isabella have a word to say to each other; and the question awkwardly persists — does Isabella forgive Claudio? And does Claudio forgive Isabella? 'Let me ask my sister pardon' he had declared to the Duke; yet he does not ask it. Viewed either as the resolution of a plot, or as the summing-up of an allegory, there is great ingenuity but lukewarm comfort in the last act of *Measure for Measure.* Among all the marriages concluded, hinted at, or shortly to be foreseen, the only one acceptable to the common sense of a modern audience is that of Claudio and Julietta; but of this no mention is made, even for the sake of symmetry.

The moral values of the play detonate with the force of great poetry, psychological truth, and dramatic tension in those passages where the allegory does not ask to be accommodated to happy endings. The modern audience, which is rightly reluctant to let Isabella marry the Duke, wrongly forbid her to place a higher price on her own virginity than on her brother's life. 'More than our brother is our chastity' is the stiffest hurdle that any actress feels called upon to face; you see them approaching it like a nervous steeplechaser. The situation — so runs the argument — could be saved by situation ethics. But situation ethics were unknown to Shakespeare, or Shakespeare's audience. For them, chastity was an absolute, and death no more than a misfortune that might come today or tomorrow, but would come inevitably. 'We shall all die, cousin' and 'the readiness is all' — these are the essential texts. To the first the Duke gives a Stoic, to the second a Christian, emphasis. Not even the besotted Barnardine can be allowed to die until he has made his peace with God[1]

> A creature unprepared, unmeet for death
> And to transport him in the mind he is
> Were damnable
>
> (IV, iii, 71-3)

and as for Claudio

> What's yet in this
> That bears the name of life? Yet in this life

---

[1] I have read the eye-witness account of an execution in Malta during the Second World War, in which the hangman would not pull the lever until the condemned man had formally forgiven his enemies.

Lie hid more thousand deaths: yet death we fear
That makes these odds all even.

(III, i, 38-41)

It is worth recalling, however, that John Donne was not above giving
Stoic advice from the pulpit of St Paul's

We are all conceived in a close prison: in our mother's wombs we are close
prisoners all; when we are born, we are but born to the liberty of the
house; prisoners still, though within larger walls, and then all our life is but
a going out to the place of execution, to death. Now was there ever any
man seen to sleep in the cart, between Newgate and Tyburn; between the
prison and the place of execution, does any man sleep? And we sleep all
the way.[1]

Claudio thinks he is reconciled — 'To sue to live, I find I seek to die'
— but he is reckoning without Isabella. Far more provocative than
her refusal to sacrifice her chastity is her want of imagination in
telling Claudio that she had the choice of doing so. This has been
defended as the courage to tell the truth; but there are occasions
when it is unnecessary, and even harmful, to tell the truth —
especially when silence cannot be said to cover even the whitest of
lies. Her anger at Claudio's pleading — and his pleading shows a rough
acquaintance with moral theology

Sure, it is no sin;
Or of the deadly seven it is the least

(III, i, 110-11)

contrasts not only with this, but with the Provost's

He hath but as offended in a dream!
All sects, all ages smack of this vice; and he
To die for't

(II, ii, 4-6)

and with her own plea to Angelo in accents nobler even than Portia's

No ceremony that to great ones' longs
Not the King's crown, nor the deputed sword
The marshal's truncheon, nor the judge's robe
Become them with one half so good a grace
As mercy does.

(II, ii, 59-63)

Isabella must learn to understand and to forgive, and Angelo to
repent. That is the excuse for the Duke's ingenious and, as it seems,
inhuman stage-management. This is what the second half of *Measure
for Measure* is about.

The subjects of Shakespeare's earlier comedies are trials which are

[1] Sermon XXVII.

overcome; the subject of *Measure for Measure* is sin, which is punishable according to its gravity, and eventually redeemed. It is about wrongs which are righted, and as easily as *Twelfth Night* or *As You Like It,* it fulfils Coghill's definition of Shakespearean comedy as a play which 'starts in trouble and ends in joy'.[1] Because its situations are painful, there is no need to postulate a dramatic poet with a psychological hang-over. Shakespeare had lived too long in London, and in close proximity both to the Court and to the stews, not to find a parallel in Duke Vincentio's Vienna

> Where I have seen corruption boil and bubble
> Till it o'er-run the stew; laws for all faults,
> But faults so countenanc'd, that the strong statutes
> Stand like the forfeits in a barber's shop
> As much in mark as mock.[2]
>
> (V, i, 320-4)

But the Duke, like Prospero, has only half a mind for state affairs; he has preferred to leave the law to its siesta. When he decides that the time has come to wake it up, the appointment of Angelo gives him the chance to investigate private as well as public morality. He thus becomes both an actual and allegorical figure, and asks to be judged in this dual perspective. The play develops into a series of tests, which circumstances or the Duke himself apply. Although, as F. R. Leavis has argued, Shakespeare did not 'feel that the prescription of pre-marital chastity might well be dispensed with',[3] his sympathies are clearly with Lucio: 'What a ruthless thing it is, for the rebellion of a codpiece to take away the life of a man!' After all, Claudio and Isabella had done no more than anticipate a formal ceremony because Julietta's dowry was not yet in the bank. Still, Angelo has the law on his side, and the possible conflict between Law and Justice now becomes apparent. Claudio must face a severer test than the natural 'heyday in the blood', and this will be the temptation to despair. It will need all the Duke's philosophy, and the white lie that Angelo was only testing Isabella's virtue, to teach him resignation. Julietta repents of a sin mutually committed, but the Duke makes the classic distinction between perfect contrition and servile fear

> Which sorrow is always towards ourselves, not heaven,
> Showing we would not spare heaven as we love it,
> But as we stand in fear.
>
> (II, iii, 32-4)

Isabella stands up with superb courage to her first testing; fails to

---

[1] op. cit.
[2] The barbers' shops were places of resort, where various regulations were posted up, usually to the derision of the customers.
[3] *Scrutiny* (January 1942).

meet Claudio's momentary weakness which her own tactlessness has provoked; and must learn to plead for Angelo before she knows that Claudio has been saved. Angelo falls at his first testing, when Pompey and Froth are brought before him; he orders them to be whipped before he has heard the full evidence. Having sinned against natural Justice in condemning Claudio, he now sins against statutory Law. His second testing is fatal; and Escalus, in asking

> Whether you had not sometime in your life
> Err'd in this point which now you censure him
>
> (II, i, 14-16)

anticipates Isabella's

> If he had been as you, and you as he,
> You would have slipt like him; but he, like you,
> Would not have been so stern.
>
> (II, i, 64-6)

His third failure is to order the law to take its course, even after Isabella has, as he thinks, agreed to his proposal. The bed-trick allows justice to be done to Mariana, as in *All's Well* it had done justice to Helena, and it shows Angelo to be no more guilty than Claudio, since a 'just compact' had previously bound him to Mariana. His penalty is public exposure, until he craves

> death more willingly than mercy;
> 'Tis my deserving, and I do entreat it.
>
> (V, i, 481-2)

before, let it be noted, sentence of death has been pronounced. There is amnesty all round in *Measure for Measure,* and it is irrelevant, allegorically speaking, to ask whether Angelo and Mariana will make a happy *ménage.* Pompey will earn an honest living as a hangman's assistant — he has admitted that his former profession did 'stink somewhat' — and Barnardine is spared to get drunk until he dies from drinking too much. Much is forgiven. Mistress Overdone for keeping Lucio's bastard by Kate Keepdown; and Lucio's scurrilous slanders must be paid for by making of Kate a relatively honest woman. Lucio, alone among the characters that need repentance, shows no sign of it; but this suits his role as the Devil's advocate, if not as an understudy for the Devil himself. It also excuses — again allegorically speaking — the Duke's severity towards his impertinence. The Devil's understudy must not be rude about an understudy of Almighty God. Lucio, like Parolles and Falstaff, is the Old Vice of the Moralities, and his privilege is to make the audience laugh in a play where laughter is in short supply. His seconding of Isabella's suit to Angelo is the tribute that vice unwittingly pays to virtue, and his light punishment of marriage to a 'punk' appropriately reflects the pardon which, in this play, virtue extends to vice.

Scholars have vied with each other in explaining, or in justifying, what Tillyard has called 'an heroic failure'.[1] We need not go so far as some in equating the Duke with God the Father, but we can recognize, with the licentious Lucio, his 'power divine', and agree that Shakespeare's *palette* is here more pervasively Christian than we have hitherto found it to be. The play is the work of a man who remembers his catechism, and knows — or well imagines — what it is like to kneel in a confessional. If, as Muriel Bradbrook has written, it is 'stiffened by its doctrinaire and impersonal consideration of ethical values';[2] if the Duke's octosyllabic soliloquy — 'He who the sword of heaven will bear' — sounds an overture to the later theophanies; if we allow Leavis's plea that in *Measure for Measure* Shakespeare shows us 'complexity distinguished from contradiction'[3] — we touch the heart of that complexity with F. P. Wilson

> The non-naturalistic temper of Shakespeare's plays admits always an element of the morality play, though this is more disguised with him than with his contemporaries because of his unparalleled gift of creating character.[4]

[1] *Shakespeare's Problem Plays* (1951).
[2] *Review of English Studies*, Vol. 17.
[3] op. cit.
[4] *Elizabethan and Jacobean* (1946), p. 117-18.

Chapter 16

'Uncleanly Apprehensions'

Othello is at once the most painful and the most perplexing of Shakespeare's tragedies. It may often happen that a great work invites one to answer back, and here the heckling has been fairly persistent. Authoritative voices from the hall — T. S. Eliot, W. H. Auden, and F. R. Leavis — are refuted from the platform by voices no less authoritative: Andrew Bradley, Dover Wilson, and Granville-Barker. It is, to some extent, a quarrel of generations; an argument between a romantic and an anti-romantic view of human nature. Shakespeare, of course, can be credited with either view, and sometimes within the scope of the same play. Bradley has been freely accused of discussing Shakespeare's characters as if they were characters in real life, of ignoring their poetic and theatrical dimension. The balance was redressed by Barker, but Barker realized — as who should not? — that we should not bother to discuss the characters at all unless we were relating them to real life. It is just because *Othello* is a domestic tragedy — though it is something more than that — and a play closer to our everyday experience, with characters to which we could find modern equivalents, that both schools of critics are forced to discuss the *dramatis personae* in terms of how such people should, or should not, have behaved.

The question did not wait for the authoritative questioners. Thomas Rymer started the debate in 1663,[1] hoping that the play might be 'a lesson to husbands, that before their jealousy be tragical, the proofs may be mathematical'. This was long before a woman in the gallery called out to Othello in the middle of a performance of the play: 'Use your eyes, you damned fool'. Towards the close of it Othello asks Iago

> Will you, I pray, demand that demi-devil
> Why he hath thus ensnar'd my soul and body?

and Iago replies

> Demand me nothing: what you know, you know;
> From this time forth I never will speak word . . .
>
> (V, ii, 303-6)

[1] *A Short View of Tragedy.*

We doubt very much whether 'torture will ope' his lips; he 'passes the buck', as the phrase goes, and so does Shakespeare. But what foxes us in *Othello* is the validity of our own response. We should like to pity Othello, because it appears that Shakespeare — not to mention Othello himself — would like us to. But is he entitled to the pity that he claims? Sense and sensibility are at odds in us, and we rarely leave the theatre or lay down the book without a twinge of aesthetic conscience. We are moved, but have we the right to our emotion?

The play followed closely on *Hamlet,* and was performed (as already noted) at Court during the Christmas festivities of 1604-5. As in the case of *Measure for Measure,* its source was the *Hecetommithi* of Geraldi Cinthio, which Shakespeare must have read in the original, or in a French translation, since no English version was then available. *Othello* did not appear in Quarto until 1622, and there are only minor variations between this and the Folio text, published in the following year. Most notable in the latter is the omission of any direct reference to the Deity consequent on the law against blasphemy promulgated in 1606. Had Shakespeare lived to revise the play, he might have removed some of its inconsistencies. For example, in Act I Cassio is surprised to learn that Othello and Desdemona are married; yet Othello later admits to Iago that he knew of their wooing and 'went between us very oft'. This suggests a degree of improvisation in the writing. Shakespeare did not quite know where his characters would lead him, and once the play had been acted he did not trouble to revise it.

Barker has argued, forcibly enough, that the inconsistency of Double Time does not trouble us in the theatre as it does when we analyse the play in print; that it was an essential part of Shakespeare's dramatic strategy. Iago's first plan was *'after some time* to abuse Othello's ear'; had he stuck to this, there would have been time for Desdemona to commit adultery, time for Iago to share sleeping-quarters with Cassio, time for Cassio to neglect Bianca 'for a week', time for Iago to ask Emilia 'a hundred times' to steal Desdemona's handkerchief. But Shakespeare evidently felt that, having already broken the time sequence between Venice and Cyprus, he could not afford to break it again so soon. If he had judged the play in print, might he not have concluded that a slight slackening of tension would have been worth an inconsistency which has occasioned so large an expenditure of ink? Othello is credulous enough, as it is; but even Othello would have seen how impossible it was for Desdemona to have committed adultery a few hours after their marriage had been consummated. Such conversation as the plot allows them suggests a couple who have settled down; and why, moreover, should Othello have been relieved of his command in

Cyprus twenty-four hours after he had assumed it? Why should a young aide-de-camp of unstable character be appointed, for no apparent reason, in place of an experienced soldier who had, only the day before, presided over the dispersal of the Turkish fleet? These questions, although we may overlook them in the theatre, trouble us afterwards; they are not irrelevant in a play where facts, and the fancies deduced from them, are of such importance. Had Iago delayed his temptation — 'after some time' — they need never have arisen. I am not convinced by the apologists for Double Time; it makes *Othello* a lesser play than it might have been.

If it is more than a melodrama — and the point surely needs no argument — what kind of a tragedy can it be said to be? It is not a tragedy of circumstance like *Romeo and Juliet*, or of ambition like *Macbeth*, or of folly like *King Lear*, or of pride like *Coriolanus*, or of misanthropy like *Timon of Athens*, or of sexual obsession like *Antony and Cleopatra*. All these are tragedies of character. *Othello*, like *Hamlet*, is more exactly a tragedy of temperament. What do we know of Othello? Little beyond what he tells us himself; that he is of royal blood, a Christian, widely travelled, of long military experience, and newly enlisted in the service of the Venetian Republic. For a long time theatrical tradition, and perhaps unconscious racial prejudice, presented him as a sun-tanned Berber chieftain; but here the evidence is unambiguous. 'Haply for I am *black*'; 'why what a fortune doth the *thick lips* owe'; '*sooty* bosom'; 'an old *black* ram' — Othello is a negro, and Desdemona had fallen in love 'with that she feared to look on'. Other things apart, a baptized negro was plausible; a baptized Moslem a near impossibility. Dover Wilson found Othello's *négritude* confirmed by Paul Robeson's performance; my reservations about that performance do not shake my conviction that Othello was an African as coloured as Robeson, or as Aaron in *Titus Andronicus*. It may be more agreeable to Western eyes to see Desdemona in the arms of a Berber chieftain, but it is less credible that a Berber chieftain would have acted so disastrously on evidence, in itself so easily refutable, which he did not even trouble to verify. It generally passes unobserved that Othello dismisses Cassio without hearing his defence. He evidently thinks that Iago's cleverly coloured report of the brawl is the best that can be said for him, and that it is not good enough. But an incident usually taken to demonstrate Othello's sense of justice shows an equal disregard for the rights of the accused; and in a more serious context this will be fatal.

We have, then, to reconcile a man as accustomed to command himself as to command other people; of boundless, and even boastful, self-confidence; trusting in others, but naturally preferring Cassio to Iago as an aide-de-camp, because Cassio is a gentleman where Iago is not; a man, though of ripe age, who is obviously in love for the first time, and with no previous experience of women beyond the casual 'vices of the blood' which he admits to — we have to reconcile this person 'whom passion could not move' with the man who falls in the space of a few hours from the seventh heaven of happiness into the nethermost hell of infamy. Can it be done without doing violence to what we know, or can reasonably conjecture, of the character?

I think it can — but only just. Othello is sure of himself when he is playing on his home ground; facing Brabantio and the police — 'Keep up your bright swords, for the dew will rust them'; quelling a brawl or cashiering Cassio; receiving the Venetian envoys with courtesy and protocol; facing the Senate where he knows that Desdemona will corroborate him, and knows that he is indispensable in a military crisis. But he is still an alien in this society. Brabantio, it is true, has invited him to dinner; but he has little doubt of what Brabantio would say to his marriage with Desdemona, and he prefers to risk an elopement. It would not be too late, even at midnight, to find a quiet chapel and an accommodating priest. He knows, too, his worth to the state and also, no doubt, the power of his own eloquence. Although he has not 'those soft parts of conversation / That chamberers have', he can 'a round, unvarnished tale deliver' of his 'whole course of love', and other tales he will not mind varnishing a little when he sees how Desdemona enjoys hearing them, no matter how tall they may become in the telling. For — like Macbeth in this respect, though unlike him in others — Othello is something of a poet. Nor is it a generalized music that he speaks, but a music consonant at every point with his character and his predicament. This, however, should put us on our guard. The music is so noble that we are tempted to confuse Shakespeare's valuation of Othello with Othello's valuation of himself.

He is simple, romantic, and — here is the chink in his armour — not a little vain. Listen to him, and it is remarkable how he refers every situation to himself. He is not a self-confessed egotist like Iago; his vanity has not the classic presumption of pride; but there is a strain of egotism in his character none the less. As Leavis has written, this egotism, which is all part of his 'noble lack of self-knowledge', is the 'essential traitor within the gates'.[1] Indeed both the difference, and the fatal collaboration, between Othello and his tempter is between one kind of egotism and another. Bradley and Dover Wilson may be right that Othello is not naturally jealous; and that the notion of Desdemona's infidelity throws him off his feet because it is

[1] *Scrutiny*, VI, pp. 259-83.

unfamiliar. Nevertheless the play is about the destructive effects of jealousy, which turns a great soldier into an eavesdropper, a gibbering epileptic, and, at the best, 'an honourable murderer'. We have to reconcile the man 'whom passion could not move' with the man who can exclaim: 'I'll chop her into messes'; and compare his own statement that he is 'not easily jealous' and Desdemona's confirmation that he is 'made of no such baseness as jealous creatures are', with Emilia's observation that jealous souls

> are not ever jealous for the cause,
> But jealous for they're jealous: 'tis a monster
> Begot upon itself, born on itself
>
> (III, iv, 163-5)

— more likely to express Shakespeare's thought about Othello since Emilia's choric role in the tragedy becomes increasingly apparent. She may represent, as Bradley put it, 'the norm of popular morality', but in a play where neither the protagonist nor his victim show much intelligence of life, she may also be talking sense.

It is altogether too much to claim, with certain critics, that Othello rushes to embrace Iago's insinuations. His trust in Desdemona is seemingly secure. Nevertheless he admits that, once that trust is gone, 'chaos is come again' — with the implication that he had some experience of chaos. By this I cannot doubt that he meant a primitive and unbridled sensuality against which Desdemona was his sole defence, and to which she also gave a certain sanction. It is not to impugn her integrity to suggest that a single night of consummated marriage may have taught Othello that there was more to those open hints under Brabantio's roof than the sight of 'Othello's visage in his mind'. She had the courage of her devotion, and also of her duplicity and her desires. If the daughter of the Senator from Alabama eloped with a negress, the shock to society would not be greater, nor the desires appear more precocious. When Othello fears 'lest her body and beauty unprovide my mind again', and exclaims 'O thou weed, that art so lovely fair and smell'st so sweet', he is not quite lost. But when he relapses into 'Goats and monkeys', and the delirium of 'Pish! Noses, ears, and lips', it is clear that 'chaos *has* come again'.

Othello is a Christian; the references are many, and not all of them incidental. When Olivier threw away the crucifix round his neck on 'all my fond love thus do I blow to heaven', the gesture rightly indicated the relapse into a pagan past. By the time he comes to murder Desdemona, Othello has sufficiently recovered his belief in God to usurp His prerogative of justice. He entreats her to pray, because he 'would not kill thy soul' — although he smothers her before she has time to say 'one prayer'. When his eyes are opened, he invokes his own damnation, but he does not formally repent. It is he, not Emilia, who should be exclaiming 'O fool, O dolt!' But he has more thought for Iago who has wronged him than for Desdemona whom he has wronged. He knows that she is chaste

> Pale as thy smock! When we shall meet at compt
> This look of thine will hurl my soul from heaven
> And friends will snatch at it
>
> (V, ii, 273-5)

the emphasis is on his own damnation. It is so with all the final speeches. Eliot was right; Othello is anxious to cut a *bella figura* to the end. He is still not above a military boast

> I have seen the day
> That with this little arm and this good sword
> I have made my way through more impediments
> Than twenty times your stop
>
> (V, ii, 265-8)

and although we may endorse his summing up

> Then must you speak
> Of one that loved not wisely but too well;
> Of one not easily jealous but, being wrought
> Perplex'd in the extreme
>
> (V, ii, 345-8)

and wish to rescue him from damnation, he is incapable of the humility which alone might have saved him. Since justice must be done upon him it is all in character that he should do it himself. Not even now will he put himself in the second place.

And yet . . . and yet, why is it that our response, as we leave the theatre, is pity rather than reprobation; 'but yet the pity of it, Iago! O Iago, the pity of it!' This is the response to tragedy; the expression of a genuine catharsis. And if we do not question our right to feel it, the reason must lie, not only in the hypnosis of the words Othello speaks, but in the recovery of his self-command and thus, in a measure, of the nobility that all the world had noted in him. But the pity is not quite the pity that Othello expends upon himself. It is pity that a man in many ways so magnificent, and a woman in every way so single-minded, should have been so immature. I do not quarrel with anyone who sees in the end of *Othello* the nemesis of a certain romanticism.

Othello's disintegration, physical as well as psychological, has appalled us; and this in turn suggested a volcanic stratum of savagery which the discipline of arms and the veneer of civilization had concealed even from himself. Baptized he may have been, but ancestral superstition lingered

> That handkerchief
> Did an Egyptian to my mother give;
> She was a charmer, and could almost read
> The thoughts of people . . .
> There's magic in the web of it:
> A sibyl, that had numbered in the world
> The sun to course two hundred compasses
> In her prophetic fury sewed the work;
> The worms were hallowed that did breed the silk;
> And it was dyed in mummy which the skilful
> Conserved of maidens' hearts.
>
> <div align="right">(III, iv, 58 <i>et seq.</i>)</div>

This is a long way from the Salute and the mosaic of St Mark's. The scenes in which Othello strikes Desdemona and treats her as the inmate of a brothel are the most shocking in the entire range of Shakespeare's work; in humiliating his wife he doubly humiliates himself. But because the dramatist raises him up halfway, so to speak, from this abjection we are prepared to remember the man he once had been rather than the man he had become. 'An honourable murderer, if you will' — we allow him the benefit of the paradox. Yet in the gleam of his dagger there is more of defiance than resignation. Like Cleopatra, he will make death proud to take him.

In the case of Desdemona we have to reconcile 'a maiden never bold' with the girl who prompted Othello's proposal, and did not shrink from a clandestine marriage, outrageous to society, which broke her father's heart. She admits to the Senate her 'downright violence and scorn of fortunes', and in the same breath proclaims that her 'heart's subdued / Even to the very quality of my lord'. A precocious strength of will is matched by a precocious capacity for submission. Brabantio's warning

> Look to her, Moor, if thou hast eyes to see
> She has deceived her father, and may thee
>
> (I, iii, 292-3)

echoes faintly on the quayside on Cyprus when she banters with Iago like any other sophisticated débutante

> I am not merry; but I do beguile
> The thing I am by seeming otherwise
>
> (II, i, 121-2)

and she can hold her own with Cassio's mild flirtation. Her strength and her submission alike contribute to her undoing. Her importunate pleading for Cassio lends colour to the supposition of her guilt. Indeed her strength is at the root of her submissiveness; her

innocence has a kind of obstinacy, which is not the obstinacy of
Cordelia — for Cordelia stood up to Lear whereas Desdemona stands
up to Othello for nothing, except for Cassio! With her last breath she
denies that Othello has killed her. Does the girl who challenged the
mores of Venice with her marriage really believe that it is unthinkable for a woman to commit adultery, or is she simply fencing with
Emilia's wordly wisdom? Can we not recognize in Desdemona the
same fatal lack of common sense that we deplore in Othello? Why
must she renew her plea for Cassio at the very moment when Othello
is enraged by the loss of the handkerchief? Why does she deny that it
is lost? Why does she not say, quite simply: 'I must have dropped it,
and I don't know where it is'? Desdemona's fate is intolerable; yet
there is something in her almost masochistic submissiveness which
irritates, very much as we are irritated by Othello's credulity.

And so we are brought face to face with the mystery of evil. When
Iago refuses to answer Othello's final question, it is because he
cannot. We must distinguish between the four Iagos who have spoken
during the course of the play: the Iago who deceives Othello; who
makes Roderigo his dupe; who plays the *faux-bonhomme* with
Emilia and Cassio; and who speaks to himself (or to the audience) in
soliloquy. The reasons he gives for his malevolence do not even
deceive himself. It is ironical that the most persuasive is applied to
Cassio, whereas it was Othello who more obviously deserved — and
perhaps unconsciously — evoked it

> He hath a daily beauty in his life
> That makes me ugly . . .
>
> (V, i, 19-20)

If a reason must be found for Iago's diabolical scheming, it is surely
the envy of pure (or less pure) goodness. He is annoyed that Cassio
has been promoted above him — the envy of a seasoned campaigner
for a young captain appointed to the Staff. It may, or may not, be
true that 'three great ones of the city' had spoken on his behalf. But
this is not the real reason; and when he is given the job after Cassio's
disgrace, he shows no satisfaction. He pretends to believe that
Othello, and Cassio as well, have been sleeping with his wife, but the
belief is soon discarded. These are not the real reasons either. He
plays with the idea of seducing Desdemona himself, but the thought
has only to be uttered to be dismissed. He can tell Roderigo 'I hate
the Moor' — and his reason may satisfy Roderigo. It satisfies no one
else. What interests him is the technique, not the excuse or, still less,
the theory, of evil.

His technique, of course, is brilliant. Not knowing, at first, where
it will lead him, he exploits every opportunity: Cassio's promotion,

Roderigo's infatuation, Othello's marriage, Cassio's disgrace, the loss of the handkerchief. His admiration is reserved for those

> Who, trimm'd in forms and visages of duty,
> Keep yet their hearts attending on themselves . . .

(I, i, 50-1)

As surely as Edmund's in *King Lear,* Iago's egotism announces the destruction of degree. Like Edmund, he is a 'plain, blunt' version of the 'new man' without allegiances but, unlike Edmund, without appetite. For him, every manifestation of nature is contemptible, in so far as it is a manifestation of humanity. His contempt for sexual impulse is unbounded; what Roderigo takes for love 'is merely a lust of the blood and a permission of the will'. His metaphor is bestial

> Even now, now, very now, an old black ram
> Is tupping your white ewe.

(I, i, 89-90)

Does this betray the itch of a cerebral and unsatisfied sexuality? It is possible; some have conjectured that Iago was impotent; others, perversely, that he was homosexual. More plausibly, such imagery is the nihilist's blasphemy of Being, which cannot rest until it has tainted and, if possible, destroyed every manifestation of normal life. Iago's cynicism is essentially atheistic; his reasoning is blasphemous whether he is aware of it, or not.

How far was he the conscious agent of evil? He bears no resemblance to the Mephistopheles of Marlowe, or the muscular Satan of Milton. There is nothing heroic about Iago; his medium is prose, or verse more or less prosaic, until the moment when he borrows Othello's music, because at last he has Othello in his power. Executioner and victim are as one; 'Now by yon marble heaven' and 'Witness you ever-burning lights above' answer each other like the antiphons of a psalm. But Iago is neither a monster nor an abstraction; he is a man. Prodigious in his artistry of evil, he is still petty as a human being. Nobody would have missed him when he was gone. Nevertheless, what is at work in him is the spirit of evil, unalloyed; throughout the greater part of the play he is a Satanist *malgré lui.* His genius is for action, or more precisely for the action he can persuade other people to undertake on his behalf. Here he is the Tempter incarnate. He persuades Cassio to drink too much, and incites Roderigo to attack him. But when he passes from words to action himself, he proves a bungler, letting off Cassio with a cut in the leg when he had meant to give him the *coup de grâce.* Once or twice, however, he seems to recognize the void which he inhabits

> Hell and night
> Must bring this monstrous birth to the world's light

(I, iii, 401-2)

> Divinity of hell!
> When devils will the blackest sins put on,
> They do suggest at first with heavenly shows
> As I do now.
>
> (II, iii, 343-6)

H. A. Mason, in a valuable study of the play,[1] gives his view that
such expressions should not be taken seriously. I think, on the
contrary, that they are to be taken very seriously indeed; and they
modify a little the opinion of Wilson Knight that 'Othello is a story of
intrigue rather than a visionary statement'.[2] Iago is something more
than the old Vice of the Moralities exchanging a wink with the
audience. Anyone watching Othello from the middle of the twentieth century will be prepared to give to his universe its proper name.
And if we find his reasons derisory and himself empty of everything
— even, at the end, of words — our own experience of evil has taught
us to know it by the signs of absence and absurdity.

Of the other characters Roderigo is wholly Shakespeare's invention. He serves as an instrument to get Brabantio out of bed, and as a
sounding board for Iago's cynicism. He is not a buffoon; only what
Iago calls him, a 'silly gentleman', but, with Iago, he provides enough
relief of comedy to have kept the Jacobean audience wondering just
what kind of play this was going to be. The whole of the first act
might have been the prelude to no more than a misalliance. Iago's
reasoning is persuasive

> It cannot be that Desdemona should long continue her love to the Moor
> . . . nor he his to her: it was a violent commencement, and thou shalt see
> an answerable sequestration . . . She must change for youth: when she is
> sated with his body, she will find the error of her choice.
>
> (I, iii, 341 et seq.)

Only in provoking Cassio to a brawl does Roderigo play a vital
part in Iago's scheming, and he disappears from the picture until it
becomes clear to him that, having failed to make Desdemona his
wife, he is even less likely to make her his mistress. When he decides
to ask her for the return of his jewels, he becomes a nuisance; but
Iago still has a use for him. Othello and Desdemona will be leaving
any day for Mauretania, but with Cassio out of the way Othello will
be obliged to remain, and Desdemona with him. Roderigo may still
have a chance. When his attempt to kill Cassio fails, he is expendable
— for now he may talk, and it is the essence of Iago's plot to leave no
time for talk.

Cassio is the jeune homme moyen sensuel. He has left behind him
a wife in Florence, and — if Iago is to be believed — has not seen

---

[1] Shakespeare's Tragedies of Love (1970).
[2] The Wheel of Fire (1962), p. 107.

active service. Call him a promising pupil from the Staff college, and
you have his measure. If he has carried letters or messages between
Othello and Desdemona, his new appointment is plausible —
although one does not see him so easily as a colonial Governor. As a
connoisseur of women he admires Desdemona, and had evidently
taken a vicarious pride in the success of Othello's suit. He knows that
on the field of matrimony she is 'our great captain's captain', and his
admiration turns him into something of a poet

> Tempests themselves, high seas, and howling winds,
> The guttered rocks and congregated sands,
> Traitors insteeped to clog the guiltless keel,
> As having sense of beauty, do omit
> Their mortal natures, letting go safely by
> The divine Desdemona.
>
> (II, i, 66-73)

He likes to envisage 'love's quick pants in Desdemona's arms', and
when she lands he gives her an uninhibited welcome. Iago takes note
of it, although his plot is still at the stage of improvisation

> He takes her by the palm. Ay, well said, whisper . . . Ay, smile upon her,
> do . . . If such tricks as these strip you out of your lieutenantry, it had
> been better you had not kissed your three fingers so oft . . . Very good,
> well kissed . . . Yet again your fingers to your lips!
>
> (II, i, 167 *et seq.*)

In his affair with Bianca, Cassio behaves like an officer, and more
or less like a gentleman; fairly decently, that is to say, in an indecent
relationship. But drunkenness provokes him to a self-disgust, in
which we catch echoes of Hamlet's disgust with Claudius, and
perhaps of Shakespeare's own revulsion from intemperance

> O that men should put an enemy in their mouths to steal away their
> brains! that we should, with joy, pleasance, revel and applause, transform
> ourselves into beasts.
>
> (II, iii, 284-7)

Emilia stands midway between the cynicism of Iago and
Desdemona's idealism. Of coarser clay than the lady-in-waiting
Desdemona might have expected to attend her under her father's
roof, or married to one of the 'wealthy, curléd darlings' of the Serene
Republic, she can pocket the handkerchief her mistress has let drop,
because her husband, improbably, has begged her 'a hundred times'
to steal it. We know nothing of her relations with Iago; she was
probably afraid of him. But this duplicity, and failure to confess it, is
consistent with the woman who 'would make her husband a cuckold
to make him a monarch'. She speaks for the common of her sex

> And have we not affections,

Desires for sport, and frailty, as men have?
                                                        (IV, iii, 101-2)

Yet it is Emilia, compromising as she does with 'the world's slow stain', who alone of the characters rises in the end to heroic stature. There is a salutary irony in this which often goes unperceived.

In its construction — except for the awkward inconsistency of Double Time — *Othello* is the most perfect of Shakespeare's greater tragedies; it is also the most impersonal. The steady exposition of the first act; the evocation of the storm which disperses the Turkish fleet, and brings out, as Leavis has written, 'the reality of the heroic Othello and what he represents';[1] the bustle and *dénouement* of the brawl; the reluctant growth of Othello's suspicion

> 'Tis not to make me jealous
> To say my wife is fair, loves company,
> Is free of speech, sings, plays and dances well;
> Where virtue is, these are more virtuous,
> Nor from mine own weak merits will I draw
> The smallest fear or doubt of her revolt:
> For she had eyes and chose me
>   (III, iii, 185-91)

the transformation of this security into an agony of indecision, and then into the bestial resolution of 'I'll tear her all to pieces'; the breathless and blinkered surrender to the daimon which has been unleashed; the quiet, yet premonitory, interlude of the 'Willow' scene; the swift confusion of the scuffle where Cassio is lamed and Roderigo killed; the action and explanations of the close, raised by the Othello 'music' to a point where the critical faculty is lulled into a contemplation of the 'chaste stars' — all this composes a rhythm more analogous perhaps to music than to architecture. If the beauty of the Othello 'music' tends to cushion its uncomfortable truth, that is only apparent if you analyse the score.

---

[1] op. cit.

Chapter 17

'This Great Stage of Fools'

After that opening performance at Whitehall, on All Saints' Day (1 November) 1604, in the presence of the King and Queen, and the Queen's brother Prince Frederik of Württemberg, *Othello* was revived more often than any other tragedy until the theatres were closed by the Commonwealth. At forty-eight Burbage was in his prime, and never seen to better advantage than in the title role

> But let me not forget one chiefest part
> Wherein, beyond the rest, he mov'd the heart,
> The grievéd Moor, made jealous by a slave
> Who sent his wife to fill a timeless grave,
> Then slew himself upon the bloody bed.
> All these, and many more with him are dead.[1]

The register of St Leonard's Church in Shoreditch records the christening of a certain William Bishoppe's daughter with the name of Desdemona — sure evidence of how deeply Shakespeare's tragedy had impressed the town. The dramatist was at the height of his fame, and also of his fortune. A pamphlet published in the following year describes how a young actor was held up by the notorious highwayman, Ratsey, and in default of ready cash was allowed to declaim a scene from his repertoire. He was then advised to try his luck on the London stage, and 'when thou feelest thy purse well lined, buy thee some place of Lordship in the Country, that growing weary of playing, thy money may there bring thee to dignity and reputation'. The young man was grateful for this advice, for he had 'heard indeed of some that have gone to London very meanly, and have come in time to be exceeding wealthy'.[2] No doubt he had heard of William Shakespeare.

On 24th July of that year Shakespeare had bought up half the tithes of his parish at Stratford for £440, a very considerable sum; and on the same day he was present at the christening of his nephew — the son of his sister, Joan Hart — in Holy Trinity Church. These visits enabled him both to feather his nest and to keep an eye on his

---

[1] Ingleby's *Centurie of Prayse* (New Shakespeare Society), 2nd edition, p. 131.
[2] See *Shakespeare — a Portrait restored*, p. 309.

family. He was as eager to become a man of property as his father
had been to acquire a coat-of-arms. Bardolaters must take this
acquisitiveness on the chin, and note besides that it was in the flush
of prosperity, and the sunshine of royal esteem, that Shakespeare set
about the composition of his most monumental tragedy — a work
which Coleridge compared to 'a painting imagined by Dante,
executed by Michelangelo'. Tragedy was fashionable; and that
Shakespeare was now sensitive to a tragic view of life does not in
itself prove that his own experience of life was tragic at a time when
he was composing tragic plays. As an eminent French novelist has
written: 'People can't imagine that during the years when I was
writing these inexplicably sombre books, I was so happy that at
times I was unable to sleep, and cried out of sheer joy.'[1]

Literary critics and theatrical interpreters have been quick to take
Coleridge at his word. If I fight shy of such comparisons, it is not
that I wish to deflate a masterpiece. I wish only to deflate a certain
conception of it. *King Lear* is a Jacobean tragedy in the sense that
The Duchess of Malfi or *The Changeling* are Jacobean tragedies. It
mirrors a period, and the thought of a period. It has nothing to do
with Stonehenge. We have seen other examples of how lightly
Shakespeare rode to his sources; that the forest of Arden was some
distance from the Ardennes, and that 'a wood near Athens' was
nowhere near the Piraeus. *King Lear* is about a King and his subjects;
about fathers and children; about life in the court and the castle and
the wild or cultivated countryside, as Shakespeare had seen or
imagined it. That it is also a microcosm of human suffering and
endurance wherever good and evil are at odds in society does not
emancipate it from its moment of time, nor does its moment of time
mute its universal resonance. The characters, though they are broadly
outlined, lose their 'local habitation' if we envisage them in a setting
of menhirs and dolmens; as Bradley put it, they give 'the feeling . . .
of a particular place which is also a world'.[2] The perspective
contracts from the general to the particular, and lengthens from the
particular to the general, so that we seem to be looking not only at
these predatory or distracted individuals, but at the epitome of all
mankind. The metaphysical anxiety which permeates the play loses
its tension if we forget that God is invoked in the plural only because
the law forbade Him to be invoked in the singular. The anonymous
play of 'King Leir' and his three daughters, though it ended happily,
provided the dramatist with a screen behind which the themes of sin
and redemption and the 'suffering servant' could be explored

---

[1] Julien Green, *Journal* (1975), p. 903.
[2] *Shakespearean Tragedy* (1904), p. 261.

without fear of censorship. But the characters make no sense whatever unless their Jacobean ancestry is taken into account. No Britons were ever less ancient then these.

I insist on this change in an *optique* which the sources of the play and long theatrical tradition have handed down to us, because Shakespeare's picture of society is obscured by it. When the young Gordon Craig was bothered about what to do with Oswald, Henry Irving replied after a magisterial pause: 'Hum-hum-m'boy — *Malvolio*'. Was Edgar thinking of Oswald when he pretended to Lear that he had been 'a servingman, proud in heart and mind; that curled my hair, wore gloves in my cap; served the lust of my mistress' heart, and did the act of darkness with her'? No one in their senses pictures Oswald — or Malvolio — in a setting of Stonehenge. Or the Fool, either. He is of the same family as Feste, and pivotal to the tragedy in the same way. Alternately bitter and pathetic, he applies the acid of reality to Lear's self-deluding folly. Where Kent's fidelity and Cordelia's devotion are justified by common sense and common decency, the Fool provides a counterpoint which is a 'critique of pure reason'. The comedian has become the chorus. He knows all the questions and most of the answers — except the last which is Cordelia's secret — but he is not called upon to act, as are the other characters in the play. To this extent he is an outsider. He is there to announce in riddles the things that Lear finds out, or to illustrate with his wit the things that Lear knows already. Simone Weil discerned an 'essential analogy' between her own intelligence — which was prodigious — and the intelligence of Shakespeare's Fools, because 'a great intelligence is often paradoxical, and sometimes a little extravagant'. There is much to support the theory that the Fool and Cordelia were played by the same boy actor, for the Fool does not appear until Cordelia has left for France, and by the time she returns he has become lost — we are not told how — on the way to Dover. This gives an intolerable pathos to Lear's 'and my poor fool is hanged' — which a Jacobean audience would not have missed. They would have seen Reason and Love strangled by the same halter.

The contrast is not only between good and evil, but between superfluity and basic need. 'Unaccommodated man' — Poor Tom in his loin-skin on the heath — faces men and women who are accommodated with far too much — the 'robes and furr'd gowns' that conceal Gloucester's lust and Cornwall's cruelty; the 'gorgeous' farthingales of Goneril and Regan reminiscent of the dead Queen in her fantastic finery, and still typical of a generation 'attracted by and wholly unafraid of overt display'.[1] The contrast is also between appearance

[1] David Mathew, *The Jacobean Age* (1938), p. 8.

and reality, between profession and practice. It had been the central theme of Shakespearean tragedy since Troilus exclaimed: 'This is, and is not Cressid!', and Hamlet asked his mother: 'Have you eyes?', and Othello could say of Iago: 'This fellow's of exceeding honesty'. In the same way Lear takes his two elder daughters at their honeyed word. The play is an unmasking of appearances, for when Lear tears off his clothes in the storm — 'Off, off, you lendings' — he is stripping himself bare of appearances that no longer accord with reality. The reality is 'unaccommodated man . . . the thing itself', and compared with a Bedlam beggar Lear and the Fool and Kent are all 'sophisticated'. *King Lear* may be read as a reduction of sophistication to simplicity, and this takes on its true meaning if it is seen in the light of Jacobean psychology and appearances. It is from the panelled luxury of Hatfield or Hardwicke that Lear is expelled into a countryside less hospitable than it is today.

There is much of Falconbridge in Edmund; both stand up for bastards; both are alive with the spontaneity of the 'natural' man. But what we see in Edmund is 'nature erring from itself'. In a society of competing parvenus, of decaying feudalism, and of ancient faiths proscribed, he is the opportunist *par excellence* — the new Machiavelli riding in triumphantly on the tide. It is interesting to note that Thomas Hobbes was seventeen years old when, as the Stationers Register informs us, *Lear* was 'played before the King's Majesty at Whitehall upon S. Stephen's night at Christmas last' — that is to say, on 26 December 1606. If he had seen the play, or read it two years later in Quarto, he would have agreed with Edmund's dismissal of Gloucester's superstition. 'An admirable evasion of whoremaster man to lay his goatish disposition to the charge of a star' — in itself an echo of Iago's 'Tis in ourselves that we are thus or thus'. For Edmund, too, is a study in pure egotism although, unlike Iago, he has appetite and ambition. Iago's egotism, like Othello's jealousy, 'feeds upon itself', and Edmund's is to that extent more human. He can plot to have his brother disinherited and condone the barbarous treatment of his father, when Gloucester has sheltered Lear from the storm. He can change mistresses when Regan is left a widow, and the chance opens up for him to become Duke of Cornwall — and, who knows? — King of Britain. He can order the execution of Lear and Cordelia; and even when he lies mortally wounded, and the bodies of Regan and Goneril are brought in — the one poisoned by the other — a spark of vanity still flickers in this insatiable *coureur*: 'Yet Edmund was beloved'. But the moment of triumph is also the moment of truth. 'Some good I mean to do / In spite of mine own nature' — and he tries, albeit too late, to save Lear and Cordelia from the death to which he has sentenced them. For once, temporal salvation is no part of Shakespeare's design, and we are left with the picture given us at the opening of the play. 'There was once an old king, and he had three daughters . . .'; only now the old king is dying, and the three daughters are dead. Let those who wonder why the dramatist troubled to bring back the corpses of Goneril and Regan wonder again at his mastery of theatrical effect.

Like Iago, Edmund is a rationalist

> Wherefore should I
> Stand in the plague of custom, and permit
> The curiosity of nations to deprive me,
> For that I am some twelve or fourteen moonshines
> Lag of a brother?
>
> (I, ii, 2-6)

Reasonable enough; but this is the reason of scepticism and revolt, a far cry from the bitter-sweet reasoning of the Fool, and the hard logic of Cordelia

> I love your majesty
> According to my bond; nor more nor less.
>
> (I, i, 93-4)

Edmund stands opposed to whatever 'custom', or 'the curiosity of nations', had established as the right ordering of human affairs. In alliance with Goneril, Regan, and Cornwall, he is the breaker of all consecrated bonds. Albany wobbles, and comes down on the right side of the fence; Gloucester, who has broken the bond of marriage, pays for the lust of the eyes with the loss of them. Lear himself breaks the bond of affection with Cordelia in casting her off, and the bond of duty to his subjects in clinging to the title and abdicating the responsibility of kingship. His refusal to serve is answered by Kent's offer of service, and his denial of love by Cordelia's devotion. But Cordelia and Kent both tell him the truth before they set about to save him, and his salvation will depend upon the facing and recognition of that truth. It is the message and meaning of *King Lear* that truth and love are inseparable; that the truth is hard, and almost invariably painful.

In contrast to the characters in *Othello,* the characters in *Lear* are uncomplicated, and further away from us. On the other hand, they bring us closer to Shakespeare himself. They have the clear outlines of allegory. 'Nature' is the norm by which Shakespeare judges them, but nature itself is ambivalent. He dramatizes — consciously or not — Bacon's teaching that 'No one can treat of the internal and immutable in nature, without rushing at once into natural theology', and Hooker's 'It cannot be but nature has some director of infinite knowledge to guide her in all her ways', and then opposes to them

Hobbes' equation of nature and appetite. 'So that in the first place, I put for a general inclination of all mankind, a perpetual and restless desire of power after power, that ceaseth only in death.' This is Edmund's philosophy, and it lay behind the greed and glory of the new acquisitive society. Ulysses had defined it, almost in Hobbesian terms, when he warned against the destruction of degree

> Force should be right; or rather, right and wrong,
> Between whose endless jar justice resides,
> Should lose their names, and so should justice too.
> Then everything includes itself in power,
> Power into will, will into appetite;
> And appetite, an universal wolf,
> So doubly seconded by will and power,
> Must make perforce an universal prey,
> And last eat up himself.
>
> (*Troilus and Cressida*, I, iii, 116-24)

King Lear is the fulfilment of Ulysses' prophecy, but the remedy was not to be found in politics, or even in the Homilies which were their Sunday dress. For Shakespeare rebellion against the state was always regrettable; it was no longer, however, 'the whole puddle and sink of all sins against God and man'. The subject of *King Lear* is the 'mystery of iniquity' rampant in the commonwealth, and in the family which is a microcosm of the commonwealth, and it required more than a Restoration to overcome it.

Nothing is restored in *Lear* except the invisible Kingdom of love, and this must be reached through crucifixion. I am raising, of course, the question that faces any interpretation of the play; is it a tragedy of redemption or of despair? Are we to believe with Kent that it is the 'stars' that 'govern our condition'; or with Albany that there are 'justicers' above that avenge 'our nether crimes'? Are we to take Gloucester at his word

> As flies to wanton boys are we to the gods;
> They kill us for their sport

or Edgar at his

> Think that the clearest gods that make them honours
> Of men's impossibilities have preserved thee . . .
>
> (IV, vi, 73-4)

In the end Edgar can give his father no better advice than Hamlet had given to himself, and it has seemed to many to enshrine the enigma of Shakespearean wisdom

> Men must endure
> Their going hence, even as their coming hither;
> Ripeness is all.
>
> (V, ii, 9-11)

In the case of Lear the denial of reason must be redeemed through the loss of reason; yet Lear never speaks more wisely than when he is on the brink of losing it, nor arraigns society more savagely than when he has lost it altogether. What he utters in prophecy when he is mad had been uttered in prayer when he was sane

> Poor naked wretches, wheresoe'er you are,
> That bide the pelting of this pitiless storm,
> How shall your houseless heads and unfed sides,
> Your loop'd and window'd raggedness, defend you
> From seasons such as this? O, I have ta'en
> Too little care of this! Take physic, pomp;
> Expose thyself to feel what wretches feel,
> That thou may'st shake the superflux to them
> And show the heavens more just.

(III, iv, 27-36)

For the first time Lear has thought of somebody beside himself, for he too is a study in egotism. The storm is needed to bring him to his senses, as it is also needed to bring him out of them. But a kind of cosmic vision, no longer personal, illuminates the dark night of lunacy

> *Lear* Thou hast seen a farmer's dog bark at a beggar?
> *Glos.* Ay, sir.
> *Lear* And the creature run from the cur? There thou
>   might'st behold the great image of authority;
>   a dog's obeyed in office

(IV, vi, 159-63)

and much more to the same point, until the man with one foot in the grave interprets the outcry of the child with both feet in the cradle

> When we are born, we cry that we are come
> To this great stage of fools . . .

(IV, vi, 186-7)

His last illusion is the prospect of life imprisonment with Cordelia

> When thou dost ask me blessing, I'll kneel down
> And ask of thee forgiveness: so we'll live,
> And pray, and sing, and tell old tales, and laugh
> At gilded butterflies, and hear poor rogues
> Talk of court news; and we'll talk with them too,
> Who loses and who wins, who's in, who's out;
> And take upon's the mystery of things,
> As if we were God's spies.

(V, iii, 10-17)

For the first, and only, time God has slipped into the singular; and the dynamics of a competitive society are answered, not by a return to the immobility of prescriptive rights and duties, which Hooker had salvaged from the medieval schoolmen, but by the *stasis* of pure contemplation. It is from this detachment that Shakespeare, at once dispassionate and deeply implicated, looks out upon the Jacobean world.

Dr Johnson found the end of *Lear* unbearable; and Nahum Tate, having conveniently widowed Cordelia, married her off to Edgar, with Lear to doze at their fireside. This version held the stage throughout the eighteenth century, and it was not until 1823 that Edmund Kean restored the original ending. In another play Cordelia and Lear would have been materially victorious, but a world which had illustrated Pascal's *'Les gens n'ont pas de coeur'* is too monstrous for the reign of innocence, and too disordered to be set right by the accident of arms — though the 'gored state' will be sustained by Albany, who has brought Edmund to book, and by Edgar whose role as the 'suffering servant' is essential to the play's redemptive pattern. In this Cordelia has an equal share, but her death is at once a release and a reproach. How should we imagine her as happy except at her father's side in the immunity of eternal sleep, which Lear's illusion of life imprisonment has prefigured? Edgar and Cordelia are the male and female, the active and passive, agents of redemption. They answer what some regard as the tragic agnosticism of the play, although neither may fully understand the significance of their words and actions. Not for the first time Shakespeare trusts his allegory.

King Lear is the only one of his tragedies in which he encumbers himself with a secondary plot. His subject is society — the 'great stage of fools' — and he requires a larger cast to play upon it. The sufferings of Lear are paralleled by the sufferings of Gloucester. Lear is made of sterner stuff, and his agony is more active and creative, taking him out of himself — from 'Your old kind father, whose frank heart gave you all' to the general question: 'Is there any cause in nature that makes these hard hearts?', and the general condemnation

> Let the great gods
> That keep this dreadful pother o'er our heads
> Find out their enemies now.
>
> (III, ii, 49-51)

Gloucester, as he totters towards the cliffs of Dover, can tell the truth about himself: 'I stumbled when I saw'; and his quickened sense of social justice is similar to Lear's, as he gives his purse to the beggar whom he does not recognize as his son

> Here, take this purse, thou whom the heavens' plagues
> Have humbled to all strokes: that I am wretched
> Makes thee the happier. Heavens! deal so still!
> Let the superfluous and lust-dieted man,

That slaves your ordinance, that will not see
Because he doth not feel, feel your power quickly;
So distribution should undo excess
And each man have enough.

(IV, i, 67-74)

Apart from this, Gloucester's passion is self-contained. He is tempted
to suicide, where Lear is not, and when the attempt has failed, he can
only resolve to

bear
Affliction till it cry out itself
'Enough, enough', and die.

(IV, iv, 77-9)

This is the blank wall of Stoic resignation, and it is something that
Gloucester should have reached it. But Lear's superior insight — a
kind of grace that is given him in the same breath that deprives him
of his wits — and his far greater vitality have shown him a window in
the wall, and Cordelia is on the other side of it. He has the strength
to kill her executioner, and we miss the point of his final speeches
unless we realize that this dying man is obstinately in love with life

No, no, no life!
Why should a dog, a horse, a rat have life,
And thou no breath at all?

(V, iii, 305-7)

I agree that 'Look on her, look, her lips, look there, look there'
betrays the illusion that Cordelia is still alive; and that although the
end of *King Lear* cannot be described as happy, Lear dies happily.

Shakespeare is so bent on following the itineraries of Lear and
Gloucester that he is forced to scamp a little the rivalry of Goneril
and Regan, and Edmund's liaison with them both. The itinerary is at
once physical and spiritual; in the case of Lear it is an exile which
turns into a homecoming. It starts — we may suppose — from Kent;
proceeds to Cornwall and Gloucestershire; and after that long trek
over windswept Cotswold, comes back to the 'sustaining corn' where
Cordelia, newly landed on the Kentish coast, is waiting for her
father. The journey of the soul is mirrored by the journey on the
map. Gloucester's itinerary is shorter, but he too is an exile and
wandering in the same direction until he falls by the wayside. 'A man
may rot even here' shows him defeated, though purged, by suffering.
Lear's purgatory has not been less, but it opens on to a paradise of
which Cordelia holds the key.

It is almost incredible that Jan Kott in his loudly trumpeted
Shakespeare Our Contemporary could have devoted forty pages to
King Lear without mention of Cordelia. As Victor Hugo put it, 'Lear

is Cordelia's opportunity. The daughter becomes a mother to the father. In her truth, which has a streak of her father's obstinacy, and in her tenderness, which has all of his strength, she represents the 'bias of nature' from which all her world has fallen, Edgar and Kent alone excepted. In a play devoted to the 'marriage of true minds' she might well, as Nahum Tate proposed, have made a good wife for Edgar, and her spirit lives on in him. For Edgar has 'exchanged charity' with Edmund, as Cordelia has exchanged charity with Lear, and Edgar survives to share with Albany in the rebuilding of the temporal kingdom. It is a shadowy and sombre prospect, and Shakespeare is not much concerned with it. Edgar, like Cordelia, is disinherited, and assumes in self-defence

> the basest and most poorest shape
> That ever penury in contempt of man
> Brought near to beast
>
> (II, iii, 7-9)

and like Cordelia becomes the suffering and sympathetic servant of the father who has done him wrong. Moreover his assumption of lunacy becomes a gesture of identity with the actual lunacy of Lear. Edgar and Cordelia are the twin poles around which the movement of *King Lear* revolves. Each is spiritually victorious, but Edgar's material victory stands in contrast to Cordelia's material defeat. It gives the familiar Shakespearean reassurance that, somehow or other, life will go on, perhaps a little better than before.

Here we are brought up against a problem which continues to tease the critics. The Folio and Quarto texts are both authoritative, but Q contains 238 lines which are not found in F, and F 100 lines which are not found in Q. The character of Albany is stronger in Q, and that of Edgar in F, where Cornwall's three servants who avenge the blinding of Gloucester are omitted. These discrepancies suggest that the Folio editors were working on an acting version of the play, and in the light of theatrical experience. The omission of the three servants — a most telling and typically Shakespearean passage — may have been due to a shortage of actors; and the growth of Edgar, now given the last lines of the play, have been suggested by the realization of what he stands for — a natural capacity for kingship. The 'hollow of the tree' in which he hides from Gloucester's pursuit has been aptly compared to the womb of a new vocation;[1] and the 'dark tower' in 'Child Roland to the dark tower came' to the place of initiation for knighthood. 'We that are young' certainly indicates that it is he, not Albany, who should bring the play to a close.

In Edgar and Cordelia reason and nature, as 'judicious Hooker'

---

[1] Barbara A. Kathe, R.S.M., International Shakespeare Association Congress, 1976.

understood them, are united; and through them the Shakespearean Paradiso, where so many antinomies are reconciled, became a distant possibility. This would be realized by new methods, after which the 'problem' plays had been fumbling, and tragedy had still to run its course. But when Lear entered with Cordelia dead in his arms, Shakespeare had reached the limit of a journey to the end of night which was also a journey to the edge of dawn. For this was not only a supreme *coup de théâtre* — the moment which has tempted all the tragedians — but the fusion, perfectly articulated, of the cosmic and the private agonies.

The metaphor of sophistication in *King Lear* is the savagery of nature red in tooth and claw. In no other of his plays does Shakespeare borrow so largely from the imagery of the animal world. Lear threatens Goneril that when Regan

> shall hear this of thee, with her nails
> She'll flay thy wolvish visage
>
> (I, iv, 329-30)

Gloucester would not see Goneril in Lear's 'anointed flesh stick boarish fangs'. Albany rounds on Goneril with

> Tigers, not daughters, what have you perform'd?
> A father, and a gracious aged man,
> Whose reverence even the head-lugg'd bear would lick,
> Most barbarous, most degenerate, have you madded.
>
> (IV, ii, 40-3)

Goneril's ingratitude is compared to a 'serpent's tooth'; for Regan, Gloucester is an 'ingrateful fox'; and for Kent, Oswald is 'the son and heir of a mongrel bitch'. As man's life becomes 'cheap as beast's' on the storm-wracked heath, Edgar fetches his illustrations from the bestiary. His 'serving-man, proud in heart and mind' that 'slept in the contriving of lust and waked to do it' is also a 'hog in sloth, fox in stealth, wolf in greediness, lion in prey'. Unaccommodated man owes 'the worm no silk, the beast no hide, the sheep no wool, the cat no perfume'. Poor Tom 'eats the swimming frog, the toad, the tadpole, the wall-newt ... and cow-dung for sallets'. The Fool declares that 'He's mad that trusts in the tameness of a wolf, a horse's health, a boy's love, or a whore's oath'. And when Lear taxes his own domestic pets with the ingratitude of his daughters

> The little dogs and all,
> Tray, Blanch, and Sweetheart, see they bark at me

Edgar endorses the accusation

> Be thy mouth or black or white,
> Tooth that poisons if it bite;

Mastiff, greyhound, mongrel grim,
Hound or spaniel, brach or lym,
Or bobtail tike or trundle-tail,
Tom will make them weep and wail.

(III, vi, 65-76)

Gloucester has brought the King who is mad, the Fool who is half-mad, Edgar who is pretending to be mad, and Kent who is their prop of sanity, to a provisional shelter. As the wind beats upon its walls, and the thunder threatens, the cosmic dimension of the play is rounded off. The whole of creation is included in it.

Francis Birrell once wrote that Shakespeare was 'jumpy about sex'. If we have read the *Sonnets* aright, he had reason to be. Sexual encounter which had once ensured the completion of personality, and was to ensure it again, now appeared the agent of its disintegration. Gertrude's adultery, equated in *Lear* with the promiscuity of the 'wren' and the 'gilded fly'; the competitive lust of Goneril and Regan; Lucio's inability to keep his hand out of plackets or his feet out of brothels; Angelo's repressions avenging themselves on Isabella; the rampant stallion in Edmund, and the conventional *noceur* in Bertram; the avuncular smuttiness of Pandarus, and the helpless frailty of Cressida — all these variants of the beast in the jungle are exhibited in plays written within a few years. That they contradict what we know of Shakespeare's life at this time does not alter the fact that his observation of other people's lives was obsessed to the limits of pessimism. Helena and Isabella are far from sexless, but they are both called upon to redeem the unbridled appetites of men. There was no reason why Lear's madness should have turned to sexual nausea, if this had not been infecting Shakespeare's imagination — for *Lear*, like *Hamlet*, is a play where he makes room for everything that is preying on his mind. The madness of Lear, like the affected lunacy of Hamlet and Edgar, and the patter of the Fool, gives him his opportunity. There is Edgar's 'Let not the creaking of shoes, nor the rustling of silks betray thy poor heart to woman, keep thy foot out of brothels, thy hand out of plackets . . .'; the Fool's 'This is a brave night to cool a courtezan', and his 'Now a little fire in a wild field were like an old lecher's heart, a small spark, all the rest on's body cold'; and Lear's merciless indictment

Behold yond simpering dame,
Whose face between her forks presages snow,
That minces virtue and does shake the head
To hear of pleasure's name
The fitchew, nor the soiled horse, goes to't
With a more riotous appetite.
Down from the waist they are Centaurs,
Though women all above:

But to the girdle do the gods inherit,
Beneath is all the fiends' . . .
Give me an ounce of civet, good apothecary, to sweeten
        my imagination . . .

                              (IV, vi, 120-9; 132-3)

There is nothing else in any of the plays to compare with this Manichean fury. No doubt, in ways possible to conjecture though not to discover, the time gave it proof. But we can summarize the future development of Shakespeare's art as a sweetening of the imagination, and overhear in Lear's plea to the 'apothecary' a cry from the abyss.

Charles Lamb's argument that *King Lear* 'cannot be acted' has been disproved many times over in recent years. Nevertheless the play does not appeal to the theatrical senses in the same way as *Hamlet, Othello,* and *Macbeth.* It lacks the excitement, never long suspended, of the first, the concentration of the second, and the intensity of the third. In spite of the dramatist's skill in organizing diffuse material and interweaving the two plots, it remains a panorama more exactly than a play. Shakespeare has too much on his plate, and on his mind, to keep our interest in the issue of the battle, and the exposure of Edmund, when our emotions are engaged, and never more deeply, with Cordelia and Lear. Why should Edgar write a letter to Edmund when they live in the same house? Why should Edmund forge a letter, where the handwriting would be easily detectable, rather than fabricate a conversation? Why does Edgar not face his father, and show the same resourcefulness when he is at home as he shows when he has left it? In short, why does Edgar behave like a fool when he is clearly nothing of the sort? Why does Gloucester traipse the whole way to Dover in order to commit suicide? Why does he exhibit no surprise when Edgar, having first talked to him like a Bedlam beggar, then talks to him like a poet in the description of Dover cliff, goes on to speak to Oswald in broad dialect, and then again to Gloucester like a gentleman? Why, more importantly, does he not reveal to his father who he is? This could hardly have added to Gloucester's shame, but it might have added to his comfort. It surely mattered as much to the central design that Edgar should have forgiven Gloucester as that Cordelia should have forgiven Lear. Kent speaks of the rumours that a French army is mustering, and attributes this to the harshness of Regan and Goneril to their father, when there had been no time for news of Regan's behaviour to reach the other side of the channel. Lear complains that fifty of his retinue have been dismissed, when Goneril has made no mention of their dismissal; and why does Kent preserve his incognito, when it would have been some consolation for Lear to know that the 'constant service of the antique world' lived on in the man whom he had banished? There was much point, as I have argued, in the Fool dying or disappearing on the way to Dover; but we might have been told about it.

I cannot help regretting the blinding of Gloucester as a lapse into melodrama — a concession, perhaps, to the blood-lust of Jacobean tragedy, and more typical of Webster or Tourneur than of Shakespeare; a mistake that he would not repeat when it came to the murder of Duncan. The scene is tolerable to read because its effect is not immediately physical; acted, it smothers pity in disgust. Gloucester blinded is a subject for tragedy, like Oedipus; Gloucester in the act of being blinded is a subject for Grand Guignol. Cordelia with a halter round her neck still leaves room for catharsis; if we had been shown 'the slave that was a hanging thee' pity would have been choked by indignation. The questions and inconsistencies I have mentioned above — rather laboriously catalogued by Bradley[1] — pass unnoticed in the theatre; more easily than the contradictions of Double Time in *Othello*, because the play, despite its Jacobean dress, is invested with the significance of myth. But the impact of *King Lear* is greater in the study than on the stage. Its matter is too momentous, and its detail too elaborate, to be fully grasped in performance. It has been compared to the *Divine Comedy*, or to a Beethoven symphony or late quartet. As with these, a single reading or hearing — indeed several readings or hearings — are not enough. One can live with a great play, as one cannot live with a performance, however great; and more perhaps than anything that Shakespeare wrote, *King Lear* is a play to be lived with. A lifetime is not too long to absorb its revolutionary and evangelical insights, its unflinching realism.

---

[1] *Shakespearean Tragedy* (1904), pp. 256-8.

Chapter 18

'Instruments of Darkness'

1

Timon of Athens is more problematical than any of Shakespeare's so-called 'problem' plays. There is no record of its performance during his lifetime, and it first saw the light of print in the Folio. We do not know when it was written. It has much in common with *Lear*, and something with *Troilus and Cressida* and *Measure for Measure*. In other respects it looks forward to *Coriolanus*; and in many passages Shakespeare's authorship has been questioned. Though magnificent in parts, it is generally agreed to be a failure. This has been explained in various ways: either that Shakespeare was suffering from a nervous breakdown, or that he sketched out the play, and that others filled it in, or that he left a rough draft and then, unsatisfied, abandoned it. I am inclined to prefer the last of these hypotheses.

The character of Timon was well known to antiquity as a *locus classicus* of misanthropy; he is mentioned a number of times by Aristophanes. He probably came to Shakespeare by way of Lucian's dialogue, *Timon*, or *the Misanthrope*; an academic play of the same name which may have been performed at Cambridge; and Plutarch's *Life of Antony*, where Apemantus and Alcibiades are both introduced. It has been suggested that the complementary hatred of mankind displayed by Timon and Apemantus was inspired by Montaigne's essay, *Of Democritus and Heraclitus*. Here a natural cynicism is contrasted with a misanthropy born of experience. That Shakespeare knew of Timon from his reading of Plutarch is already evident from *Love's Labour's Lost,* and Plutarch appears to have been his principal source.[1]

Not only the general mood, but certain passages of the play echo or anticipate *King Lear*. Apemantus asks Timon: 'What things in the world can'st thou nearest compare to thy flatterer?' and Timon replies: 'Women nearest; but men, men are the things themselves'. This recalls Lear to Edgar: 'Thou art the thing itself' in the disguise of 'unaccommodated man'; and Timon's subsequent speech wishing Apemantus' transformation into a beast is packed with the same kind

[1] See Bullough, Vol. VI, pp. 227-42.

of imagery which we have noted in *Lear*. The lion, the fox, the ass, the wolf, the horse, the unicorn, and the leopard, are all enumerated. Apemantus' invocation to the creatures

> whose bare unhouséd trunks
> To the conflicting elements expos'd
> Answer mere nature
>
> (IV, iii, 229-32)

carries a similar echo of the storm. Among the puzzles of the play is the sudden appearance, and as sudden disappearance, of the Fool. It looks as though Shakespeare intended him for a role similar to that of the Fool in *Lear* and then discovered that, with Apemantus well established as a successor to Thersites, the character could be dispensed with. Varrius' line: 'Thou art not altogether a fool' is an almost exact repetition (or anticipation) of Kent's comment on the other Fool's diagnosis of Lear's folly: 'This is not altogether fool, my lord'. Moreover the obsessions are similar; ingratitude which is central to both plays, and lust which, in *Timon*, is only peripheral. For there is no reason why Alcibiades should arrive before Timon's cave in the company of two prostitutes, except to give Timon an excuse for his ferocious invective

> Hold up, you sluts,
> Your aprons mountant; you are not oathable,
> Although, I know, you'll swear, terribly swear
> Into strong shudders and to heavenly agues,
> The immortal gods that hear you, spare your oaths,
> I'll trust to your conditions: be whores still;
> And he whose pious breath seeks to convert you,
> Be strong in whore, allure him, burn him up.
>
> (IV, iii, 135-42)

Here is the same whiff of the stews that provoked Lear's plea for 'an ounce of civet'. One is not surprised that Shakespeare had moved house to the north bank of the river, and that Stratford was beginning to call more loudly.

But Timon is not redeemed from his misanthropy as Lear is cured both of his folly and his pride. This leads me to guess that the play was written just before *Lear* rather than just after it. I find it difficult to believe that the undisciplined violence of *Timon* would have followed closely upon a work so carefully organized, despite its incidental discrepancies, as *Lear*, and one that ends, however painfully, upon a note of reconciliation and release. It seems to me more probable that *Timon of Athens* was a first attempt to say certain things about man and society; that it was left unfinished; and eventually published to fill a gap in the Folio, or to provide entertainment for a special audience.

How can one explain otherwise the fragmentary treatment of Alcibiades? Here was evidently the germ of an important sub-plot, in which the ingratitude of Athens towards Alcibiades would run parallel to its ingratitude towards Timon, very much as the sufferings of Gloucester run parallel to those of Lear. Alcibiades makes only a momentary appearance in Act I, and then in Act III, Scene 5 — perhaps the finest scene in the play — we find him pleading for a man's life before the Senate, and turning against the city when his plea is refused, and he is himself banished. The dialectic of justice and mercy is here examined in a depth which *Measure for Measure* had led us to expect, and its articulation is equally impressive. The man, known for his 'comely virtues', had committed a murder 'in hot blood', but Alcibiades argues that 'pity is the virtue of the law', and beseeches the Senators

> As you are great, be pitifully good
>
> (III, v, 53)

and again

> To be in anger is impiety;
> But who is man that is not angry?
>
> (III, v, 56-7)

When the Senate reply to his reasoned plea in mitigation with a sentence of banishment, he strikes an essential keynote of the play

> Banish me!
> Banish your dotage; banish usury
> That makes the senate ugly
>
> (III, v, 100-2)

and later in passionate self-justification

> I have kept back their foes,
> While they have told their money and let out
> Their coin upon large interest.
>
> (III, v, 108-10)

Shakespeare probably knew Thomas Wilson's *Discourse upon usury,* where he would have read that usury 'defaceth chivalries, beateth down nobility'; and when Flavius assures Timon of his loyalty, he is met with the question

> Is not thy kindness subtle, covetous,
> If not a usuring kindness and as rich men deal gifts,
> Expecting in return twenty for one?
>
> (IV, iii, 515-17)

The use or misuse of money, and the use or misuse of adversity, are what *Timon of Athens* is about. Alcibiades is not concerned with money, except in so far as money is the god of his senatorial opponents. He represents the aristocratic principle of honour against a legalistic and bourgeois materialism – very much as, forty years after the play was written, a royalist might have defied the Pyms and Hampdens of the Parliament. But he meets the test of adversity with better sense than Timon. His revolt is implicitly approved and, as he stands invincible at the gates of the city, he repays ingratitude with magnanimity. His situation looks forward to *Coriolanus,* but he saves it differently. Timon, on the other hand, misuses both money and adversity. As Terry Eagleton has pointed out, his generosity is a form of 'projected egoism'[1] and his hospitality a mode of self-indulgence. If you had asked Shakespeare what he thought about money, he would probably have replied, like any other sensible person, that money was to be respected but not worshipped, and that usury was as sinful as the medieval moralists had formerly regarded it. Timon does not respect it since, as Flavius – his steward – reminds him, the money is not there to pay for his parties or his presents

> What will this come to?
> He commands us to provide, and give great gifts,
> And all out of an empty coffer.
>
> (I, ii, 200-2)

This recalls Robert Greene on the largesse of Sir Christopher Hatton

> He fed a rout of yeomen with his cheer,
> Nor was his bread and beef kept in with care . . .

When Timon's friends refuse to come to his rescue, he is denied payment in one sense, and in another sense is repaid in his own coin. His subsequent curses on gold – the 'dear divorce / 'Twixt natural son and sire' – are of course an echo of his misanthropy. He is cursing what he had used without discrimination, and his misanthropy is just as indiscriminate

> Thou ever young, fresh, lov'd, and delicate wooer,
> Whose blush doth thaw the consecrated snow
> That lies on Dian's lap! thou visible god,
> That solder'st close impossibilities.
> And mak'st them kiss! that speak'st with every tongue
> To every purpose.
>
> (IV, iii, 388-92)

We may read in these lines something of what Shakespeare as an actor-manager and dramatist must have felt about the Puritan burghers who were amassing great wealth on the other side of the Thames. Flavius, whose loyalty to Timon recalls the fidelity of Kent,

---

[1] *Shakespeare and Society* (1967), p. 174.

probably speaks for a Shakespeare who, though reasonably prosperous himself, had noted the effects of prosperity in other people

> Who would not wish to be from wealth exempt,
> Since riches point to misery and contempt?
>
> (IV, ii, 31-2)

Timon complains that

> all is oblique;
> There's nothing level in our cursèd natures
> But direct villainy
>
> (IV, iii, 18-20)

and Apemantus' rejoinder hits the nail on the head: 'The middle of humanity thou never knewest, but the extremity of both ends'. *Timon of Athens* is a scaffolding rather than a structure, and it fails because Timon is a character too thin in substance to carry the weight that is put upon it. Indeed he is hardly a character at all. Unlike any other of Shakespeare's tragic protagonists, he exists in a social vacuum. We are not told whether he has a wife, a family, or a mistress. Conceived in black and white, he does not develop; he is merely transformed from one moment to the other. He is an instrument with only two strings, and only two themes — without variations — are played upon it. As the figure in a 'Jacobean morality' — to borrow Professor Bullough's description of the play — he fills his niche, but Shakespeare generally knew how to clothe a morality, or an allegory, with flesh and blood. Timon is unidimensional; the more he speaks — and he speaks a great deal — the less we know about him, and the less we care what happens to him. The same is true of the other characters, with the exception of Apemantus and Alcibiades. But in the version of the play that has come down to us Alcibiades has been elbowed out of his proper place. The fact that the last scene is given to him suggests that his role should have been more important than it turned out to be. *Timon of Athens* would have been a better play if the author of *Volpone* had written it; and I am tempted to guess that Shakespeare, realizing this, threw in his hand.

Yet it sheds much incidental light on the rat race and the musical chairs of early Jacobean society. We see the Poet and the Painter currying favour with a wealthy patron. We learn that

> Men shut their doors against a setting sun
>
> (I, ii, 152)

— the reasoning of Ulysses on the rancorous lips of Apemantus. One of the Senators instructs us that 'policy sits above conscience', and Timon learns to his cost that 'there is boundless theft in limited professions', and that 'many so arrive at second masters / Upon their first lord's neck'. The gods are constantly irvoked, as they are in *Lear,* and with a merciless irony in the grace before the banquet of tepid water which is offered to Timon's ungrateful debtors. 'You great benefactors sprinkle our society with thankfulness'. The blank verse, at its best, has the suppleness and variety of the dramatist's later style, although the number of rhymed couplets indicate either that he was working on old material, not yet refashioned, or that another hand was here at work. Timon's closing speech has the roll and rhythm of the waves breaking on an Aegean shore

> Come not to me again; but say to Athens
> Timon hath made his everlasting mansion
> Upon the beachéd verge of the salt flood
> Who twice a day with his embosséd froth
> The turbulent surge shall cover . . .

(V, i, 219-23)

This, as Bully Bottom might have said, was 'lofty'; and Shakespeare's apparent unawareness that the Mediterranean is a tideless sea should not be held against him. What he had in mind, no doubt, was the 'turbulent surge' of the English Channel as it lashed the cliff near Dover that still bears his name.

2[1]

On 17 July 1606, King Christian IV of Denmark arrived in England on a visit to his sister, Anne, and his brother-in-law, James I. The occasion was one for royal festivities, and it appears likely that a performance of *Macbeth* formed part of them. The Gunpowder Plot was fresh in people's minds, and other conspiracies had followed it. A play showing the overthrow of a usurper was likely to appeal to a monarch who claimed his descent from Banquo, and who had actually attended, incognito, the trial of the Jesuit Henry Garnet, suspected of complicity with Guy Fawkes. At his trial on 28 March 1606, Garnet had fallen 'into a large Discourse of defending Equivocations, with many weak and frivolous Distinctions'; and the Porter's macabre joke about the 'equivocator, that could swear in both the scales against either scale, who committed treason enough for God's sake, yet could not equivocate to heaven' is an obvious allusion to this, indicating that Garnet had been executed by the time *Macbeth* was presented at Court.

It may, of course, have been performed publicly elsewhere,

---

[1] For much of this section I am indebted to J. Dover Wilson's introduction to, and annotation of, the play in the Cambridge edition (1947), although his stage directions are not always to be relied upon.

perhaps in competition with Marston's *Sophomisba* at the Blackfriars
with which it has certain resemblances. If, as scholars are generally
agreed, the play which has come down to us in Folio was the
abridgement, mainly by Shakespeare himself, of a fuller text, the
reason may well have been that long plays were unsuitable for the
double or triple bill of a royal entertainment. James, in any case,
liked his plays to be short and sharp, and in this respect, as in many
others, *Macbeth* would not have disappointed him. Shakespeare, as
we know, was strangely indifferent to the printing of his plays, and
an actor's impertinence or compositor's carelessness may have been
responsible for the obscurities and discrepancies of *Macbeth*. These
are particularly evident in Act I, Scenes 2, 3 and 7. In the first we
learn that the Norwegian army has been assisted 'by that most
disloyal traitor / The thane of Cawdor'; yet in the following scene,
when the title falls on Macbeth, he is quite unaware of Cawdor's
treachery, describing him as 'a prosperous gentleman'. In Act I,
Scene 7, the following lines of Lady Macbeth have excited much
speculation

> What beast was't then
> That made you break this enterprise to me?
> When you durst do it, then you were a man;
> And, to be more than what you were, you would
> Be so much more the man. Nor time nor place
> Did then adhere, and yet you would make both:
> They have made themselves, and that their fitness now
> Does unmake you.
>
> (I, vii, 47-54)

When could this conversation have taken place? Clearly at some
point between Macbeth's encounter with the witches and his meeting
with Duncan at Forres, because by then both 'time and place'
promised to 'adhere' as firmly as he could have wished — Duncan
having invited himself to stay at Macbeth's castle. (So casually indeed
that here one suspects an omission in the text.) I suggest, therefore,
the following reconstruction of events. Macbeth, having discovered a
little more about the witches — 'I have learnt by the perfect'st
report' — writes to his wife the letter which she reads on her entrance
in Act I, Scene 5; and arrives at the castle fully determined to 'break
the enterprise'. The conversation to which she later refers then takes
place. He at once proceeds to Forres, where circumstances play into
his hand; and it is wholly in keeping with his character, and his still
sensitive conscience, that when Duncan is under his roof the
enormity of his projected crime should appear in its true colours. If
the play had been designed in this way, the roles of Macbeth and

Lady Macbeth would have alternated, with the initiative passing from one to the other, and Lady Macbeth's 'Had he not resembled my father as he slept' have seemed a less surprising access of compassion. The lines from Act I, Scene 7 quoted above can only be explained on the hypothesis that Shakespeare forgot about a scene already written, which he had been compelled, for reasons perhaps of brevity, to omit. Such carelessness was not unusual with him. He knew what he could get away with in the theatre, and this particular discrepancy went unnoticed until 1865.

The compression is especially marked in the earlier part of the play, where we should have expected the murder of Duncan to come at the close of the second act rather than at the beginning of it. How account, on the other hand, for the excessive length of the scene where Malcolm tests Macduff's loyalty, taken almost literally from Holinshed, except to give the impression of time passing — which is does, slowly enough, for the average audience — until Ross arrives hot-foot to bring Macduff the news of his wife's murder? In this wonderfully moving passage there is not a word too many; and Malcolm's flattery of James I in his description of how the 'pious Edward' miraculously cured the sick — a gift bequeathed to the 'succeeding royalty' — could have been accommodated to a scene half the length. This is the only case in *Macbeth* of Shakespeare going off at a tangent, of which we noted so many examples in *Hamlet*. Hecate, and her trivial couplets. were certainly an interpolation by Middleton; echoes of *The Witch of Edmonton* are too obvious to be accidental. The 'weird sisters' were an invitation to the theatrical display, now coming into fashion, and by the time Simon Forman saw Macbeth and Banquo riding on to the stage of the Globe in 1611 they were given a full run for the money that was paid to see them. Burnt resin was used to produce the fog into which they vanished, either into the trap or, as Nevill Coghill has maintained, on wires into the 'filthy air'. Hecate certainly descended in a 'foggy cloud' of 'billowing light material',[1] supposed to add mystery to supernatural flights. As visual aids came to the questionable relief of drama, dramatic coherence and propriety were easily forgotten; and the Folio editors took them in their stride, with the text of the play as it had been performed before James I, and with James I very much in mind. Shakespeare and his fellows owed him a great deal, and the debt was not forgotten.

Of all the plays in the canon *Macbeth* is the most literally Jacobean, and to recover the intention and the effect of its first performance it should be so presented — although a production

[1] J. Dover Wilson, *Macbeth*, Cambridge edition (1947), p. 144.

designed by Goya is among the more tempting 'might have beens' of theatrical history. Malcolm's

> What, man! ne'er pull your hat upon your brows
>
> (IV, iii, 208)

gives the costumier his cue. From 1599 there were 'English comedians' playing in Scotland, and Dover Wilson has hazarded the guess that Shakespeare might have been among them. They were led by Laurence Fletcher, whose name later appears as one of the King's Men. Nothing is known of Shakespeare's movements immediately following the fall of Essex, and the trouble over the revival of *Richard II* might have led him to absent himself. If there is any substance in Dover Wilson's conjecture, he made good use of the *genius loci*, although Holinshed and his principal source, the *Scotorum Historiae* of Hector Boethius, would have been enough to excite his imagination. The hopes of Essex's partisans were already fixed on James VI of Scotland and portions of the play may even have been written before James was called to the English throne. There is a certain parallel between Hamlet with whom thought was an impediment to action, and Macbeth with whom imagination coloured the deed both before and after it was done. Moreover the versification in the scene between Malcolm and Macduff has, to my ear, an earlier ring than the rest of the play; Shakespeare is here writing at the leisure that he allowed himself in *Hamlet,* but not elsewhere in *Macbeth.*

However this may be, *Macbeth* flattered the King's interest in demonology, as well as in his own heredity and Divine Right. On 27 August 1605 the students of St John's College, Oxford, greeted him dressed up as three Sibyls, and saluted him as the descendant of Banquo. The Witches' prophecy

> Though his bark cannot be lost
> Yet it shall be tempest-tost
>
> (I, iii, 24-5)

would have reminded him that in 1589 his own ship has been held up by contrary winds believed to have been unloosed by witchcraft. 'In a sieve I'll thither sail' would have recalled the story that 200 witches had put to sea in sieves from the Firth of Forth; their reference to the 'master o' the Tiger' is an obvious allusion to the ship of that name which had arrived back at Portsmouth on 9 July 1606 after a particularly hazardous voyage; and in Macbeth's 'Though you untie the winds . . .' James would have caught a reference to the storm, supposedly raised by witchcraft, which delayed his voyage to Denmark. He might also have remembered that a witch had confessed to hanging up a toad for three days and collecting its venom to lay her spell upon him. The eight Kings shown to Macbeth are, of course, the sovereigns of the Stewart dynasty; the 'two-fold balls' refer to the raised portions of the English and the Scottish crowns; and the 'treble sceptres' to the two used for an English, and the one for a Scottish, coronation. James must have especially appreciated Macduff's outcry

> Most sacrilegious murder hath broke ope
> The Lord's anointed temple
>
>   (II, iii, 65-6)

because this echoed, almost literally, the doctrine of the Divine Right.

Having situated *Macbeth* in its moment of time, we have still to explain its unique hold on the imagination, for many would consider it Shakespeare's greatest purely dramatic achievement. It is the most intensely sustained, as it is the shortest, most concentrated and in some respects the most classical, of his tragedies. The influence of Seneca is very marked, disposing of the curious heresy that Shakespeare was an uneducated man. Lady Macbeth has something in common both with Clytemnestra and Medea. When Hercules Furens exclaims that although

> The waves of all the Northern sea on me shed out now would,
> And all the water thereof should now pass by my two hands
> Yet will the mischief deep remain[1]

we catch a faint anticipation of Macbeth's

> No; this my hand will rather
> The multitudinous seas incarnadine
>
>   (II, ii, 60-1)

and Lady Macbeth's 'All the perfumes of Arabia will not sweeten this little hand'. There are many similar parallels, and Shakespeare turns them all to his advantage, avoiding the fatalism which would remove from his two protagonists the responsibility of a fearful choice. Yet the history of the stage, at least in recent years, is littered with the failure of *Macbeth*. It beckons and then, almost inexplicably, betrays — so constantly indeed that theatrical superstition forbids one to quote from it. One reason, maybe, was given by Laurence Olivier, a superb exponent of the principal part, when he observed that Macbeth is a man 'whose arm you would hesitate to take as he was crossing the street'. Macbeth is unapproachable in a way that Hamlet and Othello, Antony and Lear, are not. He does, it is true, even to the end, excite a measure of pity; and so, more powerfully, does his Lady. But neither of them is ever lovable. We grant to the one his

---

[1] Translation by Jasper Heywood (1561).

heroism, and to the other her resolution. We sympathize, to some degree, with the nightmare-ridden retribution they have brought upon themselves. We have been taken down into the depths of outraged conscience with Macbeth, and with Lady Macbeth into the void of a conscience deliberately anaesthetized. We see into their souls, but as persons they stay remote from us. The imprisoning fantasy of his ambition keeps Macbeth at arm's length from everyone except his wife until, as he goes deeper into crime, they draw apart — each dying, as they had come to live, in the loneliness of the loss of God. What had moved and united them was ambition — and ambition in other people leaves one cold, whatever warmth it may generate in oneself. Macbeth's sin is, more precisely, the sin of exorbitance. In his own place, on the battlefield, he is splendid; but in usurping another's place he defeats his own intention. 'To be thus is nothing but to be safely thus' — the truth comes quickly home to him; yet he will 'let the frame of things disjoint', and 'nature's germens tumble all together / Even till destruction sicken' because this, applied to the city and the cosmos, is the logic of the anarchy he has let loose within himself.

Just as he has denied his own better nature — for there was much good in him — so Lady Macbeth has denied hers. Even in the act of invoking 'the spirits that tend on mortal thoughts', she admits the 'compunctuous visitings of nature'; she knows 'how tender 'tis to love the babe that milks me'; even her ambition is vicarious. But her deliberate choice of evil leads her to insomnia, and then to suicide. As Freud put it, 'Macbeth and Lady Macbeth exhaust the possibilities of reaction to the crime, like the disunited parts of the mind of a single individual.' The sleep which Macbeth had murdered has its revenge upon them both. 'Nature seems dead', he had murmured when the 'air-drawn dagger' had ceased to beckon him. He spoke more truly than he knew, for in himself it was dead indeed. The 'unruly night' of regicide saw Duncan's horses — 'beauteous and swift, the minions of their race' turn 'wild in nature'; and this, like similar portents, was 'unnatural, like the deed that's done'. For it was in the nature of things that Duncan should live out his term of kingship, and that Malcolm should succeed him. And with Malcolm's coronation nature, having imposed the chastisement of *hubris*, resumes her reign.

We must look, therefore, beyond the disintegration of Macbeth and his Lady, wonderfully conveyed as it is, to appreciate the dimension of the play. Its dramatic power makes its minor obscurities of small account; the identity of the Third Murderer, or the number of Lady Macbeth's children, should not matter to us. By the time he had finished the play, Shakespeare may well have forgotten that she had any. What stick in our minds are, first, the master-strokes of dramatic irony; moments when the word, or the event, carries a meaning beyond itself. Macbeth's 'So fair and foul a day I have not seen' echoes, unwittingly, the Witches' 'Fair is foul and foul is fair' — before he has caught sight of them. Banquo's

> And oftentimes, to win us to our harm,
> The instruments of darkness tell us truths,
> Win us with honest trifles, to betray's
> In deepest consequence
>
> (I, iii, 123-6)

looks forward to their specious reassurances when Macbeth visits them in their cave. Duncan's reference to Cawdor

> There's no art
> To find the mind's construction in the face:
> He was a gentleman on whom I built
> An absolute trust
>
> (I, iv, 12-15)

immediately precedes Macbeth's entrance, his mind dizzy with the Witches' prophecy and his mouth protesting overmuch a loyalty he is far from feeling. When he declares, a few moments later, that he will

> make joyful
> The hearing of my wife with your approach
>
> (I, iv, 45-6)

the words mean one thing to Duncan and another to Macbeth. The late afternoon sunshine that greets Duncan's arrival at Inverness — the only sunlit moment of the play — and Banquo's evocation of the 'temple-haunting martlet', rebuke the sacrilegious crime in preparation, and the owl 'that giv'st the stern'st good-night'. Macduff, knocking at the door on his errand to arouse the King, is in fact sounding the first note of retribution for a crime of which he is unaware, and which it will be his mission to avenge. The Porter's maudlin patter about the equivocator who 'could not equivocate to heaven' is more applicable — and again unwittingly — to Macbeth than to Henry Garnet; and his reference to 'those of all professions who go the primrose way to the everlasting bonfire' applies to him no less, although the primroses will not blossom there for long. When Banquo replies to Macbeth's 'Fail not our feast' with 'My lord, I will not', he little knows, and neither did his first audience, in what manner he will keep his promise. Simon Forman described how, on his second appearance, he occupied the chair immediately *behind* Macbeth, who only saw him as he turned round — in a terrifying proximity. Ross assuring Macduff that his children 'were well at peace when I did leave them' means one thing to himself and the audience, and another to Macduff. Lennox, replying to Macbeth's casual 'I did hear the galloping of horse. Who was't came by?'

> 'Tis two or three, my lord, that bring you word
> Macduff is fled to England

$$(IV, iii, 140-2)$$

is unaware of Macbeth's intention to 'surprise the castle of Macduff' just as Macbeth was unaware that Macduff had not been 'of woman born', and therefore remained a threat to him. The 'galloping of horse', we learn, was easily simulated on the Jacobean stage, and here it strikes a note more chilling than the bizarre ritual which has gone before.

This is only one of many passages that send a shiver down the spine; others stab you with pity. Macbeth's 'This is the door' when Macduff asks the way to the chamber where Duncan lies dead; and his terse ''Twas a rough night' after Lennox has recalled the 'lamentings heard i' th' air, strange screams of death'. 'Men must not walk too late' was all the advice that needed to be given to a population cowed by despotism, when 'confusion' had all too evidently 'made his masterpiece'. In such passages as these Shakespeare gains his effect by the simplest of means and the minimum of words. Macbeth's 'Tomorrow and tomorrow and tomorrow'; Lady Macbeth's 'All the perfumes of Arabia will not sweeten this little hand'; Macduff's 'He has no children', surely a reference to Macbeth and not, as Bradley maintained, to Malcolm who has been trying to console him. These moments stand out against the chiaroscuro of imagery where the poetry, though never irrelevant, seems to exert its power independently, as it does not in *Hamlet, Othello,* and *Lear,* and as it will presently do, most notably, in *Antony and Cleopatra.* From the first appearance of the 'weird sisters' it creates a climate of evil – a nocturnal ambience – which is proper to the play. They hover through 'the fog and filthy air'. Lady Macbeth calls upon 'thick night' to make itself even thicker 'in the dunnest smoke of hell', and imagines her 'keen knife' plunging into Duncan through 'the blanket of the dark'; 'the moon is down' when Banquo and Fleance pass across the stage to bed; only the owl interrupts the silence of the castle while Macbeth is about his ghastly business; Lennox relates how 'the obscure bird / Clamoured the livelong night'; and the next morning Ross endorses what appears to be the reaction of the elements to crime

> Thou see'st the heavens, as troubled with man's act
> Threatens his bloody stage: by th' clock 'tis day,
> And yet dark night strangles the travelling lamp:
> Is't night's predominance, or the day's shame,

> That darkness does the face of earth entomb,
> When living light should kiss it?
>
>   (II, iv, 5-10)

Banquo will be murdered as dusk is falling

>   ere the bat hath flown
> His cloistered flight, ere to black Hecate's summons
> The shard-born beetle with his drowsy hums
> Hath rung night's yawning peal
>
>   (III, ii, 40-3)

and how casual, yet how premonitory, is his observation, while the assassins wait in ambush: 'There will be rain tonight'. The same night is 'almost at odds with morning, which is which', as Macbeth is left alone, and exhausted, with his wife after Banquo has kept his engagement to 'fail not our feast'. The skies, one feels, are leaden as Birnam Wood advances towards the battlements of Dunsinane, and Malcolm hopes 'the days are near at hand / That chambers will be safe'. Only the light that Lady Macbeth 'has by her continually' pierces, and at the same time intensifies, the gloom that presides over the closing scenes of the play.

The gloom, let it be emphasized, is metaphysical. *Macbeth* is a theological tragedy, which is not to say that Shakespeare was a theologian. 'In the great hand of God I stand' exclaims Banquo, and the two protagonists stand, even more perilously, in the same place. Macbeth measures the risk; he would 'jump the life to come' if he were certain retribution would not meet him in the here and now. Lady Macbeth would sell her soul to the Devil, and her body, no less than her soul, pays the price. Critics, and actresses too, have been divided as to whether she actually faints when Macbeth is rather too verbosely excusing his killing of the grooms, or whether she only pretends to in order to stop him talking too much. I am inclined to believe that the faint is real — the first sign that nature is getting its own back. Neither she nor Macbeth is capable of true contrition; she, for her part, can only re-enact in her insomnia a crime that cannot be undone, and for Macbeth what remains to him of life is no more than

>   a tale
> Told by an idiot, full of sound and fury
> Signifying nothing.
>
>   (V, v, 27-9)

No philosopher of the absurd could have put it better.

Shakespeare's familiarity with the Bible and the Book of Common Prayer is evident: it suggests that he was at least a conforming Anglican

Heaven's cherubim, horsed
Upon the sightless couriers of the air

(I, vii, 22-3)

recalls Psalm XVII: 'He rode upon the cherubims, and did fly; he
came flying upon the wings of the wind'. When Lady Macduff asks
her little boy how he will live without a father, and he replies 'As
birds do, mother', Shakespeare is remembering Matthew 6:26.
Macbeth's invocation

Thou sure and firm-set earth
Hear not my steps, which way they walk, for fear
Thy very stones prate of my whereabout

(II, i, 56-8)

echoes Luke 19:39: 'I tell you that, if these should hold their peace,
the stones would immediately cry out'. From the moment Macduff
has fled to England the two countries compose a diptych where sin
and redeeming grace are seen in contrast. The possibility of salvation
derives directly from the piety of the 'holy King' who has received
Macduff

with such grace
That the malevolence of fortune nothing
Takes from his high respect

(III, vi, 27-9)

and will give every assistance to the *émigrés*. Historically, this is
Edward the Confessor, in whose borrowed robes Shakespeare is
pleased to flatter the reigning monarch. What matters, however, is to
have clearly in view the three Kings: Duncan, the innocent and saintly
victim; Macbeth, the guilty usurper; and the saintly Edward, from
whose territory and with whose help — 'and Him above to ratify the
work' — temporal salvation can go forward. Like *Hamlet*, *Macbeth* is
a play about society as well as about a pair of individuals; divisions in
the soul are mirrored by divisions in the state. And in both, supernatural agencies play their part.

Just as it is important to look beyond James I to Edward the
Confessor, so we should look beyond the 'weird sisters' to the
'masters' whom they serve. They have the gift of foreknowledge, but
they are not Fates. Macbeth remains captain of his soul until he loses
it by his own volition. The witches echo his temptations, but it is he
who gives way to them. He faces and weighs his choice. To the
Jacobean audience the witches were real in a way that they cannot
be to us — although Bradley seemed to think they could be found in
Bond Street! Theirs is 'the equivocation of the fiend / That lies like
truth'; when Macbeth sees Birnam Wood in motion, and learns that
Macduff 'was from his mother's womb untimely ripped', he sees

them for what they are: creatures

> That keep the word of promise to our ear
> And break it to our hope.

(V, viii, 21-2)

Banquo had got it right. The 'weird sisters' are precisely the 'instruments' of that metaphysical 'darkness' which envelops the play; of those unseen 'spirits that tend on mortal thoughts', and are mortal to mankind. They make of *Macbeth* what Dover Wilson has defined it to be

> ... the history of a human soul on its way to Hell, a soul at first noble, humane, innocent; then tempted through ambition to commit an appalling crime; and last, passing through the inevitable stages of torment and spiritual corruption that precede damnation.[1]

---

[1] *Macbeth*, Cambridge University Press (1947), XLVI.

Chapter 19

Roman Questions

1

For Coleridge *Antony and Cleopatra* was the 'most wonderful' of Shakespeare's plays. Not least among the reasons for wonder is the fact that it was probably written — though we have no record of its performance in the poet's lifetime — during the winter of 1606, only a few months after James I had been applauding *Macbeth*. No two plays could be more different. *Antony and Cleopatra* is technically a tragedy because the two protagonists die before it is over; but how different are their deaths to those of Macbeth and his Lady! And how different, so to speak, is the weather! Shakespeare has emerged from the nocturnal gloom of his Scottish *Walpurgisnacht* into the broad sunlight of Mediterranean day. We may suppose, it is true, a few shadows in Cleopatra's monument, and the night is 'shiny' when Enobarbus stumbles out to die. But then, as I shall hope to demonstrate, the death of Enobarbus is tragic in a way that Antony's and Cleopatra's is not.

With Plutarch at his elbow, Shakespeare must have had a play on the subject in mind when he set Antony and Octavius at odds in the last act of *Julius Caesar* — although mention of Cleopatra would have been tactless in a work intended to show that dictators may rule by political necessity, if not by Divine Right. Why then did he not proceed to write the sequel when, as we saw in *Troilus and Cressida*, the interlocking themes of love and war — or 'wars and lechery' — were clamouring for treatment? We may be thankful that he refrained from doing so, for if *Antony and Cleopatra* had been written in the vein of *Troilus* it would have been a much lesser play. Dramatists had to watch their steps after the fall of Essex, and a tragedy showing how a great general was let down by a capricious queen might have been too near the knuckle for Elizabeth — for Essex had many partisans. As Professor Bullough suggests, the woman who had exclaimed: 'I am Richard, know ye not that?' might have found reason to exclaim: 'I am Cleopatra'.[1] It was in fear of

---

[1] See Bullough, Vol. V, p. 216.

such a reaction that Fulke Greville had destroyed his play on the same subject.

Shakespeare could have found all he needed in Plutarch, but he may well have looked at other sources, of which there were not a few, and out of them he created his own inimitable Cleopatra. For Chaucer, in his *Legend of Good Women,* she was an example of true love, and Antony a man 'of discrecion and of hardynesse'. Shakespeare denies him the first and allows him the second. Chaucer stands in amiable contrast to Spenser who consigns both lovers to his House of Pride for their 'wastfull Pride and wanton Riotise'. Giulio Landi's *Life of Cleopatra* (1551) gave the dramatist, with much else, the silver oars that ferried the 'barge she sat in' and 'when they struck the water . . . gave out a musical sound, various and sweeter than flutes or other such instruments'. From Samuel Daniel's *Cleopatra* (1594) he got the episode where Seleucus admits to Octavius that Cleopatra's inventory of her treasures is incomplete; and also the contrast between Rome where everything must give way to duty, and Egypt where everything gives way to desire.

But the play is as inalienably Shakespeare's as anything he wrote; yet differently so. The tension of *Macbeth* is like the tautened strings of a violin; the movement of *Antony and Cleopatra* is swelling and relaxed — musical with a sumptuous imagery and dramatic in its contrast between two civilizations, and the seduction of one by the other. The multiplicity of scenes and minor characters form a coherent pattern on a stage which does not interrupt their comings and goings with irrelevant indications of locality. One quite naturally groups *Antony and Cleopatra* with the other Roman plays because Rome is one of its chief characters

> Let Rome in Tiber melt and the wide arch
> Of the ranged empire fall.
>
> (I, i, 33-4)

These lines, and many others like them, have a brazen resonance, and they describe the map on which the action of the play will be deployed. But there are other instruments in the orchestra which Shakespeare has assembled for this supreme occasion

> I am dying, Egypt, dying; only
> I here importune death awhile, until
> Of many thousand kisses the poor last
> I lay upon thy lips.
>
> (IV, xv, 17-21)

There is nothing like this in *Julius Caesar* or *Coriolanus,* where the passions are of a different kind — pride, envy, and ambition. It would not be too difficult, I think, to stroll through the British Museum or the Museo Nazionale in Naples and pick out the busts of Brutus and Cassius, Caius Marcius and Menenius, Portia and Volumnia, and many others; but the Mark Antony of *Antony and Cleopatra* I do not imagine as a bust at all. These other characters I have mentioned are fixed — you can circumscribe them in a phrase as you could circumscribe them in stone or terracotta — but Mark Antony is fluid. You never know what he is going to do next. He is a battlefield of conflicting fidelities, not in the sense that he wilfully does wrong, but in the sense that he is quite simply without the principles which will make him do right. When I speak of Antony behaving rightly, I am speaking of him behaving Romanly — and it is the whole paradox and grandeur of the play that in Shakespeare's eyes, it would seem, right and Rome are not quite certainly the same thing. There is no clear confrontation of right and wrong in *Antony and Cleopatra,* as there is in *Macbeth*; there is only a confrontation of Rome and Egypt. In *Coriolanus* Rome is not yet the *res Romana* and she is at odds only with a neighbouring tribe. In *Julius Caesar* the *res Romana* is at odds only with itself. In *Antony and Cleopatra* it is at odds with 'the serpent of old Nile'.

'I am all fire and air' she says, as she bids her grosser elements farewell. 'And water, too' she might have added — for she also is fluid, more mercurial even than her master and her slave. Water is a prime constituent of the play's cosmic décor. When Cleopatra first met Mark Antony, we are told, 'she pursed up his heart upon the river of Cydnus'. Nothing stable in that fatal exchange; these lovers are always in movement like the sea that separates them — the sea that bore the treacherous flight of Cleopatra's ships. In *Julius Caesar* and *Coriolanus* we are always on *terra firma,* but in *Antony and Cleopatra* the whole Mediterranean occupies the scene, so that we view the battles and the embassies and the embarkations through a kind of golden mist which the transcendent poetry supplies — very much as we might have viewed them in a landscape by Claude Lorrain. This is the most *public* of Shakespeare's tragedies; intimacy always has its spectators

> Take but good note and you shall see in him
> The triple pillar of the world transformed
> Into a strumpet's fool.

                                                            (I, i, 11-13)

There you have the picture in three lines. Antony's prestige is imperial; with Octavius and Lepidus he sustains — and disputes — the only world that was worth the knowing. It was not the solid manageable world of the Republic which Brutus had murdered his best friend to save. The seas battered or lapped its shores; the seas were part of it; and the seas were unaccountable. Beyond them was

Egypt — and strange fish, like the crocodile and Cleopatra. Again like Cleopatra, the seas had depths and shallows and could be whipped into sudden storms. Of course in one sense — in the Roman sense — Antony was indeed a fool and Cleopatra a strumpet. It is a Roman who tells us so. But this is only a single aspect of the kaleidoscopic commentary which Shakespeare casts upon his twin protagonists. By the end of the play, Antony is as big a fool — in the Roman sense — as he was at the beginning, but Octavius is also 'ass unpolicied'. The scales have been held even; or so even that it is up to anyone to say on which side they have come down. It rather depends on how you feel about the *res Romana.*

'Take but good note' Demetrius had said, and you will observe that all through *Antony and Cleopatra* people are taking notes. We see the central characters through other people's eyes, because other people are always standing around. Shakespeare is here turning to commodity the disadvantages, or at least the conditions, of his stage. The first Cleopatra, if indeed she was acted at all, was necessarily played by a boy, and there were certain kinds of scenes which a boy could not decently enact. Moreover Cleopatra was quite capable of dressing up as a boy — perhaps she did so when they wandered through the streets, the pair of them, and noted 'the qualities of people'. This would not have been beyond the whims of a reigning sovereign who could 'hop forty paces through the public street', and look more seductive when she was out of breath than when she was in it. The boyish gamesomeness of Cleopatra not only suited her first interpreter; it provided a counterweight to an eroticism that might have been oppressive, so that the contrast with the 'dull Octavia' — not so dull perhaps to an appetite less exorbitant than Antony's — is less between coldness and heat than between stillness and movement, consistency and caprice, work and play, duty and desire, proportion and extravagance. The contrast is even more marked — because it is more central — between Antony and Octavius; and it is Octavius who lets us see what the 'triple pillar' looked like when it still stood upright

> on the Alps
> It is reported thou didst eat strange flesh,
> Which some did die to look on: and all this —
> It wounds thy honour that I speak it now —
> Was borne so like a soldier that thy cheek
> So much as lank'd not.

> (I, iv, 66-71)

Yet in all this, magnificent as it may have been, there was a want of proportion that prepares us for the sequel

from Alexandria
This is the news: he fishes, drinks, and wastes
The lamps of nights in revel: is not more manlike
Than Cleopatra, nor the queen of Ptolemy
More womanly than he: hardly gave audience, or
Vouchsafed to think he had partners.

(I, iv, 3-8)

And why had he not given audience to Caesar's messenger? The excuse is unblushingly typical

Sir
He fell upon me ere admitted: then
Three kings I had newly feasted and did want
Of what I was i' the morning . . .

(II, ii, 4-7)

And so the argument goes on, with Antony's reluctant apologies and Octavius declaring that

if I knew
What hoop should hold us staunch, from edge to edge
Of the world I would pursue it

(II, ii, 16-18)

until Agrippa has the bright idea that the best hoop will be a wedding ring, and suggests that Antony shall marry Octavia. His agreement registers a shift of policy, but not a change of heart

I will to Egypt
And though I make this marriage for my peace
I' the east my pleasure lies.

(II, iv, 38-40)

Poor Octavia! She did not have much of a honeymoon.

Shakespeare must have calculated — if calculation is not too rational a word for the swift intuitions of his genius — where exactly to place the famous description of Antony's first meeting with Cleopatra. We have already heard how he is besotted with his serpent of old Nile and we have seen how she wriggles when he is recalled to Rome. Octavius has told us that his capacity for physical endurance is equal to his capacity for self-indulgence and we have seen that when it comes to policy Octavius is the stronger man. These are Roman voices, and none of them sympathetic to Cleopatra. They are the voices of men who simply cannot understand how Antony can make such a fool of himself. But now, just when Antony and Octavius have gone out, more or less arm in arm, it is Enobarbus, Antony's loyal lieutenant, who tells us how Antony and Cleopatra met and explains to us why they can never be parted. The rectitude of Enobarbus is not such that he cannot understand how another man can fall from it; not is his cynicism so sour that he cannot appreciate, and even perhaps envy, the sweets that another man enjoys. The muscular verse of the previous argument relaxes into prose — for Enobarbus generally makes his counterpoint in prose — and one imagines him unbuckling his belt and doing whatever a Roman officer did in lieu of filling his pipe. Two senators stay behind to talk to him. The great description is cunningly prepared and in the most casual way we are whisked back to Egypt

> Maec. Eight wild boars roasted whole at a
> breakfast, and but twelve persons there;
> is this true?
> Eno. This was but as a fly by an eagle: we had
> much more monstrous matter of feast, which
> worthily deserved noting.
>
> (II, ii, 183-7)

So far the picture is orgiastic in its suggestion of gluttony unrestrained. Then it begins to lighten as Maecenas comes to the point

> Maec. She's a most triumphant lady, if report be
> square to her.
> Eno. When she first met Mark Antony she pursed
> up his heart, upon the river of Cydnus.
>
> (II, ii, 190-2)

If we analyse the passage we shall discover most of the things we need to know about Antony and Cleopatra, and a great deal also about Shakespeare's poetic art in a play where the poetry is more consistently incandescent than in any other that he wrote, with the possible, though very different, exception of *Macbeth*. It varies widely in intensity, as well as in style, from play to play. There is a great poetry in *Romeo and Juliet* and *A Midsummer Night's Dream*: there is almost none in *Much Ado About Nothing*. Shakespeare always employs his verse for a dramatic purpose — to paint a scene or to illustrate a character — and the purposes of *Antony and Cleopatra* demand that the poetry shall be at a consistently high pitch; that it shall be lavishly descriptive of people and place and situation, and at the same time that it shall not weary or surfeit the listener.

I have said that the *mise-en-scène* of the play is global; and the unlocalized stage of the Globe theatre would have been well suited to it. If there is a key word to follow throughout its five acts it is the word that we should expect: *earth* or *world*. Antony is the 'triple pillar of the *world*'; 'a third o' the *world* is yours' he tells Pompey; 'The *world* and my great office will sometimes divide me from your bosom' he tells Octavia in what is at least an understatement; the triumvirs are 'the senators alone of this great *world*'; war between Antony and Octavius 'would be as if the *world* should cleave'; when

Pompey is defeated, Enobarbus concludes, 'Then, *world,* thou hast a
pair of chaps, no more'; Antony has 'given his empire up to a whore;
who now are levying the kings o' the *earth* for war'. Cleopatra is
Antony's 'day o' the *world*'; and when Antony, whose sword had
'quarter'd the *world*', is brought dying to Cleopatra, he allows
himself a retrospect on the 'former fortunes wherein I lived the
greatest price o' the *world*'. We remember Cleopatra's lament: 'The
crown o' the *earth* doth melt', and Octavius' tribute to the rival who
had been his friend

> The death of Antony
> Is not a single doom; in the name lay
> A moiety of the *world.*

(V, i, 17-19)

These two could not 'stall together in the whole *world*' − Octavius
knew it; and Cleopatra, too, addressing him as 'Sole sir o' the *world*'
when they find themselves face to face in the fifth act.

Here, then, as nowhere else in Shakespeare, 'all the world's a stage'
and the world looks on. So let us return to Enobarbus' description
and see how it relates to a play which is concerned with the public
consequences of a private passion. First of all, then, Cleopatra must
be seen as splendid as well as seductive; she must have her setting

> The barge she sat in like a burnished throne
> Burnt on the water; the poop was beaten gold;
> Purple the sails and so perfuméd that
> The winds were love-sick with them . . .

Notice the broad vowels and the bold alliteration; the solidity of gold
contrasted with the shimmering fluidity of water; and then the light,
sibilant ripple of the fourth line followed by

> the oars were silver.
> Which to the tune of flutes kept stroke and made
> The waters which they beat to follow faster,
> As amorous of their strokes . . .

Both eye and ear are now conditioned for the centrepiece

> For her own person
> It beggared all description

and Shakespeare is as good as his word. He does not describe
Cleopatra, any more than Homer describes Helen in the Iliad; he
describes her setting − the cloth of gold pavilion − and her effect
upon other people

> On each side her
> Stood pretty dimpled boys, like smiling Cupids,
> With divers-coloured fans, whose wind did seem

> To glow the delicate cheeks which they did cool
> And what they undid did

— the light vowels again supplying a prophylactic to a sensuality which might have become too lush. By the time we have been introduced to the gentlewoman — 'so many mermaids' — and seen how 'the silken tackle swell with the touches of those flower-soft hands' we are ready for the great encounter — and comedy

> The city cast
> Her people out upon her; and Antony
> Enthron'd in the market place, did sit alone
> Whistling to the air; which, but for vacancy,
> Had gone to gaze on Cleopatra too,
> And made a gap in nature.

Shakespeare, having created the *ambiente* so that we not only see but smell it, now takes a deep dive into psychology and twists the verse with irony

> Upon her landing, Antony sent to her,
> Invited her to supper: she replied,
> It should be better he became her guest
> Which she entreated: our courteous Antony
> Whom ne'er the word of 'no' woman heard speak,
> Being barber'd ten times o'er, goes to the feast,
> And, for his ordinary, pays his heart
> For what his eyes eat only.

One of the senators succinctly rejoins with 'Royal wench': for Cleopatra is just exactly everything we understand by those two words — as Enobarbus now precisely underlines

> I saw her once
> Hop forty paces through the public street;
> And having lost her breath, she spoke, and panted,
> That she did make defect perfection
> And, breathless, power breathe forth

— a feat which Shakespeare, with his unfailing dramatic tact, was careful not to ask even his most gymnastic boy actor to accomplish on the stage. But in the telling it imprints a romping and pranking Cleopatra unforgettably on the mind; and when Maecenas hints that Antony must now 'leave her utterly' because he is to marry Octavia, Enobarbus is ready with his summing-up

> Never: he will not:
> Age cannot wither her, nor custom stale
> Her infinite variety: other women cloy
> The appetites they feed, but she makes hungry
> Where most she satisfies: for vilest things
> Become themselves in her, that the holy priests
> Bless her when she is riggish.
>
> (II, ii, 195 *et seq.*)

I have analysed the speech in some detail because it is much more than an *aria* put into the mouth of a character not given to that kind of vocal exercise; it contains and condenses the play through the dispassionate commentary of its chorus — until the spectacle of his master's folly strains to breaking point the loyalty of Enobarbus, and death seals his lips.

It may be useful to consider here Shakespeare's handling of two themes always dear to him — loyalty and reason. Enobarbus is the last in a line of strong men who have at the same time supported and seen through a weak and errant master. The strength and lucidity of Enobarbus — his cynicism even — can be traced back to Kent in *King Lear* and Falconbridge in *King John*. But there is this important difference, that with Enobarbus loyalty fails through excess of reason

> The loyalty well held to fools does make
> Our faith mere folly: yet he that can endure
> To follow with allegiance a fall'n lord
> Does conquer him that did his master conquer,
> And earn a place i' the story.
>
> (III, xiii, 42-6)

By the time Antony's rage with Octavius' messenger is spent and he has decided to restore the situation with a party — 'Come, let's have one other gaudy night' — Enobarbus can stand the strain no longer

>   I see still,
> A diminution in our captain's brain
> Restores his heart: when valour preys on reason
> It eats the sword it fights with. I will seek
> Some way to leave him
>
> (III, xiii, 197-201)

and when we next see Enobarbus he has gone over to Caesar's camp, already wondering what sort of job he will get there, and whether he ought to have gone over at all: 'Canidius and the rest / That fell away have entertainment, but / No honourable trust.' His foreboding is confirmed when he learns that Antony, with no word of reproach, has sent after him all his treasure 'with his bounty overplus'. Faced with this magnanimity and largesse, Enobarbus can only creep into a ditch to die. The one character in the play who seemed almost to belong to comedy is the one whose tragedy is unrelieved. 'A master-leaver and a fugitive', he has no empyrean to look forward to where 'souls do couch on flowers'; not for him to 'make the ghosts gaze'. Having chosen the head against the heart, he dies despairing and alone.

It is not quite accurate to say that Shakespeare holds the scales even between the *res Romana* and the serpent of old Nile. What he does is to throw the whole weight of his genius first on one side and then on the other. Silly and superficial people in the middle of the twentieth century can jeer at establishment; let them see the results of disestablishment and they may laugh on the other side of their faces. Shakespeare knew better; for a man whose grandparents remembered the Wars of the Roses the state was a serious matter. Yet in this play he suggests that other things may be more serious; and he does more than suggest that statesmen may be silly. He makes it quite clear that statesmen can be drunk, and that when they are drunk they are food for laughter, just as when they are dead they are food for worms. What is the point of the hilarious scene on Pompey's galley, placed as it is plumb in the middle of the play, but to show us the silly side of the power game — so that a modern spectator cannot help steering the galley to the northern shores of the Black Sea and imagining Stalin, Roosevelt and Churchill trying to hold their vodka! For it is not only that Enobarbus can say of Lepidus, when they carry him off, 'A bears the third part of the world'; not only that Antony drivels on in his cups about Egyptian crocodiles; but that even the cool Octavius can admit

> You see we have burnt our cheeks; strong Enobarb
> Is weaker than the wine; and mine own tongue
> Splits what it speaks
>
> (II, vii, 129-31)

and that Enobarbus comments, as the others are led down into the dinghy: 'Take heed you fall not.'

All this is surely to prepare us for the moment when Cleopatra can call Caesar 'ass unpolicied', although in the meantime Antony's besotted folly has played into his hands. The fifth act of *Antony and Cleopatra*, with the last scene or two of the fourth, is the greatest rescue operation in dramatic literature. Antony, twice betrayed by Cleopatra in the middle of the battle, and hearing the false news of her death, bungles his own suicide; and then, learning that she is, after all, alive, is brought to her in the monument and hoisted up into her arms. It is from this nadir of catastrophe that Antony and Cleopatra, without ever ceasing to be themselves, must be hoisted from one kind of failure to another kind of success — so that we wonder whether the play ought to be called a tragedy at all; whether it ought not rather to be called a triumph.

Let us look at its conclusion a little more closely. Antony's death — since die he must — is a cosmic disaster against which the universe itself should veil its face

>   O sun
> Burn the great sphere thou movest in! Darkling stand
> The varying shore o' the world.
>
> (IV, xv, 9-11)

The dying Antony has quite shed his shame

> Not Caesar's valour hath o'erthrown Antony,
> But Antony's hath triumphed on itself
>
> (IV, xv, 14-15)

and the insatiate lover reasserts his rights

> Only
> I here importune death awhile, until
> Of many thousand kisses the poor last
> I lay upon thy lips.
>
> (IV, xv, 19-21)

Cleopatra's reply to this is wholly characteristic. Even though the time for kissing is running short, she does not leap at the suggestion. The nightmare of a Roman triumph is always at the back of her mind

> I dare not, dear,
> Dear my lord, pardon, I dare not,
> Lest I be taken
>
> (IV, xv, 21-2)

and she cannot forbear a final barb of jealousy

> Your wife Octavia, with her modest eyes
> And still conclusion, shall require no honour
> Demurring upon me.
>
> (IV, xv, 27-9)

But then she throws caution to the winds and in a moment Antony is in her arms

> die where thou has lived,
> Quicken with kissing: had my lips that power
> Thus would I wear them out
>
> (IV, xv, 38-9)

and it only remains for Antony to sketch with what breath is left to him the *bella figura* with which so many of Shakespeare's tragic heroes like to redeem the mess that they have made of their lives — 'a Roman by a Roman valiantly vanquished'. But Antony is luckier than most since he has not only Cleopatra but Caesar himself to pronounce his epitaph. For Cleopatra

> O withered is the garland of the war,
> The soldier's pole is fall'n
>
> (IV, xv, 64-5)

and for Agrippa

> A rarer spirit never
> Did steer humanity; but you, gods, will give us
> Some faults to make us men.
>
> (V, i, 31-3)

All this adds up to a plenary absolution, and it stands in immediate contrast to Caesar's petty scheming. Cleopatra must be saved from suicide at whatever cost in duplicity

> Go and say
> We purpose her no shame; . . .
> Lest in her greatness by some mortal stroke
> She do defeat us; for her life in Rome
> Would be eternal in our triumph.
>
> (V, i, 61-6)

The rest of the play belongs to Cleopatra, and in order that the queen of harlots shall be transformed into the queen of heroines, she must put off her royalty for a while

> No more, but e'en a woman, and commanded
> By such poor passion as the maid that milks
> And does the meanest chares.
>
> (IV, xv, 72-4)

Nothing matters now but the right moment to die — and as for Caesar, and the pinnacle of power on which he now stands unchallenged

> 'Tis paltry to be Caesar;
> Not being Fortune, he's but Fortune's knave,
> A minister of her will
>
> (V, ii, 2-4)

and for the rest, death is a mightly leveller; to die is

> To do that thing that ends all other deeds;
> which shackles accidents and bolts up change:
> Which sleeps, and never palates more the dug,
> The beggar's nurse and Caesar's.
>
> (V, ii, 5-8)

When Proculeius comes to her with Caesar's intentions on a silver plate, she remembers that Antony had said, almost with his dying breath, 'None about Caesar trust but Proculeius'; but she also remembers that Antony's judgment was not infallible. It was certainly not infallible here, for no sooner have she and Proculeius exchanged courtesies than he signals to the men who ascend the monument from behind and take her prisoner. Once again the vision of Octavia in the imperial box comes up to torture her

> Know, sir, that I
> Will not wait pinioned at your master's court,
> Nor once be chastised with the sober eye
> Of dull Octavia
>
> (V, ii, 52-5)

and when Octavius' second envoy, Dolabella, comes in and she has

painted for him the cosmic Antony whose 'legs bestrid the ocean'
and whose 'rear'd arm crested the world', she puts the question to
him bluntly

> *Cleo.* He'll lead me then in triumph?
> *Dol.* Madam, he will; I know't.

> (V, ii, 108-9)

By now, we shall agree, the *res Romana* is beginning to look rather
shabby as, with Caesar's entrance, the issue stands clear. His words
are honeyed, but their threat is unmistakable. When Cleopatra offers
the inventory of her riches, her treasurer Seleucus informs Caesar
that she has kept back enough to purchase what she has made
known. He has learnt to recognize the glint in the panther's eye when
it is about to spring, and he prepares a hasty exit. But Cleopatra will
'catch' his eyes 'though they had wings'. For some extraordinary
reason actresses often try to cut this episode; they think it takes the
gilt off the death bed. They fail to see that Cleopatra's fishwife fury
is all in character, and that if we are to accept the sublimities which
lie just ahead, the serpent of old Nile must still retain its sting, and
must still know how to wriggle

> say,
> Some nobler token I have kept apart
> For Livia and Octavia, to induce
> Their mediation.

> (V, ii, 167-70)

She — to ask for Octavia's mediation! But Caesar now thinks he has
his triumph in the bag; he is 'no merchant to make prize with you of
things that merchants sold'; he will dispose of Cleopatra as Cleopatra
shall give him counsel; let her 'feed and sleep'; he will remain her
friend. It all sounds very royal and magnanimous, but Cleopatra is
not taken in for a moment — 'he words me, girls, he words me' — and
in a minute or two Dolabella is back with the news that within three
days she and her children are to be sent on ahead of Caesar to await a
Roman triumph. But the asp is ready and in allowing its gentle bite
to conduct her to the ulterior shore, Cleopatra lets drop a word
which indicates the extent of her sublimation. 'Husband, I come' — it
was not thus that she had been used to think of Antony; and again,
in words written, as John Masefield has said, in a 'gush of the spirit
when the man must have been trembling'[1]

> Peace, peace!
> Dost thou not see my baby at my breast
> That sucks the nurse asleep?

> (V, i, 311-13)

[1] *William Shakespeare*, p. 207.

It was not thus, either, that Iras and Charmian — or we, the spectators of this play — had been used to think of Cleopatra. Finally, in order that the regality of this death-bed shall not want for realism, there is Charmian's: 'Your crown's awry; I'll mind it, and then play.'

Bradley was right not to include *Antony and Cleopatra* among the other Shakespearean tragedies, because it is not tragic as they are tragic. Antony and Cleopatra are, each in their different way, too fallible to realize the love which at the same time unites and so nearly destroys them. Shakespeare does not skimp its ambivalence; yet his purpose is not to moralize but to mediate, and the instrument of his mediation is a poetry which I can only describe as sacramental, in the sense that material things are invested with spiritual meaning without losing anything of weight or shape or colour. Death, for Antony and Cleopatra, is not the doom that it is for Macbeth, the release that it is for Hamlet or Lear, the self-imposed retribution that is for Othello. It is the passport to eternal life; not the punishment but the purification of love, and the condition of love's perpetuity. And as for the *res Romana* — one doubts whether Caesar would have been very gay company on that long journey back through Syria. Perhaps, after all, he went by sea; perhaps he was sea-sick; perhaps he was even drunk, as he was certainly disappointed. 'Ass unpolicied'? No, he had not overheard her saying it, and in any case there were certain things that one did not repeat to the man who was shortly to become Augustus.

The *res Romana* — I think Shakespeare would have said — was a fine thing in its proper place; but it somehow did not flourish in the shadow of the Sphinx, and it was not so great a thing that it could not afford to be made a fool of by a woman who was as clever as she was beautiful. In one of his broadcast talks E. M. Forster called for 'Two Cheers for Democracy', and added that the only thing that deserved three cheers was Love, which he described as the Great Republic. In *Antony and Cleopatra* Shakespeare says very much the same thing about the *res Romana* and the *res-publica amoris*.

2

Coriolanus has proved its topicality whenever political debate grows heated. In 1938 its performance at the Comédie Française was suspended at the request of President Doumergue, because the militants of Action Française had seized the occasion to demonstrate their anti-democratic sentiments. Cries of 'Vive Boulanger!' went up from every part of the house, and the curtain had to be lowered twenty times. In 1958, when General de Gaulle was recalled to power, François Mauriac, writing in *L'Express*, borrowed his commentary from *Coriolanus*

> I had rather be their servant in my way
> Than sway with them in theirs.

(II, i, 219-20)

Wisely, he did not push the parallel any further; de Gaulle was a consummate politician, whereas it was part of Coriolanus' tragedy that he was not.

The play was no less topical in 1608 — to assume a probable date for its composition. For two successive years the harvest had been bad, and during the great frost of 1607-8 the Thames had been frozen over, with pans of coal set in the fairway and stabbing the winter darkness. Marcius refers to 'the coal of fire upon the ice' (I, i, 74). Moreover social unrest was brewing. The enclosure of common land by the gentry had become increasingly unpopular, and the peasantry of Northamptonshire protested to their Members of Parliament against 'the excessive conversion of tillage into pasture'. Prices rose, and open rebellion broke out in the Midlands, spreading into Warwickshire. The dissidents were described as Levellers, and in 1608 the citizens of Northampton requested that the King's Progress through the city be cancelled. He 'progressed' nevertheless, but with a good deal less pomp and circumstance. The stage was set for a conflict between 'Peers and People', reminiscent of Lloyd George's war cry in 1911, and Shakespeare was quick to take his cue from it. Another cue he may have taken from the death of his mother in September of the same year. *Coriolanus* is a play about the relationship of a mother and her son — the only occasion on which he had treated such a theme, except in *Hamlet*. And how different, there, were both the mother and the son, and how different the relationship! In *Coriolanus* pride is overcome by a mother's pleading, not by the pressure of one political faction or another.

The play is not a miracle, like *Antony and Cleopatra*, and it is sparing of poetic flights after the largesse of its immediate forerunners. These are so rare that we remember them; why, one asks, should Valeria, a quite subsidiary character, be suddenly apostrophized as

> The moon of Rome; chaste as the icicle
> That's curded by the frost from purest snow
> And hangs on Dian's temple.

(V, iii, 65-7)

For no reason, except that Shakespeare could not help himself. Nevertheless, in its quite different, steely vein, *Coriolanus* is a masterpiece — technically almost perfect, with our sympathies impartially solicited. If we do not see inside Caius Marcius, as we see inside Antony or Macbeth, it is because there is not so much to see. He is a simple character — much too simple for the role he allows himself to assume; a *locus classicus* of the soldier mistakenly strayed into politics under the illusion that he can treat citizens like a recalcitrant peasantry or a bunch of raw recruits. The setting, and also to a large extent the subject, is Rome in the adolescence of its civic growth and territorial expansion. The balance of power in the republic has yet to be worked out, as it still had to be worked out in seventeenth-century England. The city is united against pressure from without, divided against pressures from within. The part of a fighting soldier suits Marcius like a glove, but as consul he is hopelessly miscast. I have spoken of his pride, which is not to be confused with vanity, and of pride he has more than enough. But this might have mattered less if he had known how to keep his temper.

The action of the play revolves around three conflicts, closely inter-related: between the patricians and the plebs, between Rome and Antium, and between Coriolanus and his mother. Shakespeare is very far from giving a charter to democracy. The people are short of food and complain that 'what authority surfeits on' would relieve them — the familiar complaint of the under-privileged against the evidence of prosperity in Mayfair or Park Avenue. Menenius, a veteran politician and sensible within the limitations of his class, replies with the parable of the organic state, where all the food goes into the belly and the belly distributes it to the members. The belly cannot distribute more than it receives, although the distribution is open to question. So far, the argument is fairly even, but when we learn that the people have been given 'the corn i' the storehouse gratis', a point is gained for the patricians. Brutus and Sicinius, the tribunes, are as unscrupulous a pair of demagogues as ever swayed the votes of a Trade Union Executive. The intemperance of Coriolanus gives them an excuse to get rid of him, and to turn his popularity into obloquy. When they are faced with his return at the head of a Volscian army, they are mute with fright. The citizens whom they cleverly manipulate are the same 'Hydra-headed multitude' that applauded the murder of Caesar and then lynched the man they mistook for his assassin. In *Coriolanus* they are as quick to change their minds; as one of them observes, 'I ever said we were i' the wrong when we banished him'; and 'So did we all', rejoins his fellow. Nor are they any more steadfast before the gates of Corioli

> The mouse ne'er shunned the cat as they did budge
> From rascals worse than they . . .
>
>   (I, vi, 44-5)

Caius Marcius puts the case (and Shakespeare's also, no doubt) for aristocracy

> and my soul aches
> To know, when two authorities are up,
> Neither supreme, how soon confusion
> May enter 'twixt the gap of both and take
> The one by the other
>
> (III, i, 108-12)

and he goes on to warn what happens

> where gentry, title, wisdom,
> Cannon conclude but by the yea and no
> Of general ignorance . . .
>
> (III, i, 144-6)

But his argument is weakened by a visceral contempt for 'the mutable, rank-scented many', and his inability to dissimulate in peace as easily as in war. As Volumnia, who shared his contempt, shrewdly reminds him

> If it be honour in your wars to seem
> The same you are not, which, for your best ends,
> You adopt your policy, how is it less or worse,
> That it shall hold companionship in peace
> With honour, as in war, since that to both
> It stands in like request?
>
> (III, ii, 46-51)

Coriolanus is neither intelligent nor mature; and his manners, abrupt with his equals and insulting with his inferiors, speak ill for the breeding on which he sets such store. Volumnia appeals to his head in vain; only when she appeals to his heart will she gain a Pyrrhic victory, losing her son with the plea that saves her city. But when it comes to a trial of strength between the patricians and the plebs, government by the people shows the sharper teeth. The patricians can do no more than escort their candidate to the city gate, earning, shortly afterwards, the contempt of the senator who bars Menenius' entrance to the Volscian camp

> Can you, when you have pushed out your gates the very defender of them, and, in a violent popular ignorance, given your enemy your shield, think to front his revenges with the easy groans of old women, the virginal palms of your daughters, or with the palsied intercession of such a decayed dotant as you seem to be?
>
> (V, ii, 41-8)

In so far as one can deduce Shakespeare's political options from *Coriolanus*, one might summarize these by saying that the people have no right to rule, and that the patricians have an obligation to

behave. No Jacobean dramatist could have been expected to go
further than that.

It is a crude error, which the theatre has too often endorsed, to
imagine the Volsces as a primitive tribe at war with a more or less
civilized city state. Antium has its senate and nobility as well as
Rome. Aufidius is a more subtle character than any of his opponents.
He knows how to play the power game — better than Coriolanus
knows how to treat the servants of the man he is seeking as an ally.
When he makes himself known, Aufidius is quick to embrace him

> Let me twine
> Mine arms about that body, where against
> My grainéd ash a hundred times hath broke
> And scarr'd the moon with splinters.
>
> (IV, v, 112-15)

But as Coriolanus assumes rather more than half of the command
allotted him, Aufidius is reminded that

> you are darken'd in this action, sir,
> Even by your own
>
> (IV, vii, 5-6)

and he cannot but agree. Coriolanus being the man he is, Aufidius
'must excuse / What cannot be amended'. Nevertheless

> be thou sure,
> When he shall come to his account, he knows not
> What I can urge against him.
>
> (IV, vii, 17-19)

After their first indecisive duel he had admitted that Marcius was as
'bold' as the Devil, 'but not so subtle'; and it is Aufidius who
analyses more acutely than anyone else what has brought him to his
present pass

> I think he'll be to Rome
> As is the osprey to the fish, who takes it
> By sovereignty of nature. First he was
> A noble servant to them; but he could not
> Carry his honours even: whether 'twas pride,
> Which out of daily fortune ever taints
> The happy man; whether defect of judgement
> To fail in the disposing of those chances
> Which he was lord of; or whether nature,
> Not to be other than one thing, not moving
> From the casque to the cushion, but commanding peace
> Even with the same austerity and garb
> As he controll'd the war; but one of these . . .
> made him fear'd,
> So hated and so banished.
>
> (IV, vii, 33-48)

Like Essex, of whom these lines must have been a piquant reminder,
Coriolanus had forgotten that 'our virtues / Lie in the interpretation
of the time' — a recipe for political wisdom if ever there was one.
Why then does he not return to Rome with his family when their
pleading has won him over? Rather strangely, they seem not to
expect him to. Had he done so, the tribunes would not have dared to
show their faces, and must have trembled for the renewal of their
mandate. Evidently he believes himself bound in some kind of
honour to Aufidius

> What peace you'll make advise me: for my part,
> I'll not to Rome, I'll back with you.
>
> (V, iii, 196-7)

But Aufidius lets us see in an aside that it is not an honour that he
recognizes

> I am glad thou has set thy mercy and thy honour
> At difference in thee: out of that I'll work
> Myself a former fortune.
>
> (V, iii, 200-1)

He works it basely by the abuse of his own hospitality. Coriolanus is
killed by a posse of conspirators, and Aufidius, to the shock of the
bystanders, sets his foot on his head

> *Sec Lord:*   Thou hast done a deed whereat
>   valour will weep.
>
> (V, vi, 136)

It is a self-defeating conquest of the man he had sworn to better in
single combat, and he can only make amends with a metallic epitaph:
'Trail your steel pikes'. This indicates that on Shakespeare's stage the
'boy', who 'like an eagle in a dovecote' had 'flutter'd your Volsces in
Corioli', would be given a Jacobean burial.

The 'family portrait' is drawn with nice distinctions; a Puritan
household, you might have said, with Volumnia and Virgilia sewing
on 'two low stools'. Virgilia wishes that Caius Marcius were safely
back from the wars, but for the older woman: 'If my son were my
husband, I should freelier rejoice in that absence wherein he won
honour than in the embracements of his bed where he would most
show love'. Had she a dozen sons, she would rather have 'eleven die
nobly for their country than one voluptuously surfeit out of action'.
Here are the *pietas* and *prisci mores* on which the republic was built;
and the Lady Valeria's prattle, when she comes to call, serves to give
us a picture of Caius Marcius' little boy who has already shown his
military temper by tearing the wings off a gilded butterfly! Valeria
asks Virgilia to go with her to visit a woman in labour, but Virgilia

has no heart to turn her 'solemness out o' door'. The scene is a conversation piece set in a Dutch interior; we are a long way from Nicholas Hilliard.

When Marcius returns in triumph the ladies are there to meet him, and Virgilia's portrait is sketched in the words with which he greets her: 'My gracious silence, hail!' It is a silence she will not break until she kneels with the others in the campagna, and caps Volumnia's

> thou shalt no sooner
> March to assault thy country than to tread —
> Trust to't, thou shalt not — on thy mother's womb
> That brought thee to this world

with

> Ay, and mine,
> That brought you forth this boy, to keep your name
> Living to time.
>
> (V, iii, 122-7)

The gestures and silences of the famous scene are as eloquent as its speech — deftly, but almost literally, taken from Plutarch. 'Speak to me, son . . . why dost not speak?' to Coriolanus; 'Daughter, speak you: he cares not for your weeping. Speak thou, boy.'

> He turns away
> Down ladies; let us shame him with our knees

and then

> Nay, behold's:
> This boy, that cannot tell what he would have,
> But kneels and holds up hands for fellowship.
>
> (V, iii, 173-5)

There is a homeliness about Volumnia's pleading, which prevails where vituperation would not

> Down: an end:
> This is the last: so we will home to Rome,
> And die among our neighbours.
>
> (V, iii, 171-3)

Hers is both the service and authority of the 'antique world'; and when Coriolanus acknowledges her victory — which is a victory both of the public and the private life

> But for your son, believe it, O, believe it,
> Most dangerously you have with him prevail'd,
> If not most mortal to him . . .
>
> (V, iii, 187-9)

She is so relieved that she does not catch his presentiment; and he will soon discover that Aufidius' notion of a 'convenient peace' is very different from his own.

To sum up the issue of the three conflicts out of which the unity of the play is woven. The plebs are defeated by the patricians, but Coriolanus is no longer there to rejoice at their discomfiture. It seems, nevertheless, that life had continued well enough in his absence, and the tribunes flatter themselves that

> Here do we make his friends
> Blush that the world goes well.

(IV, vi, 4-5)

Rome is saved from the Volsces, but Coriolanus is no longer there to threaten them; and it is Volumnia who receives, with unsuspected irony, a victor's welcome

> *First Sen.* Call all the tribes together, praise
> the gods,
> And make triumphant fires; strew flowers
> before them:
> Unshout the noise that banish'd Marcius
> Repeal him with the welcome of his mother.

(V, v, 2-5)

The welcome will resound hollowly when she receives the news from Antium. I have emphasized that *Coriolanus* is a play about pride as well as about politics; and although pride had had its fall, she had not expected it to fall so far.

The play is exceptional for the precision of its stage directions. The 'mutinous Citizens' enter with 'staves, clubs, and other weapons'; the ladies 'set them down on two stools and sew'; Marcius returns from Corioli to the Roman camp 'with his arm in a scarf'; he enters Rome 'crowned with an oaken garland'; the Citizens are later described as a 'rabble'; the ladies appear 'in mourning habits' for their trial of supplication. The seven scenes devoted to the siege of Corioli can only make theatrical sense in terms of an Elizabethan stage, or one that obeys its pattern. The rear wall and balcony represent the city. I conceive the Roman army entering from the yard and the two Senators appearing 'on the walls' — that is to say, on the upper stage. The Volsces 'issue forth their city' from the two entrances in the back wall; the Romans retreat to the edge of the platform; Caius Marcius urges them forward, and himself enters the gates, represented by a centre opening. Ladders have been called for, and these may well be set up against the balcony. The open stage must now serve for the streets of Corioli, and then for the camp of the Roman forces under Cominius' command (Scenes 5 and 6). Titus Lartius, the other Roman general, comes out of the gates (Scene 7), and the open stage becomes a neutral ground between Corioli and the Roman camp, until Aufidius and his allies are driven back into the city (Scene 8). Such it remains, while Marcius receives his new surname, and with a mixture of pride and modesty makes light of his wounds (Scene 9). When the Romans have dispersed to their camp — probably through the yard — the stage is clear for the Volsces, and Aufidius wonders

> What good condition can a treaty find
> I' the part that is at mercy?
>
> (I, x, 6-7)

Chapter 20

New Directions

1

On 9 August 1608 Richard Burbage took back the lease of the Blackfriars Theatre. The Kings Men now had a second place of their own, and for their winter seasons a roof over their heads. They began to play there regularly in January 1609-10. Shakespeare had a seventh share in the enterprise which allowed him the same share of the receipts, and made him liable for a similar proportion of the expenses. The Blackfriars soon became the most fashionable play-house in the city, and the parking of coaches in the street outside presented difficulties with which we find it easy to sympathize. The house had a seating capacity of 1,200 — about half of what we may reasonably allow to the Globe — and admission was more expensive. It was spoken of as 'the great Hall or Roome'; and had, as Sir Edmund Chambers has calculated, a length of sixty-six feet from north to south, and a width of forty-six feet from east to west, with the stage at one end of the hall. Leaving eight or ten feet for a passage and property space behind it, the main stage could hardly have been more than twelve feet in depth, although it might well have occupied the entire width of the hall. If we suppose that ten feet of this, on either side, were taken up by the stools for privileged spectators, we are left with an acting area of approximately twelve feet by twenty-six. The hall may well have been high enough to accommodate a gallery at one end, and some kind of upper stage at the other; and although the later plays of Shakespeare, written evidently with the Blackfriars in mind, have less use for this, there must have been facilities for Jupiter, in *Cymbeline*, to descend 'astride an eagle' — and presumably to deliver his message suspended in mid-air. No divinity could be expected to appear otherwise than from 'above'.

How the shape, size, and style of the Blackfriars affected the presentation of Shakespeare's plays can easily be conjectured. The 'houses' — Professor Hotson's 'transpicuous mansions' — which had always been a feature of performances at Court, could now be accommodated if they were called for — which I suspect was not very often. The masque was coming into fashion, and the Blackfriars welcomed it more warmly than the Globe. With the spectators all facing the stage, an 'inner stage' comes into its own, and the proscenium arch is at least foreshadowed. Intimacy was secured by a smaller, candle-lit auditorium, and the amenity of a roof. Nevertheless the same plays were given at both theatres, with the minimum adaptation of the *mise-en-scène*; and the company was augmented by the more talented of the 'little eyases' — now emerging from adolescence into manhood — whom Burbage had taken over from the previous lessee.

We have no record of Shakespeare as an actor after 1603 when his name is in the cast list of Ben Jonson's *Every Man in his Humour*. The prodigious creative effort represented by the plays discussed in the last few chapters would have left him little time for the wear and tear of stage performance, and for the touring of which the King's Men did a good deal. No date can be fixed for his so-called retirement to Stratford, but it seems likely that from 1608 onwards he spent more and more of his time there. His mother's house in Henley Street had been lent, or leased, to his daughter, Joanna Hart, and his interest in real estate was still keen. The mood of the final plays suggests not so much a rupture with the theatre as a more distant view of it. They certainly indicate that he had in mind the possibilities of a different kind of stage; and for this the acquisition of the Blackfriars surely had much to do. A more convincing sign of his periodic detachment is the fact that in many of the plays still to be treated here another hand can be seen at work. If Shakespeare felt the need of assistance, the reason may have been that distance, and possibly fatigue, kept him out of touch with his old associates. But collaboration should not be confused with the revision of another man's work when the King's Men required a play — perhaps at very short notice.

What, for example, are we to make of *Pericles*? On 20 May 1608, a play of that name was registered at Stationers Hall for Edward Blount, but it was not published. Later in the same year George Wilkins' narrative *The Painfull Adventures of Pericles, Prince of Tyre* was advertised as 'a true history of the play ... by the King's Majesty's Players excellently presented', thus indicating that Shakespeare's play, or a previous version of it, was already in the repertoire of Burbage's men. In 1609 the first Quarto was published as 'The Late and much admired play called Pericles, Prince of Tyre as it hath been divers and sundry times acted by his Majesties' Servants, at the Globe on the Bankside, by William Shakespeare'. A second Quarto came out in the same year and a third in 1611 — three in Shakespeare's lifetime — and others followed in 1619, 1630, and

1635. Yet, in spite of its popularity, the play was not included in the First Folio. From this we can only deduce that the editors considered the Quarto texts unworthy of their author, and that no other copy was available.

All are agreed that the last three acts of *Pericles* are superior in quality to Acts I and II, but a copyist's or compositor's errors are flagrant throughout. The problem has been minutely examined by Professor Philip Edwards,[1] and I cannot do better than briefly summarize his findings. In Acts I and II only 10 per cent of the verse is faulty, whereas in the remainder of the play the proportion is no less than 70 per cent, with 415 lines printed as prose. Professor Edwards shows with much ingenuity that three compositors were at work on a text supplied by two 'reporters', who had copied down and imperfectly remembered the play they had seen in the theatre. Whether the play registered by Edmund Blount was the same as that published by Henry Gosson remains uncertain, since Shakespeare's name was not attached to the former. The first reporter appears to have welded into very mediocre verse what he recalled from the original, and is much closer to Shakespeare when he writes in prose. The second has a more accurate memory, but his ear for verse is exceedingly capricious. Professor Edwards admits the possibility that the lost *Pericles* was wholly Shakespeare's work. It may be, however, that the play registered by Blount was by another hand; that Shakespeare revised it for Gosson, becoming more interested in the theme as he went on; and that reporters, copyists, and compositors made a pretty mess of the revision. As it is, the *Pericles* that Bankside flocked to see comes to us through a mist which is sometimes impenetrable, and at other times clears away altogether. Why so faulty a text was republished without correction, and twice within the author's lifetime, remains a mystery.

Shakespeare must often have paused by the tomb of John Gower in Southwark Cathedral, and Gower's *Confessio Amantis* may well have been already familiar to him. This and Laurence Twine's *The Patterne of Painfull Adventures* (1576) were the source of *Pericles*, whether it were Shakespeare or another who first lighted upon them. They gave him the cue for a new departure; but this was also a return to the chronicle play, fashionable during the last quarter of Elizabeth's reign, of which his own *Henry V* was a good example. The change could not have been more abrupt from the severe architecture of *Coriolanus*. He was moving towards a different kind of play where themes mattered more to him than character; where tension — not to be confused with the grip of a good story — could

---

[1] *Shakespeare Survey*, 5 (1953).

be relaxed, and where the gods would take a hand in the business. He was developing a new style as the instrument for an extreme sophistication and a crystalline simplicity; a poetry which is at once evocative, concentrated, and colloquial; images that shine and phrases that bite, rather than rhythms that carry you along. Even in the early and least satisfactory part of *Pericles* we are suddenly dazzled by

> The blind mole casts
> Copp'd hills toward heaven, to tell the earth is
> thronged
> By man's oppression; and the poor worm doth die for't
>
> (I, i, 100-2)

one of many places where Shakespeare's verse reminds us of Balzac's definition of painting: *'l'art est la nature concentrée'*. And in a simpler mode the scene of Marina's restoration to her father touches a Matterhorn of sublimity.

In a chronicle play, held together by a Chorus, the poet was not afraid of plain straightforward exposition, and Gower himself supplies it, illustrating his narrative with Dumb Show: Pericles with Cleon at Tarsus receiving the letter which calls him home, and rather quaintly knighting the Messenger who brings it to him; departing from Pentapolis with Thaisa; on his knees before the supposed tomb of Marina at Tarsus. These, with the elaborate stage directions for the mooring of Lysimachus' barge alongside the vessel in which Pericles has berthed at Mitylene, indicate a use of spectacle, with which the Chorus in *Henry V* might have been glad to embellish his descriptions. The masque has not yet taken possession of the theatre, but one has the impression that Inigo Jones is waiting in the wings.

The new departure was also a return to a theme which had haunted Shakespeare from the beginning, and was to haunt him to the end; a theme where the sea is envisaged as a fairway for human fortunes. It had washed up Aegeus and Antipholus at Ephesus, and thus provoked the 'comedy of errors'; it had supposedly wrecked Antonio's argosies in *The Merchant of Venice*; it had thrown up Viola on the Illyrian coast, and whipped up the storm which, in *Othello*, had scattered the Turkish fleet. Its opportunities and perils were a subject of daily conversation and concern to men who remembered the Armada, admired the explorations of Raleigh, and applauded the piracies of Drake. It was a theme upon which, in *Pericles*, the dramatist played every possible variation. The hero escapes by sea from Antiochus' incestuous *ménage*, and then from Tyre to Tarsus, where his 'portly sail of ships' is descried from Cleon's palace. Fearing the pursuit of Antiochus' agent, he again

> put forth to seas
> Where when men been, there's seldom ease
>
> (II, i, 27-8)

and is wrecked on the shore at Pentapolis. The unmistakable Shakespearean voice is heard in the prose of the three fishermen — not least in their surnames, Pilch and Patchbreech. The occasion is seized for standing up for the poor against the rich

> *Third Fish.* Master, I marvel how the fishes live
> in the sea.
> *First Fish.* Why, as men do a-land; the great ones
> eat up the little ones: I can compare
> our rich misers to nothing so fitly
> as to a whale; 'a plays and tumbles,
> driving the poor fry before him, and at
> last devours them all at a mouthful:
> such whales have I heard on o' the
> land, who never leave gaping till
> they've swallowed the whole parish,
> church, steeple, bells, and all
>
> (II, i, 30-9)

and when Pericles is hauled ashore, Patchbreech calls out 'Help, master, help! here's a fish hangs in the net, like a poor man's right in the law.' Pericles, having won Thaisa from King Simonides, and warned that if he does not return to Tyre the faithful Helicanus will be obliged to assume the crown, once more commits himself to 'Neptune's billow', and the organ notes of late Shakespearean verse swell with the overture to the third act

> Thou god of this great vast, rebuke these surges . . .
>
> (III, i, 1)

Marina is born at sea

> For a more blustrous birth had never babe . . .
>
> (III, i, 28)

Thaisa dies in the storm; her coffin is consigned to the waves; and Pericles puts about for Tarsus where, after a twelve months' stay, he leaves Marina in the care of Cleon and Dionyza, and returns to Tyre. Again, it is by the sea that Marina, now grown to young womanhood, walks with Leonine whom Dionyza, jealous for her own daughter, has suborned to murder her. How casual, and yet how sinister, is their conversation; Leonine, like Hubert in *King John*, shy of coming to the point

> *Mar.* Is this wind westerly that blows?
> *Leon.*   South-west.
> *Mar.* When I was born, the wind was north.
> *Leon.*   Was't so?

> *Mar.* My father, as nurse said, did never fear,
> But cried, 'Good seamen!' to the sailors, galling
> His kingly hands, haling ropes;
> And, clasping to the mast, endured a sea
> That almost burst the deck.
> *Leon.* When was this?
> *Mar.* When I was born.
>
> (IV, i, 51-9)

The rhythm is infallible. Never, from first to last, does Marina speak a syllable that is out of character: not for her to 'rebuke these surges'. Rescue, on this occasion, comes from the sea as the pirates save her from Leonine, but wears an uglier look when they sell her to the brothel in Mitylene. 'Well-sailing ships and bounteous winds' favour, ironically enough, Pericles' return to Tarsus 'to fetch his daughter home', only to kneel in sackcloth before her monument. But the winds drive him to Mitylene, where she is restored to him, and then

> In feather'd briefness sails are fill'd
> And wishes fall out as they're willed
>
> (V, ii, 280-1)

as father and daughter proceed to Ephesus. Piety brings Pericles to Diana's temple, and Thaisa, magically restored to life by Cerimon, is there to recognize him — for she, too, had been rescued from the sea where husband and daughter had supposed her buried.

Such then are the ways in which Shakespeare, using his favourite image, sets the fortunes of his characters afloat. But Pericles is more than a chronicle of chance; it is an allegory of good and evil. Incest drives Pericles from Antioch; the remorse of Cleon and the answering contempt of Dionyza recall *Macbeth*

> *Cleo.* Were I chief lord of all this spacious world,
> I'd give it to undo the deed . . .
>
> (IV, iii, 5-6)

> *Dion.* I do shame
> To think of what a noble strain you are
> And of how coward a spirit
>
> (IV, iii, 23-5)

and Marina's steady, unsentimental innocence strikes a note of pathos in the brothel scenes, which are otherwise rancid with Hogarthian realism. T. S. Eliot used to take the Pandar's single line: 'The poor Transylvanian is dead that lay with the little baggage' as an example of Shakespeare's indefectible ear. It has always seemed to me that an entire short story by de Maupassant is contained in it. Yet a discrepancy in the behaviour of Lysimachus, the Governor of Mitylene, suggests a copyist's omission. He arrives disguised at the brothel, reminiscent of the Duke in *Measure for Measure*, but he behaves at first like Bertram in *All's Well*. When Marina refuses to play his game, however, he admits

> Had I brought hither a corrupted mind
> Thy speech had altered it

(IV, vi, 111-12)

and a moment later 'be you thoughten / That I came hither with no ill intent'. Is he trying to excuse himself? Did he really come to 'spy out abuses' in the red light district of Mytilene? Or has he suddenly been converted? If the latter, so swift a change of heart required more careful preparation. Beyond the antinomies of good and evil, each portrayed in primary colours, the presiding gods are constantly invoked in *Pericles*, and it is 'Celestial Dian, goddess argentine' who speaks for them in a brief theophany. Whoever may have pointed the way to Shakespeare's treatment of this theme, and confused his footprints, there is no wonder that he found it irresistible.

2

Although *Pericles* continued to please the many — a writer[1] in 1646 took it as his text to compare Shakespeare with Sophocles — it was censured by some of the judicious few. Ben Jonson described it as a 'mouldy tale'; and in face of *Cymbeline*, which followed it, his great and later namesake declared that he would not 'waste criticism upon unresisting imbecility, upon faults too evident for detection, and too gross for aggravation'. This was the eighteenth century's reply to Shakespeare, and to a good deal else besides. The play is certainly a further step in a new direction, but what sort of play can it be said to be? A fairy tale, or simply a farrago? A metaphor, or merely a muddle? Something of all of these; and a new kind of poetry, where the poet — or his collaborator — sometimes misses his footing. For want of a better word, *Cymbeline* passes as a romance where even sinister happenings are not to be taken too seriously, and where assurance is never far from the surface that all will come right in the end. It is not the work of a tired man, but of a man relieved, maybe, not to have Burbage breathing down his neck. Professor Wilson Knight has rightly seen it as a theophany in which Jupiter gives his blessing to a marriage between Roman order and British independence — and idea flattering to James I who even flirted with the idea of a marriage between the Church of England and the Church of Rome. But let Professor Knight tell that to Dr Johnson and see what sort of an answer he gets from the autocrat at the breakfast table.

[1] S. Shepherd.

In the early summer of 1610 the Court was *en fête* for the investiture of Prince Henry as Prince of Wales. The royal family themselves took part in a masque, Daniel's *Thetys Festival*, where the Queen referred to her visit to Milford Haven. The constant references to Milford Haven, and the Welsh presence and vocation in the play, make it probable, at least, that *Cymbeline* was composed for these festivities.[1] If it were principally designed for the Blackfriars, the baroque prosody would have appealed to sophisticated tastes, and the inner stage have proved its usefulness. This would have served for Imogen's bedchamber, and Belarius' cave — with a scenic accessory enabling the outlaws to 'stoop', as they are bidden; for Posthumus' cell, and Philario's house in Rome. Shakespeare, when he chose to exercise it, had the gift of plunging us straight into the heart of a situation; here, as in *Pericles*, he introduces it, like a chronicler, through the dialogue of the two gentlemen — as if he were saying to us, 'This is an old story about far-away times'. He will use the same technique in *The Tempest* when Prospero's narration of his wrongs sets Miranda dozing, and a certain nervousness may be felt lest the audience may be dozing too. The art of the novel and the art of the theatre are beginning to coalesce; except in the hands of a master, the coalition is rarely a happy one.

When Shakespeare is writing below his best — and much of *Cymbeline* is a long way below his best — it is tempting to suspect the signature of another hand. Furness and Granville-Barker were among those who have scented a collaborator here. I find it hard to believe that the same man wrote the wonderful dirge over Imogen's supposed corpse, and the hack-work rhyming of Posthumus' Roman ancestors. I suggest that Shakespeare did not find the play altogether easy to write; that the theme captured him by fits and starts. I am struck by the absence of humour, although the gaoler in Posthumus' cell does not disappoint. 'O, the charity of a penny cord' rings true to the man who had written the brothel scenes in *Pericles*, and was shortly to create Autolycus. On the other hand the use of irony is striking. Imogen's beauty is brought before us obliquely through Iachimo's cold-hearted desire

> the flame o' the taper
> Bows towards her and would underpeep her lids
> To see the enclosed lights, now canopied
> Under those windows, white and azure, laced
> With blue of heaven's own tinct.
>
> (II, ii, 19-23)

---

[1] See Professor Glynne Wickham, 'Shakespeare's Investiture Play', *The Times Literary Supplement*, 18 December 1969.

Here, and throughout the soliloquy, is the master's hand, clinching the nervous rhythms with a rhyme

> Swift, swift, you dragons of the night, that dawning
> May bare the raven's eye! I lodge in fear;
> Though this a heavenly angel, hell is here

and then a final drop into the colloquial, as the clock strikes

> One, two, three: time, time.

(II, ii, 48-51)

Again, it is over a body supposedly dead but actually alive that Arviragus and Guiderius speak their dirge; and over the headless corpse of Cloten that Imogen evokes her husband's martial physique. One critic has suggested that Shakespeare could not have written 'Golden *lads* and girls', and I have a horrible hunch that Johnson might have agreed with him.

The point about Iachimo's soliloquy is that, although it is so cunningly varied, it is perfectly clear. So is Imogen's impatience to get to Milford Haven, where she expects Posthumus to meet her — irony again, since we know that there is little prospect of his doing anything of the kind

> O for a horse with wings! Hear'st thou, Pisanio?
> He is at Milford-Haven: read and tell me
> How far 'tis thither. If one of mean affairs
> May plot it in a week, why may not I
> Glide thither in a day? . . .
> . . . Prithee, speak,
> How many score of miles may we may well ride
> 'Twixt hour and hour?

(III, ii, 49-54; 68-70)

Here there is hardly a line in the whole speech that you would describe as strictly poetical, and yet the poetry of the heart is in every word of it. Compare it with Juliet's 'Gallop apace' — an aria, pure and simple, winged with the same impatience, not undramatic but lyrical, and addressed to herself alone. Imogen's 'Milford-Haven' has the same throb of longing, but the poetry is practical; what matter for the moment are ways and means. These are questions that Pisanio must answer, and all he can say is, 'Madam, you're best consider'; but Imogen is past consideration

> I see before me, man: nor here, nor here,
> Nor what ensues, but have a fog in them
> That I cannot look through.

(III, ii, 80-2)

It is a marvellous passage; Shakespeare, having fallen in love with Imogen, is himself again. In his mastery of a new prosody, he reminds one of a veteran jockey on a young filly taking Bechers Brook in an easy leap, with the rest of the field left nowhere.

The verse, except when Shakespeare is nodding or has handed over to someone else, is variously simple or extremely complicated. Posthumus, in the manner of a Greek Messenger, describes in a speech, bristling with parentheses, how Belarius and the boys had held the invading Romans at bay in a narrow pass. Like Imogen, he is breathless with excitement but far less easy to follow. Then his interlocutor sums up the incident succinctly

> This was a strange chance
> A narrow lane, an old man, and two boys.
>
> (V, iii, 51-2)

Many of the themes in *Cymbeline* are common to the later plays: jealousy and fidelity, simplicity and sophistication, court and countryside, repentance and reconciliation. But they are less skilfully integrated than we expect from Shakespeare, until they are resolved in the final scene which is a masterpiece of stagecraft. We know the answers, as we knew them in *Romeo and Juliet*; the interest, here, is all in how the characters will react to them. But Cymbeline and his wicked queen are too long out of sight and mind before they reappear; Belarius and the boys — what I have called the Welsh 'vocation' — are not announced until the third act; nor is the political theme of Rome and Britain until the end of the second. The first two acts are geared, securely enough, to Iachimo's wager and Cloten's clumsy wooing; they reach a climax with Posthumus' explosion of jealousy

> Is there no way for men to be, but women
> Must be half-workers?
>
> (II, v, 1-2)

But Posthumus does not appear again until the beginning of the fifth act, by which time we have ceased to care very much about him. Not, indeed, that we ever cared a great deal. Although he has pretty solid circumstantial evidence for suspecting Imogen, we do not enter into his jealousy because Shakespeare has failed to bring him alive. If Iachimo is a pale reflection of Iago, Posthumus is not even Othello's shadow. He certainly does not deserve, dramatically speaking, the ceremonial visit of his ancestors and the spectacular descent of Jupiter.

But with Imogen it is a very different matter. She is irresistible because Shakespeare could not resist her either, once she had leapt to life out of the old story from which he took the play. 'I have done this sort of thing before', one can imagine him saying, 'it is not too late to do it again.' In a sense it *was* too late because Imogen, in assuming masculine attire, sheds a good part of her personality. She becomes, in Belarius' cave, a conventional figure of romance, without the definition of her sisters in the late 'romances'. Not a passive sufferer like Hermione; not a waif preserving her innocence like Marina; not a castaway like Miranda or Perdita meeting Prince Charming on a sea coast or a desert island; but a pale variation on Viola or Rosalind, though not to be mistaken for either of them. Nor does she have the same luck with her men. The jealousy of Posthumus, the importunity of Cloten, and the Machiavellian trickery of Iachimo belong to a harsher world than Arden, or Illyria, or Belmont. If the three caskets come out of one kind of fairy-tale, Iachimo's trunk comes out of another. Moreover Imogen is called upon to exercise a magnanimity of which those earlier heroines had no need, and how gentle is her reproach

> Why did you throw your wedded lady from you?
> Think that you are upon a rock, and now
> Throw me again

and Posthumus answers as they embrace

> Hang there like fruit, my soul,
> Till the tree die.
>
> (V, v, 61-4)

This has the ecstatic brevity of Leontes' 'O she's warm!' when he takes the reanimated Hermione in his arms.

And yet, if you compare Imogen with the other heroines who have challenged misfortune in man's attire, she seems lighter, swifter, more aerial, more delicate, than they. This impression is confirmed by the images used by her, or about her. She is, one feels, something of a bird-watcher. She speaks of the 'crow' and 'the puttock'; describes Britain as a 'swan's nest'; the story of Philomel is her bedside reading; and it is some 'jay of Italy', she thinks, who has wronged her. For Arviragus, as he stands over her body, 'the bird is dead', and he thinks of the 'ruddock with his charitable bill' strewing her grave. 'Hark hark! the lark at heaven's gate sings' is the opening line of Cloten's aubade. She herself is equated with 'a piece of tender air', as if, like the birds, the air were her native element — and that is something you would not say of her sisters in the canon of Shakespeare's romantic comedy. She does indeed, in all essential matters, have her feet on the ground; yet she stands, as it were, on tiptoe and is always ready to leave it. One sees her thus, as she follows with her eye the departing figure of Posthumus

> I would have broke mine eye-strings, cracked them, but
> To look upon him, till the diminution
> Of space had pointed him sharp as my needle

> Nay, followed him, till he had melted from
> The smallness of a gnat to air, and then
> Have turned mine eye, and wept.
>
> (I, iii, 18-22)

And there is one other crucial difference between Imogen and her elder sisters. Their problem was to get their man, and the getting him was the subject of the plays. Imogen has got him when the play begins, and her problem was to keep and to recover him. Between her and them lies Shakespeare's knowledge of the world, and other women with whom she claims no kinship — the weakly wanton Cressida, and the 'serpent of old Nile'.

Shakespeare drew part of his story from Boccaccio's *Decameron*, Day 2, Novella 9, part of it from a late fifteenth-century German version of this, *Frederyke of Jennon*, and part of it from Holinshed. From these he constructed an ancient British-classical Roman-high Renaissance amalgam which invites the stage director to do pretty well anything he pleases. But where did the wicked stepmother with her brew of poisonous herbs come from, and the stealing of the young princes by Belarius, and Fidele's life with them in the cave? It has been suggested that Shakespeare was here obliged to the folk story of 'Little Snow-white'. In the tale, as in the play, we find a weak king, surrendering his child to a cruel stepmother described as 'beautiful, but proud and haughty'; in the best versions of it the 'cottage' of the dwarfs is a cave; and Snow-white enters it uninvited. 'Oh heavens, Oh heavens,' cried the dwarfs, 'what a lovely child!' 'By Jupiter, an angel' cries Belarius 'or if not, an earthly paragon.' Just as Snow-white cooks and keeps house for the dwarfs, so does Fidele for Belarius and the two boys

> But his neat cookery: he cut our roots
> In characters
> And sauced our broths, as Juno had been sick
> And he her dieter.
>
> (IV, ii, 49-51)

Both in the play and in the tale the stepmother's poison sends the girl into a death-like trance; but in the latter she is really dead. 'The dwarfs' we are told 'laid her upon a bier, and all seven of them sat round it, and wept for her, and wept three days long.' The queen in *Cymbeline* is straight out of fairy-tale or folk lore; a 'Queen of the Night' without the aria to improve a rather weak libretto.

The social and political themes of *Cymbeline* may well have meant more to an Elizabethan audience than they do to us. Britain is in a poor way, and Cymbeline himself, shadowy figure though he be, is a bad king. He has banished Belarius, as Lear banished Kent, and thereby incurred the loss of his two sons. He has married, *en deuxième noce*, an adventuress determined that her son, Cloten, shall marry Imogen, the King's daughter by a former marriage. He has banished Posthumus, a kind of ward in chancery, because Imogen has married him instead. So Britain is pretty rotten at the top, however sound it may be at bottom. Posthumus represents this soundness to a certain degree, although even with him it is not unflawed. The essential soundness of Britain has fled to Wales, and here we find the same contrast between court and countryside, purity and corruption, that we found in *As You Like It*. Belarius states it without more ado

> Hail, thou fair heaven!
> We house i' the rock, yet use thee not so hardly
> As prouder livers do.
>
> (III, iii, 7-9)

But Shakespeare insists that one life must be reconciled with the other, and Arviragus seems to suspect it

> What should we speak of
> When we are old as you? When we shall hear
> The rain and wind beat dark December, how
> In this our pinching cave shall we discourse
> The freezing hours away? We have seen nothing.
>
> (III, iii, 35-9)

But Belarius has seen too much

> Did you but know the city's usuries,
> And felt them knowingly: the art o' the court,
> As hard to leave as keep; whose top to climb
> Is certain falling, or so slippery that
> The fear's as bad as falling . . .
>
> (III, iii, 45-9)

The meeting between Imogen and the boys discloses layer upon layer of meaning. Like Belarius, she knows all about the court and has fled from it. Like Belarius, and also like the boys, she belongs to it by birth; but she does not know that they too belong to it, and the ignorance is mutual. What they discover is a brotherhood of heart and mind, unaware that it is also a brotherhood of blood. 'Are we not brothers?' Arviragus asks her; and she replies

> So man and man should be:
> But clay and clay differs in dignity,
> Whose dust is both alike
>
> (IV, ii, 3-5)

and the boys take up the theme in the dirge over her body — they whose royalty of nature requires no insignia. As Belarius puts it

> 'Tis wonder
> That an invisible instinct should frame them

To royalty unlearn'd . . .

(IV, ii, 176-8)

Shakespeare is responding to these princely outlaws, as he had responded to Imogen, and as they respond to her when they suppose her dead

> Stark, as you see:
> Thus smiling, as some fly had tickled slumber,
> Not as death's dart, being laugh'd at; his right cheek
> Reposing on a cushion.

(IV, ii, 209-12)

It is a wonderful picture; yet in these comparisons of man's estate Shakespeare is never bitten by the egalitarian itch. Imogen, in bidding the boys carry on with their daily routine of hunting, had spoken for her author in observing that 'the breach of custom is breach of all'; and even the ridiculous Cloten must be buried according to his degree

> Our foe was princely:
> And though you took his life as being our foe,
> Yet bury him as a prince.

(IV, ii, 249-51)

From ancient Britain, at the opening of the play, we are transported to Renaissance Italy — for although the scene is set in Rome, there is as yet no hint of the *res Romana*. The nationalities — Italian, French, Spanish, and British meet in Philario's house, the Frenchman reminding Posthumus that they had met in Orleans when Posthumus was 'a young traveller'. Slashed doublet and ruffles are the wear, one feels; togas can wait; and the prose ripples along with the elegance of Shakespearean comedy at its best. The distinction between Rome and Italy is capital for an understanding of the play. Posthumus, though his role is to have a foot in both camps and to bring them together, is here the strong and silent Britisher challenged, amiably enough, by the voluble Italian. It is not until later that Rome, as distinct from Italy, emerges as a prominent theme. The legions have withdrawn from Britain, but Britain still owes tribute to Augustus which Caius Lucius is sent to collect. He is politely received and, with equal politeness, sent back empty-handed; and the legions are mobilized once again for a channel crossing.

So the play's emphasis shifts between four distinct localities — the Britain of Cymbeline, Cloten, and the 'Queen of the Night'; Renaissance Italy represented by the 'yellow' Iachimo; classical Rome, not to be confused with it; and 'wild Wales' which has the integrity of Britain in its keeping. But notice how Posthumus and Imogen, in all good faith, change sides. Lucius, landed in Wales, is promised victory by the Soothsayer, and immediately discovers Imogen beside the corpse of Cloten whom she still mistakes for Posthumus

> A very valiant Briton and a good
> That here by mountaineers lies slain.

                                                    (IV, ii, 368-70)

No longer, as she thinks, under any obligation to Belarius and the boys, or still less to Cymbeline, she takes service under Lucius. Meanwhile we learn that 'the gentlemen of Italy', under the command of Iachimo, are mustering in the same cause. Posthumus, who has arrived with Lucius, believes the evidence of a 'bloody cloth' that Pisanio has done his bidding, and that Imogen is dead. Struck with remorse

>   brought hither
> Among the Italian gentry, and to fight
> Against my lady's kingdom

                                                    (V, i, 17-19)

he resolves to change sides

>   I'll disrobe me
> Of these Italian weeds, and suit myself
> As does a Briton peasant: so I'll fight
> Against the part I come with.

                                                    (V, i, 22-5)

In the ensuing battle — the stage directions suggest that it is more like a ballet than a battle — Iachimo is disarmed by Posthumus, but the Romans appear to have won and Cymbeline is taken prisoner. Belarius, however, and the boys come to the rescue of the British; Posthumus has sought death as a Briton but not found it; and now that the British have won, he will cheerfully accept it as a Roman. He is duly taken prisoner, and only awaits 'the charity of a penny cord'. The point of the ancestral vision, accompanied by solemn music, and of Jupiter's descent is to make it clear to him — and to us — that he is, in fact, a Roman; and that when he and Imogen are united, all wrongs forgiven, Rome and Britain will be at one again. Nor will Cymbeline even quibble about sending that cheque to Augustus, whatever damage it may do to his balance of payments. Theophany certainly helps to resolve the discords in *Cymbeline*, but it also provides a convenient exit from a theatrical impasse.

Nevertheless, Shakespeare's sense of political justice has been satisfied. Britain has been saved by Belarius whom Cymbeline had rejected, and by the two boys who did not know they were his sons. Cloten and the 'Queen of the Night' are dead. Classical Rome has its rights — but freely given, not forcibly seized; and even the 'Italian gentry' in the person of Iachimo, having fought bravely and said they were sorry, can return to their spaghetti and their wild oats. A modern critic[1] has compared the transition from Shakespearean tragedy to Shakespearean 'romance' to the transition from Caravaggio to Rubens; from the Renaissance to the baroque. *Cymbeline* is a strange, beautiful, and uneven play, with its 'odd and distinctive music derived from the interplay of contrasting themes and modes'.[2] And there are many passages where it leaves one inclined to paraphrase Orlando and exclaim: 'But heavenly Imogen!'

[1] Nicholas Brooke.
[2] F. R. Leavis.

Chapter 21

Redeeming the Time

1

In 1609 Shakespeare's *Sonnets* were published by Thomas Thorpe, and no other edition appeared in his lifetime — a strange contrast to the popularity of *Venus and Adonis* and *Lucrece*. But narrative verse was no longer in fashion, and Shakespeare's poetry was now enshrined in his plays. His fame, and perhaps his personal fortune, were further attested by the painting of his portrait[1] by Martin Droeshout in the same year. Droeshout was a Dutchman, who had become a British subject in 1608. It is not a very lively portrait, but it tempts one to exclaim with Hamlet: 'See what a grace was seated on this brow ... the front of Jove himself / An eye like Mars to threaten and command', balanced by the sensitivity of the nose and mouth.

He did not want for relations and friends at Stratford. His brother Richard lived with his sister, Joanna Hart, in Henley Street. William Reynolds, a wealthy farmer and wool merchant, and unrepentant Papist, had a large house, with twenty-two servants and a clandestine chaplain, only a few yards from New Place. Hamnet and Judith Sadler, the godparents of Shakespeare's twins, also lived near by. At Clifford-Chambers, a short distance from Stratford, Michael Drayton lodged with Sir Henry and Lady Rainsford; they were all three patients of Dr Hall. There is no reason to question Nicholas Rowe, the poet's first biographer, when he writes that

> The latter part of his life was spent, as all men of good sense will wish theirs may be, in ease, retirement, and the conversation of his friends ... His pleasurable wit, and good nature, engaged him in the acquaintance, and entitled him to the friendship of the gentlemen of the neighbourhood.

The picture is both pleasing and deceptive; it suggests not only a player who had discarded his motley, but a poet who had laid down his pen. In fact the quill can hardly have scratched the last lines of *Cymbeline* before it was busy on *The Winter's Tale* — a work of far more explosive originality. Simon Forman was in the audience at the

---

[1] Now in the Memorial Gallery, adjoining the Royal Shakespeare Theatre.

Globe on 15 May 1611, and gave a detailed résumé of the plot. He was unlikely to have done so unless he were referring to a fairly recent production. In the Office-Book of Sir Henry Herbert, Master of the Revels in 1623, *The Winter's Tale* is mentioned as an old play 'formerly allowed by Sir George Buck, and likewise by me on Mr Heming's word that there is nothing added or reformed, though the allowed book was missing . . .' Now Sir George Buck took office in August 1610. Ben Jonson mentions the play in the Induction to *Bartholomew Fair* (1612-14); and Professor Glynne Wickham has suggested[1] that it was written for performance in the autumn of 1610 before the King and the Prince of Wales shortly after the latter's investiture in June. A flattering parallel is indicated between Hermione's statue and the statue of Mary, Queen of Scots, which James had commissioned for her tomb in Westminster Abbey. Her body was interred there on 11 October 1612, but the statue had probably been completed by the autumn of 1609. Even if he had not seen it, Shakespeare must have known that the sculptor, William Cure, was at work on it. Professor Bullough is inclined to think that the play was composed 'between June 1610 and May 1611, later rather than earlier'.[2] This leaves room for Professor Glynne Wickham's hypothesis. We know that it was acted at Court to celebrate the marriage of the Princess Elizabeth to the Elector Palatine in February 1613.

Shakespeare took the skeleton of his plot from *Pandosto* — a popular story by his old enemy Robert Greene. 'If you accuse me of plagiarism,' one can imagine him thinking with an unembittered smile, 'here is further grist to your mill.' In several respects, however, he had departed from his source or added to it. The localities of Bohemia and Sicily are reversed; a Chorus, in the person of Time, bridges the gap of sixteen years between Acts III and IV; Leontes' jealousy is a sudden stroke of near insanity instead of being more carefully prepared for, and he does not cast a lascivious eye on Perdita, and then commit suicide; Hermione does not die when she hears of the death of her son; Leontes takes the initiative in consulting the oracle; and Polixenes is present to lend a dramatic climax to the sheep-shearing. Paulina, Antigonus, and Autolycus are all the dramatist's invention — the latter taken from Ovid's *Metamorphoses* (Book XI), and Homer had mentioned him in the *Odyssey* (Book XIX) as one who had 'the art of theft and swearing'. The bear that kills Antigonus and, most importantly, the animation of Hermione's statue, with the recognitions and reconciliations of the

---

[1] *The Times Literary Supplement*, 18 December 1969.
[2] See Bullough, Vol. 8, p. 117.

final scene, are entirely Shakespeare's work. The latter is so reminiscent of Euripides' *Alcestis* that one cannot help wondering if Shakespeare knew the story from those better versed in Greek than he was himself — for no translation of the *Alcestis* was then available.

The masque now coming into fashion, especially for performances at Court, was often followed by an anti-masque, where satire answered back, so to speak, to sentiment or ceremony. In *The Winter's Tale* Shakespeare turned this formula to his own purposes, opposing the pastoral comedy of Act IV to the apparent tragedy of Acts I to III, and joining them together in the romantic resolution of Act V. The current popularity of Beaumont and Fletcher — both now writing regularly for the King's Men — had doubtless helped to divert Shakespeare from tragedy to romance. Francis Beaumont came from an old Leicestershire family, and John Fletcher's father was Bishop of London; they were a social as well as a professional asset to the company, and Shakespeare was certainly not above taking a cue from the fashion they had set. The tone of *The Winter's Tale*, as indeed of *Cymbeline*, had also much in common with Sidney's *Arcadia*, which was bedside reading for every educated man. But Shakespeare was resolved to wear his romanticism with a difference. Rupert Brooke described the tragedies of Fletcher as 'a sea of saccharine'; the Shakespearean sea had plenty of salt in it, and *The Winter's Tale* combines the remoteness of romance with the sting of reality.

The play, despite its contempt for the unities, is carefully structured. Tension is high throughout the first three acts; nor is it absent altogether from the sheep-shearing when Polixenes denounces the troth-plight of Florizel and Perdita. This usefully alienates our sympathy from Polixenes just when Leontes is shortly to regain it. The tension mounts again, with expectation stretched to breaking point, in the scene before Hermione's statue, having been relaxed during the hectic rapportage of the four gentlemen. This last has been criticized, but the reason for it is not far to seek. To have shown the reconciliation of the two Kings, and the identification of Perdita as Leontes' daughter, would have blunted the impact of the solemn climax, very much as the restoration of Thaisa to Pericles was blunted by the previous restoration of Marina. Irony is still a powerful weapon. In the opening dialogue Camillo tells Archidamus that Leontes and Polixenes 'were trained together in their childhoods; and there rooted betwixt them then such an affection, which cannot choose but branch now' — when a few minutes later it will branch in opposite directions. Archidamus tells Camillo that Mamillius 'is a gentleman of the greatest promise that ever came into my note' — when shortly afterwards Mamillius is to die. Antigonus vows to 'pawn the little blood that I have left' to save the life of the infant Perdita, little guessing how grotesquely he will lose his own. In the last act Paulina speaks of Hermione as 'she you killed', and Leontes echoes her, not knowing — and neither did the play's first audience — that Hermione is still alive.

Theophany in *The Winter's Tale* plays its part more subtly than in *Pericles* or *Cymbeline*. Its first expression is atmospheric, in the short scene where Cleomenes and Dion recall their visit to Delphi. As a breathing space in the headlong impetus of the plot, this has much the same effect as the entrance of Duncan under the battlements of Macbeth's castle

> *Cleo.* The climate's delicate, the air most sweet,
>   Fertile the isle, the temple much surpassing
>   The common praise it bears.
> *Dion.*   I shall report,
>   For most it caught me, the celestial habits
>   Methinks I so should term them, and the reverence
>   Of the grave wearers. O, the sacrifice!
>   How ceremonious, solemn, and unearthly
>   It was i' the offering.
>
> (III, i, 1-8)

This would have recalled the solemn liturgy of the Mass for anyone who remembered what it had been like; for the classical setting of *The Winter's Tale* is a very thin screen for what I am not alone in taking as a testament — the more persuasive, maybe, if it were only half intentional — of Christian humanism.[1] The voice of the gods is heard with dramatic immediacy when their verdict is delivered to Leontes; and this is the first turning point of the play. The second is where the Shepherd discovers the infant Perdita on the 'sea coast of Bohemia', and his son describes how the bear had mangled Antigonus. 'Now bless thyself: thou mettest with things dying, I with things new-born.' In other words, he tells his son to make the sign of the Cross; however improbably Bohemia may have extended its frontiers, it is evidently some way from Delphi.

Nor is it only in these casual echoes of a Christian way of life — Perdita's reference to 'Whitsun pastorals', and the Shepherd's anticipation of the priest who will 'shovel dust' into his grave, showing Shakespeare's acquaintance with the rubrics of the first Prayer Book of Edward VI — that demonstrate a Christian ethic and spirituality. The theme of the play is an innocence lost and recovered, and an innocence that does not need recovery. The boyhood friendship of Leontes and Polixenes had been perfect; the 'world's slow stain' had not yet come to smirch it

---

[1] See the valuable essay by S. R. Bethell, *The Winter's Tale* (1947).

```
        we knew not
The doctrine of ill-doing, nor dreamt
That any did, nevertheless
Had we pursued that life,
And our weak spirits ne'er been higher rear'd
With stronger blood, we should have answer'd heaven
Boldly, 'not guilty'; the imposition clear'd
Hereditary ours.
```

                                                    (I, ii, 69-75)

Original sin had taken its toll; the subsequent reference to Leontes' 'vices' indicate a secret perversity that gives a shadowy excuse for the *coup de foudre* of his jealousy, although Hermione evidently had no inkling of it. Bernard Shaw was right in seeing the jealousy of Leontes as more plausible than the jealousy of Othello, because Leontes is naturally and pathologically jealous; and with Hermione nine months pregnant, and Polixenes' reminder that he has been nine months their guest, it was fatally easy to put two and two together. Having sinned against love, Leontes sins against justice; and then, in full knowledge of his fault, he must do penance. This, with Hermione's resignation, stand for the necessary, albeit life-denying, *ascesis* of medieval morality, just as Paulina stands for the severity of the old dispensation. They are met, however, by the sane and life-enhancing sensuality of Florizel and Perdita, where chastity is preserved but only for so long as it need be. Florizel's 'desires / Run not before mine honour, nor my lusts / Burn hotter than my faith'; Perdita, in giving her flowers to Florizel, longs for him to be 'quick and in mine arms'. Her language, as she distributes them to the other girls at the feast, has the frankness and fearlessness of innocence

```
        and yours, and yours,
That wear upon your virgin branches yet
Your maidenheads growing . . .
```

                                                    (IV, iv, 114-16)

Perdita, one feels, would have followed Romeo to Mantua, since she has no hesitation in following Florizel to Sicily; and Florizel has the excuse of a mind and heart made up for the lies with which he explains their arrival. Perdita has come 'from Libya' the daughter of a King who has given his tearful blessing to their union, and Florizel has dismissed his 'best train' from the 'Sicilian shores'. When Polixenes comes hot-foot in pursuit of the eloping couple, their resourceful mendacity goes unrebuked; and as Hermione is reawakened into life an old marriage is mended and a new marriage is announced. I do not think it is unduly fanciful to see in the stirring of Giulio Romano's statue an analogue of the resurrection of the flesh; and in the union of Bohemia and Sicily an analogue of the union between the English and the Scottish crowns.

The contrast is vivid between the sophistication of Sicily and the simplicity of Bohemia; nevertheless the two must be brought together in a synthesis of civilized living. Perdita disdains the 'carnations and streak'd gillyvors' because

> I have heard it said
> There is an art which in their piedness shares
> With great creating nature

and Polixenes replies

> Say there be;
> Yet nature is made better by no mean,
> But nature makes that mean; so, over that art
> Which you say adds to nature, is an art
> That nature makes.
>
> (IV, iv, 86-92)

Here is social as well as aesthetic criticism. The Shepherd, like Adam in *As You Like It*, stands for the 'constant service of the antique world', recalling how his wife

> was both pantler, butler, cook,
> Both dame and servant; welcomed all, served all:
> Would sing her song and dance her turn; now here,
> At upper end o' the table, now i' the middle;
> On his shoulder, and his; her face o' fire
> With labour and the thing she took to quench it,
> She would to each one sip.
>
> (IV, iv, 55-62)

This, like the roguery of Autolycus, is rustic realism, not Arcadian romance. But while the Shepherd survives the transformation of his fortunes, his son does not; the one behaves like the gentleman he has always been by nature, the other like a country bumpkin transformed into a city bounder. Shakespeare, though he was moderately rich himself, had a sharp eye for the *nouveaux riche*.

The language of the play, in its concrete and sometimes brutal imagery, its smooth or tortured rhythms, disposes, like so much else in the later plays, of a Shakespeare divorced from quotidian reality. Lytton Strachey's picture of the bored Bard of Stratford is responsible for this misleading legend. What has changed — we saw it in *Pericles* and *Cymbeline* — is the perspective. Shakespeare has widened, not his own distance from life, but the distance between his audience and his play. Three times, in the last act, the strange happenings are compared to 'an old tale'; and when Mamillius responds to Hermione's 'tell's a tale' with 'A sad tale's best for winter' he throws out a hint to the spectator that *The Winter's Tale* will be sad before it can be merry, and strange before it can be moving. The man who 'dwelt by a churchyard' carries a faint foretaste of the chapel where Hermione will live immured for sixteen years. This is improbable enough, and I take the 'sea-coast of Bohemia' to be no more than the dramatist's invitation to a further suspension of disbelief. The storm that Antigonus narrowly escapes, and the bear that dines off him, introduce a change both of key and climate. Antigonus has deserved death for discharging the 'ungentle business' that Leontes has put upon him, and the bear — not, I think, a live one, though the bear-pit and the Globe were next door neighbours — is as good an intrument as any other for dispatching him. As G. B. Harrison has reminded us, 'a bear rampant is of all beasts the most easily personated by a man'. To the Jacobean audience the famous stage direction 'Exit, pursued by a bear' would, I suggest, be macabre rather than amusing, symbolizing 'the revenge of nature on the servant of a corrupted Court'.[1] The change of key comes immediately afterwards with the entrance of the Shepherd and the transition from verse to prose; and it turns to broad comedy with his son's relation of 'how the poor gentleman roared and the bear mocked him, both roaring louder than the sea or weather'. Observe that the son is described as a 'Clown' — evidently a part for the comedian — and we are not invited to shed any tears for Antigonus. In the fullness of time Paulina will console herself with Camillo; and Time itself, in the Chorus to the fourth act, puts the first part of the play in the perspective of 'a sad tale' — not forgotten but remote, until the plot brings it closer again. The 'disease' of Leontes' jealousy, purged by prayer and fasting, is countered by 'great creating nature', eloquent in the health and innocence of Perdita. The first three acts of *The Winter's Tale* are a tragedy of denial; the last two are something like a Divine Comedy of affirmation, and beatitude beckons when they are over.

Of characterization there is all that there needs to be, but this is much. Shakespeare could have met Autolycus at any 'Whitsun pastoral' in Warwickshire, where he had doubtless possessed himself of many purses. Paulina, from her brusque entrance into Hermione's cell to her unforgiving reminders to Leontes, when it is balm and not blame that he requires, is among the dramatist's finest portraits of mature womanhood. She stands out in brush-strokes as broad as her speech, like a figure from a canvas by Frans Hals, shrewish though finally compassionate. As a study in morbid psychology, Shakespeare did nothing more masterly than Leontes. Where the waves of Othello's jealousy swell like a symphony until they dissolve into the babbling of epilepsy, the speech of Leontes shivers and splits into syncopation from the moment the thunderbolt has struck him

[1] Nevill Coghill, *Shakespeare Survey* 2 (1958), pp. 31-41.

> Too hot; too hot!
> To mingle friendship far is mingling bloods.
> I have tremor cordis on me: my heart dances;
> But not for joy, not joy
>
> (I, ii, 108-11)

and so to 'paddling palms and pinching fingers'; and the image which embodies for all time the self-created hell of jealousy

> I have drunk and seen the spider
>
> (II, i, 45)

until the mind is debased to the level of its own delusion

> It is a bawdy planet, that will strike
> Where 'tis predominant; and 'tis powerful, think it,
> From east, west, north and south: be it concluded,
> No barricado for a belly; know't:
> It will let in and out the enemy
> With bag and baggage! many thousand on's
> Have the disease, and feel't not . . .
>
> (I, ii, 21-7)

This is the language of delirium, and merits Hermione's later riposte

> My life stands in the level of your dreams . . .
>
> (III, ii, 82)

The line illustrates Shakespeare's power of setting complexity and clarity in contrast, each appropriate to the speaker and the situation. Once the oracle has proclaimed Hermione's innocence, the verse given to Leontes, which has foamed and choked like a raging torrent, broadens out like the same torrent received into the bosom of a lake, whose still depths are differently troubled. So, as he reflects on his treatment of Polixenes: 'How he glisters / Thorough my rust'; and in the last act, when his courtiers are urging him to take a second wife, Paulina warns him that, were she the ghost of Hermione

> I'd bid you mark
> Her eye, and tell me for what dull part in't
> You chose her; then I'd shriek, that even your ears
> Should rift to hear me; and the words that follow'd
> Should be 'Remember mine'

and Leontes replies in monosyllables charged with the weight and ache of memory

> Stars, stars,
> And all eyes else dead coals.
>
> (V, i, 63-8)

One might have thought, after *Antony and Cleopatra*, that there was nothing more for Shakespeare to do with language, or with dramaturgy after *Coriolanus*. But in *The Winter's Tale* both poetry and drama discover a new development. The new directions, explored a little fumblingly in *Pericles* and *Cymbeline*, reach their goal with complete assurance. Not even in *The Tempest* does Shakespeare generate an equal variety and excitement, or distil a riper wisdom. If the tale is wintry, and much of its colouring autumnal, the freshness and energy of spring are in the treatment of it.

2

Many of Shakespeare's acquaintance had an interest in the Virginia Company, founded in 1606 — Southampton and Pembroke, and his Stratford neighbour, Lord Carew. He had certainly been shown the news-letter from William Strachey, describing how the *Sea Adventure*, with Sir George Somers and a party of colonists aboard, after leaving Plymouth Sound on 2 June 1609, had been driven ashore at Bermuda by a hurricane of exceptional severity — fortunately, however, with no loss of life. The other eight ships, with their five hundred colonists, were all dispersed by the gales. The reading of this letter undoubtedly inspired *The Tempest*. Strachey's picture of St Elmo's fire 'like a faint star trembling and streaming along with a sparkling blaze half the height upon the mainmast and shooting sometimes from shroud to shroud . . . sometimes running along to the very end and returning' gave Ariel his cue for

> Now in the waist, the deck, in every cabin,
> I flamed amazement: sometime I'd divide
> And burn in many places; on the topmast,
> The yards and bowsprit would I flame distinctly,
> Then meet and join.
>
> (I, ii, 197-201)

The play was given at Hallowmas, 1611, and revived on 14 February 1613, to celebrate the betrothal of the Princess Elizabeth — 'th' eclipse and glory of her kind' — to the Elector Palatine. Whether it was shortened for this occasion — events previous to the shipwreck being now related by Prospero — is an open question. I incline to the view of E. K. Chambers that the play, as it has come down to us, is the play that Shakespeare originally planned.[1] He may well have concluded that if brevity were the soul of wit, there were occasions when it might also be the spice of drama. The 'sea sorrow' and the 'green world', which are alternating themes in Shakespearean comedy, meet and are reconciled when shipwreck brings Prospero's enemies to his fertile island, and 'calm seas' and 'auspicious gales' take them off it.

---

[1] *Shakespearean Gleanings* (1944).

The Tempest is a recapitulation, but how far may we describe it as an autobiography? Nothing that we know or can guess about Shakespeare suggests the slightest resemblance to Prospero; yet what Prospero does is analogous to the 'shaping spirit of imagination', and in the abdication of his magic it is not fanciful to read a hint that Shakespeare has not very much more to say. The play is a synthesis of much that he has said already. To begin with — and for the first time since *The Comedy of Errors* — he obeys the unities, although Ben Jonson, to judge from a snide observation in *Bartholomew Fair,* was not to thank him for it. Then there is the double stranding on a foreign shore — first of Prospero and Miranda, and then of their enemies — and the magical command of the elements which Oberon and Puck had exercised for a mischievous, and Prospero and Ariel now employ for a moral, purpose. Where Puck was earth-bound, Ariel has the freedom of the sky; Shakespeare seems to have derived him from Shrimp in Anthony Munday's *John a'Kent and John a'Cumber* (1594) — a play in which he may have performed himself when the Lord Chamberlain's Men and the Lord Admiral's Men had temporarily joined forces. The magic in *A Midsummer Night's Dream* was neither white nor black; in *The Tempest* it could not be whiter. The play is unashamedly didactic, and loses thereby a little of entertainment value. Prospero is not necessarily a bore, but the actor must see to it that the play marches to the pulsation of his 'beating mind'.

Next is the theme — recurrent through histories and tragedies alike — of usurpation, or the killing of the King.

> *Seb.*   I remember
> You did supplant your brother Prospero.
> *Ant.*   True:
> And look how well my garments sit upon me;
> Much feater than before; my brother's servants
> Were then my fellows; now they are my men.
> *Seb.* But, for your conscience —
> *Ant.* Ay, sir; where lies that? if it were a kibe
> 'Twould put me to my slipper; but I feel not
> This deity in my bosom: twenty consciences
> That stand 'twixt me and Milan, candied be they,
> And melt ere they molest.
>
>   (II, i, 267-77)

He will presently feel it outside his bosom when Ariel spirits away the banquet before the conspirators have time to sit down to it

> You are three men of sin, whom Destiny —
> That hath to instrument this lower world
> And what is in't — the never-surfeited sea
> Hath caused to belch up you . . .
>
>   (III, iii, 53-5)

It is the moment of the particular judgement, and Ariel speaks with the voice of the Recording Angel

> But, remember —
> For that's my business to you — that you three
> From Milan did supplant good Prospero:
> Expos'd unto the sea, which hath requit it,
> Him and his innocent child: for which foul deed
> The powers, delaying, not forgetting, have
> Incens'd the seas and shores, yea, all the creatures
> Against your peace.
>
> (III, iii, 68-75)

The Shakespearean 'tempest', which has been put to so many uses, is here the instrument of Divine retribution, and what now awaits the conspirators is 'lingering perdition' from which nothing can deliver them but 'heart-sorrow' / And a clear life ensuing'. Here is the Christian doctrine of contrition defined in four words, and no theologian could have put it better.

It is an error to equate Prospero with Almighty God; his function is sacerdotal. He uses Ariel in a sacramental way, very much as the priest uses the bread and wine at Mass. The elements, divinized by the words of consecration, are still dependent on him, even while they are accomplishing a work that he could never accomplish by himself. Discovered and liberated by Prospero, Ariel operates the Divine powers which are lent to his master. In one respect he is above Prospero, since he performs what Prospero cannot; in another respect he is below him, since, for the time being, he obeys his instructions. It is not fanciful to see in Ariel a personification of imprisoned grace, set free at last for the service of mankind, but always hankering for the pure, unfettered liberty which is only to be found in Paradise. If Ariel is subject to Prospero, that is only because Prospero, through his mastery of magic, has borrowed the Divine prerogatives. It is as a priest, not as a man, that Ariel obeys him; and when the conspirators are 'all prisoners', and apparently penitent, it is Ariel who teaches Prospero forgiveness. The priest returns to the community of sinners

> Though with their high wrongs I am struck to the quick,
> Yet with my noble reason 'gainst my fury
> Do I take part: the rarer action is
> In virtue than in vengeance.
>
> (V, i, 25-8)

But with the reminder of Caliban's plot against his life, anger returns. Abruptly he dissolves the masque, and it is with a 'beating mind' that he proclaims his message that 'our little life is rounded with a sleep'. The famous lines are a far cry from a serene philosphy.

The role of Prospero is not unlike that of the soi-disant psychiatrist in T. S. Eliot's *The Cocktail Party*, although Shakespare has not helped him with a sense of humour. Having set himself, and his world, to rights, as far as he can, he returns half-heartedly to Milan; and if every third thought is to be his grave, there is little indication that the other two will be dedicated to affairs of state. Perhaps Prospero was not a very good Duke; it was characteristic of Shakespeare to leave the question open.

If we should beware of identifying Prospero too closely with his author, we are justified in seeing here a reflection of James I himself. In 1611 James was eagerly in search of a bridegroom for the young Elizabeth. Still haunted by the dream of a reunited Christendom, his thoughts had turned to the widowed Philip III of Spain. The memory of Ferdinand of Aragon who, with Isabella of Castile, had united Spain may have been in Shakespeare's mind when he chose that name for the young man upon whom Prospero's hopes are set. In the event, however, things turned out differently, and by the time the play was revived a Protestant prince had been chosen, and the ecumencial dream was fading. The end of the play is tempered with realism. If Prospero's island is equated with Britain, the wrecking of Alonso and his fellow-usurpers with the wreck of the Armada, and the failure of Caliban's conspiracy with the failure of Guy Fawkes, Antonio, though forgiven, is unrepentant, Ariel is on the wing to freedom, and the island is left to Caliban. He will 'seek for grace', but from whom is he to seek it?[1]

We misread *The Tempest* if we see in it a pattern of Utopia. What Bonamy Dobrée wrote of Kipling is true of Shakespeare: 'He is, one may perhaps claim, romantic by impulse; but then he tries his romance seven times in the fire of actuality, and brings to it the clearness of crystal.' Old Gonzalo is allowed to indulge his nostalgia for an Earthly Paradise, but Gonzalo is a sentimental anarchist and Shakespeare answers him with Prospero's pedagogic realism. It was a hundred years since More had published his *Utopia*, and history had given it a dusty answer. The massacre of St Bartholomew, the Peasants' Revolt, and the Northern Rising had discouraged ideas of the good society. The speech, placed where it is, throws up into relief the regicide that Antonio and Sebastian are preparing to commit. And what of Caliban? The Elizabethans, in the first flush of colonial expansion, had scant regard for aboriginal rights. Prospero owes his title to the intrinsic superiority of civilized man over savages; yet it was not in the nature of Shakespeare to create a character like Caliban and never once to stir our sympathies. But despite his gropings towards the sublime, he remains the incurable primitive who

---

[1] See Glynne Wickham, *Essays and Studies* (1975).

perverts the instruction he has received. Like all demagogues, and most democracies, unless they are strongly protected by local custom, he uses his intelligence to flatter his instincts. The scene in which he swears allegiance to the drunken Stephano has a Swiftian edge to its satire; the monster, the drunkard, and the clown are linked by a common ambition — to uproot authority. Having deprived Prospero of his books (to hell with culture!): 'for without them / He's but a sot, as I am' — the levelling jealousy of all superior attainment — they must get possession of Miranda, and the end of the conspiracy will be moral as well as political anarchy. But the plotting of the 'common men' is brought to nothing through their own stupidity; the rich stuffs displayed before the entrance to Prospero's cave distract them from their more sinister intent. Very significant is Stephano's drunken refrain: 'Thought is free!'; what Shakespeare is here attacking is the notion that thought can be divorced from discipline, and again in Stephano's 'This will prove a brave kingdom to me, where I shall have my music for nothing' the illusion that pleasure need not be paid for. Almost every heresy which has ravaged the modern world, and in particular those fathered by the sentimental genius of Rousseau, were pulverized in *The Tempest* centuries before they were born.

The future, in Shakespeare's penultimate vision, is not with Caliban or Prospero, but with Ferdinand and Miranda. The play which began with a tempest, is directed towards an epithalamium, and the masque of goddesses, with their celebration of a love which seems to be sacramental from its first flowering. The religious images abound

> *Mira.*   I might call him
> A thing divine; for nothing natural
> I ever saw so noble.
>
> (I, ii, 423-5)

> *Fer.*   Most sure, the goddess
> On whom these airs attend!
>
> (I, ii, 426-7)

In her perfectly instructed innocence, Miranda stands for the Beatific Vision, and the way to her lies through a gentle Purgatory. Yet she is not incapable of desire; even through the emotional sobriety of the verse, one feels it grow in her. But her primary instinct is compassion

> If you'll sit down,
> I'll bear your logs the while. Pray, give me that,
> I'll carry it to the pile.
>
> (III, i, 23-5)

It has been a long step from the lyricism of Romeo and Juliet to this colloquial simplicity; yet the poet has found his way back to the moment when Romeo could exclaim: 'O she doth teach the torches to burn bright', and when Rosalind could ask: 'Why talk we of fathers, when there is such a man as Orlando?' In a play that is full of music, the first notes of it are heard as Ariel, unseen, invites Ferdinand to 'these yellow sands'. If the sentences of Divine judgement have been announced by the storm, if the crimes against natural law have been avenged by natural agencies, these convulsions require their antiphon; and music answers the storm very much as grace comes to the aid of nature. For Ferdinand, it seemed literally to spring from the heart of the tempest

> Sitting on a bank,
> Weeping again the King my father's wrack,
> This music crept by me upon the waters,
> Allaying both their fury, and my passion,
> With its sweet air . . .

> (I, ii, 393-7)

In the same way Pericles and Marina (and they alone) had heard the 'music of the spheres', and Paulina called for music to awaken Hermione. And just as in *The Winter's Tale* the future belongs to Florizel and Perdita, so in *The Tempest* it belongs to Ferdinand and Miranda. 'Sweet music' is commanded to consecrate their betrothal; but then, having built up his edifice of nature's plenty, Prospero levels it to the dust. 'We are such stuff as dreams are made on . . .' — why does he choose this moment to compose an immortal poetry on the mortality of the world? Is he speaking for his dramatist, or only for himself?

For twelve years he has worked for the betterment of his little world, and he is leaving it, all things considered, a better place than he had found it. But not even the Earthly Paradise, not even Gonzalo's Utopia, could last for ever; not even a redeemed nature could escape the logic of its own laws. And man, with the works of man, was doomed to perish. Is it his essence, or merely his mortal experience, that has no more substance than a dream? The question — and it is the greatest question of all — is left tantalizingly open; but however we answer, or decline to answer, it, a certain detachment will be the mark of the philosophic mind; a detachment not only from the things that are evil, but also from the things that are good. 'Heaven and earth shall pass away' Prospero seems to be saying — and he would have had the right to complete the quotation.

Chapter 22

Death and Apotheosis

1

The notion of Shakespeare laying down his pen with the gesture of Prospero renouncing his magic is a romantic fantasy for which there is no scrap of evidence. I do not believe that he was that kind of self-conscious artist. True, he was now less prolific; enjoying the amenities of New Place; and content to leave the stage of his triumphs to younger talents, among whom Fletcher and Massinger were prominent. Nevertheless, if there were a job to be done he was not the man to shirk it, and an occasion was generally at hand. On 26 October 1612 the Elector Palatine, Prince Frederick Simmern, anchored at Whitehall with his retinue of fifty noblemen; and the King's Players — Shakespeare certainly among them — composed a guard of honour to welcome them. Southampton escorted the Prince into the throne room, where the Princess Elizabeth curtseyed to him and allowed him to kiss her cheek. But the subsequent festivities were clouded by the sudden death of Prince Henry, the Heir to the Throne, and they were not resumed until the New Year. At least six of Shakespeare's plays were performed in honour of the bridal pair, and although *Henry VIII* was not among them, it was probably inspired by the mood of the moment. The marriage took place in February 1613, and the Elector with his 'winter Queen' left for Germany in April.

It was only in the nineteenth century, with James Spedding, that Shakespeare's authorship of *Henry VIII* was seriously questioned. Its inclusion in the Folio, and its steady popularity on the stage, seemed a guarantee that he had written it. But this was to reckon without the higher criticism. Browning, Tennyson, and Emerson were among those who detected the hand of Fletcher in the delayed caesuras and the feminine or pronominal endings of *Henry VIII*, although Swinburne sprang to Shakespeare's defence. By and large, however, the higher criticism established its own orthodoxy, but the wheel has now come at least half circle. Peter Alexander, Wilson Knight, R. A. Foakes in his introduction to the *New Arden* edition of the play, and Geoffrey Bullough have all argued in favour of Shakespeare's substantial authorship. The historical sources — Hall, Holinshed, and Fox's *Book of Martyrs* — had long been familiar to him, and to these were added *The Life of Cardinal Wolsey* by George Cavendish. Mr Foakes observes that 'If two authors wrote the play, they read the same parts of these authorities with a strangely similar attention to detail.'[1] Dr Bullough discerns the characteristic Shakespearean magnanimity in 'the absence of polemical rancour and the air of generosity and sincerity with which actions not easily condoned are glossed over'.[2] Professor Arthur Humphreys, in his perceptive and judicious introduction to the play for the New Penguin, allows Fletcher a somewhat larger share.

> A prologue warns the public not to expect
> a merry bawdy play,
> A noise of targets, or to see a fellow
> In a long motley coat guarded with yellow.
>
> (14-16)

This probably refers to an earlier play by Samuel Rowley, *When You See Me You Know Me*, in which there was a good deal of clowning by the court jesters, and where the King was imprisoned for brawling in the London streets. Shakespeare, with his eye on Buckingham, Wolsey and Katharine is concerned to show 'How soon this mightiness meets misery' (30). If the audience 'think it well', they may 'let fall a tear', but the play must still end on a festive note. One way of paying a compliment to the Princess Elizabeth and her Protestant consort was to celebrate the birth, and eulogize the reign, of the Queen who had been her godmother, and had secured the Protestant succession. But to organize his 'chronicle-pageant' — for that is what the play amounts to — around the most controversial of the Tudor Kings put a strain on Shakespeare's theatrical tact. History must not be falsified, but humanity must be allowed its rights. He solved the problem by writing a play in which there are no villains — merely the alternation of human fortunes — and by abstaining from any judgement on the issues around which they rose and fell. The fulfilment of Cranmer's prophecy is not an endorsement of his theology, and the beheading of Anne Bullen is not referred to. The Jacobean audience would have concluded that although everything had come right in the end, everything had been far from all right in the beginning. If, and where, it had gone wrong the spectator must decide for himself.

The play starts with a vivid narrative — where no one has questioned the master's hand — of the Field of the Cloth of Gold,

---

[1] New Arden, XXIII.
[2] See Bullough, Vol. IV, p. 449.

but the excuse is taken afterwards for the kind of gratuitous chauvinism which evidently went down with the public. The French are censured for the 'pagan cut' of their clothes, and for their sexual prowess

> A French song and a fiddle has no fellow . . .
>
> (I, iii, 41)

Henry is the bluff 'King Harry' of popular tradition, wilful, good-natured, and impetuous with his characteristic 'Ha?' There is something in him of Falstaff, and something of Falconbridge. Superficially, at least, he is the kind of man whom Shakespeare had always rather liked, and his mistreatment of Katharine stops short of brutality. He can speak, when need be, for England against the Papacy, and with a better right to do so than King John. He is allowed his natural longing for a male heir, but when

> It seems the marriage with his brother's wife
> Has crept too near his conscience . . .

this earns the reply

> No, his conscience
> Has crept too near another lady . . .
>
> (II, ii, 17-19)

There is more mention of conscience, Professor Humphreys has noted, than in any other of Shakespeare's plays. The treatment of Anne is strikingly sympathetic. When we meet her in conversation with the Old Lady — an aristocratic version of the Nurse in *Romeo and Juliet*, and like Lord Sands, inimitably Shakespearean — her thought is all for the Queen whom she is presently to supplant

> O, now, after
> So many courses of the sun enthroned,
> Still growing in a majesty and pomp, the which
> To leave a thousand-fold more bitter than
> 'Tis sweet at first to acquire — after this process,
> To give her the avaunt! it is a pity
> Would move a monster.
>
> (II, iii, 5-11)

There is a touch of Emilia's worldliness in the Old Lady's admission that she would 'venture maidenhead' to be a queen, and a disingenuous irony in Anne's

> I swear again, I would not be a queen
> For all the world.
>
> (II, iii, 44-5)

Dr Johnson held that Shakespeare left the play with Katharine. This was not fair on the picture of the London crowd that presses into the palace yard for the christening of Princess Elizabeth — 'the youths that thunder at a playhouse and fight for bitten apples' — where the racy vernacular makes Cranmer's prophecy seem a somewhat laborious compliment to the crowned heads and contented commonwealth in question. But Katharine is among the triumphs of Shakespeare's later portraiture; one has only to compare her speech before the Cardinals with Hermione's defence before Leontes, to see that they were written by the same man, and to feel in Katharine a sharper characterization. Hermione is wronged and noble, and not much else; Katharine can lose her temper and still preserve her dignity. When Wolsey opens the proceedings in Latin, she cuts him short with 'O, good my lord, no Latin'; and translates into plain English Feste's tag from *Twelfth Night, 'cucullus non facit monachum'* — 'But all hoods make not monks'. Having appealed to Rome, she prepares to leave the court, but is called back by the Gentleman Usher, and replies to him with an authority that does not desert her in misfortune

> What need you note it? pray you, keep your way,
> When you are call'd, return. Now the Lord help!
> They vex me past my patience. Pray you, pass on.
>
> (II, iv, 128-30)

Nor does she forgive the lapse in protocol when the King's messenger, sent to introduce Capucius, forgets to kneel to her

> Admit him entrance, Griffith: but this fellow
> Let me ne'er see again.
>
> (IV, ii, 107-8)

These touches of quick temper humanize the portrait and detract nothing from its pathos; and the absence of recrimination against the King accuses him more effectively than the invective which she reserves for Wolsey. Katharine does not forget that the Emperor Charles V was her nephew, and the audience is not allowed to forget it either. Eloquent but not rhetorical, she is not the least regal of Shakespeare's queens, because she is the most recognizably a woman.

Wolsey is shown as seeking the divorce, but not in order that the King shall marry the daughter of a commoner — and, as she turns out, a 'daughter of the game'. His pride is Luciferian, 'and when he falls, he falls like Lucifer / Never to hope again'. But misfortune teaches him 'the blessedness of being little', and even Katharine can honour him after he is dead. The priest, so neglectful of his calling, is allowed to rise from the ashes of the parvenu; and in spite of his disgrace, he bears no resentment against the King. 'I know his noble nature' — how far, one asks oneself, could the Jacobean audience stretch its notions of nobility? It is the same with Buckingham, who has

> had my trial,
> And must needs say, a noble one
>
> (II, i, 118-19)

and whose

> vows and prayers
> Yet are the King's, and, till my soul forsake,
> Shall cry for blessings on him.
>
> (II, i, 88-90)

Nothing but the facts of history — speaking as loudly or as softly as the spectator had ears for them — is allowed to testify against the King who had six wives, divorced one, and beheaded two of them. Henry VIII was a far cry from Richmond on the field of Bosworth, and Shakespeare cannot help himself. But he seizes with consummate artistry on the one moment when the King can rightly engage our sympathies. Anne is in labour, and he is longing for a boy. The Old Lady enters with Lovell

> *King*   Now, by thy looks
> I guess thy message. Is the queen deliver'd?
> Say, ay, and of a boy.
> *Old L.*   Ay, ay, my liege;
> And of a lovely boy: the God of heaven
> Both now and ever bless her! 'tis a girl,
> Promises boys hereafter. Sir, your queen
> Desires your visitation, and to be
> Acquainted with this stranger: 'tis us like you
> As cherry is to cherry
> *King*   Lovell!
> *Lov.*   Sir?
> *King* Give her a hundred marks. I'll to the queen.
>
> (V, i, 161-70)

To have allowed Henry to express his disappointment at the birth of Princess Elizabeth was unthinkable. Yet Shakespeare knew just how much Burbage or Lowin could say without uttering a word.

The play stands on its own and, in the theatre, steadily enough where four fine acting parts have generally guaranteed its success. Yet we miss the pressure of Shakespeare's 'giant power in its strength of vigour and maturity',[1] the complexity and pregnancy of phrase which are so evident in the plays of his later period. The characters, for the most part, speak at one remove from the emotions they fluently express. *Henry VIII* proceeds; it does not develop and progress. As one protagonist after another fall from grace and favour,

---

[1] S. T. Coleridge.

they slip out of sight and mind. Cranmer's prophecy is a ceremonial conclusion, not an inevitable climax. Alone among the historical plays in the Folio, *Henry VIII* is described as a 'history', as if the dramatist were content, or constrained, to let history speak for itself. This lack of urgency and organic design was doubtless the result of collaboration. If Shakespeare had been gripped by Henry VIII as he was gripped by Henry IV, he could have dispensed with Fletcher, or declined to lend him his support.

On 29 June 1613, *Henry VIII* was acted at the Globe with every embellishment of ceremony, the Knights of the Garter wearing their full insignia and the Yeoman of the Guard their embroidered coats, and the stage matted for the occasion. What then happened is described by Sir Henry Wotton

> Now, King Henry making a Masque at Cardinal Wolsey's house, and certain Canons being shot off at his entry, some of the Paper, or other stuff wherewith one of them was stopped, did light on the Thatch, where being thought at first but an idle smoke, and their eyes more attentive to the show, it kindled inwardly, and ran round like a train, consuming within less than an hour the whole House to the very grounds.
>
> This was the fatal period of that virtuous Fabrique; wherein yet nothing did perish, but a few forsaken cloaks; only one man had his Breeches set on fire, that would perhaps have broyled him, if he had not by the benefit of a provident wit put it out with bottle ale.

Sir Henry made light of the disaster, for it seems more than probable that many of Shakespeare's MSS went up in the flames. Ben Jonson was in the house that afternoon and wrote in his *Execration against Vulcan* of the god's cruel stratagem

> Against the Globe, the glory of the banke,
> Which though it were the Fort of the whole parish,
> Fenc'd with a ditch and fork'd out of a Marish:
> I saw with two poore Chambers taken in,
> And rais'd ere thought could urge . . .

The King's Men did not repine. In March 1614 Shakespeare was in London to raise capital for the rebuilding of the Globe. Fourteen hundred pounds were subscribed, of which £100 came out of his own pocket. The second Globe, now octagonal in shape and roofed with tiles, was reopened exactly a year after the first had been destroyed. John Taylor, the 'water poet', echoed the general admiration

> As gold is better that's in fire tried
> So is the Bank-side Globe that was late burn'd:
> For where before it had a thatchéd hide
> Now to a stately theatre is turn'd.[1]

---

[1] For a persuasive reconstruction of what the Second Globe was like, see C. Walter Hodges, *The Second Globe Playhouse* (1973).

2

Shakespeare is generally agreed to have lent a hand to Fletcher in *The Two Noble Kinsmen*, published in 1634 as having been 'presented at the Blackfriars by the King's Majesty's servants with great applause' and 'written by the memorable worthies of their time, Mr John Fletcher and Mr William Shakespeare, gentlemen'. The main plot was derived from Chaucer's 'Knight's Tale', in which two friends, prisoners of Theseus, become estranged by love for the same lady. One of them dies, and the two survivors are happily united. Ben Jonson, in *Bartholomew Fair*, confirms the dual authorship, and among later critics Lamb, Coleridge, de Quincey, and Swinburne detected Shakespeare's hand in the better passages of the play, although it is nowhere Shakespeare at his best. It looks as though he may have touched up, here and there, a text that Fletcher had submitted to him. If so, that was further proof of his generosity; and his name would hardly have been attached to the play unless he had admitted to a share in it. On 9 September 1653, Humphrey Moseley obtained a licence for the publication of a play described as the *'History of Cardenio,* by Fletcher and Shakespeare'. In fact, the play was never published, but it was probably the lost piece twice performed at Court by the King's Men in 1613. In both these cases Shakespeare's reputation was such that quite a slender excuse would have been seized upon to credit him with an authorship which was a valuable advertisement.

To sum up, then — for we have now reached the term of Shakespeare's achievement — a distinction can be drawn, I think, between writers who seem to have the answers pat, and those who are content to sit quiet or questioning before 'the mystery of things'. Among the former, Dante and Milton come to mind; among the latter, Shakespeare is supreme. To say that he has no mind of his own, that his mind was a species of blotting-paper which registered rather than revealed, would be a patent absurdity. His was the creative power to impose order and significance upon sensation and phenomena; to show us what we did not know, and to show us in a fresh light what we thought that we knew already. But he does not bring down the tables of the Law from Sinai; he presupposes, at least directly, no straight answer as to why we are here and whither we are going; he leaves us with our own beliefs, or lack of them. What stand out, however, are the values that he evidently prizes beyond any other dramatist of his time. Order in society, honesty in dealing between man and man, good faith between man and woman. He does not look beyond the boundaries of the world he knows; yet his knowledge, like the knowledge of Mozart, is also a kind of innocence. His consecration of 'order' is a recall to normality, to a 'centre' that he is resolved shall 'hold', whatever else may be crumbling around it. He had escaped, through the late 'romances', both the sentimentality of Fletcher and the blood-shot morbidity of Webster and Tourneur. The satire and one track-mindedness of Jonson were never his natural vein. By what he tells us about other people, he tells us a good deal about himself; and in the last analysis it is all that we need to know. The rest is a secrecy that it will always be fruitless to disturb, to whatever lengths we may be tempted to push our curiosity.

Shakespeare never lost touch with his fellow-sharers in the Globe and the Blackfriars. Of these Heminge, the company's business manager, Condell, and Burbage were his closest intimates. Heminge is reputed to have created Falstaff, and Burbage was to Shakespeare what Alleyn had been to Marlowe. In 1613 they were associated in devising an emblematic decoration for the Earl of Rutland's equipment for a Court tournament in honour of Princess Elizabeth's wedding. Burbage, who was an accomplished painter, executed the design and Shakespeare contributed the verses, or motto, which accompanied it. What he wrote has not come down to us, but they were each paid forty-four shillings for their pains.

In the same spring of 1613 Shakespeare purchased a two-storied building, with a yard attached to it, within a few hunded feet of the Blackfriars Theatre. It stood on the west side of St Andrew's Hill, more or less opposite what is now the Mermaid Theatre. This had long been a nest for recusants, with secret passages leading down to the river. Shakespeare bought it as an investment in partnership with three other trustees, including William Johnson, 'Mine Host' of the Mermaid. The ground floor was leased to a mercer, and the second to John Robinson, a London friend of the poet. The property was immediately mortgaged for £60. In acquiring it, Shakespeare was following the example of the Burbage brothers who had also bought land or houses close to the Blackfriars; for the last time he had succumbed to the itch for real estate. Two years later he was associated with other owners of property near by in the recovery of documents relating to his title in the Blackfriars building. Matthew Bacon, the former proprietor, was compelled to deliver up the deeds in question, which had come into his hands on the death of his mother, although he denied any knowledge of their contents. This successful litigation shows that Shakespeare was a stickler for his legal rights, and that within a year of his death he would come to London to enforce them.

For some time now he had broken the journey at Oxford, lodging at a tavern near Carfax —afterwards the Crown Inn — with its proprietor, John Davenant. The association seems unlikely since

Davenant was reputed to be of a 'melancholic disposition and was seldom or never seen to laugh'. On the other hand he was a keen playgoer and cultivated the society of dramatists; and his wife, 'a very beautiful woman of a good wit and conversation', made up for what he lacked in liveliness. They had a numerous family. Robert, later a Fellow of St John's College, Oxford, used to recall how Shakespeare 'had given him a hundred kisses', and the second son, William, became a well-known playwright and ardent royalist. He was baptized in St Martin's Church on 3 March 1605/6, and there is good reason to believe that Shakespeare was his godfather. He was certainly very attached to the boy, and the rumour, fanned by Aubrey's gossip, spread that William was his natural son. If the charms of Mistress Davenant and William's devotion to the memory of Shakespeare, lent some colour to this, the story is contradicted by the verses composed shortly after Mistress Davenant's death in 1621. These spoke of John Davenant's good fortune in the 'happy issue of a virtuous wife'. The impression remains, however, that Mistress Davenant may well have been gayer company than Ann Shakespeare, now well on into her fifties, and that Shakespeare found his youth renewed by her teeming nursery. His own married life defies conjecture. Doubtless Ann was a good housekeeper; with New Place on her hands, she had need to be.

As one who knew every inch of the road from Stratford to London, Shakespeare was naturally concerned for the upkeep of the public highways, and we find his name among those of his fellow townsmen who were collecting a fund to 'prosecute' an amending bill in Parliament to ensure their better repair. On 3 February 1611/12, a 'Gilbert Shakespeare, adolescens' was entered in the burial register of Holy Trinity Church. This was probably a son of William's brother, Gilbert; and a year later his brother Richard was buried in the churchyard. His elder daughter, Susanna Hall, had one child, Elizabeth, who was baptized in the parish church on 21 February 1607/8. In 1613 Susanna was accused of immoral conduct by a certain John Lane, the son of a prominent local citizen. He reported that she 'had the running of the reins and had been naught with Rafe Smith and John Palmer'. Susanna brought a charge for defamation of character before the Bishop of Worcester's Consistory Court; but Lane refused to appear when the case was heard, and was excommunicated.

The growth of Puritanism in Stratford was a foretaste of the trouble in store for the profession which Shakespeare had done so much to make respectable. William Combe, a friend of the dramatist, denounced his fellow-townsfolk as 'Puritan knaves', and Dr Hall himself admitted Puritan leanings. The town council passed a resolution declaring plays to be unlawful, and imposing a fine of forty-one shillings on those responsible for their performance. When a large part of the town was devastated by fire in the summer of 1614, and all Shakespeare's property was spared, he might have been forgiven for concluding that Providence shared his own opinion of the killjoys who were bent on the destruction of what remained of 'merrie England'. William Combe was the nephew of John Combe, a prominent landowner, who increased his fortune by money-lending on a large scale. John died on 12 July 1614, leaving Shakespeare five pounds in his will. He was buried in the Stratford church and is commemorated by an altar-tomb in the east wall of the chancel. This was carved by Garret Johnson, who was afterwards commissioned to execute Shakespeare's monument. Both Aubrey and Nicholas Rowe reported that Shakespeare was the author of some facetious verses attached to the tomb, but subsequently erased. According to Rowe the lines ran as follows

> Ten-in-the-hundred lies here ingrav'd,
> 'Tis a hundred to ten his soul is not saved.
> If any man ask, who lies in this tomb?
> Oh! ho! quoth the devil, 'tis my John-a-Combe.

Aubrey's version was similar, and both — if their authorship be admitted — testified to Shakespeare's detestation of usury. At the same time they were a scurvy joke at the expense of an old friend, and a poor return for even a modest legacy.

In the early autumn of 1614 the two newphews, William and Thomas Combe, declared their intention of enclosing some of the borough's common land in the direction of Welcombe, Bishopton, and Old Stratford, which adjoined their own property. This was strongly opposed by the Town Council, and particularly by their newly appointed clerk, Thomas Greene. Shakespeare preserved a neutral attitude in a controversy where both sides tried to enlist his support. He owned the freehold of 127 acres adjoining the threatened land, and he was a joint owner with Thomas Greene and others of the tithe-estate of Welcome, Bishopton, and Old Stratford. He was therefore not directly menaced by the Combes' proposal. But his hands were tied by an agreement with their agent which would indemnify him and his heirs against any loss they might incur if the scheme went through. On the other hand he met Greene in London and gave him his opinion, shared by Dr Hall, that 'nothing would be done at all'. In September 1615 he told Greene's brother that he was totally opposed to the 'enclosing of Welcombe'. The dispute dragged on, and was not settled until two years after Shakespeare's death when the Combes' proposal was condemned by the Privy Council.[1]

---

[1] For a full account of this rather tedious controversy, see Lee, pp. 475-81.

On 10 February 1615/16 Shakespeare's younger daughter, Judith, was married to Thomas Quiney, the son of Richard Quiney, an old friend of her father. She was thirty-one years of age, and four years older than her husband. Thomas was a prosperous vintner, and judging from the inscription on his monogram

> *Heureu celui qui pour devenir sage*
> *Du mal d'aultrui fait son apprentissage*[1]

had a taste for French literature. Judith does not appear to have shared her sister's brilliance, although a portrait shows that she had inherited her father's high domed forehead and hazel-green eyes. The wedding took place in Lent, without the necessary licence, and when the newly married pair were twice summoned before the Bishop's court to explain their failure to obtain one, they refused to attend, were excommunicated, and fined seven shillings.

The wedding had in fact been hurried forward on account of the rumour that a certain Margaret Wheeler was with child by Thomas Quiney. The child died at birth a month later, and on Tuesday, 26th March, Quiney appeared in court and admitted his paternity. He was sentenced to do public penance in a white sheet during Morning Prayer on three successive Sundays. This would have been an appalling disgrace for Shakespeare's son-in-law, and Thomas was spared the worst of his humiliation. He was allowed to perform his penance in the relative privacy of the chapel at Bishopton, and in his ordinary clothes. But the scandal cast a shadow over the last months of Shakespeare's life. The changes made in his will appeared to protect Judith against a husband who was to justify all her father's misgivings. He was reputed to be 'given to fornication and to taverns'; was fined for allowing disorderly drinking on the premises of his shop; and ran into such financial difficulties that trustees were appointed to act for his wife and their three sons. The eldest of these was rather presumptuously given 'Shakespeare' as a Christian name and died when he was only six months old. The other two died respectively at twenty and twenty-one, and neither had issue.[2]

That Shakespeare's health was failing in January 1615/16 is indicated by the making of his will, although this was not signed until 25th March in the presence of five witnesses, all friends of the poet and much about his own age: Francis Collins, a solicitor from Warwick; Julius Shaw, the Stratford bailiff; Hamnet Sadler, who had been godfather to Shakespeare's son and given him his name; Robert Whatcote, who had testified for Susanna in her action for defamation of character; and John Robinson, not to be confused with the lessee

---

[1] Octavien de Saint Gelais.

[2] For those details see E. R. C. Brinkworth, *New Light on the Life of Shakespeare* (1975).

of the testator's house in Blackfriars. The preamble to the will followed the formula used by many of those attached to the old faith, although this evidence of Shakespeare's final dispositions should not be pushed too far

> First I command my Soul into the hands of God my creator, hoping and assuredly believing through the only merits of Jesus Christ my Saviour to be made partaker of life everlasting, and my body to the earth whereof it is made.

Richard Davies, the Archdeacon of Coventry and Vicar of Sapperton, reported, later in the seventeenth century, that Shakespeare 'died a Papist'. This should not be taken as gospel truth, but neither should it be dismissed as idle gossip. Davies was a zealous Protestant, and he was unlikely to have stated that Shakespeare died a Roman Catholic unless he thought he had good reason for his belief. Upon what it was founded we shall never know; but it would have been natural, as he felt his end approaching, that Shakespeare's mind should turn to the religion of his mother's family, and that some echo of this should be caught in his conversation.

He left twenty pounds and his whole theatrical wardrobe to his sister Joanna Hart, with the house and outbuildings in Henley Street, and five pounds to each of her three sons. His silver plate was bequeathed to Elizabeth Hall. Ten pounds were given to the poor of Stratford, and various friends were also remembered. Heminge, Condell, and Richard Burbage received money 'to buy them rings'; for Shakespeare had not forgotten that Augustine Phillips, one of the original sharers, had left him a gold ring on his death-bed. The bulk of his property went to Susanna Hall who, with her husband, was appointed executrix. It was to pass, by order of primogeniture, to their children; then to the children of their daughter, Elizabeth; and if Elizabeth had no heirs, to the children of Judith Quiney, or, failing these, to the posterity of Joanna Hart. Anne Shakespeare was legally entitled to a third of all revenue brought in from her husband's property, and needlessly heavy weather has been made over the bequest to her of their 'second-best bed'. The 'best' bed was normally reserved for guests; what Shakespeare left to his wife was the four-poster in which they had slept together, albeit intermittently, at least from the time of their establishment at New Place.

Nothing can be known for certain about the circumstances of Shakespeare's death. John Ward recorded in his diary that 'Shakespeare, Drayton, and Ben Jonson had a merry meeting, and it seems drank too hard, for Shakespeare died of a fever there contracted'. This is not in the least improbable, for Drayton was constantly at Clifford-Chambers, and if Ben Jonson were paying him a visit they would naturally have called upon their old friend. On the other hand an epidemic was taking its toll in Stratford at the time, and Thomas Hart was among those who died from it. He was buried on 17th April, and if Shakespeare attended the funeral, as he would have wished to do, this may have hastened his end. Death came to him at New Place on 23rd April, and he was buried two days later, seventeen feet below the flagstones, in front of the altar in Holy Trinity Church. As a part owner of the tithes, he had the right to be interred within the chancel. The funeral was conducted according to the rites of the Church of England by John Rogers, and among the churchwardens were Shakespeare's brother-in-law, Bartholomew Hathaway, and John Hathaway his newphew. One of the sidesmen was Richard Horneby, an old acquaintance who kept the black-smith's shop in Henley Street, and another was Abraham Sturley, a brother-in-law of Richard Quiney. The north wall of the chancel was uncomfortably close to the charnel house outside, and it was probably to safeguard his own remains that Shakespeare had com-posed the inscription which has deterred posterity

> Good friend, for Jesus' sake forbeare
> To dig the dust enclosed heare;
> Blest be the man that spares these stones,
> And curst be he that moves my bones.

It is ironical that the last lines said to have been written by Shakespeare might have been written by anybody, as if to remind us — and perhaps to remind himself — that he was, after all, of common clay.

3

Among the first voices raised in eulogy of the poet was that of his godson, William Davenant, then only eleven years old. To anyone walking on the banks of the Avon he warned that

> each flower
> (As it ne'er knew a sun or shower)
> Hangs there the pensive head.

To those who wished Shakespeare's body to be interred in West-minster Abbey, Ben Jonson, who was eventually to lie there himself, replied

> I will not lodge thee by
> Chaucer or Spenser, or bid Beaumont lie
> A little further, to make thee a room:
> Thou art a monument without a tomb
> And art alive still, while thy book doth live
> And we have wits to read and praise to give.

Nevertheless the family commissioned the monument which hangs on the north wall of the chancel in Holy Trinity Church. The same sculptor had carved the effigies of Thomas Combe and Sir Thomas Lucy. It is an improbable picture of the poet in the act of composition, with his right hand on a cushion and holding a golden quill; nothing to suggest the haste and ecstasy, the purely practical genius, of the actor-dramatist. A Latin inscription underneath described him as one who 'united the wisdom of Nestor and the genius of Socrates to the Art of Virgil, and on earth elicited the admiration of the multitudes and has his place on Olympus'. If the popular playwright was dead, the Bard of Stratford-upon-Avon had been born. Some verses in English followed, and here the author came closer to the truth when he wrote that with Shakespeare's passing 'Quick nature died'.

Richard Burbage played his last part in 1618, and it was left to Heminge and Condell to take in hand the preparation of the First Folio. This was financed by four members of the Stationers Company: William Apsley who held a half-share in the selling rights of Thorpe's edition of the *Sonnets*, and had himself published the quartos of *Henry IV* and *Much Ado About Nothing*; John Smethwick who had produced reprints of *Hamlet* and *Romeo and Juliet*; Edward Blount who had initially acquired the rights of *Pericles*; and William Jaggard whose imprint was on several Quarto texts. The Folio was published in 1623 and dedicated to the Earl of Pembroke. It was prefaced by a long introduction by the editors, who admitted that hitherto the public had been 'abused with divers stolen and surreptitious copies, maimed and deformed by the frauds and stealths of injurious impostors that exposed them'; and claimed that 'even those are now offered to your view cured and perfect in their limbs'. This still left the field open to the higher critics, and it is open to them still. But the Folio was a monument both of piety and editorial discretion on the part of two actors whose only literary experience was in the handling, and the merciful preservation, of prompt-books.

The frontispiece of the Droeshout portrait was guaranteed as a true likeness by Ben Jonson, and followed by his memorial Ode, so misleadingly criticized by Dryden as lacking in sincere admiration. It had never been easy for the great classicist to digest the sheer fecundity of Shakespeare's genius. Of his personal affection there was no doubt. 'I loved the man, and do honour his memory on this side idolatry as much as any. He was, indeed, honest, and of an open and free nature; had an excellent phantasy, brave notions, and gentle expressions, wherein he flowed with that facility that sometimes it was necessary it should be stopped ... His wit was in his own power;

would the rule of it had been so, too!' But in addressing Shakespeare
as 'Sweet Swan of Avon', Jonson seemed to recognize a charm which
he could never hope to rival; a charm which had ensured that
Shakespeare, for many people, shall be loved even before he is
admired. If Jonson had been tempted to regard his great contemporary as an untutored genius, that judgement could no longer stand

> Yet must I not give Nature all; thy Art
> My gentle Shakespeare, must enjoy a part.
> For, though the poet's matter Nature be,
> His Art doth give the fashion; and that he
> Who casts to write a living line must sweat
> Such as thine are and strike the second heat
> Upon the Muses' anvil, turn the same
> (And himself with it) that he thinks to frame;
> Or for the laurel he may gain a scorn;
> For a good poet's made as well as born.
> And such wert thou.

Nearly a hundred years before Nicholas Rowe stood first in the line
of Shakespeare's biographers, Jonson indicated where that biography
was to be found

> Look how the father's face
> Lives in his issue, even so, the race
> Of Shakespeare's mind and manners brightly shines
> In his well turnéd and true filéd lines . . .

It was Jonson who supplied the text for his immortality:— 'not of an
age, but for all time' — and the English poets have been competing
ever since to preach from it

> some spirits start
> Upwards at once and win their aureoles.[1]

---

[1] Gerard Manley Hopkins.

Select Bibliography

The books listed below will give the reader many alternative or complementary insights into aspects of Shakespeare's life and work, which I have not found space to discuss in detail, or even to discuss at all. I would suggest that the general and less academic treatments, such as those of John Masefield, Middleton Murry, Peter Quennell, and Mark van Doren, are not the least valuable; and that the list is very far from being exhaustive.

J. Cranford Adams, *The Globe Playhouse* (London and New York, 1961).

C. L. Barber, *Shakespeare's Festive Comedy* (Princeton, 1959).

Roy W. Battenhouse, *Shakespearean Tragedy* (Bloomington, 1971).

G. E. Bentley, *The Profession of Dramatist in Shakespeare's Time* (Princeton, 1971).

S. L. Bethell, *The Winter's Tale* (London, 1946; New York, 1947).

M. C. Bradbrook, *English Dramatic Form* (London and New York, 1965).

A. C. Bradley, *Shakespearean Tragedy* (London, 1924; New York, 1905).

Ivor Brown, *Shakespeare and the Actors* (London, 1970; New York, 1971).

Ivor Brown, *How Shakespeare Spent the Day* (London and New York, 1963).

Geoffrey Bullough, *Narrative and Dramatic Sources of Shakespeare*, 8 vols (London and New York, 1975).

E. K. Chambers, *William Shakespeare*, 2 vols (London and New York, 1930).

E. K. Chambers, *The Elizabethan Stage*, 4 vols (London and New York, 1923).

E. K. Chambers, *Shakespearean Gleanings* (London and New York, 1944).

Clara Longworth de Chambrun, *Shakespeare — a Portrait Restored* (London and New York, 1957).

Wolfgang Clemen, *The Development of Shakespeare's Imagery* (London and Cambridge, Mass., 1951).

Nevill Coghill, *Shakespeare's Professional Skills* (London and New York, 1964).

S. T. Coleridge, *Shakespeare and the Elizabethan Dramatists*.

John F. Danby, *Shakespeare's Doctrine of Nature* (London, 1949; New York, 1966).

Mark van Doren, *Shakespeare* (New York, 1939).

J. Dover Wilson, *The Essential Shakespeare* (London and New York, 1960).

J. Dover Wilson, *What Happens in Hamlet* (London and New York, 1951).

J. Dover Wilson, *Shakespeare's Sonnets* (London and New York, 1964).

Terry Eagleton, *Shakespeare and Society* (London and New York, 1967).

Una Ellis-Fermor, *Shakespeare the Dramatist* (London and New York, 1961).

Henri Fluchère, *Shakespeare* (London and New York, 1953).

H. Granville-Barker, *Prefaces to Shakespeare*, 4 vols (London and Princeton, 1946).

F. E. Halliday, *The Life of Shakespeare* (London and New York, 1961).

C. Walter Hodges, *The Globe Restored* (London and New York, 1968).

Martin Holmes, *Shakespeare and his Players* (London and New York, 1972).

Martin Holmes, *The Guns of Elsinore* (London and New York, 1964).

Leslie Hotson, *The Wooden O* (London, 1959; New York, 1960).

Leslie Hotson, *The First Night of Twelfth Night* (London and New York, 1954).

Leslie Hotson, *Shakespeare versus Shallow* (London and Boston, 1931).

G. Wilson Knight, *The Wheel of Fire* (London and New York, 1962).

G. Wilson Knight, *The Imperial Theme* (London, 1931; New York, 1951).

G. Wilson Knight, *The Sovereign Flower* (London and New York, 1958).

G. Wilson Knight, *The Crown of Life* (London and New York, 1947).

L. C. Knights, *An Approach to Hamlet* (London, 1960; Stanford, 1961).

L. C. Knights, *Some Shakespearean Themes* (London, 1959; Stanford, 1960).

Sidney Lee, *A Life of William Shakespeare* (London, 1916; New York, 1969).

Clifford Leech, *Shakespeare, the Tragedies* (London and New York, 1950).

Harry Levin, *The Question of Hamlet* (London and New York, 1959).

John Masefield, *William Shakespeare* (London and New York).

H. A. Mason, *Shakespeare's Tragedies of Love* (London and New York, 1971).

Peter Milward, *Shakespeare's Religious Background* (London and Bloomington, 1973).

Kenneth Muir and Sean O'Loughlin, *The Voyage to Illyria* (London and New York, 1937).

J. Middleton Murry, *Shakespeare* (London and New York, 1936).

Joseph C. Price (ed.), *The Triple Bond* (University Park, Pennsylvania, 1975).

Peter Quennell, *Shakespeare: the poet and his background* (London and New York, 1963).

Anne Righter, *Shakespeare and the Idea of the Play* (London, 1962; New York, 1963).

A. L. Rowse, *William Shakespeare* (London and New York, 1963).

A. L. Rowse, *Shakespeare's Sonnets* (London and New York, 1973).

S. Schoenbaum, *Shakespeare's Lives* (London and New York, 1970).

Theodore Spencer, *Shakespeare and the Nature of Man* (London and New York, 1967).

A. C. Sprague, *Shakespearean Players and Performances* (London, 1954; Cambridge, Mass., 1953).

Caroline Spurgeon, *Shakespeare's Imagery* (London, 1961; New York, 1952).

Ashley Thorndike, *Shakespeare's Theatre* (New York, 1960).

E. M. W. Tillyard, *Shakespeare's History Plays* (London, 1948; New York, 1946).

E. M. Tillyard, *Shakespeare's Problem Plays* (London, 1951; Toronto, 1949).

Derek Traversi, *An Approach to Shakespeare* (London, 1957; New York, 1956).

Derek Traversi, *Shakespeare: The Roman Plays* (London and Stanford, 1963).

John Vyvyan, *The Shakespearean Ethic* (London, 1959; New York, 1960).

John Vyvyan, *Shakespeare and the Rose of Love* (London and New York, 1960).

John Vyvyan, *Shakespeare and Platonic Beauty* (London and New York, 1961).

John Wain, *The Living World of Shakespeare* (London and New York, 1964).
Ronald Watkins, *Moonlight at the Globe* (London, 1946).
George Wyndham, *The Poems of Shakespeare* (London and New York, 1898).
Walter Raleigh *et al.* (eds), *Shakespeare's England*, 2 vols (London and New York, 1970).

The best editions of Shakespeare's separate plays, currently available, are the New Arden, the New Cambridge, and the New Penguin.

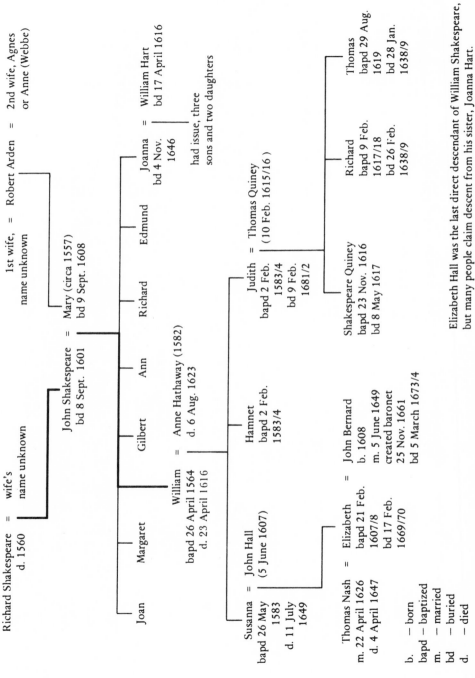

SHAKESPEARE'S GENEALOGY

Richard Shakespeare = wife's = 1st wife, = Robert Arden = 2nd wife, Agnes
d. 1560   name unknown   name unknown   or Anne (Webbe)

John Shakespeare = Mary (circa 1557)
bd 8 Sept. 1601   bd 9 Sept. 1608

Joan   Margaret   Gilbert   Ann   Richard   Edmund   Joanna = William Hart
                                                              bd 4 Nov.   bd 17 April 1616
                                                              1646
                                                              had issue, three
                                                              sons and two daughters

William = Anne Hathaway (1582)
bapd 26 April 1564   d. 6 Aug. 1623
d. 23 April 1616

Susanna = John Hall   Hamnet   Judith = Thomas Quiney
bapd 26 May (5 June 1607) bapd 2 Feb.   bapd 2 Feb. (10 Feb. 1615/16)
1583   1583/4   1583/4
d. 11 July   bd 9 Feb.
1649   1681/2

Elizabeth = John Bernard   Shakespeare Quiney   Richard   Thomas
bapd 21 Feb.   b. 1608   bapd 23 Nov. 1616   bapd 9 Feb.   bapd 29 Aug.
1607/8   m. 5 June 1649   bd 8 May 1617   1617/18   1619
bd 17 Feb.   created baronet   bd 26 Feb.   bd 28 Jan.
1669/70   25 Nov. 1661   1638/9   1638/9
               bd 5 March 1673/4

Thomas Nash
m. 22 April 1626
d. 4 April 1647

b.   – born
bapd – baptized
m.   – married
bd   – buried
d.   – died

Elizabeth Hall was the last direct descendant of William Shakespeare,
but many people claim descent from his sister, Joanna Hart.

Index

OTHER COOPER SQUARE PRESS TITLES OF INTEREST

THE WAR OF 1812
Henry Adams
New introduction by Col. John R. Elting
392 pp., 27 b/w maps & sketches
0-8154-1013-1
$16.95

THE LANTERN-BEARERS AND OTHER ESSAYS
Robert Louis Stevenson
Edited by Jeremy Treglown
320 pp., 27 b/w maps
0-8154-1012-3
$16.95

TOLSTOY
Tales of Courage and Conflict
Edited by Charles Neider
576 pp.
0-8154-1010-7
$19.95

THE TRAVELS OF MARK TWAIN
Edited by Charles Neider
448 pp., 6 b/w drawings
0-8154-1039-5
$19.95

LIFE AS I FIND IT
A Treasury of Mark Twain Rarities
Edited by Charles Neider
343 pp., 1 b/w photo
0-8154-1027-1
$17.95

THE SELECTED LETTERS OF MARK TWAIN
Edited by Charles Neider
352 pp., 1 b/w photo
0-8154-1011-5
$16.95